Judaism and World Religions

Previous Publications

Thinking God: The Mysticism of Rabbi Zadok of Lublin (2002).
Judaism and Other Religions: Models Of Understanding (Palgrave Macmillan, 2010).

Judaism and World Religions

Encountering Christianity, Islam, and Eastern Traditions

Alan Brill

palgrave
macmillan

JUDAISM AND WORLD RELIGIONS
Copyright © Alan Brill, 2012.
All rights reserved.

First published in 2012 by
PALGRAVE MACMILLAN® in the United States – a division
of St. Martin's Press LLC, 175 Fifth Avenue, New York, NY 10010.

Where this book is distributed in the UK, Europe and the rest of the world,
this is by Palgrave Macmillan, a division of Macmillan Publishers Limited,
registered in England, company number 785998, of Houndmills, Basingstoke,
Hampshire RG21 6XS.

Palgrave Macmillan is the global academic imprint of the above companies
and has companies and representatives throughout the world.

Palgrave® and Macmillan® are registered trademarks in the United States, the
United Kingdom, Europe and other countries.

ISBN 978–0–230–10369–6

Library of Congress Cataloging-in-Publication Data

Brill, Alan.
    Judaism and world religions : encountering Christianity, Islam, and
Eastern traditions / Alan Brill.
        p. cm.
    Includes bibliographical references and index.
    ISBN 978–0–230–10369–6 (hardback)
    1. Judaism—Relations.   2. Religions.   I. Title.
    BM534.B745 2012
    296.3'9—dc23   2011035975

A catalogue record of the book is available from the British Library.

Design by MPS Limited, A Macmillan Company

First edition: March 2012

10 9 8 7 6 5 4 3 2 1

Printed in the United States of America.

Contents

Preface

In much of the Western World, people believe they will not encounter other faiths and will never have to make intellectual space for those of different religions. Chaim Potok offers us a fictional account of his own reaction to his unexpected meeting with other faiths as a Jewish chaplain in the Korean War:

> A young rabbi from Brooklyn, on leave from his post in Korea during the Korean War, travels for the first time in Japan. One afternoon he stands with a Jewish friend before what is perhaps a Shinto shrine with a clear mirror in the sanctum, or maybe it was a Buddhist shrine with an image of the Bodhisattva of Compassion. We are not told which, and it really does not matter. The altar is lit by the soft light of a tall lamp. Sunlight streams in the door. The two young men observe with fascination a man standing before the altar, his hands pressed together before him, his eyes closed. He is rocking slightly. He is clearly engaged in what we would call prayer. The rabbi turns to his companion and says,
> "Do you think our God is listening to him, John?"
> "I don't know, chappy. I never thought of it."
> "Neither did I until now. If He's not listening, why not? And if He is listening, then—well, what are we all about, John?"

In the above passage from his novel, *The Book of Lights*, Potok describes the beginnings of the meetings between American Judaism and world religions during the Korean War. At that time, Jewish soldiers who were returning home from the war had shifted their views on world religion as a result of living and fighting with Christian soldiers and together experiencing firsthand an encounter with Eastern religions. That encounter served as a model for their homecoming to the suburbia of the 1950s where American Protestants, Catholics, and Jews met and learned to identify with each other. The Jewish soldiers returning home to the United States worked hard to fit in among Christian neighbors as part of the unified three American religions of democracy.

Today, Christians and Jews are meeting Muslims, Sikhs, Hindus, Buddhists, Jains, and many more as a result of living in a global age. As a result, many people discover other faiths through encounter with their classmates, coworkers, some through travel, others through study, and only a small number through formal interfaith encounters. These informal encounters vary from gentle meetings in suburbia to tumultuous confrontations that occur after natural disasters or the events of 9/11. In the United States, citizens meet the diversity of religions in their daily lives as a direct outcome of migration and travel, as well as globalization and multiculturalism. We live in a new religious America, one that is multifaith and has an abundance of houses of worship in every neighborhood. As Americans, we try to accommodate this multifaith patchwork; for example, New York traffic regulations have expanded from respecting Christian and Jewish holidays to also accommodating Muslim and Hindu holidays.

Globalization leads to an erosion of clear boundaries, involuntary confrontation with the other, and a new need for a hermeneutic of the other. We need to think about where are the possibilities of enriching mutual recognition, and enhanced love of God. This period of globalization has created many contact zones where we come to know the other faith in a transcultural space. There will be new attention to the hybridity in our religious thinking because for the many that are crossing borderlines, globalization is a game changer for those involved.

We live in a new golden age of interfaith encounter. God is back in the media and political speeches for public discussion. Far from being a public sphere naked of religion, it now seems as if every story has a religious angle. Noting this change, Jürgen Habermas has discussed how we live in a post-secular age; as I see it, after 2001, we were already discussing political and social issues based on the religious aspects. All the religions are interested in putting themselves forward to be known by others. On the collegiate and young professional levels interfaith encounter organizations are growing by leaps and bounds.

This book is more intellectual and theological than the aforementioned, informal encounters. It asks the important question of: how do I be true to my own faith and still speak about another religion in a way that rings true both for them and for me? I write as a Jewish thinker who has begun to glimpse something of the richness and importance of the world beyond Jewish frameworks. This is a moment that can be enhanced for new thinking as we advance into a new age. Theology of other religions is not universal but is cultivated from one's commitment to his own faith. One starts with the teachings of one's own tradition and with a desire for having one's own faith confront others with different commitments.

At this point in my life, I keep busy with many interfaith activities through many levels and am surprised at the continuous need for interfaith speakers required to deal with new topics, to explain new issues that were not dealt with in prior encounters. We are in a period of openness and acknowledgement that creates ample opportunity to promote border crossings between the faiths. At a junction like this, we need to recognize commonalities without losing sight of the differences. We must move beyond simple dichotomies of same or different or pluralist and exclusivist.

New Questions

The new issues around the borders of religion are shown in the types of question that I receive from people who are, for the first time, looking to formulate topics relating to other religions. How do we relate to the Evangelical concern with end time? What do Catholics mean when they claim Jews share in the covenant of Abraham? Can one practice meditation, yoga, or tai chi without practicing the religious faith to which they are central? Can one visit a Sikh or Jain Temple grounds? Can one buy for resale native Inuit art?

In the recent Orthodox Jewish controversy, over using Temple hair to make women's wigs. (see Chapter eight for more details). I served as a minor border crossing of knowledge. On the day before the ban on the wigs was going to take effect, one of the Israeli rabbinic figures involved frantically called me as an outside expert. As I started to approach my answer by setting up an explanation of Hinduism and the role of temples, I was cut off with the question, "Hindu, Buddhist, what difference does it make?" The question clearly indicated that there was no basic conceptual category of Hinduism, religion, or other religions. Nor was there any rubric, outside of the Talmud's presentation of Greco-Roman offerings to the gods, to frame unfamiliar activities. The only question was whether this presumed idol was worshiped through a hair offering or not. Afterward, when consulting with another colleague who had received the same phone call, I was told that he, too, had received the same reaction.

This book asks what to do when we gain knowledge of the other religions in relation to Judaism? This book starts with the fact that there is a category in our era called religion and expands into the concept and the fact that there are many religions. Most importantly, this book asks: what to do when we gain knowledge of other religions? Do we compare other religions to Judaism? As will be demonstrated below, both medieval texts and modern scholars have offered insights into whether we share monotheism, Biblical narrative, or human religious expressions.

But, what does the Jewish tradition say? To answer that question, we need to ask: Is there wisdom among gentiles? Do we have commonalities and convergences? Maybe we have completely different paths that do not intersect at all? The response will emerge only by means of a patient and painstaking investigation of particular texts, doctrines, liturgical practices, and moral precepts. This process demands a sense of humility that Judaism endorses in principle an openness to the wisdom of others. The investigation needs to note both differences and similarities between Judaism and other religions. Only in this way can there be a mutual understanding, full of challenge, correction, and enrichment, for both Jews and non-Jews.

We need to come to the table with the breadth and depth of our conviction and grounding in a given religious tradition. There are many positions and many sources. Different situations require different texts. All of them do play a role and all of them continue to be used in the community. Knowing what the Jewish texts say about other religions means that Judaism does indeed have different rules, opinions, and beliefs than other religions. Nor do our own commitments mean that we should stop studying and exploring other religions. We need to appreciate what the wide palette of traditional texts says about other religions and stop thinking that we already know the full range of opinions. Our religious community has a robust tradition of varying interpretations of the texts, often yielding competing understandings. We have to be open to the multiple voices that can speak to the various sides of this discussion.

Encounter

This book also assumes that there is a current need to go out and learn how to understand ourselves as part of a multifaith world for our own self-understanding as well as learning to work with others. We must be humble and honest in the acceptance of who others are and of who we are. I reject a simplistic view of all religions in some collective approach where differences are minimized. Rationality and theology are important in accomplishing anything we can transmit and make use of for self-understanding.

Theology of the other is not dialogue. In order to realize that, we should not confuse the public policy decision of whether to engage in actual theological dialogue in a given situation with the theoretical question of whether Judaism actually has a theology of other religions. Why should one engage in interfaith understanding and encounter? In essence, what purposes does discussing religion serve? For starters, I can list a few. First, good neighborly relations, learning to tolerate, accept, recognize, and show hospitality to the other all create an atmosphere in which a successful interfaith encounter can take place. Second, it helps overcome prejudice and misconceptions. Ignorance of the other breeds contempt. If not taken care of, antagonisms smolder. Third, political diplomacy, it allows groups to meet whether they are considered backdoor politics, back channel, or even not as official politics. Interfaith activity is a means of letting countries talk to one another when their politician cannot, it allows hostile groups to meet, and it serves as a means for petitions to get though. Fourth, and for many this is primary while for some this is not a concern at all, we engage in interreligious encounter to sanctify God's name. To present ourselves to a wider world in a dignified and respectful manner clears up misconceptions on both sides but also illuminates our sincere and committed endeavor to work with others. Finally, interfaith encounter cultivates better religious self-understanding (whether as Jews or otherwise) and also aids in the bettering of Jewish relationships with other faiths. I assume and hope that the reader will find this last goal is the most immediate gain from the book. It is crucial to understand that this last goal of self-understanding supports the other four goals.

Knowing the best in other religions creates a desire to emulate and learn from the higher aspirations. Maimonides's son, Abraham ben haRambam, used Sufism to help him formulate his Jewish piety. Jews will discover that they may have things to learn from Christians and Muslims, a thought that would not have occurred to those who think purely in the historical context. Avoidance is a consequence of lack of sufficient intellectual and spiritual presence to the challenges. It proclaims to others and even more to ourselves: We are afraid and may not be up to the challenge.

In order to encounter another faith with respect, one needs to acknowledge that she has no power to ignorantly point the finger and judge others of a different faith, in addition he/she misses out on the opportunity to learn something worthwhile. If one approaches another with a top-down, literally holier-than-thou position that assumes that "your" comprehension can never match "mine," then we will have overstepped what we can possibly know, as well as betray that sense of humaneness about religious commitment that we want others to see. One must be emphatic as well as eager, not afraid, to embrace and learn from the other.

We cannot delude ourselves. If we think religion has only one side and that we are on that side, this only harbors misconceptions and needs to be corrected. Before one can judge or even refuse dialogue, he/she must seek to address his/her own distortions, pathologies, and imperfections. A better way to look at the religious faith of other people is with an attitude or stance characterized by several different adjectives, words such as open, respectful, and hospitable. Indeed, the creation of such an attitude may enhance relations with co-religionists as well.

Tenzin Gyatso, the fourteenth Dalai Lama, in a recent *New York Times* op-ed, "Many Faiths, One Truth" (*NYT* May 24, 2010) advocated such an open appreciation of other religions even though he remains exclusivist about his own faith. The goal is not to deny differences, just to find enough convergence to allow people to work together. He describes his visit to a synagogue and what he learned that was unique to the Jewish experience:

> I first visited a synagogue in Cochin, India, in 1965, and have met with many rabbis over the years. I remember vividly the rabbi in the Netherlands who told me about the Holocaust with such intensity that we were both in tears. And I've learned how the Talmud and the Bible repeat the theme of compassion, as in the passage in Leviticus that admonishes, "Love your neighbor as yourself."

He learned the story of Judaism, discovers familiarity with Judaism, and is able to find universal commonalities with Judaism. He does not equate the two, rather the act of openness, education, and hospitality is the current interfaith encounter. He writes:

> When I was a boy in Tibet, I felt that my own Buddhist religion must be the best—and that other faiths were somehow inferior. Now I see how naïve I was, and how dangerous the extremes of religious intolerance can be today . . . Granted, every religion has a sense of exclusivity as part of its core identity. Even so, I believe there is genuine potential for mutual understanding. While preserving faith toward one's own tradition, one can respect, admire and appreciate other traditions.

Even though he thinks his religion is the best (as we all do), he thinks that one can respect, admire, and appreciate other traditions. Moreover, he believes than that it is the only way to prevent violence.

Leaving the Comfort Zone

Hospitality, a term stressed by the French Jewish philosopher Emmanuel Levinas, is an openness to new perspectives and to leave one's safe precinct. An important element in approaching other faiths is the need to go out of one's comfort zone. One needs to actually meet someone of another faith and place oneself in a situation where you may learn. One needs to see, meet, talk, and enter the realm of the other. If not, one may still be just projecting one's own prejudice onto the other side and the stance becomes segregated into "my" religion and "yours" with much more appreciation for the former rather than listening to the latter.

A big hindrance to encounter and hospitality is a pluralism in which all religions are just personal choice or individual faith commitment so one does not really need to know or learn anything from the other faith. Why is this a hindrance? First, the concept of individual choice turns all religions into a Western construct, rather than their original approach as being about people, community, and obligation. Second, it does not go out and show curiosity, hospitality, or encounter. One does not actually encounter anyone. Third, it makes all details of religions disappear. To use an analogy that does not completely work but is worth using in this case: to say that all cooking is a matter of personal taste and that one cannot argue with taste is really about offering individuality. It tells us nothing about the cuisines of the world, nor improve our cooking skills, or offer any insight into the ways that different cultures use the same spice differently. The pluralist can use the same stump speech when approaching any religion without having to change anything in the speech.

I used to teach a course called "The Sacred" at an Orthodox University where there could not officially be an introduction to a religions course. Before I taught the course the first time, the dean, who needed to watch over his shoulder from those who would consider such a course idolatry, asked me to have the syllabus religiously vetted by the *mashgiah ruhani* (spiritual supervisor) for the school. The rabbi said that, of course it would be no problem since the emblemic Rosh Yeshiva Rav Soloveitchik studied William James, Max Scheler, Rudolph Otto, and Karl Barth. Rabbi Soloveitchik's positions framed the issue as a confrontation between academic history of religion that studies natural phenomena as contrasting to the particular revelation of the Orthodox framework outside of any naturalism.

But this dichotomy is actually widespread in the Jewish or even non-Jewish world. When most people think of other religions, they tend to move to one of two default positions, either to the supposed universalism of the study of religion typified by Mircea Eliade or to a focus on one's own theology based on the theologian Karl Barth. The former creates a perennialism in which each religion shares the same quest for the sacred, while the latter assumes that all religions are cultural constructs and only one's own revelation is real. I have discussed the tension with students who majored in religion at various universities, which confirmed they had no means to connect what they studied in the university to their own personal belief. This book will show the complexity of the lines between the universal of religion and the particular of theology.

As noted first after WWII and reiterated by many scholars since, a fundamental, existential attitude matters more for many people than content. In a time of conflict, even the smallest difference between two religions can be harnessed to justify prejudice and stereotyping. And in time of cordial relations, even conflicting theological accounts that do not allow room for any commonality can serve as a point of mutual respect and hospitality toward the other. Now that Jews are in a post-polemic period with Christianity, there is no need to turn differences into polemics. In short, any judgment a Jew makes about Christianity, Islam, Hinduism, or Buddhism, involves a judgment about the world Jews now inhabit. The same can be applied for a different religion in light of the others. Book knowledge alone of the other religion does not say much about one's attitude toward the other faith.

Many Jews have internalized a narrative in which Christians are still the oppressive, pervasive presence that their medieval ancestors experienced in the form of Christendom. I have spoken to educated Jews-those who might even have a degree in Jewish history- and they see Christianity as essentialized at its most violent points or its most anti-Jewish forms. These educated Jews are still of the mind that Christianity teaches the anti-Judaism of John Chrysostom and that current Christians are still waiting to be crusaders ready to slaughter the Jews. They create a direct line between medieval anti-Judaism and any Christian theology. I once even met a rabbi with a doctorate who was so proud to tell me of his Jewish–Christian interfaith work, yet he considered twenty-first century Catholics as hiding their true John Chrysostom positions. Jews should recognize when Christians change. In discussing Islam, they considered the worst actions or pronouncements of the Taliban or Salafi preacher as reflecting all members of Islam. I do not want to reproduce their rabid Islamophobic positions. The Jewish perspective can quickly turn any discussion to the worst passages of Christian and Muslim texts and return every discussion to the worst moments of historical encounter with those faiths. These Jews seem more intent on blaming the other rather than understanding or recognizing the other side.

Further, many Jews also have little knowledge of the other faiths. On the lay level Jews cannot seem to differentiate within the Christian faith and do not know the difference between a Catholic, Calvinist, Greek Orthodox, Lutheran or Pentecostal, or Unitarian, and they blur the lines between evangelical and main-line. Muslims are discussed without distinction as to Sunni or Shiite, and the many cultural and legal distinctions are largely overlooked. The two faiths that make up 22% and 33% of the world's religious base are treated with numbing indifference and ignorance.

Jews have barely begun to look at their attitudes toward other faiths, albeit this reluctance was forged in an era of persecution. But they do not look at their own problematic and nasty texts about gentiles; they ignore their own traditional visions of destruction of the other faiths at the end of days. They frequently stigmatize other faiths in a totalizing way and call other faiths idolatry, Amalek, or Molekh based on current political attitudes. They judge other faiths by their worst and cite Judaism at its best. Jews consider Jewish extremists as aberrations and non-Jewish extremists as the norm. They cite modern sanitized Jewish approaches that show how wonderful and tolerant Judaism is toward others, and disown their own anti-gentile texts written over the millennia. At the same time, however, they assume that other faiths are shackled to their prior texts as understood in prior ages, and do not allow the possibility that other religions have modern under-standings of themselves.

Jews have never internalized Maimonides who said not to judge a faith on its historical actions rather than on its theology (see the chapter on Islam below). They will even judge another faith based on their own projected fears of the other. Other faiths need to learn to encounter and recognize Judaism, but so do we need to learn to encounter and recognize other faiths.

No religion has a perfect attitude toward other faiths and there is continuous recurrence of heterophobia, the fear of the other when having to share space. Part of the interfaith encounter is to overcome fear. The goal today is to avoid any religion turning into its worst potential and to increase the moderates on each side. Many Jews remain reluctant to listen and know about other religions. In the twenty-first century, there is no effective isolation. In the twenty-first century, there can be no peace in the world without peace between religions.

More fundamentally, many Jews have not kept up on the changes in the encounter between faiths of the last half century. While I was writing this book, the *New York Times* columnist Sam G. Freedman wrote an article entitled "Amanda's Wedding" discussing his Catholic friend Tim, whom he meet when they were both 11-years old in 1966 (*Jerusalem Post* 2/5/09). The boys became good friends and Sam attended his friend's wedding, the Christening of his friend's daughter Amanda as well as decades later he attended Amanda's wedding. His purpose in these reminiscences about his childhood was to make a point about the change in the ways that Jews and Catholics relate to one another. "We were the children of that revolution in Catholic-Jewish relations. I never had anyone chase me home from school for killing Christ. I never knew any Jews of my age who had that experience." His argument is that no diplomatic mistake or foot-dragging on the part of the Vatican can, should, or will change the new relationship of Jews and Catholics and in its wake with most of Christendom. As someone younger than Freedman by several years, I share his experiences of a new religious reality. Many are still isolated in their memories of prior decades, be they those of pre-Vatican II or current Jewish provincialism.

In the weeks before finishing this book, people asked me: what I was working on? I said *Judaism and World Religions*. They replied in confidence and with dismay: "We have nothing to say about other faiths except how bad they are." Most of these naysayers were in their early sixties and told me of growing up with the common experience of being called a "Christ-killer" and being roughed up; in the ensuing discussion their Islamophobia and disdain for Eastern religions as superstition were also dredged up. Yet, on the other hand, the same week, when I told someone thirty years younger than the first group what I was working on, he said that his major issue in his faith concerns the Jewish attitude towards gentiles. Specifically, "that we need to know other religions" and that the central issue of our age was overcoming our negative assessments. He wondered why the question of other faiths was not dealt with before. I responded that the lack of interest was mainly due to persecution but also in the past there was less travel and contact. In addition, Jews did not have a missionary interest in contact with other faiths. In our age of globalization we encounter other faiths all the time. The younger man listened, and then confided that his father completely disagreed and did not understand the need for any thought about other religions. I write this book for those living now who do think this is a vital topic. This work is not of an historian of religions method where I suspended my own belief. This is not joint theology; This is a Jewish work and I am only presenting the Jewish side.

This Book

This book is a continuation of my last book, *Judaism and Other Religions*. In that work, I discuss the return of religion into public discussions in our era of globalization and the need to face the challenge of the new religious diversity in the United States. Specifically, I dealt with the need to formulate a theology of other religions, especially in the four categories of inclusivist, universalist, exclusivist, and pluralist. It also dealt with the need to acknowledge that Jews have good and bad texts about other faiths.

When I finished the book, I saw that not everything fit into the four categories I set up. This book goes beyond those internal categories and seeks to actually understand the diversity of other religions and that we need to have familiarity with the wider world. This book begins to ask questions about the differences from Judaism, the similarities, and even the commonalities and interconnections. Two extensive topics that did not fit into the last volume were the idea of a Jewish–Christian covenant as well as those who reject it, along with the Eastern religions of Hinduism and Buddhism.

The categories of my last book were entirely based on how Jews view other faiths in general. This companion volume provides the first extensive collection of traditional and academic Jewish approaches to the religions of the world, Christianity, Islam, Hinduism, and Buddhism—that is, it moves beyond the theory of inclusive/exclusive/pluralistic categories and looks at Judaism's interactions with other faiths *in practice*. Starting from within was an essential starting point for moving people beyond the simple dichotomy of exclusivism or pluralism. It also reminded people that other faiths do contain teachings and practices that are similar to those of Judaism.

In this book, I start with the basic sense that there is something in our era called religion and that there are many religions in the world. I am not starting with interfaith dialogue, but the internal Jewish theological issue of how we view other religions. This book is still at the level of looking at what has already been written about the specifics of other faiths. Through evaluating the past opinions and then seeing what categories need to be used, we can begin to develop a Jewish theology of other religions. The book is still on the level of learning to be open and empathetic to the other as a necessary first step. It is a continuation of my last work and should be read in conjunction with it.

In chapter one, I deal with the need to let Jewish theology and the study of religion meet to create a richer Jewish theology of other religions. I ask the questions of the relationship of our particular faith in light of the universal. How can we learn from other faiths? Can we create commonalities and when should we admit that we have divergent paths? I also clarify some of the linguistic difficulties Jews have with the various concepts of encounter and dialogue.

Presenting the Jewish approach to several religions in a single setting allows one to ask if these differences are intrinsic or accidents of history. Debates over the use of yoga and meditation have a different resonance among Jews than the debate of Paul's vision of salvation. The question is not whether we are the same or different nor is it about pluralism or exclusivism. The question thus is how do we show interest in the other and overcome the Jewish sense that other religions are inscrutable. Jews need to learn where the universal human quest ends and where the other faiths start.

Chapter two addresses what Judaism says about the very concept of religion. The chapter starts in the rabbinic period texts and surveys opinions throughout the early modern and modern periods. It shows how the medieval categories move into the quite varied categories of modernity.

Chapters three–five are on Christianity, focusing on the twentieth-century changes. Chapter three is on the rapprochement over the last fifty years moving both sides from disputation to dialogue. It focuses on the existential attitude of the encounter. Chapter four focuses on the idea of a common covenant and the Judeo–Christian tradition as well as its critics. Chapter five is on how we discuss similarity and difference today, which should serve as a basis for further discussion.

Chapters six and seven focus specifically on Islam. Chapter six presents the medieval Jewish foundations to the encounter from sources in philosophy, law, piety, and poetry. Chapter seven is on contemporary Jewish ideas of Islam in Koranic scholarship, history, and contemporary polemic. For Islam, the theological commonalities are easy, but post 9/11 the politics are difficult.

Chapter eight discusses Hinduism and Indian religion from medieval texts to travelogues to modern contemporary approaches. Buddhism and Chinese religions are covered in chapter nine. These chapters had the fewest classical texts to use and rely more on modern discussions. I included the contemporary journeys as a means of opening up discussion of where the lines are drawn and differences are located. Much of the current Jewish debate still either enjoys the novelty of encountering Eastern religions or distains it as pantheistic syncretism. These chapters will serve as starting points for moving the discussion forward.

This book as a whole is an introductory work in a conversation that I hope will go much further. This book is limited to prior encounters and has much on certain groups and little on others. The book does not discuss, for example Mormons, Shiites, Pentecostals, Jains, or Shintoists. I have collected the texts from prior authors with an eye toward future discussions. I am concerned with the closeness as well as the openness, the differences, the boundaries and the border crossings. Several of the chapters end with the start of what may look like my working out a solution. The interested reader may want to know: what do I think? What do I think should be the Jewish attitude toward Christianity or Islam? I have already given several talks on my opinion, but the answers will be in future essays.

Like my last book, this volume will cover both good and bad texts. It will present texts useful for future harmony as well as those that show us at our most exclusive. Only by casting the net wide in this manner can we discover the contours of Jewish thinking on a topic and know the historic and philosophic background to our encounter with other religions. Both the good and the bad texts still frame contemporary discussions.

I will not be dealing with history, ethnicity, or persecution except when needed by the discussion. Most Jewish relations with other faiths are conducted at the historical level—consisting of acknowledging prior anti-Semitism, based on minority status under crescent and cross, reconciliation to address the past and forgiveness to repudiate the past. It is an aggressor and victim meeting, rather than a meeting of religion or theology. If we are historical, then we can never ask what we can learn from the other religion. Hence, this work will discuss theological ideas when Jewish thought encounters Christianity, Islam, and Eastern religions.

Seton Hall University has been a wonderfully productive work environment allowing both the time and support for writings and research. This work came to be through attending and speaking for, and with, many organizations including the Council of Centers on Jewish-Christian Relations (CCJR), the Center for Christian-Jewish Understanding, The Elijah Interfaith Institute, National Council of Synagogues, American Jewish Committee (AJC), Interfaith Encounter Association (IEA), Gulan Society, International Council of Christians and Jews (ICCJ), Boston Theological Institutes, Catholic Theological Union, and Florida International University. In addition, I wish to thank everyone who read parts of the manuscript and offered useful comments or answered e-mail questions: Herb Basser, Daniel Boyarin, Marshall Breger, Philip Cunnigham, Alon Goshen-Gottstein, Adam Gregorman, Ann Heekin, Isrun Engelhardt, Nathan Katz, Robyn J Lemanski, Deborah Lerner, Donald Lopez, Zvi Mark, David Michaels, Moshe Y. Miller, Yehudah Mirsky, Len Moskowitz, Rori Picker-Neiss, Dovid Sears, Marvin Simkovitch, Shimon Steinmetz, Gisella Webb, Ronit Yoeli-Tlalim, P.V. (Meylekh) Viswanath, and Peter Zaas. I deeply thank my undergraduate assistant, Amanda Frankel, whose talented editing abilities, as well as her footnoting skills, made for a much clearer and concise book. Despite her dream of becoming a novelist, she has efficiently and graciously done much of the dirty work for this volume. Jon Baker gets credit for scanning the page of Talmud for the cover graphic. I thank Fr. Lawrence Frizzel as head of our department for his professional support and Jay Wolferman who administers our department. I thank all my ever-patient editors at Palgrave Macmillan. Once again, I dedicate this volume to my wife Debi, for her continuous love, patience, and encouragement.

I

Recognizing Others

We have inherited great advances in Jewish-Christian reconciliation and are at the start of bringing Islam, Hinduism, and Buddhism into the encounter. This book is the beginning of a Jewish theology of other religions, it addresses and takes seriously the diversity of religious expression. In our age of globalization, people regularly travel to other continents and are engulfed by other cultures and are able to witness a diversity of faiths. This topic is one of the new dimensions of our era, leaving many questions:

- How should Jews think about these other faiths?
- Can Judaism have an appreciation of other religions?
- How do we strike a balance between similarity and difference?
- What should be the relationship between the academic findings and theology?

In this chapter, we will present the problem of recognizing other religions. First, the broad topic of the tension between the academic and theological approaches. We will present the questions presented by the empirical study of religion and then offer the foil of those who only understand other faiths though theological concepts such as revelation.

Second, I will summarize my prior book that presented a non-empirical approach of a Jewish theology of other religions.

Third, this chapter will carry the discussion of the prior book forward by looking at four complimentary approaches toward a comparative theology of religions, meaning a theology that takes account of empirical differences.

Fourth, we will return to the problem of diversity, we will explore the fundamental question about the ability to make comparisons between conceptions of God.

Fifth, and finally, this chapter will present a discussion of the concept of dialogue and encounter in order to help the reader distinguish dialogue from theology.

- ❖ Academic Encounter
- ❖ Revelation: General and Specific
- ❖ Theology of other Religions

❖ Four Approaches to a Comparative Theology: Clooney, Heim, Ricoeur, and Panikkar
❖ Do we Worship One God?
❖ Encounter and Dialogue

Academic Encounter

For many, the first encounter with the beliefs and practices of another faith is derived only from academic books, and as a consequence, many people have little means of connecting this new knowledge to their own religious beliefs.

Wilfred Cantwell Smith (d. 2000), a long time professor of religions at Harvard, asked his students the important question once one recognizes that there are other faiths:

> We explain the fact that the Milky Way is there by the doctrine of creation, but how do we explain the fact that the *Bhagavad Gita* is there? If it is the task of theological reflection is to be as all-embracing as possible in trying to comprehend the religious dimension of culture, then the very fact of religious plurality surely cries out for interpretation. How do religious believers explain the will of God for diversity?[1]

Smith told his students that "no statement about religion is valid until it is recognized by the adherents of this religion itself." One cannot consider one's own theological understanding of another faith as actually and accurately reflecting that religion without encountering the other religion. We need to learn about other religions in order to describe the world that we live in. In our era, when many people are meeting other religions for a first time, we need to be self-conscious in the way we think about other faiths. We need to show justice to the facts but more so, justice to the faith, experience, and history of others who do not share the same beliefs and thoughts. This includes a basic familiarity with the structure of the other faith. This book assumes that there is already a century of empirical works to turn to about other religions; the goal now is to return to our faith communities with that knowledge.

In the nineteenth century, Max Müller, the great Indologist and one of founders of the field of comparative religion, proclaimed that, "He who knows one religion knows none." To this he meant that in order to have self-understanding of one's own religion, one needs a comparative outside perspective. The academic study of the history of religions does not intentionally privilege one religion. Rather, it seeks to describe the history, context, and basic forms and structures of the religious life. What is gained by learning about other faiths? First, one gains the ability to understand that there is a diversity of religions in the world with unique qualities. Second, one is able to see what is unique in one's own faith compared to others. Third, a believer gains through the use of comparative categories a rigor of thought of religious theology, ritual, and prayer.[2]

But what happens when we return with this knowledge to the realm of theology? Theologians ask what are the implications of the knowledge of others' faiths for one's own faith.

Ernst Troeltsch (c. 1865–1923), a German Christian theologian, was one of the first modern theologians to stress the need for theology to embrace empirical knowledge of other religions and also to formulate the complex questions of the relation between theology and the study of other religions. For Troeltsch, there are two operative questions: what, if any, influence should other religions have on contemporary systematic theologians? And, if it were concluded that the doctrines of other religions should be taken into consideration by systematic theology, how precisely might such a consideration be undertaken? Judaism has not given extensive thought to these issues.[3]

Furthermore, Troeltsch asked: How can one study another faith without disloyalty to one's own religious beliefs? He answered with the Protestant theologian Søren Kierkegaard's position that religion is primarily a matter of experience and subjectivity, but philology and historical conditions are mere knowledge without belief. Knowledge of another religion is objective and universal like any other field, it is only faith that is private and requires loyalty. Genuine faith "lifts the individual subject above its own limitations and brings it into full and living contact with the divine life for the first time." In contrast, academic study remains human and not divine.

In contrast, Phenomenologists of religion, from Geradeus van de Leeuw in the 1920s to the humanist observations of Tsevetan Todorov in the 1990s, emphatically note that one can gain an understanding of others through actually entering their perspectives. The religions are mutually enriched in the sense that by passing over into the consciousness of the other, each can experience the other's values from within the other's perspective. This can be enormously elevating, for often the partners discover in another tradition values that are submerged or only inchoate in their own.[4]

Prior to World War II, many scholars of religion such as Wach, Sonderblum, and Heiler still sought a theological answer in addition to their empirical work. Since then, the academic study of religion has sought to move away from any theological questions. Yet, the progress in creating departments of religion went hand and hand with Vatican II, leading to religion departments and the desire for knowledge of other faiths. The newly formed departments of religion broke away from theology departments in an attempt to present religion in a light that was outside of creed and religious institutions. They integrated social scientific research and featured a strongly naturalistic philosophy that supported religion as part of the natural cultural life of humanity.[5]

For most people of the last generation, the knowledge of other religions was found in the 1960s introduction to religion course, which at the time of its creation was the most popular college course in the United States. Usually, the departments taught the colorful works of the prolific phenomenologist of religion, Mircea Eliade (1907–1986). These works illustrated that there is an irreducible element called the sacred found in every religion and consists of sacred time, sacred space, and the human quest for meaning. Religion is ritual, a myth, and a symbol outside of organized religion. Eliade's theory of religion presupposes that humans have an innate drive for transformation, seeking a " . . . fundamental mystical experience, that is, transcending the human. This approach is associated with the great historian of religions, Mircea Eliade, but others including the scholar of Jewish texts Gershom Scholem were part of this new approach."[6] Eliade sees differences between the roles of a *historian* of religion and that of a *theologian*. The former concentrates primarily on religious symbols, and completes his/her analysis of religious phenomena as phenomenologist or philosopher of religion, whereas the latter aims to see in the content of a religious experience the clearer and deeper understanding of the relationship between God-Creator and man-creature.

Yet, for most who took courses on comparative religions, it almost by default created an equation between them because in some of the weaker versions of these comparative studies the details of the religions were never sufficiently covered and the differences were elided. The academic study of religion has many times generated a universalist approach to other faiths. This approach colors many media presentations of religion as spirituality with its implicit naturalism, quest for personal bliss, and a common humanity. However, it must be stated emphatically that usually the goal of contemporary history of religions is to show the differences between religions and to aid in the overcoming of the cultural limitations by pointing out variation. Therefore, it is important to note that many with a superficial impression of the historical study of religion, gained from magazines or certain types of survey courses, assume that comparative study teaches that all religions are essentially one, with the same myths and symbols. In the popular perception, the universalism discussed by Joseph Campbell in his *Bill Moyers* interviews is the goal of comparative religion. Campbell presents religion as the universal myths that evolved in the history of the human race. But that is not true of the majority of the academic study of religion nor of theology.[7]

Some theologians actually created theologies for this universalism. The Protestant theologian Paul Tillich considers anything that serves as man's ultimate concern as religion. Tillich argues that the theologian must accept that revelatory experiences are common to all religions and revelation is received under finite human condition. Based on this universality, W. C. Smith proposed a single world theology as one religion for one world and that symbols are a universal human phenomena. This approach ignores the scriptural, doctrinal, communal, and authoritative elements.[8]

This book is a return to answering theological questions needed for historical and religious questions. But this work acknowledges that it is written from a faith commitment of writing a Jewish theology of other religions as part of the trend of interfaith encounter of our century.

Revelation: General and Specific

Does the fact that our human narratives now involve encountering other religions affect our sense of a unique revelation? Can one acknowledge other religions and still believe in truth and revelation? These questions, not covered in a class on the history of religions, are the subject of this section.

Early nineteenth century thinkers, such as Friedrich Schleiermacher (1768–1834), considered other religions as a prologue of a natural human quest, but not as part of Christian faith.

In the twentieth century, many in European theology followed Karl Barth (d. 1968), who rejected finding God in human culture in any way, so the human religious quest is not true. The only true form of religion is from revelation of God's own self-knowledge, of a God who cannot be discovered by humanity simply through its own intuition. To the theological followers of Barth, God's word can only be known through the revelation of the Bible. All other religions, and even the human elements of the Church, are solely human products. This choice between these two extremes of either revelation or human culture caused many theological authors to consider world religions as products of human culture, thereby not letting the encounter with world religions affect their theological view. Revelation is unique and limited to a single religion, while the human experience contains a wide variety of experiences, including religion, poetry, and philosophy. At its extreme, a Barthian position has no human element to religion and no divine sense within man. Jews know this position from the writings of Soloveitchik and other German Jewish émigrés.[9]

There are two names, however, that the average Jewish reader will be unaware of that play a role in any discussion of the relationship of theology and the academic study of religion: A.G. Hogg and Hendrik Kraemer.

A.G. Hogg (1875–1954) was a missionary in India and professor of Indian religion. Hogg had an empirical temperament toward religions and saw Indian religions comparable in many ways to Christianity. Hence, even though he could not place the Hindu faith on equal footing with Christianity, he was willing to grant that Indian religions are due to natural revelation. Hogg privileges the revelation of the Bible as direct and offering a special unique message. In addition, God offers a general revelation to all humanity not unique to the specific faith. For Hogg, there is an actual finding of God in other religions. All religions are not false but various mixtures of revelation and human. In 1937, Hogg wrote, "The Barthian bull destroyed many valuable things in pursuit of the matador of modernism." Hogg thought that one must have a direct empirical understanding of the religious life of other religions, and that one could see the workings of Biblical faith in their faith. If there is one revelation, then one willy-nilly must understand others through one's faith.[10] Hogg insists that both Christianity and non-Christian religions have a dimension of purely human consciousness, as well as a revelatory element.[11] However, unlike the phenomenology of religion of Eliade, Hogg considers similarities and points of contact between religions as well as the concept of religious experience of little regard. Only the revelatory elements are of value.[12]

Hendrik Kraemer (1888–1965) was a missionologist and prominent figure in the ecumenical movement.[13] Kraemer taught exclusivity without Barthianism, and based his studies more on Pascal, Kierkegaard, and his vision of direct Biblical faith. Kraemer thinks Barth surrenders biblical realism for sterile intellectualism. Other religions do not have revelation, rather, a human religious consciousness's natural sense of the divine and natural theology. Kramer criticizes Otto and Wach for confusing the psychological religious experience with revelation. Otto's *tremendum* is not the Biblical God of wrath and mercy. The modern study of religion has created natural "classical experiences" with Biblical tie-ins, but it is still not a true presentation of revelation. The modern conception of religious experience

ude sin and atonement (John H. Newman had the same complaint
rative religion). Kraemer is against the fact that mysticism and inner
e treated as the highest form of religion and more conservative elements are given shorter shrifts.

Lesslie Newbigin (1909–1998), Church of Scotland missionary author, accepts
the uniqueness of the Bible, yet he strives to create as much continuity with the
faiths of the world. Newbigin works from the premise that the whole cosmos is
ruled by a wise and loving God who would not ignore most of His creations. In
the human condition, there are dark mysteries and there is a God-given ability
for the human grasping of goodness, a potential for universal ethics outside of
revelation.

My Previous Book

The first approach to resolving the tension of one's own faith and the acknowledgement of the diversity of religions is to develop a theology of other religions.
Does Judaism have a theological approach to other religions? Emphatically, yes.
Judaism has a wide range of texts that offer thoughts on other religions. In my
previous book, *Judaism and Other Religions*, I presented a broad range of traditional sources bearing on this question of the theological relationship between
Judaism and other religions in order to start a discussion about a Jewish theology
of other religions.

In 1982, Alan Race, a British academic and Protestant reverend, created these
categories and they were popularized in the writings of John Hick (b. 1922), a
British philosopher of religion. They have been used in the field of theology for
the past twenty-five years.[14] My previous book was the first extended application
of these categories to a wide variety of Jewish opinions.

The categories are exclusivist, inclusivist, universalist, and pluralist. Jewish
thought does not ask when approaching these discussions whether gentiles have
access to God or whether other religions are saved. For Jews, these categories are
ways of looking at and examining other faiths.

The exclusivist maintains, *"There is only one true religion."* Exclusivism states
that one's own community, tradition, and encounter with God comprise the one
and only exclusive truth; all other claims on encountering God are, *a priori*, false.
There is only one way to reach God and salvation. Thus, one religion is uniquely
and supremely true and all other religions are false. Those who accept exclusivism
usually affirm that other religions possess some elements of wisdom but do not
teach "the truth" of salvation and revelation.

The pluralist, on the other hand, is of the belief that, *"All major world religions
have some truth."* Religious pluralism accepts that no one tradition can claim
to possess the singular truth. All groups' beliefs and practices are equally valid,
when interpreted within their own culture. Thus, no single religion is inherently
better or superior to any other. For pluralists, there may be differences in rituals
and beliefs among these groups, but on the most important issues, there is great
similarity. Most religions, they claim, stress love for God, and have a form of the
Golden Rule.

The inclusivist seemingly takes the middle path between the two aforementioned stances and believes, *"One religion is best but weaker forms of religion are possible in other religions."* Inclusivism, in other words, situates itself between these two extremes, where one acknowledges that many communities possess their own traditions and truths, but maintains the importance of one's comprehension as culminating, subsuming, or perfecting all other truths. One's own group possesses the truth; other religious groups contain parts of the truth. They do believe, though, that truth, wisdom, and even revelation can be found in other religions. The inclusivist position usually uses a lens of historical mission in which knowledge of God and His will play themselves out in the wider world of other religions. Halevi, Maimonides, Nahmanides, Emden, Hirsch, and Kook all look to biblical history in which the other nations play a role in the unfolding of God's plan.

Universalists maintain, "The truth is One." Universalism is the midpoint between inclusivism and pluralism, where one acknowledges that the universal truths of God, soul, intellect, and ethics have been made available by God to all people. This is usually a God-centered approach in which theism transcends the other elements of religion. In the Universalist approach, the universalism of the prophets is joined with the philosophic monotheism of the Middle Ages. They accept a universal truth that is available to all humanity beyond, but does not go against revelation. In a universal truth there is no need to refer to Judaism as the single truth; rather all knowledge is grounded in a higher divine knowledge, or a unified sense of rationality, or the natural abilities of the mind and soul. Thinkers in this category include ibn Gabirol, Moses Narboni, Immanuel of Rome, as well as Shadal and Moses Mendelssohn. This category does not exist in the standard Christian typology since historically they required salvation through Christ.

Jewish exclusivism assumes that the sole domain of truth is the Torah, and Judaism is the sole revealed religion, which differs in meaning from traditional Christian use of the word exclusivism, in that it does not usually deny salvation to gentiles. For the Jewish exclusivist the universe is Judeo-centric and the other religions are not relevant; at best we can speak of individual gentiles as righteous and understand there is wisdom among the nations. We find the restrictive position among some of the halakhic approaches that require the gentile to submit formally and publicly to Judaism and enter into a semi-conversion of a separate religion of the seven Noahite laws as defined by the rabbis. Some Jewish texts of late antiquity and the middle ages include the debate about *Verus Israel* (The True Israel) and contain mockeries of Christianity, such as Kalir and Rashi. Others, such as Maharal and many Hasidic texts, continue the rabbinic approach of viewing the gentile as the opposite of the Jew. Some, such as Bar Hiyya continue the apocalyptic eschatological visions found in the book of Ezekiel and suggest that the gentile will be eradicated at the end of days.[15]

Jewish pluralists place limits to human knowledge and do not credit revelation as offering a truth greater than any specific faith. Rabbis Irving Greenberg, Elliott Dorff, and David Hartman all limit human knowledge to make room for other faiths. The pluralist position distinguishes between reality as known in concrete particular ways and ultimate reality as being beyond human comprehension. Each group makes their own unique covenant with God, but they all seek to add mean-ing to life and to sanctify human existence. In the final analysis, all traditions are rafts, a means to an end, and they conceptualize these symbols according to the best lights they have.

Many have noted that in practice, most theologians do not fit tightly into one of the following categories. Only philosophers who construct their theories *a priori* can fit totally into a single category; theologians who work with the com-plexity of textual traditions and social circumstance cannot be thus restricted; and lived communities of faith can never operate in a single mode. Some figures will be included in one, two, three, or all four categories.

Theological Interconnection

Besides a theology of other religions consisting of the categories of exclusivist, inclusivist and pluralist, there are a variety of other approaches that are worth discussing. My goal is to move past my previous work and consider methods that allow for a Jewish discussion of specific religions. We are going to look at four approaches to creating interconnection between one's academic knowledge and theology, as wisdom (Clooney), as separate goals (Heim), as recognition of an other (Ricoeur) and as parallel convergence (Panikkar). We also return to the role of revelation as a limiting function (Ratzinger).

Clooney

Francis X. Clooney (b. 1950) is a contemporary theologian at the Harvard Divinity School. Clooney asks comparative questions to create a theology of what he calls "Comparative Theology." According to Clooney, he proceeds by comparison, ful-filling the basic goal of "faith seeking understanding" precisely in the intelligent juxtaposition of theological texts from different traditions. He starts with com-parative questions and then as faith seeking understanding; however, comparative theology eventually involves the theologian in questions of faith, particularly in finding a response to the other tradition's experiences. The goal of the process is not dialogue but self-understanding of one's own faith. Comparative theology is where I ask what can I learn about my own faith from this text of another religion. I do not say anything about them or where they fit into my larger questions, but how do their poems, piety, and ritual shed light on the similar elements in my faith. This approach allows me to say that they are different than my faith but they still have something to teach.

The comparative theologian is familiar with, relatively at peace with, and rooted in one of the traditions compared. Comparative theology is the acquisi-tion of a new literacy, in which one's theology is enriched and made complex by reception of the vocabulary, methods, and choices of the other tradition, and by one's assimilation of these into one's home tradition. He wants to know how other traditions read, how we might read with them, and then, how we might re-read our own tradition thereafter. Comparative theology is detailed, deeply reflexive, and self-corrective in the course of its own investigation, even in regard to its basic questions, methods, and vocabulary.[16]

Clooney reads Hindu texts from his own position of Christian faith. He found himself drawn into the world of the intensely emotional, devotional poetry of the saints of south India. This made impartiality and distance problematic, and the possibilities of transformation and conversion became more real, as research and identity became more closely intertwined.

The method is able to confront central religious symbols in a religiously pluralistic world, since it can address questions of religious pluralism on explicitly theological grounds without relinquishing the critical tools of modernity. This approach is one of the most fruitful from a Jewish perspective because Judaism states that there is wisdom among the gentiles. "If someone says to you that there is wisdom among the gentiles, believe him. If he will say that there is Torah among the gentiles, do not believe him (*Eichah Rabbah* 2)." The application of Clooney to Judaism is that there is a religious wisdom. Everyone acknowledges that there is something to learn, but the question is what are the limits? Does saying that there is Torah, mean no revelation or just no special revelation like the Sinai Torah? When Maimonides writes that it is forbidden to learn from the books of the idolaters (Hilkhot Avodah Zarah 2:2), does that apply to what I can learn in sacred envy about their philosophies, poetry, and scripture? Can the Jewish discussion about wisdom in other faiths be softened using the insights of Clooney? At points in this book, I will implicitly rely on Clooney for my own self-understanding of Judaism.

Heim

A different approach is offered by S. Mark Heim, a contemporary theologian at Andover Theological Seminary, who locates the plurality of religions theologically by emphasizing a plurality of salvations where salvation may not be the same for everyone, nor need we say that every salvation, even when real, be equal to others in its completeness. In this situation, where plurality is to be taken very seriously, and where our personal encounters matter theologically, there is an urgent need for a post-pluralist and inclusive conversation that yet draws on the consciousness of the modern West and its deepening awareness of pluralism.[17]

Heim wants to preserve the maximum number of religious experiences, as a "radical religious pluralism." Different religions have different goals, and each faith has its own uniqueness. This way he preserves the differences between the faiths, and requires the maximum knowledge to understand the marked difference of the other religion.

Heim criticizes pluralism for its lack of recognition of actual religious difference, both metaphysically and practically. Neither the exclusivist nor the pluralist position is completely satisfactory in integrating the two goals of an authentically Christian and historically viable theology of religions. Heim moves the theology of religions project beyond taking sides on exclusivist and pluralist views. The crux of his argument is this: that it makes more sense to speak of salvation in the plural, to maintain that the ends of various religions are indeed varied and significantly constituted by the paths taken to reach them. At the same time, all paths—Christianity included—can and must make or require exclusive commitments on the part of those that hold them.

Heim believes that all pluralist approaches to religion, do not respect the actual content of the traditions themselves. They instead acknowledge, or in Hick's case postulate, only that which each has in common, in order to avoid the conflict that often arises as a result of difference. So Heim calls into question the hypothesis based on the fact that it allows for only one eschatological end. Heim wishes to affirm the religious traditions themselves, to "acknowledge in the various traditions not merely some abstracted common object or attitude, but the concrete availability of some or all of the specific religious fulfillments they affirm."

Heim approaches each religion individually, affirming what it says and accepting its religious end as a valid one. What does Heim mean by a religious end? "A religious end or aim is defined by a set of practices, images, stories, and concepts" which "provides material for a thorough pattern of life," is "understood to be constitutive of final human fulfillment and/or to be the sole means of achieving that fulfillment," and "is in practice exclusive of at least some alternative options." In this sense there undoubtedly are a variety of religious ends. Christian salvation and Buddhist nirvana are different religious ends.

In a similar manner, Stephen Prothero of Boston University writes that one should not reduce one religion to another one. Yes, all religions preach compassion but it is false to claim that compassion is the reason for being the great religion. The Buddha did not sit down under a Bo tree in India in order to teach us not to kill our brothers. The Hindu milieu in which he was raised already knew that. He came, according to most Buddhist thinkers, to stamp out suffering and pave the path to nirvana. He does suggest there are no convergences, or shared fundamental values in the major world religions. Religions have different aims, different expected outcomes: so Christian love is not the same as Buddhist compassion; and Christian justice is not the same as Muslim justice, and so on. We cannot, therefore, assume that we are all united, even in the realms of ineffability. There just are differences.[18]

There are commonalities and difference, openness and borderlines, we are all negotiating how we are going to be Jewish—with what mix of beliefs, practices, experiments, border-crossings—and thus too, how we learn from our religious, and where we draw the limits on that learning. For example, we may be practicing yoga, but not submitting to a Hindu guru; we may learn from reading the *Bhagavad Gita*, but not worship Krishna; we may find Hindu insights helpful in rethinking gender and the divine, but not actually pray to a Goddess. Similarly, many of us are learning from Islam or Buddhism, or Native American traditions. This book will implicitly rely on Heim in later chapters when I stress that one should not assume the similarity of all faiths.

Ricoeur

Paul Ricoeur (d. 2005) was a major Continental philosopher whose work touches on many aspects of our discussions. First, he avoids the distinction between academic knowledge and personal faith that troubled twentieth-century discussions of religion. He shows that contemporary religion is expressed in texts, or other products of culture. He does not look for the faith commitment of the author but rather treats texts as understandable by themselves. He insists upon the need for interpretation of texts; by this he means "to appropriate here and now the intention of the text." According to Ricoeur, there are no "textless" worlds, therefore unlike Kierkegaard—there are always rival and competing interpretations of texts based on the appropriation. One cannot claim that one's faith is private and incommensurate with other faiths or that the texts and rituals of other faiths are not understandable.[19]

A second useful insight offered by Ricoeur overcomes the distinction between the two elements to understanding religion, the academic and the theological, by claiming that they are complimentary, not opposites. It is not a dialectic, either/or choice. For Ricoeur, human culture does not work with untranslatable abstractions outside of that culture. If religion was above culture then it could not affect anyone in culture. For Ricoeur, Karl Barth admirably described this realm of hearing the voice of revelation, greater than any human experience. Nevertheless, we can only hear the proclamation within our own human experience. Revelation itself is expressed in myth, symbol, and narrative. The narrative element captures the human experience of religion, ever changing and capacious of meaning. For Ricoeur, the research of Mircea Eliade and other scholars capture this human realm splendidly.

The third contribution Paul Ricoeur makes to our discussion is to replace the word and concept of dialogue with recognition, in which one recognizes the other side. He moves the emphasis from mutuality and commonality to a recognition of our differences and the sharp recognition of otherness of the other faith. Ricoeur sets out three primary meanings of recognition. These are: (1) recognition as identification of the other side; (2) recognizing oneself in the mirror of the other side; and (3) the mutual recognition gained from the encounter. Recognition amounts to transcending simple given characteristics and taking the risk of error in order to truly recognize the other side that will shift our perceptions and view of reality. In interaction with another religion, there is a reciprocal learning or apprenticeship, and it is just here that one discovers a dynamic subjectivity of the other. Our common constitution demands mutual recognition. Nonetheless, because vulnerabilities are never eliminated, we must constantly struggle in the act of recognition to overcome them.[20] For Ricoeur, our sense of self is developed as a reflection of our experience of others and of the expectations of others. In the interfaith relation that calls us to a radical awareness of the other, one should expect to find reciprocity of impact and to reconsiderations of innermost selves.

Panikkar

Raimon Panikkar (c. 1919–2010), a Roman Catholic theologian whose 1961 *The Unknown Christ of Hinduism* and embrace of Hinduism and Buddhism made him an influential voice for promoting dialogue among the world's religions, was one of the pioneers in opening up to other religions and learning from them. He wrote, "The whole history of Christianity is one of enrichment and renewal brought about by elements that came from outside itself," adding that, "If the church wishes to live, it should not be afraid of assimilating elements that come from other religious traditions, whose existence it can today no longer ignore."[21]

The main thesis is that the name and experience of God is universal. This focus on *experience* is central to Panikkar's thought. The unique aspect of experience is a measure of the *concreteness* of God for us. Since God is God, he is beyond all specific names. God is convergence with divine grace in our human attempts. If it is universal, then we can see elements of our own faith in the other religions. Ewert Cousins (1927–2009), a colleague of Panikkar, developed a theology based on a convergence of mystical paths and initiated projects in comparative mysticism and spirituality.[22] We need to acknowledge that those inclined to spirituality, prayer, and mysticism do not have trouble comparing notes on the human elements in their experiences. For the spiritually adept, the theological question is an epistemological choice between being a mystic and a rationalist. Some types of mystics have a certainty of the universality of the same empirical reference to an oneness of God greater than any theological scheme. This universalism is not a pluralism in which religions are all partly right, but are of empirically learning to respect the other on their own terms. To be a person that can give witness to other acts of faith. He or she must recognize the common phenomenology of spiritual techniques. The empirical mystic knows that he can compare techniques with other mystics, but does not make it a principle of his theology.

Academia at its best functions as an inductive interfaith agent in its activities of finding connections between rationalists, mystics, or jurists. As academics, we have no trouble presenting, in a cognitive way, Maimonides in the context of Farabi and Aquinas, or Soloveitchik in the context of Karl Barth and Emil Brunner, or comparing Rav Nahman of Bratzlav to Ramakrishna and St. Francis of Assisi, or even cognitively comparing *teshuvah* to reconciliation. These comparisons and contextualizations, however, are not discussions of faith, belief, or commitment, but public presentations of topics in academic settings. In the classroom Panikkar seems true in that we have no trouble discussing convergences of techniques.

This book argues that if Maimonides learned from Plato, Aristotle, Ibn Sina, and Farabi to better understand the Bible, and if Rabbi Soloveitchik learned from Søren Kierkegaard and Karl Barth, then perhaps Jews may be able to learn from the Buddha and other great religious thinkers and traditions, which contain wisdom that can help them more clearly understand God's revelation and Judaism. I try to be true to the texts of my faith, but in the classroom I certainly understand universal perspectives. Nevertheless, I distinguish faith statements from phenomenology, which allows one to speak about universals.

Jacques Dupuis (d. 2004), Jesuit theologian, further developed Panikkar's ideas on how *Nostra Aetate* tended to focus not on the differences between the Catholic faith and other religions, but on what they had in common. It stated that "the Catholic Church rejects nothing which is true and holy in these religions." Dupuis took the council's thinking further, as he sought the significance of other religions in God's plan for mankind. Dupuis, however, was arriving at the conclusion that divine revelation is not limited to the Judaeo-Christian tradition but extends also to other faiths. His faith underpins the hope that all the diverse religious paths will converge toward the final, universal reign of God.[23]

Ratzinger

Joseph Cardinal Ratzinger, now Pope Benedict XVI, rejected acknowledging revelation outside of Christianity and Judaism. This returns the discussion to the concerns of Hogg and Kraemer. For Ratzinger, Christians are not and never have been obliged to say that no truth comes through the other faiths, or from people of other faiths. It is perfectly consistent to say that Christ is the Way and the Truth, the one Mediator, and to say that we do not know how exactly, in the fullness of time, this unique mediation will unfold for the good of the world. This sensitivity to the difference between the "order of being" and the "order of knowing" leaves a space where attentiveness to the faith of others may take its due place. The transformation in Jewish-Catholic relations over the past fifty years owes much to this admission that God, in working with his Chosen People, acts in ways "known to himself."[24]

Pope Benedict acknowledges that Muslims "adore the one God," a phrase he crafted to avoid acknowledging their prophecy and revelation. He also acknowledges that they use "countless Biblical figures, symbols, and themes" without acknowledging any revelation on their part. Concerning Eastern religions, he acknowledges a Catholic respect for them, as well as an acknowledgment of their concern for the transcendental, family, and ethics. The major point is that one can recognize in Eastern religions admirable religious traits. "In Buddhism, respect for life, contemplation, silence, simplicity; in Hinduism, the sense of the sacred, sacrifice and fasting; and again, in Confucianism, family and social values." The Hindu community immediately applauded this statement that moved them from a human quest for transcendence to having religious wisdom, in which there are things that westerners can learn from, admire, and emulate in Indian religions. The ability to meditate, have silent retreat, and even the desire for sacrifice are recognized as positive methods. The value is not just the existential human quest, but also the conclusions reached and the methods developed.

Can we learn from Pope Benedict to acknowledge that there are virtues and wisdoms in other faiths? Can we learn that some religions have a virtuous practice of contemplation and silence, not found in Judaism? We can acknowledge it in Jewish terms as "wisdom among the gentiles," but we also then need to say it needs a Jewish theological understanding.

Do We Worship the Same God?

Before concluding a discussion of the background needed for a theology of other religions, I need to ask one more question. Do we worship the same God? I am looking to present the issues needed to open up such a discussion.

Sefardic Chief Rabbi Eliyahu Bakshi-Doron, and Rabbi Michael Melchior, as well as Christian and Muslim religious leaders, were able to sign the "first Alexandria declaration of the religious Leaders of the Holy Land: 2001." The declaration states:

> In the Name of God who is Almighty, Merciful and Compassionate, we who have gathered as religious leaders from the Muslim, Christian, and Jewish communities . . . According to our faith traditions, killing innocents in the name of God is a desecration of his Holy Name.[25]

In this statement, three faith communities have united in acknowledging God and what Jewish traditions declare to be the most important Divine attributes: the Omnipotent Creator, the Compassionate Commander of Morals, and the Holy One whose name can be praised or desecrated. These signatures relied on the many medieval Jewish sources recognizing that Jews, Christians, and Muslims worship one God.

Prior to any discussion of this question of whether we worship one God, however, it is worth restating one of the underlying assumptions of all the sources quoted in this book, a principle that is crucial to reaching the conclusion of commonality: God is real! All traditional Jewish theological positions assume that we pray to a living God. Conversely, God is not just a concept; therefore, different languages or conceptions applied to God are not creating different deities, they are rather disputing aspects or conceptions of God. For a universalist, the conceptions are pointing to different perceptions of a unity that is too great to be contained by any one observer. Inclusivists look to the common monotheism. For many exclusivists, the different faiths share the philosophic monotheism of God as creator, but that does not overcome the substantive differences in God as revealer and redeemer.

When two Jewish theologians have different conceptions of God, do they have two different Gods? Does a Jewish theologian consider a follower of Hasdai Crescas, Moses Cordovero, Maharal, or Rabbi Kook as having a different God? This theological premise of an oneness of God differs from the academic premise where one can distinguish different concepts of God within Judaism. An academic can distinguish between the God of the Bible, even the many different personas of God in the Bible, from the philosophic abstract God of Maimonides and then distinguish both the Bible and Maimonides from the dynamic, theosophical God found in medieval Kabbalah. An academic can consider these as three concepts of God. Yet, these distinctions would in the course of real life be rejected by both the religious philosopher and the Kabbalist.

Judaism accepts various formulations of a Logos, Divine glory (kavod), and hypostatic elements to the Divine. In Medieval thought, even Jewish philosophers, including Saadyah, Ibn Ezra, Yehudah Halevi, Maimonides, and Narboni, formulated theories of the Divine glory. These statements are essential for any comparative metaphysics that is not creating an unfair analogy by comparing medieval metaphysics of Islam and Christianity to modern Jewish theological formulations, which are not metaphysical, thereby ascribing metaphysics to the other side and historical narrative to the Jewish side.

What of Maimonides's view that one must have the correct conception of God to call it God? If one solely follows Maimonides then his approach cannot be selectively used. For him, Nahmanides, Crescas, and Rabbi Kook have the wrong view. For the most radically monotheistic rational sources, such as Maimonides, plenty of Orthodox rabbis with positive descriptions of God and His will or those who deliver anthropomorphic sermons would be considered idolatrous by its rational standards. There is also little question that Maimonides would regard contemporary wonder working, as well as magical and superstitious rabbis and their followers, as idolatrous. Idolatry applies not just to other religions but also to false conceptions of God within one's own religion. According to Maimonides, God remains an unknown essence, he is existent, volitional, and knowing, yet incorporeal, a unity, and non-representational. Any other formulation would be unacceptable, including those formulations, by Jewish Neo-Platonists, Kabbalists, Midrash, Modern Jewish thinkers, and Christians.

Nevertheless, that different faiths agree upon the essence of God does not mean that we accept mutual formulations of God's attributes and actions, or that our formulations are all compatible. From a Jewish perspective, the Catholic formulation of God is theologically problematic, especially regarding incarnation, iconic images, the personhood of God, and the multiple essences of God. From a Catholic perspective, Jewish formulations and denial of the essential of Christian faith and revelation are equally problematic. Nevertheless, disagreements concern the same, singular God of creation, compassion, and commandment. The Jewish objections to the Trinity, when not from a polemical context, are predominately against incarnation and the mediation of the infinite in the finite. Thus, for academic purposes, Judaism would be considered as Docetic and Arianistic, but this would not imply that Judaism worships a different God than Christianity.

Some modern authors do not respond to the traditional realist, nominalist, and idealist arguments for one God, rather they define God as a protagonist in biblical narrative or His function in Jewish law. But then one would not be a theologian speaking about God, then one is defining religion by narrative or law, not by theology. Without the theological position, one cannot deal with the positions of this book. In fact, the medieval thinkers did assume at least a nominalist connection between faiths; the word Nominalism, from the word *nomen* (name) means that one can ascribe a common name to diverse concepts. Whereas moderns use the word "nominal" to mean in name alone, sans a real commonality like "nominal damages" or "nominal observance." Almost every medieval Jewish thinker started with either realist and idealist commonalities or at least nominal commonalities and then worked to the specifics of attributes. "God exists" is the commonality and then they ask how is God described. Descriptions and attributes applied to God must return to the original common object being described.

Many today reverse the medieval approaches and consider the descriptions, narratives, and attributes as primary, thereby considering any commonality elusive and of little theological consequence. They see God as a literary character relating to Abraham, Isaac, and Jacob and avoid the God of the theologians or the philosophers. They also tend not to see commonalities of stories. They do not consider Abraham the father of three faiths but as different images created by three traditions with more differences than overlaps. Few engaged in interfaith activities would want to be forced to say that the difference in religions is that there are two, or more, Gods at battle.[26]

Diane Eck, a leading professor on religious diversity who teaches at Harvard, in her profound work on encountering other religions, *Encountering God*, asks: do we consider the God of other religions as having a different God? If so, then there would be two Gods in the world. Or do we see a common core to all religions? In that case, there would only be one God. Or can there be a third option in which we can still encounter our own God in the other religion?[27] The Bible keeps asking whose God is greater, but our modern idiom is not one of competition; we recognize the prayer act of others while still questioning whom they worship.

The important question in an age of global contact is: What do the realities of the other religion mean to me? The traditional texts, such as those of Gikkitila or Emden, allow me to ask: What does the worship that I see in other religions mean in my system? I can acknowledge that the doxologies of the world contain many names of God. In the empirical observations of other religions, one can recognize piety while at the same time theologically understand one's own religion of Judaism in a way that makes room for the other.

Eck points to the diversity of Hindu names of God to remind each of us of the diversity of naming God in one's own religion. The ancient Jewish hymns and *piyyutim*, even the popular *Aderet ve Emunah*, and *Shir Hakavod*, offer a plethora of divine names, and present a litany of diversity opening up the reader to the limits of human language in reaching the Divine. The many names of God, even internally within Judaism, reveal the role of human language in naming God, which from a Jewish perspective all point to a single Deity. When the Bible honors God as king, mother, groom, bride, warrior, ancient of Days, and Kavod, from a Jewish perspective, they all point to a single Divine. While traditional rationalists minimalized the use of divine language, much of the Midrashic, theosophical, and liturgical traditions did not.

A Common Word: Miroslav Volf

The recent series of interfaith encounters between the Catholic Church and Muslim world leaders offers new models for dealing with our issues. Whereas Vatican II turned everyone's attention toward the question of finding room for other faiths in one's theological rubric. The new question is: how do we speak of commonalities and differences? Miroslav Volf of Yale Divinity School continues this line of thinking and states that we do not worship different warring Gods. If we have different stories then do we have different Gods?

Volf thinks that we *do* worship one God, the character may be different but the object of worship is the same. They have overlap in descriptions of God and similar values. There is no inevitable clash due to theology. He rejects making religious belonging and religious labels more significant than allegiance to one true God. The word God is not a symbol or a marker of identity, like a flag in which each group has its own symbol. Rather, God symbolizes the sole creator of the universe that is not to be confused with pagan demi-gods, house deities, or tribal gods. God is not an idea of our community aspirations but is the source of the true and the good, the source of our deepest values. We share a common source of what it means to have values, even if we interpret them differently. But "if God is a marker of identity, then the Gods of the two communities must be different." And conversely "any similarity between them is immaterial."[28] Specifically, Volf thinks that at least four aspects of the question of commonality must be analyzed in pursuit of an answer: (1) Linguistic terms, the word "God" is used across languages and cultures. Is using "God" in English equivalent to using "Elohim" in Hebrew or "Allah" in Arabic?; (2) Referents, is the object of such linguistic terms the same. Do they refer to the same metaphysical object of God?; (3) Description, are the characteristics [attributes] of God close enough between two faiths to warrant the conclusion that they are the same God?; and finally, (4)Worship and the way of approaching God. Even if Jews, Muslims and Christians believe in the same monotheistic God, do Muslims and Christians worship/approach God in the same way?

There are two ways to decide whether the terms refer to the same object: (a) historical usage and (b) theological comparison. Through historical usage, Jews distinguish themselves from Christians by focusing on the difference between God in the form of a Trinity, or God that includes God's Son, Jesus Christ. From the Jewish perspective, medieval inclusivists and universalists acknowledge that the Christian God is a form of monotheism but a defective one. The exclusivist tradition, on the other hand, treats the Christian God as equivalent to the pagan gods, which is condemned by the Bible. If one only used history and polemics, then one would increase the sense of difference. Instead of asking do we share one God, this approach that looks to polemics asks: Are you a second person of the Trinity or Jewish monotheism?

In a theological comparison of Jewish, Muslim, and Christian monotheism, each claims to believe in one sovereign, creator God who is categorically different than His creation. Therefore, on monotheistic terms there is no metaphysical room for *another* God besides the one, the *only* God. In other words, if monotheism is true, then there is only one God. And if two religions believe in monotheism, then in general terms they *must* believe in the same one God.

One cannot expect more commonality between two different faiths than within a single faith. This is a famous discussion in philosophy: when two people each refer to the evening star and the morning star, they refer to the same planet Venus. Why do we consider it the same object? In terms of a description of God's characteristics, is there enough similarity between how Jews and another faith each understand the attributes of God in order to warrant the claim that we believe in the same monotheistic God? In broad, general terms, both religions share very similar features (i.e., monotheism, revelation from God in holy books, eschatological judgment, etc.) but differ on the details. Volf points out if one's beliefs are not *contrary* then one can know the monotheistic God even with wrong details. For example, Jews can acknowledge Christians as sharing the same God, even if we reject the Trinity. In spite of these wide differences among various theologians and traditions, all are referring to the same monotheistic God, seen through a glass darkly.

There is still a difference between *identifying* God truly and *approaching Him in worship* truly that is approaching God on His own terms. In other words: one cannot rightly worship the wrong God (this is idolatry); but, neither can you wrongly worship the right God. This works well in the Jewish case that Catholicism is the wrong worship of the right God, wrong in its concept of the Trinity, and wrong in its use of representation. But right in its love and fear of God, respect for scripture, love of neighbor, and many characteristics we recognize in Judaism. Volf reminds us not to create false dichotomies or to create distinctions that are not there.

Dialogue

Dialogue was originally a humanistic term based on Martin Buber's thought, which encouraged each side to put away its theological differences before a common human mutuality and understanding. Then it became a term for looking for commonality between faiths. Now, people are explicit in the retention of their own beliefs and when engaged in interfaith work more often use the words encounter, hospitality, or consultation. Many times the word is used solely as synonym for meetings between divergent groups. This section will help the reader distinguish between creating a theology of other religions and dialogue.

Already in the 1930s, Hans Schoeps (1909–1980) stated that the modern age of dialogue is a major change from the past era. So, too, Jacob Neusner astutely points out that between faiths, attitude is everything. And Marc Tannenbaum stated clearly that book knowledge alone does not change attitudes, one needs to encounter the other religion. If two religions see themselves at loggerheads, even commonalities and similarities will be downplayed before the imagined chasm. On the other hand, if two faiths are on the road to reconciliation then no amount of differences in theology will stand in its way. A person's existential attitude toward another religion determines what one sees. Is the person positive or negative, fearful or friendly, seeking bridges or barricades? Is one engaged in hospitality and openness? Prior historical encounters play a big role in this level of contact. The first type of dialogue is the existential attitude of Jews, Judaism and Jewish texts toward the other faith. This is not to just find similarity and differences but to discuss the fundamental initial perception toward the other religion. Are we conditioned from prior periods of persecution, contempt, or debate?

Do we now live in a post-polemic age with Christians? For example, until recently, Jews have viewed Christians as heirs of the crusaders. Alternatively, contemporary Jews view Buddhism with an overly positive veneer with no connection to Mongol warriors. How do we viscerally react to the rituals and symbols of another faith? If we see meditation, yoga, or a Gregorian chant, are we comfortable with it? Do we treat the other as idolatry, as an opposite, or as part of my faith? Many will call this sense of living in a post-polemic age as living in an age of dialogue. When one meets another faith, people use the word dialogue.

Whether it is called dialogue, encounter, hospitality, recognition, or consultation, many Jews seem to have trouble focusing on the event in front of them and not conjuring up grand events of dialogue like Vatican II and the proclamation of *Nostra Aetate*. Jews confuse grassroots initiatives with political, social, and theological dialogue. They don't keep clear the differences. Collectively working together after a disaster or local interfaith councils that serve as community building activity are not the same as joint political work or working to make the work better, and neither of these are the same as theological dialogue or mystical dialogue. The Catholic Church divides dialogue into four categories, but even those categories are foreign for Jews. For example, the Church might propose a program for Jews and Christians to collectively examine the history of anti-Semitism. The Church will call the program dialogue while the Jewish participants will call it a seminar on history. There might be a joint trip to visit a Holocaust memorial or to a death camp, which the Church will call dialogue and Jews will call memory and commemoration. Or a third example, a seminar on knowing other faiths if done under Church auspices would be considered as dialogue while Jews would use the academic term of studying other religions. So, in order to help some of my Jewish readers gain a sense of this over-stretched word dialogue, I will present the definitions of the Church, and compare that to intergroup or political dialogue.

The Pontifical Council for Interreligious Dialogue (PCID) has the following responsibilities: (1) to promote mutual understanding, respect, and collaboration between Catholics and the followers of others religious traditions; (2) to encourage the study of religions; (3) to promote the formation of persons dedicated to dialogue. In the language of the Catholic Church, the 1991 guidelines, issued as "Dialogue and Proclamation," have colored the field ever since. The list differentiates four types of dialogue: everyday life, joint action, theological, and religious experience.

> Dialogue requires both listening and active communication. It can take many forms: a) The dialogue of everyday life, where people strive to live in an open and neighborly spirit, sharing their joys and sorrows, their human problems and preoccupations. b) The dialogue of action, in which Christians and others collaborate for the integral development and liberation of people. c) The dialogue of theological exchange, where specialists seek to deepen their understanding of their respective religious heritages, and to appreciate each other's spiritual values. d) The dialogue of religious experience, where persons, rooted in their own religious traditions, share their spiritual riches, for instance with regard to prayer and contemplation, faith and ways of searching for God or the Absolute.[29]

They say that in dialogue "these traditions are to be approached with great sensitivity, on account of the spiritual and human values enshrined in them." They command our respect because over the centuries they have borne witness to the efforts to find answers "to those profound mysteries of the human condition"[30] and have given expression to the religious experience, and they continue to do so today. Other religions can be given credit for divine grace, holy spirit, mystery of God's salvation, wisdom, or the mystery of the unity of mankind. To say that the other religious traditions include elements of grace does not imply that everything in them is the result of grace.

In encountering other religions, Len Swindler (b. 1929), academic specialist in dialogue, offered the following advice, which many integrate into their work. One ought not to assume in advance where points of agreement or disagreement will exist. Instead, listen with empathy and sympathy and avoid presumptions about what the other will say. See how much is held in common while maintaining the integrity of your own tradition. If there is a real point of disagreement, it must be respected. However, it may be at a different point than that which was originally expected.

But much, if not most, dialogue is of a social or political nature in which the very act of meeting and socializing breaks the ice to lose the heterophobia of the unknown other. Professor Mohamed Abu Nimer of the American University School of International Service is a leading expert on the group dynamic of political dialogue and conflict resolution. Nimer shows that in political dialogue, the goal is for deep forms of hostility to be overcome, at least temporarily, and to identify where is there a resistance to change.[31] There is a need for stereotypical images, prejudices, and past injustices to be safely discussed, and overcome the fear and avoidance of the other. Each side needs to be able to hear the religious narrative of others including how each side describes their rituals, holidays, and beliefs. Therefore, in political dialogue, we start with the universal or religious secondary language for what we share, such as peace and love. This helps to discover similarities and allows differences to slowly be discovered over time.

In the initial meeting of Phase One, there is an excitement to be at the event combined with a tension of representing two different groups. The conversation has an undue politeness. People see themselves as ambassadors of their religion, and present ideal versions of their own religion.

In Phase Two, after the initial speeches and icebreakers, there is an appeal to broad similarities and the creation of universals like children of Adam or the image of God. This is a period in which both sides reveal stereotypes that need to be overcome, and to create through informal contact a secondary language applicable to both groups.

In Phase Three, the differences are accentuated and there is a discussion of the frustration, mistrust, suspicion, and blame. At this point, after the creation of informal contacts, it can be handled by personal discussion. The theme of tolerance is reiterated.

In Phase Four, there is a recognition of the limits of meeting and encounter as well as an appreciation for its advantages. In an ideal situation, both sides are more trusting of the other side and feel empowered to continue the informal contacts for further discussion. One can commit to continue exploring alternatives to conflicting positions. One tries to arrange common activities for the future. Both sides map the issues onto the landscape of resources available through the current inter-religious organizations. Participants may return to their fears and stereotypes. Jews may continue to find anti-Semitism everywhere and to find either Christianity or Islam as inherently antagonistic. But, at the very least, those of the other religion in the room who participated in the dialogue are considered good or at least better than their coreligionists outside the room. Yet, dialogue excludes those not in the room so they too have to be acknowledged.

According to Nimer, if this meeting is done well then once you meet—you will never return to the same awareness—you join a new society. One's former sectarian judgment, on the other hand, allowed no room or need for negotiation. But now, one has new information for an alternate cognitive process—for a change in the mindset; second, one has positive emotional experience for a change in heart to a safe and trusting place; and finally, one has worked together with the other group leading to an attitude change.

By almost all accounts, interfaith encounters and dialogues are yielding fruits of shared spiritual questing, mutual learning, and common actions for local and national good. It has led to a greater respect and recognition for the "other" and has helped to overcome hatred.

Conclusion

Former Chief Rabbi Israel Meir Lau (b. 1937) delivered a speech at the Inter-religious Meeting at the Pontifical Institute in 2000. Rabbi Lau acknowledges the other faiths and calls on all faiths to adopt a humanistic approach of listening to one another and working together for peace, friendship, and understanding:

> Everyone has his way of serving the Almighty, but one way is common and must be common for all mankind, all the believers of all the religions, especially the brother of the monotheistic faith. Peace, friendship, understanding, listening to one another, even though we do not agree with everything. In spite of all obstacles and differences, to overcome obstacles and differences, we have to speak, we have to listen. We are ready to go from place to place, from one continent to the other, from one century to another, offering a hand, speaking about peace.

These public statements have important effects in molding open communities and softening the ground for encounter, self-understanding, and dialogue.

Rabbi Sha'ar Yashuv Cohen (b. 1927) was the Chief Rabbi of Haifa, and the rabbinic liaison of the State of Israel to the Vatican and for interfaith dialogue, and he is currently at the forefront of the Orthodox Jewish encounter with other religions. His family background, rabbinical and political positions, and open personality as a whole make him an important contemporary voice. Rabbi Cohen accepts that there have been forty years of dialogue, that there was a Fundamental Accord between the Vatican and Israel in 1992, and he has responded to all the new calls for dialogue in the twenty-first century. He engages in theological dialogue with Christians and the Vatican as a representation of Israel.[32]

Rabbi Cohen envisions a tolerant application of Rav Kook in which the messianic age is not an age of greater distinction between faiths but of expansiveness of Judaism to embrace the world. Until now, Judaism's universalism was only in potential, but now that we live, according to Rabbi Cohen, in the potentially messianic age, Jews need to fulfill the Biblical destiny of universalism. Just as in Rav Kook's vision, every Jew will return to Judaism, so too will every gentile return to God. Sha'ar Yashuv Cohen remains within the inclusivist world of the medieval texts:

> We need to find the best in each nation [. . .] and they need to be able to respect us. A nice garden is not just one flower but a variety [. . .] the world is God's garden—it needs many flowers and we are God's gardeners.

His acknowledgement that the other nations have things that we do not have and those novel aspects create variety in the world is a major concession to acknowledging diversity, but at the same time he envisions everyone under Israel's banner. This metaphor is a good test case for the chapter. Is the sense of a bouquet self-aware responsibility or apologetics? Sha'ar Yashuv Cohen uses the metaphor of different variegated flowers, for religions, and a "basic tradition of tolerance" growing in harmony to produce a beautiful garden. He called Haifa's residents "outstanding in working together despite different creeds and approaches." This harmony offers "a ray of hope [that] people can change their way of relating to each other."[33]

We have come a long way from the Jewish soldier described by Chaim Potok as having never thought about other faiths before, but we still have a great deal of work to create a Jewish theology of other religions.

2

Jewish Views of Religion

The world is comprised of a variety of diverse religions. What does it mean to observe a person of a different faith performing a ritual, engaged in prayer, or seeking mystical experience? People were always aware of the practice of others. In modern times, the word "religion" implies the differences and diversities of many different religious communities, each with their own faiths and practices. This concept is something rare in pre-modern texts, which use different categories of thought to describe religion than do modern texts.

Religion through the Ages

During the Roman era, religion referred to "respect for what is sacred, reverence for the gods"; alternately, it could be defined as "obligation, the bond between man and the gods." The term was still used throughout the medieval period and during the Reformation to designate true "piety" or "religiosity." It did not signify a system of beliefs that made it possible to discern a true system from a false one. Rather, a set of obligations upon a given community. The Rabbinic texts reflect awareness of the fact that others are engaged in the performances of obligations to the gods, but they were not bound by Jewish obligations. In the medieval Islamic world, Jews used the word *dat,* meaning religious community, and it focused on the organized entity rather than on piety.

In the middle ages, the questions about my religion, and the religion of others, were of functionality: Does it work? And, is it of divine origin? (I dealt extensively with the medieval texts in my previous book, *Judaism and Other Religions.*)

Medieval thinkers spoke of false religion as incorrect doctrine. Early modern views of false religion considered them idolatry and polytheism From the sixteenth century onward the word religion came to be used in the plural, referring increasingly to Islam as well as to the traditions of India and the Far East. Between the seventeenth and eighteenth centuries, the questions shifted to the new ideas of many religions and polytheism. Other religions were seen as superstitious, and there was more emphasis on one's own faith being correct than extending the olive branch to other religions. This concept of polytheism and superstition is not found in Rabbinic texts, but has crept into Jewish use from the vernacular.

In the nineteenth and twentieth centuries, however, religions were credited with different abilities to convey an Abstract Spirit that was universal to all of them. The nineteenth century saw evolutionary and Hegelian schemes. It is only in the twentieth century that we have religious experience and a comparison among the faiths. In modern times, the word "religion" implies concepts of difference and diversity of many different religious communities, each with their own faiths and practices. This concept is something nontraditional to pre-modern texts, which used different categories than what we use today. This chapter will survey some of the categories used by Jewish texts.

- ❖ Rabbinics—Civic religion, Magic, and ritual objects
- ❖ Early modern—Idolatry, Philosophic Religion, Deism- de Costa and Spinoza
- ❖ Modern—Idolatry as sensuality and materialism – Hirsch
- ❖ Hegelian religion—Kook, Emil Hirsch, Grossman
- ❖ Evolutionary Theism—Michael Friedlander
- ❖ Religious Experience—Scholem, Heschel, and Soloveitchik

Rabbinics

In the Roman Empire, piety was considered fulfillment of obligations to the gods. This widespread religious performance by non-Jews was observed by rabbinic literature. They considered praying, offering votives, and making petitions by gentiles as natural human phenomena. With regards to the human phenomenon of ritual, there seems to be somewhat begrudging respect given to the foreign observance.

Most of the Rabbinic legal restrictions dealt with avoiding the false worship of representation by avoiding statues of the gods. The rabbis of this time were more worried about participation in the urban Greco-Roman life including its dedication to deities as part of the city: temple, bathhouse, library, brothel, monuments, and civil authority. Ancient worship in civic life consisted of statues of the gods and offerings, which meant the Jews did not take part. In Jewish texts, there is almost no discussion of the religious beliefs of the philosophers and their private religion during these times. (For more on the prohibition of foreign worship in the rabbinic age, see my prior book *Judaism and Other Religions.*)

Moshe Halbertal and Avishai Margalit in their book *Idolatry* showed the use of the term *avodah zarah* (idolatry) varied in Rabbinic metaphor from (1) Idolatry is about what is permitted representation, or image of God; (2) idolatry as myth or wrong story; (3) idolatry as error; (4) idolatry as having the wrong God; and finally (5) idolatry as an immoral lifestyle associated with the practices of the worship of Canaanite deity *Baal Peor* and following one's evil inclinations. I will look more at the rabbinic attitudes toward the practice of Roman holidays, practices, and objects, not the use of the metaphor.

Talmud Yerushalmi

In most cases, the legal parts of the rabbinic corpus, Mishnah, Tosefta, and Talmuds are concerned with the parameters of distancing from gentiles or avoiding foreign worship practices. Occasionally, the texts give indirect insight into the rabbinic view of religion in general. In the following excerpt of a rabbinic discussion, there is rabbinic linkage and taxonomy of various types of foreign worship specifically between the varied religions of the Romans, Persians, and the Egyptians. They knew that the worship of the Greco-Roman gods was connected to the Roman public life of amphitheaters, fairs, and circuses.[1]

The passage below acknowledges that there are several separate communities of religious practices and that Rab in Babylon sees a natural human element in religion, either in fear of natural phenomena or in royal kingship rituals. The Romans named the first day of the month after the new moon, Kalends. This passage refers to the January 1st holiday that is equivalent to a winter solstice date. Saturnalia was celebrated the week before lasting from December 17th to the 23rd and consisted of gift giving, wearing festive garments, and participating in role reversals. The etiology of the holiday Kalends Januarius here does not fit the ethnographic description of the year-end festival, but it seems to loosely reflect a holiday to celebrate the triumph of Augustus over Marc Antony. Kratesis is defined as the ascension to the throne and possibly refers to a specifically Eastern festival of the ascension of Augustus over Egypt or another Emperor's triumph over a certain country. The historian Fritz Graf, in his study of these pages of the Talmud, finds a precise knowledge of certain details combined with a lack of knowledge of the range of festivals. Graf is inclined to think that the rabbinic knowledge was of the early Mishanic era and does not reflect the reality of the later centuries.

The Talmud has knowledge that Diocletian (Roman Emperor from 284–305) was associated with the restoration of the Temples, especially the Tyre Fair, which was dedicated to Hercules. Diocletian, according to Christian literature, was a horrible persecutor of Christians but here he receives a neutral cameo appearance:

Rab said, "Kalends did the first man found.
When he saw that the nights were getting longer, he said, 'Woe is me. Perhaps him concerting whom it is written, "He shall bruise your head and you shall bruise his heel" (Gen. 3:15)—perhaps he is going to come and bite me.' 'Even the darkness is not dark to thee,'" (Ps. 139:12)
   "When [the first man] saw that the days were growing longer, he said, 'Kalendes— *Kalondeo!* Praise be to God!'"[1]

The kingdom of Egypt and the kingdom of Rome were at war with one another. [The Talmud recounts a story in which the King of Rome sacrificed himself and his sons grieved for him.]
   Thus then did his sons cry out for him, 'Kalendes Januarius!' From the day following and onward, they mourned for him, 'The black day!'"
   R. Yohanan said, "With reference to both Kalends and Saturnalia, it is forbidden only [to do business] with those who worship on that day."

R. Abba in the name of Rab: "There are three festival seasons in Babylonia, and three festal seasons in Media. The three festal seasons in Babylonia are Mahuri, Kanauni, and Banauta. The three festal seasons in Media are Nausardi, Tiriasqi, and Mahirkana."

Kratesis: It is the day on which the Romans seized power.

The emperor's anniversary: "On the third day, which was Pharaoh's birthday, he made a feast for all his servants." (Gen. 40:20)

His birthday and the day of his death: To this point [the Mishnah periscope refers] to public [celebrations]. From this point forward it refers to individual [celebrations].

"I, Diocletian the emperor, have founded the fair of Tyre for the fortune of Archeleus, my brother, for eight days" [so the fair was indeed for the sake of idolatry].[2]

It is important to note that Roman religion mixed loyalty to the emperor with the world of the markets, theaters, and bath houses, which existed across the empire. Did Romans treat this civil mixture the way Christians treated their faith as something requiring personal affirmation? The answer according to scholars is clearly no, and this will color the rabbinic response. Anthropologist Dan Sperber notes that the goal of Roman worship of statues was to show civic allegiance and no one, except a philosopher, would articulate dissent based on belief or fail to offer homage. Historian Paul Veyne shows that they did not believe their myths as literal and thus, the stories of the gods were treated as part of the general culture and used to refer to the organizations of family, social, and political life.[3]

Rabbinic Ritual

The Greeks and Romans were cognizant of demons as disembodied spirits acting as both instruments of vengeance and products of magic. In the accounts of Josephus, the New Testament as well as Greco-Roman literature generally, Jews were experts in the process of casting off demons. Josephus, for example, shows this widespread talent among Jews by referring to King Solomon's talent for exorcisms. In his account of Eliezer, , who in the presence of Vespasian, his family, and soldiers, was able to cure those who were possessed by using both a magic ring and herbs placed under the nose. In response to this account and others, the satirist Lucian ridiculed the credulousness of the widespread belief in demons and the spiritual realm.[4]

The Jewish position moved from first century acceptance of the Greco-Roman practice of exorcism to the sixth and seventh centuries' view of Judaism as entirely separate from the realm of demons and its former embeddedness in its era. In the passage below, R. Johanan Ben Zakkai is portrayed as responding to a gentile who associates religious ritual with the questionable realm of magic by connecting the ritual with the more socially acceptable process of exorcism. The gentile asks Rabbi Yohanan ben Zakkai about the red heifer, asking if this is magical. The answer is no, rather it is a simple exorcism known universally in late antiquity. The story concludes with the Rabbi's disciples asking about this comparison. His own answer to his students is that ritual is God's decree transcending cultural categories. Rabbi Yohanan's denial of any commonality with exorcism of other religions is meant to show that what the Jews do they perform as God's decrees and not to be associated with any magical, pagan practice. This story can be found in various post-Talmudic Midrash collections such as the *Pesikta de-Rav Kehana Tanhuma* and *Numbers Rabbah.*

> A gentile asked R. Johanan Ben Zakkai: "These rites that you perform look like a kind of magic. You bring a heifer, burn it, pound it, and take its ashes. If one of you is defiled by a dead body you sprinkle upon him two or three drops and say to him: 'You are clean!'"
>
> R. Johanan asked him: "Has the demon of madness ever possessed you?"
>
> "No," he replied.
>
> "Have you ever seen a man possessed by this demon of madness?"
>
> "Yes," said he.
>
> "And what do you do in such a case?"
>
> "We bring roots," he replied, "and make them smoke under him, then we sprinkle water upon the demon and it flees."
>
> Said R. Johanan to him: "Let your ears hear what you utter with your mouth! Precisely so is this spirit a spirit of uncleanness. Water of purification is sprinkled upon the unclean and the spirit flees." (Zachariah 13:2)
>
> When the idolater had gone, R. Johanan's disciples said to their master: "Master! You have thrust off that heathen with a mere reed of an answer, but what explanation will you give to us?"
>
> Said he to them: "By your life! It is not the dead that defiles nor the water that purifies! The Holy One, blessed be He, merely says, 'I have laid down a statute, I have issued a decree. You are not allowed to transgress My decree.'"[5]

Helios

During the second and third centuries, there was a rise in the worship of the sun as "Sol Invictus" (Invincible Sun). Its origins appear to have diverse origins in an older Roman sun god, second century Jupiter worship, as well as in a Syrian sun god that possessed elements of ancient Baal worship. In 274, Aurelian made it an official cult alongside the traditional Roman cults. Julian the Apostate had also offered speeches in honor of the sun. However, Augustine, the fourth century Church Father, still felt the need to preach against the cult.

The imagery of Sol Invictus is also found in several Jewish synagogues, leading to the questions of whether Jews used the imagery for aesthetic reasons, if they actually worshiped the sun, or if they used Helios as a symbol for the biblical God. The Rabbinic E. E. Urbach considered the sun imagery as merely figurative whereas the scholar of Hellenistic Jewry Erwin R. Goodenough considered these synagogues as inhabited by non-Rabbinic syncretic Jews. Emmanuel Friedman, a contemporary scholar, thinks that there were Jews who did indeed worship the sun. He notes that the Bible finds the worship of the sun as a continuous temptation for Israel and that the Talmud had to warn against the sun imagery (Deut 4:19 17:3, 2 Kings 21:5, 23:11-12 Jer 8:2, Ezekiel 8:16). "You should not make the likeness of My attendants who serve me, such as the sun and the moon, the stars or astrological signs" (RH 24b AZ 43a). Friedman also collects syncretic texts such as the fourth century Jewish magical work

Sefer ha Razim, which includes a hymn, "I revere you, Helios." While Friedman himself does not have any clear evidence about actual Jews worshipers of Helios, the idea that non-Jews worship the sun, the moon, or the stars is widespread in rabbinic literature.[6]

Pillars: Genesis and Deuteronomy

Early rabbinic texts point out a difference in religious practice between Genesis, where the patriarchs used stele pillars as a sign to God similar to the Canaanite practice, and Deuteronomy, where they are forbidden. This can be seen in the following passages:

> Jacob set up a pillar in the place where He spoke with him, a pillar of stone, and he poured out a drink-offering thereon, and poured oil thereon (Genesis 35:14).

> Nor shall you erect for yourself a pillar which the Lord your God hates. (Deut. 16:22)

> Do not erect a pillar that the lord your God hates. It only states pillar, how do I know that it applies to all idolatry is it not [logically] correct that if the pillar which was beloved by the patriarchs is hated for the children, the idolatry that was hated by the patriarchs is it not so that it is forbidden to the children.[7]

A modern historian would assign the Biblical texts to two dates or two traditions; however, even though the rabbinic text was aware of the change, the passage does not concern itself to explain why it was changed. Rashi proffers his own explanation of the text based on the *Sifrei,* which notes a change due to an adoption of the practice by the Canaanites. Due to this, now it has to be forbidden. "For it was the practice of the Canaanites; and even though He liked it in the days of the patriarchs, now it is hateful to Him, since idolaters took over the practice." Abraham Ibn Ezra offers a more concise harmonization. He suggests Genesis refers to the practice of erecting a pillar and Deuteronomy only forbids idolatrous pillar so there is no contradiction with Genesis.

Nineteenth century traditionalists Rabbi S. R. Hirsch and Rabbi A. I. Kook use this text to differentiate between worship of God during the period of the Patriarchs, and His worship by their descendants. Genesis was seen as a sensual and materialistic form of worship because that was required in the early era. For Hirsch, after Sinai, man's worship of God should no longer use natural objects. For Kook, later in the Deuteromistic age, the abstract dimension of God needed to be introduced.[8]

Egyptian Religions

The Bible paints Egypt as having magicians, priests, and many false Gods. The rabbinic texts of the first centuries turned to their contemporary Egypt in order to expand on the biblical account. The texts consider the Nile as one of the Egyptian gods, as both "Pharaoh and the Egyptians worshiped the Nile. Therefore, God said that he would smite their god first" (*Exodus Rabbah* 9:9). The Nile's annual overflow is therefore the occasion for "the ministers (*sarim*) to go and celebrate at the river, as a festival of idolaters" (Pesiq. Zut Gen. 39).

According to Midrash scholar Rivka Ulmer, the Egyptian term for the overflow of the Nile is Hapy (h pj), which is translated to a divine figure personifying the overflow, which brings abundance and prosperity to the land. "The rabbis assumed that the Egyptians worshiped the Nile. However, the transformation of the Nile into a divinity with a major cult transpired only during the Greco-Roman period. Prior to this era . . . fecundity figures related to the Nile overflow . . . were not major gods." In the times of the Romans, there was only one Nile god: Neilos. The "Nile Festival" mentioned in rabbinic texts seems akin to the Egyptian Opet festival, in which the "people joined in a dramatic procession honoring Amun that commenced at the Karnak Temple and ended at the Luxor Temple." The Midrash below offers a glimpse into both types of worship in Roman era Egypt: a festival dedicated to worshiping Neilos as well as serving as a dramatic procession to Amun.[9]

> It came to pass on a certain day, when he went into the house to do his work (Gen. 39:11). [R. Judah and R. Nehemiah, each has his own explanation of this]. R. Judah said: [On that day] there was a day of idolatrous sacrifice to the Nile; everyone went to see it, but he [Joseph] did not go. R. Nehemiah said: It was a day of a theatrical performance, which all went to see, but he went into the house to work on his master's accounts.

The Mishnah warns against objects with "the image of a breastfeeding woman or of Serapis" as amulets with the Egyptian-Hellenistic deity, Serapis, and his consort, Isis. There are other representations of *Isis lactans* (Isis as a breastfeeding mother) as well that were prevalent in late antiquity.

Rabbinic texts acknowledge that the Bible may still be using terms from the Egyptian language as a means to show the God of the Israelites displaced the Egyptian gods. The best example is the Hebrew word Anokhi as the first word of the Ten Commandments in its association with the Egyptian ANKH, the symbol for eternal life possessed by all deities.

> R. Nehemiah said, What is anokhi (Ex 20:2)? It is an Egyptian word. Why did God find it necessary to use an Egyptian word?
> The Holy One used the word anokhi ('nky),which is a form of the Egyptian "nwk so that the Holy One began His inauguration of the giving of the Torah with Israel's acquired way of speaking;" *I am (anokhi [nky]) the Lord, your God. Pesiq. Rab. Kah* 12:24

In some rabbinic texts, Egypt has become a typology for assimilation or immorality rather than a real place, an emblem of the ultimate rejection of one's heritage. The typology of the opposition of the powers of Egyptian magicians to the powers of Moses and the biblical monotheistic God are already intrinsic to the biblical story and there are innumerable discussions of the magical religion of Egypt in rabbinic texts and later commentators throughout the middle ages.

Early-Modern Era: From Idolatry to Polytheism

In the sixteenth century, new worlds were being discovered by the Europeans, scholastic thought was declining, and there was a Protestant reformation. Each event helped lead to a dissolution of the former hierarchical categories that distinguished between faiths based on how close they were to the medieval definition of truth. During this time as well, the famous Sepulvada-Las Casas debate (1550–1551) occurred. The former, using medieval categories, ruled that the people in the new world must be non-believers and worshiping a false god. The latter, however, asked, "who has ever thought of offering sacrifice to any being other than the one whom he knew, believed or imagined to be God?" This question led Las Casas to his new conclusion about the nature of idolatrous worship: the heathens of the world are following a universal natural religion; all people have a natural law and natural reason. (Parenthetically, he considered Jews as tainted by Egyptian magical and idolatry, hence pagan.)

During this time, the term "idolatry" moved from its original reference of icons and false representation and transformed into a variety of modern meanings. The first use of the new definition was as a rallying cry by Dutch Calvinists against the Catholics. The latter were compared by the Protestants to the priests and cults of the ancient Egyptians, the ancient Romans, and the polytheistic cults in the new worlds. Idolatry was also used by Deists and Catholics to refer to any superstitious religious practice.[10] In the seventeenth century, Bernard Pickart among others, wanted to show that the rituals of the different religions were all different. His ethnography described and condemned the religions of the world at the same time.

A second change in this century was the invention of word "polytheism." The term was first used by John Selden in 1619 in Greek, and then popularized in English by Ralph Cudworth. As Unitarian Protestants, both men considered anything but pure monotheism as idolatry.[11] Medieval thinkers accepted that humanity has had devolution from the Biblical truth to idolatry. This was replaced by John Spenser's theory of progress from paganism to Protestantism. During this era, the biblical approach of viewing all humanity as diffusion from Noah was breaking down through the use of non-biblical materials.[12]

Third change: Henry Moore, the Cambridge Neo-Platonist defined idolatry as polytheism, equating both with the multiplicity of sensuality and materialism. Moore saw this sensuality in the rites of Indies and Catholicism. He saw Judaism as filled with Egyptian pagan rites, only removed by Jesus.[13]

In the eighteenth century, religion was conceptualized as natural theology and that was in contrast to calling one's opponents pagan, and thereby immoral and backward. There was always one single true religion and the others all have defects leaving one's faith without rivals.[14] Voltaire states that idolatry never occurred but polytheism did. People never believed in idols, but rather they worshiped many gods. For Voltaire, religions are popular or elite, rather than true or false; Voltaire warned not to judge religions by the superstitious masses but rather by the elite. He makes it solely a choice of philosophic monism or polytheism.[15]

Isaac de Castro

Balthazar (Isaac) Orobio de Castro (1617–1687), was a Jewish philosopher, physician, and apologist. Born to a Converso family in Portugal, de Castro returned to Judaism upon moving to Amsterdam where he became a prominent member of the Sephardic community and authored anti-Christian texts. De Castro is a widely read prime example of Jewish participation in Enlightenment irreligion.[16] The early modern period defined idolatry as falsehood and superstition compared to Enlightenment thought. There was no need to polemicize against doctrines of God, prophecy, or Divine providence. Other religions, sans Judaism, were by definition considered as superstition.

Castro no longer uses the word idolatry in reference to the worship of images themselves but rather as an umbrella term for any false belief. For him, Christianity was the prime case of false doctrines, rites, and sham mysteries. The Bible did not have to mention Christianity by name, just as it had no need to mention Greco-Roman religions by name. Divine law kept Israel away from all the idolatries and ignorance. Castro thinks that "in the five books of the law, God warned Israel about all the idolatries of the gentiles, about the philosophers, and about the trinity that the Christians would invent."

> First of all, in response to the proposed argument, in no sense was it necessary that God our Lord should express himself, as the divine oracle, on the Christian sect, naming it, and identifying it as preparing to impose itself on humanity, nor go so far as identifying its false doctrines, rites and sham mysteries, just as he did not do this with respect to the fictitious deities of the ancient pagans: he did not speak of Saturn, Jupiter, Mars, Bacchus, Venus and the others, nor did he mention the superstitions of their false cult, although this idolatry was no less famous or widespread, and in no small terms harmful to Israel; but this has passed, as (will) the present, as the lord God forewarned his beloved people in the divine law that is the archive and sum of all prophecy: there they were clearly taught enough not to accept and to dismiss the many idolatries and superstitions that could be invented by the wickedness or the ignorance of men in all ages, and how this was to become very diverse; in opposition to all these the divine wisdom was able to and knew to give a general doctrine, refuting all these with general precepts—whatever evil might be invented or feigned in the unfolding of time, declarations that his mighty hand or his divine love created the heavens and the earth, humanity and all other creatures, and explanations of how he put in place this universe in all its perfection, thus excluding the vain opinions of the future philosophers of the gentiles.

> Passing through the intermediate eras and arriving at the divine gift of Sinai, which intimated to the people God's ineffable unity, that God, the lord of Israel, was one God, which is a doctrine repeated many times by the creator, and which does not require arguments.[17]

The rejection of many gods applies both to the ancient pagans and the modern Christians. Any numerical counting about God implies multiplicity. God is not comprised of multiple persons, and things are either of a single divine essence or multiplicity. De Castro accuses Christianity of tritheism. He ridicules Christianity and declares that God does not have a son and there cannot be a meek personified God who obeys a higher God or suffers. His form of antireligion means attacking Christianity and declaring Judaism as truth:

> With this divine conclusion the mighty lord locked the gate to the children of Israel, so that they should not enter into the false credit of a multiplicity of Gods, and he excluded not only the past sects of the Chaldeans, Greeks and Romans, and all the other nations that in different parts of the world worship these or many Gods, but also in the present the Christians, who claim to split God and divide him into three propositions, or truly distinct people.
>
> If they examine his own words, can believe in three Gods, because this is impossible, and is incompatible with the natural mode of speaking that is our own interior understanding; to say that God is three, and thus that there are three Gods.
>
> Israel was also warned in many places in the sacred scripture that God did not depend on another in his divine actions, and was the master of all that he might wish to do, and whoever told God what to create or to do was his advisor only, since just as he is independent in his existence, so is he in his actions, which cannot be distinguished from his existence . . . thus it cannot be possible to believe the Christian, who proposes that God the father sent God his son to the world to die for mankind, as is affirmed in an infinity of places in the Gospels . . . How could an Israelite believe in such a meek, obedient God, so dependent in his being and in his actions, being taught by the same all-powerful God that he is independent in his being and his actions and without dependence or alien advice.

Baruch Spinoza

Benedict (Baruch) Spinoza (1632–1677) is considered one of the greatest of all philosophers. He was also a free thinker, Biblical critic, and political theorist. Similar to De Castro, Spinoza was a descendent of a Portuguese Converso family who moved to Amsterdam. His beliefs led him afoul of the Jewish community, and according to popular accounts, he was excommunicated in 1656.

Spinoza did not exclude his own birth religion of Judaism from his critical comments about religion in general. He started his rational critique closest to home and declared that Biblical religions are the greatest threat to philosophic thought due to their attempts to make truth and political claims. For Spinoza, a true religion is one that practices and promotes justice and charity combined with a love of God. No ritual is needed and no religious law is needed. The Law of God commands only the knowledge and love of God and the actions required for attaining that condition. Such love must arise not from fear of possible penalties or hope for any rewards, but rather derive solely from the goodness of its object. The ceremonial laws helped preserve the Jewish kingdom and insure its prosperity, but were valid only as long as that political entity lasted.

Spinoza begins the treatise by alerting his readers to those superstitious beliefs and behaviors that the clergy, by playing on ordinary human emotions, encourage in their followers. A person guided by fear and hope, the main emotions in a life devoted to the pursuit of temporal advantages, turns, in the face of the vagaries of fortune to behaviors calculated to secure the goods he desires. Thus we pray, worship, make votive offerings, sacrifice, and engage in all the various rituals of popular religion. Ambitious and self-serving clergy do their best to utilize this situation and give some permanence to those beliefs and behaviors:

> Immense efforts have been made to invest religion, true or false, with such pomp and ceremony that it can sustain any shock and constantly evoke the deepest reverence in all its worshippers.
>
> Scriptural doctrine contains not abstruse speculation or philosophic reasoning, but very simple matters able to be understood by the most sluggish mind.
>
> There is a Supreme Being who loves justice and charity, whom all must obey in order to be saved, and must worship by practicing justice and charity to their neighbor.
>
> Every person is in duty bound to adapt these religious dogmas to his own understanding and to interpret them for himself in whatever way makes him feel that he can more readily accept them with full confidence and conviction.[18]

For Spinoza, everything is based on the natural order. There are no miracles and so, there is no revelation or Divine status given to the Bible. He stresses that God, as monotheism, is a principle of the universe and does not need any priests, theologians, or jurists. Many modern Jews follow this approach and freely combine it with the critiques of Biblical religion by Hobbes, Hume, and Renan.

During the twentieth century, Spinoza's approach was combined with treating Judaism as a people, not as a religion. In 1954, Albert Einstein wrote a letter to Eric Gutkind reflecting the view of many modern Jews toward other religions. Such an approach may be tolerant, but it does not encourage the investigation or discussion of other faiths:

> The word God is for me nothing more than the expression and product of human weaknesses, the Bible a collection of honorable, but still primitive legends which are nevertheless pretty childish. No interpretation no matter how subtle can (for me) change this. These subtilised interpretations are highly manifold according to their nature and have almost nothing to do with the original text. For me the Jewish religion like all other religions is an incarnation of the most childish superstitions. And the Jewish people to whom I gladly belong and with whose mentality I have a deep affinity have no different quality for me than all other people . . .
>
> But a limited causality is no longer causality at all, as our wonderful Spinoza recognized with all incision, probably as the first one. . .[19]

Moses Mendelssohn

Moses Mendelssohn (1729–1786) was a German Jewish literary critic, community leader, and philosopher. His writings, together with his Jewish heritage, placed him at the focal point of the German Enlightenment debates for over three decades. Mendelssohn contributed significantly to the life of the Jewish community and letters in Germany, campaigning for Jewish civil rights, and translating the Pentateuch and the Psalms into German. As a Jew, he had an unwavering belief in the harmonizing effects of rational analysis and religious discourse. His book, *Jerusalem, or on Religious Power and Judaism,* was a forceful argument for conceiving Judaism as a religion founded upon reason alone.

Mendelssohn provides a model for universal religion that does not require a specific revelation. Mendelssohn postulated that belief in God, revelation, and reward and punishment were universal.

> The voice that was heard at Sinai on the great day did not proclaim, "I am the eternal, your God, the necessary autonomous being, omnipotent and omniscient, who rewards men in a future life according to their deeds." This is the universal religion of mankind not Judaism, and this kind of universal religion— without which man can become neither virtuous nor happy—was not and, in fact, could not have been revealed at Sinai. For who could have needed the sound of thunder and the blast of trumpets to become convinced of the validity of these eternal verities?[20]

Many twentieth-century Jews believe, in a similar manner, in a rational or even in a mystical God available to all, but consider that all religions are just reflections of that universal truth.

Samson Raphael Hirsch

Rabbi Samson Raphael Hirsch (1808–1888) published *Horeb* during his time as Chief Rabbi of Oldenberg in 1837. This work became a widely read catechism and modern definition of Judaism.

Rabbi Hirsch defines idolatry as considering the natural world as separate from God. The world is filled with natural forces and internal forces of man, some seen some unseen. One should appreciate that there is a Divine law of nature and God's providence for human destiny. According to Hirsch, humans are given moral freedom, which can triumph over the tyranny of ruthless power or over the bondage to the passions. Moral freedom, to Hirsch, is seen as a gift of God and one must use to it to subordinate to God's laws for humanity.

The quests for wealth, power, and knowledge are all forms of idolatry in that one does not subject their forces to a higher purpose. Idolatry, the treating of anything besides God as absolute, consists of a loss of human dignity; this loss is not an intellectual mistake. Rather, one must beware the idolatrous human bondage of sensuality. Polytheism takes the form of one believing he does not have to follow God's duty and can instead follow passions. For Rabbi Hirsch, seeing the world as gods or forces is polytheistic, which is idolatry (*avodah zarah*).

Rabbi Hirsch's discussion of idolatry is seen elsewhere in his works. He portrays the idolatry of Egypt as sensual, as slavery without freedom, and as the power of mammon and the state. Roman society is portrayed as idolatrous due to the brutality of the state and its emphasis on militarism. Christianity and Islam both depend upon the religion of the Hebrews; without the latter, there would never have been a Bible or a Koran.

From the seventeenth century onward, idolatry moved from its original reference to icons to false attitudes toward life. European sermons preached against the major forms of polytheism as materialism, the world of commerce, and sexuality. Henry Moore, the Cambridge Neo-Platonist, defined idolatry as a combination of polytheism, the multiplicity of sensuality, and materialism. Hirsch places tremendous emphasis on the dangers of sensuality (*Sinnlichkeit*) in his writings. He easily finds support in the rabbinic statement "What is the strange god within a man's body? It is none other than the impulse to evil" (TB Shabbat 105b).

In the nineteenth century Weimar Classicism, polytheism came to mean the worship of nature or man himself and not the higher duties. *Schiller's Letters on the Aesthetic Education of Man* (1795) warns against imagination and sensuality. Man should use his freedom and take charge of his destiny. In Schiller's early work, "Mission of Moses," he argues that "Reason's victory over those coarser errors assured, and the ideas about the Supreme Being necessarily ennobled. The idea of a universal connection among things must lead necessarily to the conception of a single, Supreme Understanding." These diverse influences are clearly seen in Hirsch's *Horeb*.

> Both heresy (*minut*) and immorality (*zenut*) lead to idolatry—riotous enjoyment leads to it directly; denial and misrepresentation of God usually over the bridge of pleasure.
> And if then, in the embrace of sensuality, you have stripped yourself of everything spiritual, no longer retaining any feeling for the Divine, you will yourself become aware in your impulses of your feebleness, your instability, your inconstancy in pleasure, and you will fall prostrate before every creature that provides you with enjoyment and itself seems to you so noble and so everlasting in its enjoyment.

> You can also reach idolatry, or rather polytheism, directly through the eye and the understanding of the senses, if Torah does not reveal to you the One and Only God; for with your physical eye and understanding you behold only particular beings and activities, but not the Invisible One with his dominating law. You see only gods, not God. This is *avodah zarah*.[21]

> You see on every side active forces and their carriers in Nature, elements and carriers of elements like the sun and the earth and the sea and the air; in the life of peoples, you see Nature, soil, rivers, mountains, and so forth; you see Nature, under the hands of man, raised to a power, and you see men with their wisdom and foolishness, power and weakness, passion and folly, fashioning, destroying and influencing the fate and the life of peoples; and an unseen force that holds sway over destiny and life. And in your own life you see the spiritual and the animal in you; you see yourself as a creative force, bestowing a blessing or a curse on everything around you.[22]

> But nothing of all this exists or acts by its own power or its own will. Nothing of all this is a god; all of it is created, the servant of the One all-ruling and omnipresent God. In Nature you see God's law hold sway; in the life of peoples God's providence supreme; in yourself a strength sent from God. You yourself, as far as your body is concerned, are subject to the laws of Nature. You enjoy your moral freedom only as a free and loving gift of the Omnipotent, and with that freedom of will you are

called upon to subordinate yourself to the universal law as God's first servant. That much you have learnt.

What you have learnt, however . . . you must recognize nothing as God apart from this universal sway of God: "you shall have nothing alongside his omnipresent and all-pervading dominion."

Beware lest, instead of building your material life of God alone, you base it on wealth or power or knowledge or cunning or the like. If you do any of these things, you sin against the law: "Thou shalt have no other gods before Me."

Nor is this idolatry merely an error, a mistaking of falsehood for truth. In that case, it would be simply an intellectual mistake, a delusion, deplorable indeed, but, even at the worst, not the worst that might happen [. . .] But this is not the case. As soon as you set anything else beside God as God, and still more as *your* God, forthwith human dignity, purity and uprightness fall to the ground, the fabric of your life goes to pieces.[23]

Hegelian Religion

Georg W. F. Hegel (1770–1831) was a major western philosopher whose books exerted an influence on an educated society for over a century. He was also the first to develop seriously a philosophy of religion that no discussion of modern religion can ignore.

Hegel defines religion as the "thinking consciousness of God." This form of thinking is distinct from philosophy insofar as it is not in the form of pure thought, but is rather found in the feeling and imaginative representation. For Hegel, this representation of feeling is limited by the senses, but when coupled with thought that "lifts up the sensuous qualities of the content to the realm of universal thought-determinations," one can truly understand the concept of religion. Religion is knowledge of God and of the relation of man to God. Therefore, as rooted in imaginative representation and not in pure idea, religion operates with symbols. These symbols are forms of empirical existence, but not the speculative content. Twentieth-century theological language used the word "symbol" for this form of thought that combines imagination and feeling and is not hindered by the senses.

Another important aspect and goal of religion, for Hegel, is its self-reflective nature. This goal is not merely self-reflective on an individual level, but also on a universal level as well. For Hegel, religion is "the knowledge which the Spirit has of itself as spirit". In Hegel's system of philosophy, mankind's consciousness is a result of the spirit (*geist*)'s drive to know itself. Through worship the Godhead enters the innermost parts of His worshipers and becomes real in their self-consciousness.

Friedrich Wilhelm Joseph Schelling (1775–1854), a major nineteenth century thinker, differed with Hegel and emphasized the roles of symbol and myth. He believed the Absolute is never really known, rather a relative monotheism, consisting of a theist with pantheistic elements, which he assumed was the basis of all religious development. This relative monotheism of the earliest historic period was henotheism that only became monotheism in philosophy. The great Indologist Max Müller shares this view and Gershom Scholem was one of the Jewish thinkers influenced by it.[24]

The Jewish philosopher Nahman Krochmal (d. 1840) who was influenced by both Hegel and Schelling writes that one must see the working of the absolute spirit in the workings of Judaism; unlike the other religions that are temporary representations, Judaism is eternal. The Reform thinker, Samuel Hirsch (d. 1889), accepts the idea of an absolute spirit but thinks that the symbolic representation changes over time even in Judaism. Hence, his support for Reform came from his seeing the era of Jewish law and the rituals has passed. As Jewish Hegelians, we will look at the Orthodox Rabbi Abraham Isaac Kook, and the Reform Rabbis Emil Hirsch and Louis Grossman.

Abraham Isaac Kook

Rabbi Abraham Isaac Kook (1865–1935) was the first Ashkenazi chief rabbi of the British Mandate of Palestine. He was the thinker of the Religious Zionist movement and was known for tackling the broad issues of modernity.

Rabbi Kook accepts religion as an absolute spirit and its manifestation in the world of ritual. But, he rejects the Reform Hegelians who think the older Jewish ritual has passed and he rejects limiting religion to what Europeans call religion. For him, all of life is pan sacramental and symbolic. The purpose of religion is to help in attaining knowledge of God. There is a unity of the absolute spirit behind all religious manifestations. All religions draw from the Divine as needed by their people. Gentiles make a distinction between secular and profane, while according to Kook the Jews do not: Some nations believe that religion allows God to shine into the collective nation, Jews, on the other hand, have the Torah as revelation within the souls of the individual Jews and also as a collective.

> The fact that God is perceived only through religion has caused the world to fall into the lowest depths. God should be known from all of life, from all of existence, and thus He will be known in all of life and in all of existence.
> *God is revealed from within religion only to the extent to which religion itself is hewn from that which is above religion.* Religion is the proper name used by every nation and tongue, but not so among Israel.[25]

Kook states that religion is needed to aid in the evolution of humanity. Religions can have sensory wonders and signs based on Divine influence in order to lead humanity forward. Mistakes in religion are due to the limits of that particular spirit of the people, but ultimately there will be a higher unity of religion. Every nation has an inner ethic and spirit to enlighten them according to their specific need. Israel, however, has absolute spirit above all limitations:

> Consider, the religion which gives the possibility to arrange the sublime evolution of mankind to be absolute truth. But with every religion that serves idolatry—there is no certain hope to arrive at this level. Only the knowledge of unity of God can

perfect humanity to congregate in a single spiritual center to create a representational central place, a place of peace and love.

Consider, that the religions that draw from their own, it is not fit to look upon them in an ungenerous manner. It is possible that from their foundations a divine influx is given in order that they should be engaged in incorporating a significant part of humanity in what is fitting to them.

However, that they contain error mixed into them is nothing according to what the limits of their principle nature as part of their guidance to the final perfection to find a single spirituality in the world.[26]

The matter is understood that except for Israel there is no nation in the world that has absolute merit over another from the perspective of spiritual acquisitions of ethics and Divine religion.

But the status of the inner ethic there is in every religion to enlighten and to benefit it is fitting to respect . . . they are engaged in the worship of God according to their arrangement.

The value of religion is to be judged based on the rise of consciousness, which Rav Kook identifies with prophecy, as the peak of the sciences, and the path to human perfection. The goal of society is to transcend Enlightenment brotherhood and reach a restoration of the unity of infinite and finite, man and animal as portrayed in the Biblical story of the Garden of Eden.

The matter is understood that the obligation of religion is from a special reception and warrant from prophecy.

Humanity still needs guidance as long as the world is not filled with a knowledge in which every individual finds complete clarification the entirety of consciousness from his own self-understanding.

The principle of prophecy is the most complete science in its clarification and necessity that is possible in the necessity of history.

He is elevated from the universal faith to clarified unified knowledge. . . . However, an era will surely come of the perfection of man in which it will not be sufficient that every person will recognize all humanity all brothers and friend. But will also recognize the sublime consciousness of which the Torah describes at the start of the creation of man.[27]

Rav Kook's associating prophecy with modern self-consciousness allows one to create a parallel to similar modern thinkers who identify self-perfection with prophecy such as the Islamic scholars Henri Corbin or H. S. Nasr.

Rabbi Kook, however, is most innovative in creating a positive role for the other monotheistic faiths. He states in unequivocal terms that God cares about the people of the world and Christianity and Islam are needed to bring perfection to the world. Here, the plan is not inscrutable but rather, it makes perfect sense since every nation needs its God as part of God's concern for humanity. According to Kook, Christianity lacks discipline, which severed it from its

Jewish roots. He also thinks that the atheism of the early twentieth century was needed as a corrective to prior religious superstition. Kook grants Christians and Muslims an independent status but subservient to Judaism; whereas Franz Rosenzweig gives the task of perfection of the world and left Jews in the eternal unity, Rav Kook sees everyone working toward the perfection of humanity. Until the eschaton, the other religions play a role in the divine plan for the world:

> Every nation has its own religion, and weakening a nation's religion weakens the state. We should support those that are organized based on their national history and national concepts. . . . Other religions are only good for those born into them since the concepts are rooted in the soul.

> The founder of Christianity was a remarkably charismatic personality, but he established his spiritual influence without first training his disciples in the existing moral and cultural disciplines. When he instructed them to cultivate their spiritual life, they easily lost their Jewish characteristics and became alienated in deed and spirit from the source whence they had sprung.[28]

Comparative Religion in America: Hirsch and Grossman

Emil Gustav Hirsch (1852–1923) was the son of the rabbi and philosopher Samuel Hirsh and a leading American Reform Rabbi. He served as the rabbi of Chicago Sinai Congregation and also as professor of rabbinical literature and philosophy at the University of Chicago. From his pulpit, he delivered rousing sermons on the social ills of the day and became well-known for his emphasis on social justice.

Hirsch delivered a paper at the 1893 Chicago Parliament of Religion on Universal Religion. He considered religion as a universal quest expressed in prayer and ritual. The vision is an evolutionary one beyond creeds, dogma, or any form of nationalism. This universal vision is a Hegelian opposite of Rabbi Kook's national religion:

> The domain of religion is co-extensive with the confines of humanity. For man is by nature not only, as Aristotle puts the case, the political he is as clearly the religious creature. Religion is one of the natural functions of the human soul. . . . Man alone in the wide sweep of creation builds altars. And wherever man may tent there also will curve upward the burning incense of his sacrifice, or the sweeter savor of his aspirations after the better, the diviner, light.

> A man without religion is not normal. And who would deny that Buddhism, Christianity, and the faith of Islam present many of the characteristic elements of the universal faith? In its ideas and ideals the religion of the prophets, notably as enlarged by those of the Babylonian exile, also deserves to be numbered among the proclamations of a wider outlook and a higher uplook.

> The day of national religions is past. The God of the universe speaks to all mankind. He is not the God of Israel alone, not that of Moab, of Egypt, Greece, or America.

The universal religion for all the children of Adam will not palisade its courts by the pointed and forbidding stakes of a creed. Creeds in time to come will be recognized to be indeed cruel barbed-wire fences, wounding those who would stray to broader pastures, and hurting others who would come in. Will it for this be a Godless church? Ah, no; it will have much more of God than the churches and synagogues with their dogmatic definitions now possess.

Four years prior, Rabbi L. Grossman of Detroit, another important Midwestern Rabbi, published *The Attitude of Judaism to the Sciences of Comparative Religions.* The book was a major Jewish statement on the new field of comparative religion. Grossman boldly concluded that Judaism can learn from the new field offering a Talmudic understanding of the Hegelian system; he states that Judaism is never final in its opinions. The Talmud is always open and therefore, it is never forced on anyone. For Grossman, fixed definition is the death of thought, and dogma and creed kill religion. Grossman extrapolated from his comparative religion studies that religion is a sociological fact in which the spirit is displayed as socialized wisdom in family and community, in awe and grandeur in the world and through myth and symbol. Mythology has fancies but also spirit and genius of the people. Judaism is the soul and wisdom of the Jewish community. He was given a favorable review in the *New York Times*, which emphasized his evolutionary optimism and universalism.[29]

Michael Friedlander

Michael Friedlander (1833–1910) was an Orientalist and principal of Jews' College in London. He is best known for his English translation of Maimonides' *Guide to the Perplexed*, and his introduction and catechism to Orthodox Judaism *The Jewish Religion* (1890). Friedlander was influenced by the progressive idealism of the era, viewing religion as positive force in human life. He divides theism into perfect and imperfect forms, encouraging his readers to adopt the perfect form:

> The notion of the existence of God, of an invisible power which exercises its influence in everything that is going on in nature, is widespread, and common to almost the whole human race. It is found among all civilized nations and many uncivilized tribes. The existence of God may be regarded as an innate idea, which we possess from our earliest days. This is the origin of Natural Religion.
>
> The first form of Divine worship of which history and archaeology give us information is *Polytheism*. The creating and ruling power of some invisible Being was noticed everywhere. Every manifestation of such influence was ascribed to its peculiar deity . . . This is chiefly the kind of idolatry mentioned in the Bible and combated by the prophets.
>
> The fact that the influence of the Divine power makes itself perceptible to the observing eye of man everywhere produced another kind of human error: Pantheism (All-God).

Pantheism, by teaching All in One and One in All, is opposed to the theory of man's responsibility to a higher Being, denies the existence of God in the ordinary sense of the word, and is in its relation to true religion, equal to atheism. In the Bible atheism is stigmatized as the source of all evils. Thus the patriarch Abraham suspected the people of Gerar, that there was "no fear of God" in the place, and was afraid "they might slay him."

Many philosophers retained the name "God" (*theos, deus*) for their "First Cause" of the universe, although it is deprived of the chief attributes of God. Thus we have as the principal religious theories resulting from philosophical investigations, Theism and Deism.[30]

Friedlander did not make use of the traditional Rabbinic discourses on idolatry, rather he used contemporary literature, especially the writings of James Freeman Clarke (1810–1888), an American Unitarian preacher, and Emerson transcendentalist who opposed the hard-shelled Calvinist positions. Among his best-known books is *Ten Great Religions* (2 volumes, 1871–1883). Clarke was one of the very first Americans to explore and write about the Eastern religions. He synthesized the emergent field of comparative religion while concurrently defending against the Enlightenment critique of religion. According to Clarke, religion is not superstition, it is not harmful, not a fraud, and not man-made. Religion supports the law of progress, for example the Hindu religion has evolved from the Vedas. Clarke's categories are important because they, rather than the European classics, are in the background of much of the popular English language literature. In Clarke's book, *Steps of Belief* (1870), he claims perfect theism is the belief in a perfect being that exists above all things, through all things, and in all things. Of these varieties of imperfect theism, include Nature-worship, Polytheism, Idolatry of the form, Pantheism, and Nescience (We cannot know anything about God).

Twentieth-Century Naturalism

In the early twentieth century, American religious thought was primarily pragmatic, optimistic, and social in its orientation. The three most widely read authors were Williams James, William Ernest Hocking, and John Dewey. James in his *Varieties of Religious Experience* pragmatically encouraged a positive value in the will to believe and for healthy minded religious experience. In comparison, Dewey (1859–1952), the philosopher and educational psychologist, took a functional approach to religion in that it provided a humanistic social collective. God is the "unity of all ideal ends arousing us to desire and to action." A less remembered figure, Hocking (1873–1966) combined idealism and pragmatism in his *The Meaning of God in Human Experience* (1912), which was reprinted fourteen times until 1962. He stressed the idea of religion as a quest for righteousness by cosmic demand, and as the finding of meaning in human experience. Hocking argues that the natural human will to power finds fulfillment in religion. Also influential was the best seller *Religion without Revelation* (1927) by biologist Julian Huxley, who argued for a modern pragmatic religion stripped of its supernatural qualities and revelation.

Many of those who trained as rabbis between 1920 and 1970 accepted this humanistic and pragmatic world created by the four authors mentioned. They might have been more directly influenced by other thinkers than the aforementioned authors, but for them, religion was not about doctrine, creed, or theology. Many of the post–World War II rabbis who had advocated interfaith activities or worked to create interfaith events specifically came from this non-theological perspective. In Chapter four, I will discuss one example of Jacob Agus's theory of the double covenant; however, I must point out that those rabbis who followed Mordechai Kaplan, Milton Steinberg, and Isaac Meyer Weiss, were pragmatic and functional, particularly when engaged in interfaith activities. They stressed Horace Kaleln's idea of cultural pluralism, as well as the twentieth century American ideals of brotherhood, cooperation, tolerance, and democracy in their discussions; they viewed religion as the highest of ideals and social aspirations. They had little need to discuss theological points such as the Trinity or Incarnation.

An approach to religion that I have seen in the field that is not useful for interfaith encounter is to consider all religions as human construction and to approach other religions from a naturalistic standpoint. This approach would question why we are arguing over what Jesus said or whether he was incarnate because it is all just symbols. Alternately, why are we concerned if Abraham was going to sacrifice Isaac or Ishmael since these stories are man-made, so let us just discuss the topic from the here and now and agree to get along. In this approach, one can simply reject any troubling texts, any theological differences or even reject basic narratives. One of the few articulations of this widespread approach was penned by Bernard Martin, prominent Reform thinker, who edited the important *Contemporary Reform Jewish Thought* (1978). Martin locates faith in existential commitment and not in scripture.

> These men and women, like their spiritual mentors, simply do not, in general, regard the Bible as the Word of God, and it is not, therefore, the ultimate authority for either their faith or their actions. They may admire certain passages in it for their religious sublimity or moral grandeur, but they do not consider it as revealed in its entirety or as providing the final norms for belief and conduct . . . What is acknowledged as "divinely revealed" or "divinely inspired" is simply that which conforms to their reason and moral sense. Hence, human capacities—reason and moral sense, or moral experience—and not Scripture itself, are the ultimate authority for their religious belief and practice. This, I submit, is an undeniable fact.[31]

Eliade from Otto to Eranos

The definition of religion in terms of ideals and society gave way to considering "the sacred" as irreducible in religion. Rudolf Otto (1869–1937) was both a Lutheran theologian and a historian of comparative religion. Otto wrote a classic work, *The Idea of the Holy* (1917), which was translated in over twenty languages and changed the field from the prior idealism. The book defines the concept of the holy as that which is numinous. Otto explained the numinous as a "non-rational, non-sensory experience or feeling whose primary and immediate object is outside the self." The numinous is a *mysterium* that is both terrifying (*tremendum*) and fascinating (*fascinans*) at the same time. It also sets a paradigm for the study of religion that focuses on the need to realize the religious as a non-reducible, original category in its own right.

Mircea Eliade (c. 1907–1986) was a Romanian historian of religion at the University of Chicago. Eliade's *The Sacred and the Profane* partially builds on Otto's previously mentioned work in order to show how religion emerges from the experience of the sacred, and myths of time and nature. Eliade approaches religion by imagining an ideally "religious" person, whom he refers to as *homo religiosus*. His theory that *hierophanies* form the basis of religion, splitting the human experience of reality into sacred and profane space and time, has been immensely influential. Eliade is noted for his attempt to find broad, cross-cultural parallels and unities in religion, particularly in myths. His positions were used by much of the post–World War II scholars of religion. On the popular level, Eliade's writings were combined with those of the psychologist Carl Jung to create universal archetypes of religion. There is an implicit Western and Christian element to Eliade's theory of religion that presupposes that humans have an innate drive for transformation, seeking a ". . . fundamental mystical experience—that is, transcending the human condition" (175).

This universalism colors many media presentations of religion as spirituality with its implicit naturalism, quest for personal bliss, and notion of a common humanity. However, we must state emphatically that the goal of the contemporary study of religions is to show the differences between religions and to help people to overcome the cultural limitations of only seeing what is proximal to them by pointing out variation and differences between religions. It is worth noting that mainstream Jewish theologians such as Eliezer Berkovits condemned Eliade for not having a correct theism or a sense of man's duty (similar to the approach of Kraemer and Hogg, discussed in Chapter 1).

Gershom Scholem

Gershom Scholem (c. 1897–1982), was a German-born, Jewish philosopher and historian. He is widely regarded as the leading figure of the modern academic study of Kabbalah, becoming the first professor of Jewish Mysticism at the Hebrew University of Jerusalem. Scholem's early writing shows a Hegelian idealism, and his later writings were written as Jewish parallels to the Eliade and Jung perspective.

In brief, Scholem's early scheme unfolds as follows: the biblical period is where Judaism struggles to free itself of pure myth and, while partially successful, never quite severs itself from the mythic world of its surroundings. This is followed by the rabbinic period of late antiquity, introducing the institutional period of the Jewish religion. The rabbis suppressed myth, magic, and cult in favor of a normalized legal system that rationalized biblical mythic motifs and presented a God who, while not entirely impersonal, was more distant from human experience than in previous periods. Scholem rejected the rationalism of the Jewish enlightenment and saw Kabbalah as a reaction against medieval rationalism that emerged to revive the biblical myth by offering myths of its own born from a reification of rabbinic Midrash into a mystical cosmology. In this new post-rabbinic stage, religion is mystical and seeks communion with God. The strain of modern thought that emphasizes myth such as Schelling overcomes the more rational elements:

> Mysticism is a definite stage in the historical development of religion and makes its appearance under certain well-defined conditions.
>
> The first stage represents the world as being full of gods whom man encounters at every step and whose presence can be experienced without recourse to ecstatic meditation. In other words, there is no room for mysticism as long as the abyss between Man and God has not become a fact of the inner consciousness. That, however, is the case only while the childhood of mankind, its mythical epoch, lasts.
>
> The second period which knows no real mysticism is the creative epoch in which the emergence, the break-through of religion occurs . . . For in its classical form, religion signifies the creation of a vast abyss, conceived as absolute, between God, the infinite and transcendental Being, and Man, the finite creature. For this reason alone, the rise of institutional religion, which is also the classical stage in the history of religion, is more widely removed than any other period from mysticism and all it implies.
>
> To a certain extent, therefore, mysticism signifies a revival of mythical thought, although the difference must not be overlooked between the unity which is there before there is duality, and the unity that has to be won back in a new upsurge of the religious consciousness.[32]
>   It did not turn its back upon the primitive side of life, that all-important region where mortals are afraid of life and in fear of death, and derive scant wisdom from rational philosophy.[33]

Scholem attended many of the Eranos conferences organized by Carl Jung, where Scholem presented numerous papers, and took part in the larger ecumenical discussions. The collective consensus was a universal mystical-mythic religion that played itself out differently in the various faiths. Jung's particular interest in religious symbolism and mythology colored the topics of the conferences and brought together other important figures such as Mircea Eliade, Henri Corbin, Karl Lowith, Heinrich Zimmer, Erich Newmann, and Paul Tillich. One critic called this consensus a "religion after religion"; a modern abstraction that allowed a return to traditional ideas but without the foundational beliefs. Following Schelling, the ultimate is unknown but each religion creates myths and visions in its attempt for an imperfect grasp of God.

> The genius of the mystical exegeses resides in the uncanny precision with which they derive their transformation of Scripture into a *corpus symbolicum* from the exact words of the text.

Why does a Christian mystic always see Christian visions and not those of a Buddhist? Why does a Buddhist see the figures of his own pantheon and not, for example, Jesus or the Madonna? Why does a Kabbalist on his way of enlightenment meet the prophet Elijah and not some figure from an alien world? The answer, of course, is that the expression of their experience is immediately transposed into symbols from their own world, even if the objects of this experience are essentially the same and not, as some students of mysticism, Catholics in particular, like to suppose, fundamentally different. While recognizing different degrees and stages of mystical experience and still more numerous possibilities of interpretation, a non-Catholic tends to be extremely skeptical toward these repeated attempts which Catholics have made in line with their doctrine to demonstrate that the mystical experiences of the various religions rest on entirely different foundations.[34]

Abraham Joshua Heschel

Abraham Joshua Heschel (1907–1972) was a rabbi, academic, and theologian who later became active in the American civil rights and antiwar movements. Heschel expressed his own philosophy of religion in two books: *Man is Not Alone* (1951) and *God in Search of Man* (1955). Heschel defined religion as an experience of God, transforming and moral, and in his later writings he defined religion as the attempt by humans to understand and answer the deepest questions about life and the universe.

Heschel's early discussions of religion were influenced by the approach of Albert Reville, Freidrich Heiler, Geradeus van de Leew, and other early twentieth-century scholars of religion who thought that the study of religion could show that there is a real divine power known by all people, thereby disproving and critiquing the widespread materialist approach to life. Heschel's thinking in many of his interfaith speeches is that religion is above dogma, his model for this approach is Nathan Söderblom, the winner of the 1930 Nobel Peace Prize for his ecumenical work. As Söderblom writes, "I know that God lives. I can prove it by the history of religion."[35] For Söderblom, the core of religion is a mystical universalism, a common "religion" meaning experience of saints that reveal God, not separate religions.[36] Söderblom considers natural religion as a nonentity, meaning all religion is a true contact with the divine, all revelation is from God. Everyone has access to the higher God, but then either misread it or fell from it into a more primitive understanding. According to Söderblom's position, historical origins are not seen as important. Therefore, Christianity is Paul's mystical vision; there is no basis for discussing Jesus as a Jew, which is only the natural side.

It is important to note that one should therefore not conflate the influence of Söderblom on Heschel's thought with Heschel's own thought. Söderblom was adamant that all ecstasy is the same. Abraham Joshua Heschel, in contrast, answers with a resounding, "No!" The prophetic experience found in Judaism is unique and superior to the experience of the Divine in other faiths. Heschel rejects the ignoring of the earthly elements of religion, and he rejects Söderblom's undifferentiated universalism. Heschel does not have an undifferentiated universalism, for he retains an inclusivism of the uniqueness of the prophet called to God's will:

> There is hardly a people on earth, at least no Oriental people, which in some form or other does not know revelations of its gods . . . These statements contain an impressive half-truth. There are phenomena in many lands which bear a strong superficial similarity to Biblical prophecy. A careful analysis, however, will reveal their essential dissimilarity and compel us to qualify these statements.

> Zoroaster was obviously an inspired man, and so was Balaam; but it was a spark lost in the darkness. What followed them was either superstition or complete oblivion. Neither Lao-Tzu nor Buddha, neither Socrates nor Plotinus, neither Confucius nor Ipu-wer spoke in the name of God or felt themselves as sent by him; and the priest and prophets of pagan religions spoke in the name of a particular spirit, not in the name of the Creator of heaven and earth. It is true that man everywhere and at all times seeks guidance and help from the divine world.

> Indeed, the various conceptions of God as they have merged in the history of religious thinking may be evaluated from the notion of pathos as a key perspective.[37]

The prophetic faith remains at the highest of various religious experiences because it proves man's relevance to God; God calls to man. For Heschel, all religions are not equal, each is diverse; all religions have an experience of God but not all prophetic or Torah.

Heschel is entirely theocentric and stressed the depth theology, the ineffable orientation from God, behind any religion's symbol.

> Are dogma unnecessary? We cannot be in rapport with the reality of the divine except for rare, fugitive moments . . . Dogmas are like amber in which bees, once alive, are embalmed, and they are capable of being electrified when our minds become exposed to the power of the ineffable.[38]

There is no essence of religion or unmediated experience. Heschel believes that our given religions are preserved in amber. There is no return to the fly; we have to get the ineffable from the said amber.

Heschel's writings follow several lines of thoughts. They contain 1) a direct universal experience of God as presented by Söderblom; 2) an inclusivist argument for the superiority of the prophets and Judaism as a prophetic religion; 3) a pluralist argument for the pre-dogmatic human experience that we all share, like music, without dogma or theology; and 4) a medieval theological inclusivism, based on Halevi and Emden, that rejects Christian dogma. (See covenant chapter for more on Heschel's view of Christianity.)

The Human Condition

Rabbi Joseph B. Soloveitchik (1904–1993) was Rosh Yeshiva at Yeshiva University in New York and was considered by modern Orthodox rabbis to be their authority. Rabbi Soloveitchik accepted the modern empirical approach of James, which suggested religious experience is part of the human condition. Soloveitchik uses James's terms to present the universal quests for inner experience, the search for God, and the choice between a happy soul and a sick soul. For Soloveitchik, religious experience is part of human experience, as further presented by Rudolf Otto's *The Holy*, Herman Cohen's *Religion of Reason*, and Max Scheler's *On the Idea of the Eternal in Man*.

Soloveitchik presents the religious figure as always torn, existentially lonely, and acutely aware of his limits.[39] Offering a broad canvas of human experiences, he acknowledges that the religious experience includes the cognitive, ethical, and aesthetic-religious experience, but also the counter movement of the irrational and the paradoxical:[40]

> The religious experience—holiness, does not bring one to harmony and synthesis . . . But it frees the believer to irrationality and existential paradox.[41]

> What is a religious experience? On the one hand, it is an experience which includes the development of the individual's spirit. It is a cognitive and moral as well as an aesthetic experience; it elevates its subject to the height of ontological consciousness, irrespective of the various theories regarding the origin of religious activity.

> How does the created seek the creator? In four domains a person returns after coming to his creator as shown in creation—existence, nature, and spirit; (1) the cosmic drama (2) spiritual experience (3) the order of a-priori concepts (4) religious events and transcendental trials.

> Judaism knows well the tensions and hesitations involved in the wearying search for God, as well as the joy and ecstasy of the search. All the prophets called upon us to observe creation, to search out the secrets of the cosmic process, to observe the well-springs of the world, and to uncover the hidden and obscure—the glory of the Creator's majesty, which hovers over mute creation.[42]

Religion as a form of natural religion is part of the human experience and offers some of the peaks of existential inwardness felt by the educated modern. But the natural approach has limits and needs to be complimented by revelation to acquire knowledge of God.

Rabbi Soloveitchik discovered through dialectic theology that the gap between natural religious experience and revelatory experience is immense. He believed that revelation is not and cannot be derived from human subjectivity and experience. His reading of James and Otto remains a secular acknowledgment of the religious element of natural human life without any revelatory or Jewish significance. Religious states, therefore, become devalued and equivalent to the other products of culture. In the end, according to Soloveitchik, a religiosity predicated on cultural consciousness alone leads to spiritual weariness, bankruptcy, and ultimately denial of God:

> The quest for God through the outer and inner worlds is not a theological question that occupies the religious scholars alone; existence is a central problem that arose at the dawn of humanity. From the Greek scholars to modern philosophers (all the

more so the theocentric eastern religions) separated the quest for God into the abyss of the intellect.

The experience of revelatory faith in contrast to the experience natural-ontological is not related to man's free spirit and is not concerned with the plurality of the formation of culture in all its manifestation.

The meaning of "revelational consciousness" is this. Man cannot come to God on his own, through the initiative of his own spirit; the world is a dead end which does not permit passage to the realm of the eternal and the absolute. Man's spirit soaring up to the heavens, propelled by massive jolts and fiery longing, reaches only the shadow of the Almighty, the image of His image; she will never rest in God's bosom and cling to her lover.[43]

Dialectic theology offers as a radical secularization of life, in that it allows for a full embrace of both the modern human condition and Western academic values. Soloveitchik does not necessarily harmonize these modern works on religious experience such as James and Otto with the traditional approaches of the medieval Jewish texts. For Soloveitchik, beyond the universal quest for religious experience, Jews meet God in Sinai, both through the laws and the fear and trembling of the Sinai event. Jews also meet God from a personal sense of suffering understood in Jewish terms. According to Soloveitchik, only the Halakhah offers the Jew norms, history, and the ability to express this experience.[44]

This approach can appreciate the writings of other faiths, including Greek mythology and contemporary theology as part of understanding the general human experience. Some of Soloveitchik's more urbane students would agree with the following statement from C. S. Lewis about studying pagan culture: "It is easier to see stars without the sun—one can see the richness of human culture—pagan culture as ante pasts and ectypes of the past gained second hand. We can see things in pagan mythology that illuminate our own understanding."[45] One does not have to discuss the role of God or revelation in the other religions because one treats them as part of a revelation-less human culture while still leaving open the rich possibility that they shine with some nebulous light reflected from true religion. In other words, human truth in non-Jewish religions helps apprehend what was already given and helps illustrate a Jewish principle by placing it in another context.

Rabbi Soloveitchik's use of dialectic theology allows Judaism to be above culture, even though religious experience is a real part of human experience. Dialectic thought cannot comment on world religions, even for an internal Jewish theology, due to the fact it relegates religion to the universal realm and does not claim any revelation source for religious phenomena. (compare Kraemer and Hogg in Chapter one.)

Religion Today

The era of Scholem, Heschel, and Soloveitchik, which relied on the concepts of religious experience, mysticism, and existentialism, has passed. After the linguistic turn, religion is considered as conditioned by language and social constructions. Currently, scholars of religion do not think that there is any trans-historical essence of religion. Scholars consider the very idea of religious experience as socially constructed, and as another passing rubric like evolutionary Hegelianism. We now treat the very category of religion as a Christian invention, which rarifies faith as its own category and then asks what are other people's faiths. It treats belief outside of ethnicity, language, and shared history. In contrast, for many contemporary academics, religion is a specific space for a set of practices against a backdrop of legal or political rubrics. In this intellectual climate, theology has moved from its role as an identity of a group to the role of being a border point useful for creating boundaries, heretics, and identities. This work, while still using the modern concept of religion, is itself a product of the shared cultural space of globalization with its tendency to perceive hybridity and allow border crossings and the potential for new understandings. The goal is not to glide into a vague universalism without sensitivity to differences or to perceive variety without gaining any understanding.

3

Christianity: From Disputation to Difference

Judaic attitudes toward Christianity vary greatly but traditionally, Jews have treated Christianity as a greater theological opposite as a result of exclusivist Christian anti-Judaism along with the concurrent persecution, massacres, and exclusion. Is it possible to advance from this prior era? Can Christianity be viewed as a theological entity?

This chapter will focus on the attitudes of twentieth-century Jewish thinkers toward Christianity. The focal point will be on how Jews moved from an automatic polemical disputation toward viewing Christendom with a sense of dialogue and tolerance. The reconciliation came slowly and with haltingness. In order to properly situate the twentieth-century rapprochement there must first be a brief introduction to the influential Christian anti-Judaism of late antiquity and the polemical disputation approaches of the middle ages.

This chapter will give some succinct excerpts from the Jewish philosophic polemics against Christianity in order to give the reader a sense of the change of the twentieth century.

The first Jewish thinkers offering a sustained engagement with Christian theology in the modern era were Martin Buber, Leo Baeck, and Franz Rosenzweig, clashing against a Lutheran anti-Judaism. Joseph Hertz is still fighting against Christian missionaries. The new existential relationship was proclaimed by Hans Schoeps and decried by Walter Wurzburger, Trude Weiss-Rosmarin, and Eliezer Berkovits. European chief rabbis, such as Leon Ashkenazi, continued to grapple with the legacy of Christian anti-Judaism nevertheless are still engaged in interfaith dialogue. Finally, Emmanuel Lévinas finds Jewish values in Christianity, yet rejects the lack of responsibility in Christianity.

For Jewish readers who are habituated to think historically, there are many topics in the history of the Jewish-Christian encounter that this chapter does not discuss such as the history of polemics, anti-Jewish statements, Roman and Christian attitudes toward Jews, and anti-Semitism My goal was to focus on the modern theological aspects. The theological focus of the chapter precludes discussion of

the role of Jesus, Paul, or Christianity in Hebrew or Yiddish authors, or in secular
Jewish intellectuals and social critics.

- Christian Anti-Judaism
- The limits of Theological Polemics
- Modernity: Universalism and Enlightenment values
- Baeck, Buber: Engage in discussing Lutheranism
- Rosenzweig—The Star and The Rays—Two opposite religions
- Schoeps considers the commonality as the very existential openness of the
  encounter
- Wurzburger considers the liturgical commitments as precluding existential
  commonality.
- Trude Weiss-Rosmarin and Eliezer Berkovits reject any commonality.
- Leon Ashkenazi have irreconcilable differences but dialogue
- Emmanuel Lévinas: Christians as Anonymous Jews, as Ethically Defective
  and the Suffering of Suffering

Historical Roots of Anti-Judaism: Historical and Theological

The Anglican James Parkes, in his 1934 classic *Conflict of Church and Synagogue*,
presents the woeful tale of the Christian roots of anti-Semitism. He places the
conflict in the social context of the first centuries in which the early Church and
the authors of the gospels saw the Jews as their competitors. The early theological issue that divided Jews and Christians was seen in the debate of *Verus Israel*:
who was the true elect people of Israel? Did God elect the Jews or the gentile
Christians? In the fourth century, the answer was that the gentiles are now the
true Israel; the Jews have lost that status through the rejection of Jesus. For
Christianity, Jews were the theological other, left to wander and remain a witness
to the Bible until the end of time.[1]

Besides questions of election, the early Church Fathers—Jerome, Justin
Martyr, Tertullian, and Hippolytus—each in their own way fiercely attacked the
Jews and Jewish practice in their writings, leaving behind a legacy of contempt
and degradation. Some of the flash points include Melito of Sardis (died, c. 180)
who initiated the charge of deicide against the Jews. And two centuries later,
the fourth century Church leader, John Chrysostom (c. 347–407), archbishop
of Constantinople, further developed the changes of deicide, placed collective
guilt on all Jews, and mandated the need to entirely avoid the depravity of the
synagogue. Chrysostem wrote, according to Parkes, "the most horrible and violent
denunciations of Judaism to be found in the writings of a Christian theologian."
In the same century, the Fathers of the Antioch Church portrayed the Jew as a
devilish monster, responsible for creating the basis of anti-Semitic images that
continued to develop for more than a millennium.

Theological divisions that separated Jew from Christian were made into an
impassible divide including: the interpretation of the Messianic prophecies in the
prophets, the need for a death and redeemer to save mankind from sin, the status

of Jesus as the messiah, and Jesus as the incarnate Logos of God, and the role of the Biblical laws in an age of the spirit. The church and synagogue divided, differentiating themselves over the day of the Sabbath, the date of festivals, the allowance to still keep the commandments, and the land of Israel. Until the twentieth century, whenever the two faiths encountered one another, the result was almost always difference, polemics, and contrast.

Jules Isaac (1877–1963), the Jewish-French historian who wrote a major history of anti-Semitism in 1947 wrote "Most Christians have *torn out* of their history books the *pages* that Jews have *memorized*." The sorrow-filled relationship between Jews and Christians is cited in many Jewish historical works. These works discuss the persecution of Jews in medieval Christian Europe by the Crusaders, blood libels, and massacres. These stories are well-known to Jews.[2] Following the tragic events of the Holocaust, Jules Isaac wanted to set out the Christian theological degradation of the Jews. He was not writing a polemic against the Church as much as a plea for the adjustment of their theological positions. Isaac shows three problematic theological claims of Christianity: (1) That Judaism was already in a state of degradation from its Old Testament peak at the time of Jesus and continues in history as pure legalism. Isaac rejects the notion that the Jews were degenerate at the time of Jesus, rather there were a variety of thriving Jewish groups at the time and continuing until the present time; (2) that the Jewish people were collectively guilty of deicide and are to be punished for crucifixion of Jesus. Isaac argues against the charge by showing that Romans and not the Jews were responsible. To this Isaac boldly states that the gospels are not history and were shaped by tensions between Jews and Christians in the first century; and (3) that the suffering of the Jewish people is proof of God's punishment for having refused to accept Jesus. As noted, Isaac is not showing where Jews disagree with Christianity; rather which Christian theological claims have deadly results.

The historian Heinrich Graetz (1817–1891) and his followers have painted the medieval era as an entirely horrific, nightmarish persecution. Yet, despite the broad contours of a Christian theological and historical degradation of Judaism, the actual history of anti-Judaism is complex and has many trends. Similarly, the history of the Jewish-Christian encounter transcends simple visions of persecution and polemics. The lachrymose accounts served to make the Christian West aware of the Jewish historical experience; however, there were periods of respect and coexistence, or at least periods of prosperity and tranquility. Current historians, such as Robert Chazan, Joseph Schatzmiller, and David Nierenberg each show the relation of medieval Jews and Christians as even more multifaceted. As Robert Chazan, the important historian of medieval Jewish history, writes:

> From the early eleventh through the end of the thirteenth century, Jewish life was relatively secure. While there was an outbreak of anti-Jewish violence in 1096, it was on balance quite limited and did not resurface during the subsequent major crusades. Toward the end of the thirteenth century, as Europe slipped into a difficult period of decline, anti-Jewish violence became epidemic, first in the northern areas of Europe and subsequently in the south as well. This violence should not, however, be generalized to the entirety of Jewish experience in medieval Europe. In fact the

Jews of medieval Europe lived in relative security throughout much of the period between 1000–1500.[3]

Note that the anti-Judaism sentiments were not there but rather issues of local politics, heterophobia, and class divisions played just as much a role as religion did. Overall, there were more good periods than bad ones and that persecution and exclusion was not continuously weighing on the Jewish community.

Folklore

Most of the time, medieval Jewish culture treated Christianity through the halakhic category of idolatry and envisioned it as causing Israel to suffer (for these approaches, see my previous book *Judaism and Other Religions*). But it also treated Christianity as a folklorist caricature.

An example of how Jews understood Christianity through Jewish folklore is the story of the Apostle Peter in the medieval counter-gospel Toldot Yeshu. Peter the apostle was a greatly learned and holy man who still believed in Judaism and was not really a Christian, rather he made up the Christian religion in order to keep gentile Christians away from Judaism. The Tosaphist R. Jacob Tam wrote that Peter, whose Hebrew name was Shimon Keifa (Cephas) was "a devout and learned Jew who dedicated his life to guiding gentiles along the proper path" while twelfth century Hasidei Ashkenaz, considered him to be a saint (*zaddik*). Later traditions suggest that at the end of his life he rejoined the Jewish community, and as an act of penance he composed the Jewish liturgical prayer *Nishmat* (He did not actually compose it.)[4]

> The Sages desired to separate from Israel those who continued to claim Jesus as the Messiah, and they called upon a greatly learned man, Simeon Kepha, for help. Simeon went to Antioch, main city of the Nazarenes and proclaimed to them: "I am the disciple of Jesus. He has sent me to show you the way. I will give you a sign as Jesus has done."

> Simeon, having gained the secret of the Ineffable Name, healed a leper and a lame man by means of it and thus found acceptance as a true disciple. He told them that Jesus was in heaven, at the right hand of his Father, in fulfillment of Psalm 110:1. He added that Jesus desired that they separate themselves from the Jews and no longer follow their practices, as Isaiah had said, "Your new moons and your feasts my soul abhorreth." They were now to observe the first day of the week instead of the seventh, the Resurrection instead of the Passover, the Ascension into Heaven instead of the Feast of Weeks, the finding of the Cross instead of the New Year, the Feast of the Circumcision instead of the Day of Atonement, the New Year instead of Chanukah; they were to be indifferent with regard to circumcision and the dietary laws. Also they were to follow the teaching of turning the right if smitten on the left and the meek acceptance of suffering. All these new ordinances which Simeon Kepha taught them were really meant to separate these Nazarenes from the people of Israel and to bring the internal strife to an end.[5]

Theological response

This historical divide between the faiths has made each side blind to any similarity between them. Jews were unable to see any logic in the foundations of Christianity and rejected the Trinity, incarnation, the messiahship of Jesus, and the resurrection. For Jews, God is immaterial, indivisible, and unknowable, therefore no Trinity is possible. In Christian theology, incarnation implies the corporeality of God; for Jews that runs counter to the very idea of an infinite creator. Judaism responds to incarnation not as a shock but more as a logical impossibility.

The theological response of Jews toward Christians mirrored that of Christians toward Jews, that is, to assume that the other faith was incorrect. Neither side investigated the other faith or sought to fairly present the other faith. Both sides had severe limitations of their knowledge of the other side. They did not consider the other side as a viable option, and they did not want to mislead people by giving too much information about the incorrect positions of the other faith.

Most of the philosophic arguments relied on arguments from scripture and common sense, but we should bear in mind that they had a different scripture; the Christian side used the Latin translation and the Jewish side used the Hebrew. The Jewish side generally worked only with the literal sense of scripture, except for the exceptions that prove the rule; the Christian side generally used the figura and typological sense. Jews found all of Christianity inscrutable and irrational, especially the Eucharist, the use of divine images, the need for human confessors, and the acceptance of lax penitence, irrational doctrine, and irrational practice. In Jewish eyes, Christian society was anything but the love and mercy they professed to find in Jesus.

Daniel Lasker points out that Saadia Gaon's (tenth century) comments on Christianity already contained the three major theological points that reoccur in the later literature. (1) What is the nature of God? Can it tolerate a Trinity or incarnation? (2) When will messianic redemption occur? Or did it occur? What is the nature of the messianic era? (3) What is the nature of the Law? Does it apply today?

To respond to the first theological point: Saadia Gaon declared the incorporeality of God means the impossibility of incarnation. "That an eternal being, that is subject to neither form nor quality nor dimension nor limit nor place nor time, can be so changed that a part of it becomes a body possessing form and dimension and qualities and place and time and other attributes belonging to corporeal beings. This is only most remotely conceivable."[6]

Jewish thinkers saw the Trinity as an incorrect understanding of monotheism, at best a misunderstanding of how Divine attributes work. According to Judaism, the divine attributes cannot matter since creation and creator are separate. On the other hand, identification of the Trinity with God's attributes is even more confusing for Jews in that attributes in Jewish thought are all predicated of the unknowable God, not as separate persons.[7] In Jewish thought, even granting the possibility of the threefold division of God; Jews do not understand why God needs to be three separate persons.[8]

Jews completely did not understand the satisfaction theory of redemption, in which the crucifixion was needed for humanity because humans owe a debt that can only be redeemed by the sacrifice of an Incarnate God. Why is the debt redeemed by offering God? And if he is incarnate, then how is it infinite?[9]

One can read the polemical literature to see how every Christian interpretation of Scripture was rejected and all statements considered as prefiguration or referring to Jesus are refuted. A late medieval work such as *The Refutation of the Christian Principles* from the 1390's by Hasdai Crescas offers full refutations, from the Jewish perspective, of Adam's sin, of the need for redemption, of the Trinity, incarnation, virgin birth, transubstantiation, coming of the messiah, and the idea of a new Torah.[10]

Modernity

The modern era witnesses a breakdown of the ghetto walls and the subsequent emancipation and enlightenment of the Jews. For the first time, in each country of Western Europe, Jews were no longer outsiders or excluded from society. Religious modernization by Jews was instituted to adapt to Western patterns, specifically Protestant services. And both Reform and Orthodox rabbis emphasized a universalism and brotherhood of mankind in which all religions are paths to God in as much as God is universally available to all humanity.

Moses Mendelssohn (d. 1786), the Jewish enlightenment figure thought that the postulates of rational religion—God, the soul, freedom, and immortality, were available to all humanity without revelation. Nevertheless, he found the principles of Christianity to be non-rational and not acceptable in the age of Enlightenment.

> I must confess that the doctrines I have just listed [Trinity, incarnation, passion, gratification of the first person of Deity by suffering of second person] strike me as an outright contradiction of the fundamental principles of reason. I simply cannot harmonize them with anything that reason and connotation have taught me about the nature and attributes of the Deity[11]

Throughout the nineteenth century, Jews find integration within the dominant Christian culture through admiring liberal approaches to Christianity that limit religion to ethics and emotions. In an era after the writings of the historians David Hume, Ernst Renan, and David F. Strauss, liberal Christian theology had a reduction of the miraculous, and a desiccation of the metaphysics of Trinity and incarnation. Since there was little metaphysics left on the liberal Christian side so Jews did not have to confront Christian theology.

Samuel Hirsch (1815–1889), Reform leader and theologian explained, or rather explained away, the positive power of Christianity by asserting first that Jesus taught nothing novel but rather, "understood, realized, and fulfilled the idea of Judaism in its deepest truth" and second, that Christianity's mission to the world was no more than the Noachide mission—the preaching of ethics and monotheism. Every Jew, for that matter every man, should be what Jesus was; that was the summons of every prophet.[12] Similarly Salomon Formstecher (1808–1889) German rabbi and theologian argued that Christianity and Islam "are the northern and southern missions of Judaism to the pagan world, they are the means used by Providence to overthrow the deification of nature and to aid the generations of man to the apex of perfection." Even the great Jewish philosopher Hermann Cohen could not directly face a Christian understanding, rather he wanted to treat Christianity as an idea that transcends any of the doctrine and theology. "When Christ becomes honored as an idea rather than a historical person or fact, then the best thoughts of ancient Christianity and the deepest characteristics of the Christian Middle Ages live on."[13]

The generally accepted approach for Jews to approach Christianity was to engage in reclamation of Jesus as a Jew. And at the same time considering Paul as the start of everything wrong with the gentile Church. The Gospel portrayal of Jesus was accepted as the ideal rabbinic Jew by Abraham Geiger (1810–1874). Claude Montifiore (1858–1938) went a little further and found positive aspects in Paul (as did Rabbi Jacob Emden, a century before). There were also famous generalized contrasts between Judaism and Christianity produced by Ahad Haam and Kaufman Kohler. Yet, these remained defenses of Judaism without a direct engagement with Christian theology.

A hundred years later we still find a roster of those who engaged in Jewish-Christian dialogue in the 1900s who offered pluralist positions but still find the tenets of Christianity to be incomprehensible. Pluralism, the assumption that all religions are equally true, is not incompatible with considering Christianity irrational and irreconcilable with Judaism.

Starting with Martin Buber and Leo Baeck, there was a sincere engagement with Christian theology. But the engagement was with Lutheranism's sharp rejection of Judaism and the law, and these thinkers were still constrained to offer more defensive contrasts than dialogue.

Judaism and Lutheranism

Martin Luther left behind many vehemently anti-Jewish statements that became part of the Lutheran Confession. The Lutheran Confession downplayed the role of law and works before the grace of faith. There is a strong almost Marcion element in Lutheranism negating any continuity or use of the Hebrew Scripture. The German theologian Adolf von Harnack (1851–1930) saw Jesus as saving humanity from the unethical submission to the Old Testament law. In the twentieth century the theologian Rudolf Bultmann (1884–1976) thought the Old Testament was a shattering failure and only useful to see the miscarriage of God's promise. Reading Harnack and Bultmann give one a sense of the issues that Buber and Baeck were confronting. Much has changed in Lutheran thought to avoid the dichotomy between the Hebrew Bible and the New Testament. The courageous interfaith pioneer Krister Stendhal (1921–2008) argues for new readings of the New Testament and for a Lutheranism that has less of a dichotomy. He also argued that there is more in Christian scripture than the narrative of sin and justification. Currently, new readings of Paul minimize his critique of the law, so that it is no longer a dichotomy of faith and works (see Chapter 5).

Leo Baeck

Leo Baeck (1873–1956) was a leading rabbi in German Reform Judaism, a survivor of Theresienstadt, and a theologian of Judaism. Baeck wrote many essays defending the honor of Judaism before the critiques contained in Protestant thought in late nineteenth and early twentieth centuries. His works include *Judaism and Christianity* and *The Essence of Judaism*. The latter volume is a polemic against Adolf von Harnack's critique of Judaism in *The Essence of Christianity*.

Baeck argues forcefully that Judaism represents the height of classical religion: an ethical system characterized by monotheism and optimism, which helps people live their everyday lives morally. Baeck's notion of ethical monotheism was much the same as Hermann Cohen's notion, but he added to this the aspect of mystery—a sense of the holy—as being part of the essence of Judaism. According to Baeck, Christianity is infused with mystical rites of sacrament in an attempt to bring heaven down to earth; Judaism focuses on raising human behavior to the level of the divine, and hence emphasizes commandments that make demands upon a person's behavior. Baeck's description of Christianity is not unlike his Christian contemporaries' description of Judaism. It tends toward caricature, being largely inattentive to the subtleties and tensions within an historical tradition.[14]

According to Baeck, the Jewish concept of the Noachide entails not recognition of the religious and truth value of the beliefs of non-Jews but rather is a "political conception." It is a category that "legally substantiates the independence of moral law and of ethical equality from all rational and denominational limitations." If the non-Jew "performs the most elementary duties of monotheism, humanity and citizenship . . . he has the same legal status as the Jewish citizen."[15]

The Essence of Judaism is a diatribe against the Lutheranism of his era. For Baeck, the point of religion is to involve all aspects of life, avoid the profane, and incorporate the divisions into the sacred; every person is holy and every act is holy if done according to God's will. Baeck rejects the Lutheran dismissal of law while at the same time he distinguishes philosophic certainty and an emphasis on faith. He paints Lutheranism as a romantic, subjective religion focusing on the abandonment of self.

> In Judaism, the attempt has been made to give life its style by causing religion to invade every day and penetrate the whole of everyday . . . Every partition of life into the profane and the sacred is to be avoided. And the sanctuary dare not possess merely one day beside all the other days. The word "remember" is inscribed above this law: "That you may remember and do all my commandments and be holy unto your God." Thoughtlessness is the true Godlessness; it is the homelessness of the soul.

> A Christian should know that it does him no harm whether he keeps the law or not, even if he does what is otherwise forbidden or does not what is otherwise commanded: it is no sin for him; for he cannot commit one since his heart is pure.

> The ideal of the romantic looks altogether different. For him the highest aim is the achieved redemption, the quintessence of being beyond the Law, of pure

abandonment of self . . . This is what Paul taught quite clearly. Redemption is the fact of salvation which has been consummated in man; man does not bring it about nor does he contribute to it: he merely experiences it.[16]

For Baeck, Judaism is the religion of action and rationality. He also finds Christianity as magical, miraculous, and a faith without intellectual struggle. To date, many Jews share Baeck's conception of Christianity.

According to Baeck's interpretation of Luther's views, original sin is the determining force and the unyielding definition of humankind. The law is surpassed by faith in Jesus Christ as the Redeemer and is of no real value in the process of gaining redemption. For Baeck, this passive redemption means rejecting individual moral freedom and the ability to actively embrace the good. The goal of life is righteousness before God: through work and achievement, through the fulfillment of one's duty and through the struggle for the commandment.

During the height of National Socialism in 1938, he hoped to uncover the Jewish foundations of Christianity that would enable Christians and Jews to forge genuine and respectful relations. Baeck describes Jesus as Jewish and Christianity as Greco-Oriental:

> We see a man [Jesus] . . . before us whose entire being demonstrates Jewish character, every aspect so clearly and characteristically revealing the purity and goodness of Judaism; he was a man who, such as he was, could only have developed out of the firm roots of Judaism, and he could only win over his students and followers, such as they were, out of these roots; he was a man who could move through his life and to his death only here, in this Jewish realm—a Jew among Jews . . . The old Gospel tradition belongs in this Jewish cultural environment with all its peculiarities.

> Paul . . . a man out of the Greco-Oriental world of Asia Minor, [where] had been fused in mysticism and Gnosticism, in the miraculous conceptions of a mystery and sacraments.[17]

Martin Buber

Martin Buber (1878–1965) was a prolific writer contributing to sociology, philosophy, education, Zionism, and Biblical commentary. He is famous for his philosophy of dialogue and dialogical work, *I-Thou*. It is important to note that the very idea of interreligious dialogue comes from Buber, who expected one to step out of personal doctrinal categories and restrictions in order to enter into an interpersonal realm of mutuality and subjectivity with the member of another faith.

Buber himself was unable to live up to his own vision. Buber was forced due to the anti-Semitism of 1930's Germany to defend Judaism by casting Christianity as the doctrinal religion and to exalt Judaism as the religion of mutuality. In his book, *Two Types of Faith*, he contrasts the doctrinal faith of Christianity pitted against the humanistic trust of Jewish faith. The former is characterized as the cold dogma of "belief that" called in Greek *pistis,* and the latter is the warm experiential "belief in" of the Hebrew *emunah.* Buber's principle of Biblical faith is an overwhelming sense of divine majesty that generates trust in a living presence of God, in contrast Buber considers the faith of Christianity as an intellectual assent. *Teshuvah* is the turn of the whole being to God; for Buber, Christian metanoia is only a turning of the mind.

> The difference between this "it is true" and the other "We believe and know" is not that of two expressions of faith, but of two kinds of faith.

> *Teshuva,* turning of the whole person, in the sphere of the world, which has been reduced unavoidably to a "change of mind", to *metanoia,* by the Greek translator—and *Emunah,* trust, resulting from an original relationship to the Godhead, which has been likewise modified in the translation to "belief", as the recognition that something is true, i.e. rendered by *pistis:* these two demand and condition one another.

> The origin of the Jewish *Emunah* is in the history of a nation, that of Christian *Pistis* in that of individuals . . . *Emunah* originated in the actual experiences of Israel, which were to it experiences of faith.

> It is evident that a considerable change in relation to the Old Testament idea of faith has here [in Christianity] taken place, and this under the influence of Iranian doctrines and Greek ways of thought.[18]

He ascribes the Christian change from Biblical values as a result of the pagan Greek and Iranian influences: In a critique of St. Paul, Buber sees Paul as responsible for introducing foreign, Greek elements into the Jewish faith of Jesus. In Judaism, Jesus exemplifies Hebraic *emunah:* total trust and reliance on God. Paul's version of faith is *pistis:* a more intellectual belief in the truth of something. For Buber, Paul interrupts the history of Jewish faith in a dialogic encounter with the living God, turning Jesus into a mediator to heal the breach in this biblical faith. The intimacy between man and God is lost; the human ability to seek that intimacy is deprecated as "works"; and the willingness of God to enter into the dialogic encounter of intimacy is restricted to those who believe in Christ.

Buber's rejection of Paul is part of a larger argument against Lutheranism and its emphasis on Pauline faith at the expense of institutions, ritual, or works. Luther's understanding of Paul is that the law is impossible to follow and thus, faith is needed. For Buber, however, law is trusting living with God. He asserts that Jesus would support the approach of the Hebrew Bible and reject the Pauline approach. Buber criticizes the Lutheran Christianity of Soren Kierkegaard as faith without works, as a solitary individual and not the Jewish communal sense, and that in the Hebrew Bible God gives man commands that correspond with our will, not tests of obedience and absurdity:

> The indivisible law which allows of no selection the "whole" law (Gal. v. 3), demands therefore according to Paul the impossible, without his differentiating between

an external fulfillment which is possible and an impossible fulfillment in the complete intention of faith; evidently he already regards the outward fulfillment as impossible.

Here not merely the Old Testament belief and the living faith of post-Biblical Judaism are opposed to Paul, but also the Jesus of the Sermon on the Mount, although from a different motif and with a different purpose.

We read: "God cannot allow His honor to be impugned"; the law itself demands from God the reaction; "God would cease to be God if He allowed His honor to be impugned". This is said of the Father of Christ; therefore it does not refer to one of the gods and rulers, but to Him of Whom the "Old Testament" witnesses. But neither in this itself nor in any Jewish interpretation is God spoken of in this way; and such a word is unimaginable from the lips of Jesus as I believe I know him.[19]

Buber was not actually in theological dialogue with Christianity in order to find commonality nor was he open to Christianity.

Buber used Jesus as a model for his spiritualized Judaism; Jesus and his community of disciples constitute an authentic moment in the history of the Jewish spirit. Yet, Buber saw Jesus as entirely within Judaism and thought that Judaism has nothing to learn from Christianity:

From my youth onwards I have found in Jesus my great brother. That Christianity has regarded and does regard him as God and Savior has always appeared to me a fact of the highest importance which, for his sake and my own I must endeavor to understand.

Whatever in Christianity is creative is not Christianity but Judaism; and this we need not reproach; we need only to recognize it within ourselves and to take possession of it, for we carry it within us, never to be lost. But whatever in Christianity is not Judaism is uncreative, a mixture of a thousand rites and dogmas; with this—we say it both as Jews and as human beings—we do not want to establish a rapprochement.[20]

Buber rejects both the belief and need for Christianity. He believes that in this side of the messianic age, Christians and Jews must necessarily misunderstand each other. The other's heart of faith can only be known within the other's community. The Church can only see Israel as blind to the evident truth of Christ just as Israel can only see the Church as presumptuous and premature in its assertion that redemption has begun.

Catholic Theologians as diverse as Karl Rahner, Hans Kung, Hans Urs von Balthasar, John M. Oesterreicher, and Avery Dulles have each used Buber's writings as the authentic Jewish voice, and his contrast of the faiths was the starting point of dialogue for decades. Balthasar states that a "Christian can only offer an answer in silence and recognize the mystery." Yet, according to Balthasar, Buber clings to this mystery of immanence "in spite of the fact that it seems to us Christians as though he cannot possibly give it a biblical foundation except by taking into account the Christian fact of the incarnation."[21]

Franz Rosenzweig

Franz Rosenzweig (1886–1929) was an influential Jewish educator and theologian. He created a systematic philosophy inheriting the rich complexity of German philosophic thought. In 1920, Rosenzweig founded The Free Jewish House of Teaching (*Lehrhaus*), which became the model forum for Jewish adult education programs to offer serious discussions of Judaism. He discusses the relationship of Judaism and Christianity in his major work *The Star of Redemption*. Additionally, his letters to his cousin Eugen Rosenstock-Huessy, whom he had nearly followed into Christianity, were published as *Judaism Despite Christianity*, offering a modern Jewish- Christian theological encounter of great profundity.

There are two divergent approaches to understanding Rosenzweig's attitude toward Christianity. This chapter will follow those commentators, ranging from Rosenzweig's contemporary Hans Schoeps to the Princeton scholar Leora Batnitzky, who believes Rosenzweig's theology is about the difference between Judaism and Christianity, not the commonality. "Real dialogue, Rosenzweig contends, produces not mutual understanding, but the harsh and harrowing assessment of one point of view over and against another." In contrast, the second approach followed by Jacob Agus, and Will Herberg among others, credits Rosenzweig with creating a connection between the two faiths, sometimes referring to it as the Double Covenant Theory of Judaism and Christianity, repeated as a truism by most introductions to Jewish-Christian relations for several decades. This American creation will be dealt with in the next chapter on covenant.[22]

Rosenzweig states that Judaism rejects Christianity; that there is no relationship between the two faiths is one of its defining tenets of Judaism. Historically it sets itself apart as different. As mentioned earlier, the medieval approach to God looks for philosophic universals, such as a monotheistic conception of God. Rosenzweig and other modern thinkers, however, start with the particularities of Jewish liturgical life. From this vantage point, Rosenzweig maintains that the church's conception of God is vastly different from Judaism and, due to this God in Christianity focuses on the Son and gives an entirely new dimension to God as the father of Jesus. Because of this, Jews should not equate the two and should not look at the Christian God as God plus Jesus.

Yet, according to Rosenzweig, Judaism is inclusivist despite itself. Even in its exclusivism, both medieval and modern Judaism treated Christianity as a daughter religion. Rosenzweig, unlike the medieval philosophic formulations, considers all relationships between Judaism and Christianity not as monotheists but as the relationship of the role of the seed to be the final destiny of the tree. The biblical connection between the faiths will only be resolved in a messianic end of time. There are not two covenants, only two groups waiting for the end of the other: Judaism thinks that Christianity will return to its Jewish origins in the end, and Christianity assumes the Jews will convert to Christianity in the end. In both religions, there is a struggle for truth. Truth, in this context, is not the true or false of scientific truth claims but of alternative existential attitudes to life with God. Jews know that they have the truth and therefore reject Christianity.

The two religions are linked in their hopes even if they conceive of these hopes in different terms. There is dependence in their source for eschatology:

> Christianity recognizes the God of Judaism, not as God, but as the "Father of Jesus Christ . . . And yet, both the synagogue and the church have borne their sufferings in the same ultimate hope . . . This hope is not merely a hope for some unconscious and coincidental rendezvous in eternity (as would be the case, for instance, between the believer and the "universal-humanistic pacifist"). For both of them this hope—the God of all time—is rooted in a common origin. This common origin is the revelation of the Old Testament . . . Synagogue and Church are mutually dependent on each other.

> But could this same idea (that of the stubbornness of the Jews) also be a Jewish dogma?

> So that Christianity is like a power that fills the world (according to the sayings of one of two scholastics, Yehudah Ha-Levi: it is the tree that grows from the seed of Judaism and casts its shadows over the earth; but the fruit must contain the seed again, the seed that nobody who saw the tree noticed). This is a Jewish dogma, just as Judaism as the stubborn origin and last convert is a Christian dogma.

> We will not make common cause with the world-conquering fiction of Christian dogma, because (however much a fact) it is a fiction (and let there be truth, and let reality perish, since "Thou God art truth") . . . we deny the foundation of contemporary culture . . . for ye shall be a kingdom of priests and a holy people [Lev 19:6]; and putting it in a popular way: that we have crucified Christ and, believe me, would do it again every time. We alone in the whole world (and Let there be the kingdom of God, and let the world pass away) for "to who will you liken me, that I am like?" [Isaiah 40:25].[23]

Christianity is part of history and the progress of the world, while Judaism is outside history as an eternal Judaism, outside the Hegelian scheme of history.

Rosenzweig associates Christianity with the living spirit of Goethe, in which he sees a residue of paganism in Christianity, as did his mentor Hermann Cohen. For Christianity, God has become divided and needs to be made whole. This is the point at which Pinchas Lapide and Jurgen Moltmann start their discussion (see Chapter 5) by looking to other sources, in Rabbinic and medieval Judaism, within its theories of the Divine glory, where the Jewish God needs to be made whole.

Rosenzweig reversed the supersession argument and argues that it is the Jewish tenet that Judaism is correct as the eternal truth and the grasping of Christianity are false. This rejection encourages Jews to redouble their commitment to exclusivism and particularism:

> We see the star, but not the rays. To encompass the whole truth one must not only see the light but also what it illumes. They, on the other hand, have been eternally destined to see the illuminated object, but not the light.

> Thus Christian belief, the witness to the eternal way, is creative in the world.

Is not part of the price that the Synagogue must pay for the blessing in the enjoy-
ment of which she anticipates the whole world, namely, of being already in the
Father's presence, that she must wear the bandages of unconsciousness over
her eyes.

The Christian conquest of the world may have something to teach the Jew about
his own salvation . . . Jews are forced to recognize that it is possible that they cannot represent the universal without Christianity.

But Judaism's self-judgment does not leave Judaism affirming the truth of
Christianity. Rather, like Christianity, Judaism becomes more committed to the
particularity of its own existence. Judaism's self-judgment makes Jews uneasy.[24]

For Rosenzweig, Judaism and Christianity share a common biblical origin that
creates a bond of mutual dependence. In Rosenzweig's scheme, Jews reject
Christianity with a resounding No!; however, later thinkers, such as Hans
Schoeps and Pinchas Lapide on the Jewish side and Walter Kasper on the
Christian side, interpret this "No!" as a negation having a positive function in
that it allowed Christianity to come to be. Rosenzweig offers the dialectics of
rejecting the opposite perspective while acknowledging that there is a greater
whole in the fullness of history and combines that with personal revelations of
the ineffable.

Rosenzweig did not believe that all faiths were incommunicable. Actually, he
reserved that distinction for the Jews. In a letter to his cousin, he wrote, "And for
the very reason that you can [show me Christianity], I cannot. Christianity has
its soul in its externals."[25] The Jews, he argued, had a fundamental responsibility
to preserve a direct and unmediated relationship with God as Creator, Revealer,
and Redeemer, unhooked from the forces of normal history. Christianity, on the
other hand, is the vehicle by which the possibility of God's redemptive spirit
is brought out into an unbelieving world. Christians must therefore eschew
community—anyone can join regardless of culture or history.[26] Christianity is
a missionary religion. For Jews, Scripture ends without redemption because it
is not so much a prescription for salvation as it is a document of the journey
from faithlessness to faith. The Bible ends and yet, history goes on. There has to
be a deeper meaning to history in Christianity as the historical religion; for him
Judaism is eternal and outside history. Today, few would conceive of an ahistoric
notion of Judaism outside of society that places it as contrasting Christianity.
We have a Jewish historical presence not just as the State of Israel but as part
of the United States and elsewhere, Jews are not outside of society. This Jewish
historical presence has been essential for the ongoing encounter with other
faiths.[27]

Hans Joachim Schoeps

Hans Joachim Schoeps (1909–1980) was an important German Jewish historian
and theologian at the university of Erlangen. His collected works are contained in

sixteen volumes but were not translated, therefore they are not widely known in the English reading orbit. Many of his formulations of dialogue played a role in the writings of other thinkers.

In Schoeps's modernist view, everything in the Jewish-Christian encounter has shifted in the modern era compared to the medieval era. Now, there is a new age of understanding; we now have the gift of dialogue and an experiential connection with God. Using terminology of the German romantics and early existentialists, he thinks that tolerance is no longer sufficient, rather we seek to reach the heart in dialogue. Even though dialogue is in the heart, Schoeps wisely cautions against creating innovations solely on whims or subjectivity. He understands Rosenzweig as passing judgment on Christianity as an alien religion that cannot be understood from the Jewish perspective. Yet, Schoeps also points out that the communication of that judgment is only information, the inner experience behind the judgment cannot be expressed. The two faiths can say they are opposites, yet still reach the other's heart.

> It would be a serious misunderstanding of this recognized fact was the progress interpreted to consist in an "abolition of dogma." In such a case it would not be progress, but disintegration. Its fruitfulness lies rather in the fact that the speaker of today undertakes to conduct a dialogue with all his heart. That is, he dares to involve himself in the discussion . . . the conflicts arising from what is acknowledged through faith are brought into sharp relief; but there is real understanding in a third realm, that of spirit and truth, from which religion developed.

> "What is to prevent us from coming up with groundless innovations of modern minds, altogether liable to whim and change?"

> For Rosenzweig is aware of the modern possibility of knowing upon reflection that there is an external view of, knowledge about, and judgment upon an alien phenomena, based on one's own standpoint of belief, but there must also be a seeing, knowing, and judgment from within, which the other possesses only in his own right. It may be communicatable, but cannot be taken over and utilized by anyone else—at most, it can be accepted only on the level of information.[28]

Schoeps thinks that Rosenzweig's use of inclusivist texts from Ha-Levi and Maimonides was a projection of modern concerns onto the past since the medieval thinkers were closed to encountering others. Openness is a quality of modernity. He acknowledges that Maimonides wrote that Christianity brought the Bible to the world, but it had no effect on his thinking. "Torah was spread to the distant islands but Jews do not formulate their consciousness based on what Christians do." According to Schoeps, Maimonides made his statement about Christianity and Islam solely for his internal reasons. In contrast, Rosenzweig, according to Schoeps was already open to an engagement.

The people of Israel do not need atonement because, as a people, as they are already with God. Schoeps notes that Judaism does not allow new revelations outside of the covenant with Israel and the revelation to Israel, even the Noahite laws are not directly considered in the Torah. There is only one covenant with the people, Israel, and no atonement for all humanity from Adam because only Jews are elect, only Israel is a nation with covenantal laws for its organization:[29]

> It is not the Church and Synagogue which confront each other, but rather, Church and the people Israel.
>
> The recognition of other covenants outside of Israel (the covenant of Christ, and, in principle, that of Mohamed) even fills a gap in Jewish knowledge, since according to Jewish belief, not only Israel, but all mankind belongs to God, is called on the path to God.
>
> Just as today we are prepared to acknowledge the witness of the Church to be true, as the truth which has been granted exclusively to the Church may also acknowledge our awareness of God and his covenant with us as true, as the truth which has been granted exclusively to us.[30]

But the dogmatic aspects, since they cannot change, must be pushed to the messianic age. For Schoeps there is no common covenant, therefore any commonality must get pushed off until the messianic era.

If one must look for a commonality; it can only be found in those groups that affirm Judaism and Christianity at the same time, such as the early Jewish-Christian groups of the first centuries, such as the Ebionites:

> They [Ebionites] associated the teaching of Moses and the teaching of Jesus by means of the idea of a primordial religion. Both were sent by God to establish covenants with mankind. Since the two kinds of teaching are identical, God accepts everyone who believes in either of them. Conversion to Jesus, therefore, is precisely the same thing as conversion to God and to the Jewish law.[31]

In 1949, after the Holocaust, Schoeps wrote his own afterward that limited the potential for any future dialogue. He could not envision the potential of the Holocaust to create a negative dialectic that propelled dialogue further in the 1960s and 1970s:

> I ask myself today whether the period of religious dialogue may not perhaps be past; whether, with these senseless exterminations, something quite different has began.[32]

But just two years prior was the founding of the International Council of Christians and Jews (ICCJ) as a reaction to the Holocaust. They issued the important 10 Points of Seelisburg in 1947 on which all later reconciliation between Judaism and Christianity has been based. The ten points condemn anti-Semitism, emphasize that Jesus and his followers were Jews, avoiding using Jew as the opposite of Christian virtue in theology or passion plays, and not to theologically condemn Judaism.[33] Hans Joachim Schoeps took part in these meetings and his earlier hopeful statements were translated for a wider audience in the 1950s, but his pessimistic coda correctly reflected the need to deal with the Holocaust before further theological work could be attempted on the Jewish side.

Walter Wurzburger

Walter Wurzburger (d. 2002) was a German born, modern Orthodox pulpit rabbi, and theologian. He served as the official representative for the Rabbinical Council of American on interfaith topics and represented the positions of Rabbi J. B. Soloveitchik.[34]

Wurzburger, in responding directly to Schoeps, shares many of the same existential premises. However, unlike his liberal interlocutor, he thinks that there is no realm of the heart to establish a dialogue. Experience of the heart is derived from the truth of one's doctrine. The rejection of commonality is not on the academic level; one can readily read and understand each other's books, rather on the non-accessibility of the existential experience of the other.

> Hans Joachim Schoeps extols the existential dialogue in which conflicting beliefs are not abolished; instead the conflicts arising from what is acknowledged through faith are brought into sharp relief, there is real understanding on the third realm, that of spirit and truth from which religion develops. Underlying this faith in the dialogue is the assumption that various particular formulations of religious truth are but inadequate attempts to appropriate a higher but rather elusive religious truth. But this is precisely what is challenged by the Orthodox position. It is the commitment to an individual particular faith that provides the believer with the ultimate standards of value. As Emil Brunner has pointed out, the believer does not use his particular faith as one of the many different modes of striving for an ultimate truth.
>
> In the give and take of an honest discussion one cannot shy away from statements that may offend the sensitivities of the adherent of another faith.[35]

Wurzburger does acknowledge that Maimonides teaches that Christians are to be given a preferential treatment over other non-Jews concerning teaching them the Bible, "There is nothing gained by maintaining that we have no special ties with Christianity." Yet Maimonides's position that Christianity brought knowledge of God to the world does not imply any involvement in the covenant of Israel or the double covenant theory. Wurzburger emphasizes that *Tosafot* does allow Christians to take an oath that mentions the Trinity; it does not create any place to ignore "all such distortions as contained in the Christian doctrine of Incarnation or Trinity." It is important to note that he defends the Orthodox position using the Christian dialectic theologian Emil Brunner to prove his point.

Wurzburger, in feeling the immense changes brought on by modernity, offers the following broad caveat to basing Jewish-Christian relations solely on prior medieval texts. The "shifting theological positions of Christianity" may make some of them complete monotheists from the Jewish perspective and others to lose their status as believers in a Biblical faith:

> In the light of shifting theological positions of Christianity it is quite possible that we can modify certain attitudes to Christianity. Just as during the Middle Ages rabbis ruled that Christians no longer qualified as idolaters it may be possible in the light of new theological positions adopted by Christianity that they may no longer even be guilty of Shituph. By the same token, we may question whether some of

these new theological stances may not imply that certain Christian groups may have to forfeit certain privileges they enjoy now over non-believers.

This later statement leaves great latitude for a reconsideration of the Christian Trinity based on modern formulations.

Trude Weiss-Rosmarin

Trude Weiss-Rosmarin (1908–1989) was an Orthodox Jewish German-American writer, scholar, and feminist activist. She cofounded, with her husband, the School of the Jewish Woman in New York in 1933, and in 1939 founded the *Jewish Spectator*, a quarterly magazine, which she edited for fifty years.

Weiss-Rosmarin was an influential critic of the Christian-Jewish dialogue. She attacks those who view Judaism and Christianity as one religion and sets out to show that they are in fact fundamentally different. She sets up a fundamental divide: Jews have an undifferentiated monotheism whereas the Christian Trinity is a concession to polytheism. Weiss-Rosmarin is probably responsible for spreading the notion that Judaism is closer to contemporary Protestantism than to Catholicism. For her, Jews think of God as a spirit in contrast with the Christians, who view God as a physical entity. Jews believe law brings goodness into the world, Christians are against the law. Jews live in the world, Christians can live monastic other worldly lives. Her big point to which she keeps returning in the volume is that Judaism is a religion of law and Christianity is a religion of faith:

> The chief and fundamental difference between Judaism and Christianity is that the former is committed to pure and uncompromising monotheism and the latter subscribes to the belief in the Trinitarian nature of the Divine Being. . . . To the unconditional monotheism of Judaism the doctrine of the Trinity is profoundly objectionable, because it is a concession to polytheism or at any rate, an adulteration of the idea of the One, Unique, Indefinable and Indivisible God.

> Judaism is an ethical monotheism not predicated on a person: the Ultimate is spirit, but not a person; he is one, but the mystery of this Oneness is unfathomable, although, of this Jews have always felt certain, it is indivisible into three-thirds, all part of the One, as Christianity teaches.

> It has been pointed out that the gulf separating Judaism from Catholicism is wider and deeper than the chasm which parts Judaism and Protestantism, for the latter abolished many Hellenistic concepts and practices which the early Church adopted. It is important, however, to understand that the differences between Judaism and Protestantism are less pronounced only in *quantity* but not in *quality*.

> The Messianic ideal is that all nations and all individuals shall know peace, justice and neighborly love. Consequently, the "saint" who withdraws as a hermit from the community does not a thing to bring nearer the Messianic age. Christianity, especially in its Catholic interpretation, regards solitude as a desirable state of piety.

The Laws of the Torah are to Judaism the quintessence of permanent goodness. Christianity, on the other hand, advances its claims on the strength that the "law" is superseded and abrogated by "Faith" in Jesus.[36]

Weiss-Rosmarin is against any attempts to find a Jewish Jesus or to place Jesus in a Jewish context. She portrays Jesus as firmly against Jewish law as he was against Judaism and sought to uproot the faith of Israel. The claim to be a religion of faith and love was used by Christians in order to directly attack Judaism.

Weiss-Rosmarin also rejects the attempts made to remove the death of Jesus from the Jews. Christians in the New Testament blamed the Jews for Jesus's death with the result that Judaism is forever condemned for deicide by the very roots of Christianity. The New Testament is entirely supersessionalist in rejecting Judaism as having been past. Modern readings that attempt to soften this rejection of Judaism are not true to the text and are inauthentic. The faith of Jesus, his followers, the New Testament, and Christianity all reject Judaism in every way. So we should abort any attempt at creating a Jewish-Christian tradition:

> There is however, even more conclusive evidence of Jesus' negative attitude to the "Law" . . . Jesus' most outspoken rejection of the Law is presented by the parable of the old and the new that cannot be combined.

> The idea that the Law had been superseded by faith gave rise in turn to the doctrine that "the true Israel" are not the Jews but the heathen who accept "the good news" of redemption through faith.

> Christianity's claim to be the rightful heir to the Prophetic religion of love, supposedly disowned by the "legalist" rabbis, is invalidated by incontrovertible facts. Judaism knows of no antagonism between the Prophets and the Rabbis.

> Of what avail are "good will" efforts and profuse acknowledgements of the Jews' innocence of Jesus' death by well-meaning Christians when the New Testament lays the guilt for Jesus' death at the door of the Jews? . . . The New Testament represents Judaism as a stunted, backward and obsolete religion without "fulfillment" and lacking "truth." Consequently it has no longer any place in the world.

> In all important respects Jesus placed himself in opposition to the faith into which he was born. It is therefore idle and futile to make room for him in Judaism which he himself rejected in theory and practice.[37]

Writing Pre-Vatican II and the changes of *Nostra Aetate,* Weiss-Rosmarin would not have believed that the document could have brought Judaism and Christianity closer together, create a spiritual link, or absolve the Jews of deicide. She would probably be more shocked that sincere Christians, like Pope Benedict, would reread the New Testament passages in order to remove potential anti-Semitic references, to remove the responsibility of death of Jesus, and to paint Judaism as the covenantal basis for Catholicism.

Memory of Contempt and Refutation to Missionaries

Joseph Herman Hertz (1872–1946), chief rabbi of the British Empire, whose most lasting monument is his English commentary on the Pentateuch, was a universalist toward all faiths.

Hertz, however, refuted Christianity and defended Judaism against assimilationist and missionary activity. Rabbi Hertz saw the other religions as inclusively part of the divine scheme, and he was also a theistic universalist seeing that all who worship are turning to the one God. But practically he emphasized Christianity's culture of violence, idolatry, and lack of a sense of biblical providence.

> The adherents of no religion have hated their enemies more than Christians. The atrocities, which they have committed in the name of religion, both inside and outside their own pale, are unexampled in the world's history. And even today it cannot be said that the various sects of Christians love one another, while anti-Semitism is a proof that they do not love those who are not Christians.

> The belief that God is made up of several personalities, such as the Christian belief in the Trinity, is a departure from the pure conception of the Unity of God.

> [T]he *Schema* excludes *the trinity* of the Christian creed as a violation of the Unity of God. Trinitarianism has at times been indistinguishable from tritheism, i.e., the belief in three separate gods.

> It is only the Jew, and those who have adopted Israel's Scriptures as their own, who see all events in nature and history as parts of one all embracing plan; who behold God's world as a magnificent unity; and who look forward to that sure triumph of justice in humanity on earth which men call the Kingdom of God.[38]

Rabbi Hertz made his theological polemic against Christianity part of the editorial rubric of his Bible commentary. He wanted to show that only Judaism keeps to the biblical faith; only Judaism upholds the Bible's concepts of God, revelation, providence, and justice. Yet, Hertz addressed Cardinal Hinsley (d. 1943), the Archbishop of Westminster, as someone who stood up for what is right among "the righteous of all creeds."[39]

Rabbi Isaac Leeser in America, a similar traditional author in nineteenth-century America made many statements preceding Rabbi Hertz's beliefs, also to fight Christian missionary zeal. The responses of Rabbis Hertz and Lesser demonstrate that when a modern society practices conversionary and missionary trends toward Jews, Jews tend to respond by affirming their own superiority. [40]

Abba Hillel Silver

Abba Hillel Silver (1893–1963), American Reform Rabbi and Zionist leader, wrote a widely read comparison between Judaism and other religions and cultures *Where Judaism Differs* (1956). The book's premise is that the Bible was the only true monotheism responsible for refining mankind's concepts of God, Temple, brotherhood, and peace among men; rabbinic Judaism continued this process of refinement. The monotheistic spirit of Israel sifted Semitic mythology—leaving the Hebraic spirit, "bringing order clarity and coherence to the spiritual life of man by banishing the moral chaos of the mythological complex." For Silver, Christianity and Islam as daughter religions were just claiming a Jewish mantle and not creating new religions. When these other faiths were not derivative, then they were mythological and pagan. Christianity is portrayed as adulterating Judaism with Greco-Oriental ideas of the need for deliverance from the evil of this world. Silver also discusses, at length, Islam, Hinduism, Taoism, and Buddhism, but in each case he paints the other faith as pessimistic, otherworldly, and deterministic, thereby hindering social progress. Silver's easy-to-read homiletic style made this work a basic source for a half-century.[41]

Eliezer Berkovits

Eliezer Berkovits (1908–1992) was an Orthodox rabbi and theologian. He spent twenty-four years in the pulpit and then became the chairman of the department of Jewish philosophy of the Hebrew Theological College in Chicago. Berkovits lectured extensively and wrote nineteen books. He was influential in his Holocaust theology of "the hiding of the divine face" and his view of *halakhah* as commonsense and reality based. He was against interfaith encounter, and his approach captured the mood among many American Jews, especially the Orthodox.

For Berkovits, "Judaism is Judaism because it rejects Christianity, and Christianity is Christianity because it rejects Judaism."[42] For Berkovits, the Holocaust shows that Christianity is morally bankrupt. For him, the evidence is clear that the New Testament and the Church are the source of the anti-Semitic and anti-Jewish teaching of contempt that led to the Holocaust. Therefore, according to Berkovits, Christianity is intrinsically anti-Semitic and any encounter, dialogue, or theological consideration of their positions is fruitless and pointless. Berkovits sees the Church in decline and scrambling to survive so statements of Jewish-Christian reconciliation made today should carry no weight. Even joint social and humanitarian activities should be questioned due to past Christian behavior as oppressors and missionaries. Thus, he concludes: "we have to go our own way."[43]

> It is our responsibility to sum up the meaning of that era, unimpressed by Christian claims, guided exclusively by our own experience. In terms of Jewish experience in the lands of Christendom, the final result of that age is bankruptcy—the moral bankruptcy of Christian civilization and the spiritual bankruptcy of the Christian religion. After nineteen centuries of Christianity, the extermination of six million Jews, among them one and a half million children, carried out in cold blood in the very heart of Christian Europe, encouraged by the criminal silence of virtually all Christendom including that of the infallible Holy Father in Rome, was the natural culmination of this bankruptcy. A straight line leads from the first act of oppression against the Jews and Judaism in the fourth century to the holocaust in the twentieth. In order to pacify the Christian conscience it is said that the Nazis were

not Christians. But they were all the children of Christians . . . Without the contempt and the hatred for the Jew planted by Christianity in the hearts of the multitude of its followers, Nazism's crime against the Jewish people could never have been conceived, much less executed. What started at the Council of Nicea was duly completed in the concentration camps and the crematoria.

There is no reason on earth why it should make itself accessible to "fraternal dialogue" with a religion which, by its very premise, declares others to be in error [. . .] Independently of all considerations of interreligious politics, we reject the idea of interreligious understanding on ethical grounds.

We reject the idea of interreligious understanding as immoral because it is an attempt to whitewash a criminal past. Further, the idea of interreligious understanding is ethically objectionable because it makes respect for the other man dependent on whether I am able to appreciate his religion or his theology.[44]

According to Berkovits, in Judaism man is called to sanctify this world using his rationality and free will. In contrast, Christianity is absurd, other worldly, and shirks human responsibility. Yet, Berkovits still considers Christians as monotheists and as individually virtuous.[45]

Rabbi Yehudah Ashkenazi

Rabbi Yehuda Leon Ashkenazi, (also known as Manitou, 1922–1996) was one of the leading educators and thinkers of post-WWII French Jewry. He was a descendent of the Lurianic Kabbalist Joseph ibn Tabul and the medieval Talmudic commentator, the Rosh. He studied Kabbalah in his native North Africa and later under the influence of Rav Zvi Yehuda Kook and Rav Baruch Ashlag. He studied philosophy, psychology, and anthropology in the University of Algiers, and in the Sorbonne in Paris.

Rabbi Ashkenazi, along with Andre Neher and Emmanuel Lévinas, served as educational directors of the Jewish school system. In 1957, they organized the Annual French Jewish Intellectuals Conferences, which sought to create academic, philosophical language for understanding the Torah and Jewish culture. Those attending his lectures included a who's who of younger French Jews, including Professor Benny Gross and Rabbi Shlomo Aviner.

Ashkenazi was active in interreligious encounter, traveling often to give lectures around Europe and Asia. He was a perennialist who saw a common primordial core to all religions. He considered this core as the Judaism taught by Abraham of monotheism and morals, rather than a generic theism. He sees Jews and Christians as sharing the Bible and its values, but differing in the interpretation by means of Talmud and New Testament. After Vatican II, since Jews are not accused of deicide, the rivalry between Judaism and Christianity can now end. An open dialogue would be when Christians learn to honor and respect Jewish teachings:

The Bible of the Jews and the Christians is the same Bible . . . Any differences in our theologies and interpretations do not originate in the Bible . . . It is not the Jewish and Christian Bibles that oppose one another but rather the Talmudist and the Evangelist, who turn their backs on one another and never communicate. If this dialogue were to open one day, it would be the day that the Christians recognize and respect the Jews as creatures worthy of love of living things and especially the day Christians recognize the honor of Judaism, whose seal is truth... It was a deicidal nation, an expression that has been rejected since Vatican II. The Church purported to be the New Israel, but mutual recognition brings the rivalry between identities to an end.[46]

Ashekenazi tries to stick close to rabbinic categories of sectarian and gentile. For Ashkenazi, first and second century Jews who became Christians are sectarians (*minim*), those of gentile decent, which are most of today's Christians, have no connection to the life of Jesus and thereof no connection to either Judaism or early Christianity. From a Jewish perspective, there is no Israel of the spirit:

> There is a basic misunderstanding. Contemporary Christians and Jews present themselves as if they were living in the Generation of the Dissociation [the Second Temple Era]—rendering dialogue impossible but so essential.
>
> For us, today's Jews, Christians are not false witness. They are simply not witnesses at all. They do not represent anything that we did not understand or that we rejected as alien to our mission. Similarly, Christianity is not responsible for the formulation of its faith. Christians inherited it from their sages ... Had they been Jews, the authentic heirs to the covenant, they would be considered idolaters who bear a message of apostasy ... They would be like any other Jew who violates the covenant ...[47]

Emmanuel Lévinas

Emmanuel Lévinas (1906–1995) was a major twentieth century philosopher who, in addition to his philosophical writings, left behind an oeuvre on Jewish texts ranging from homiletics on the weekly Torah reading to works on the Talmud and the Lithuanian rabbinic tradition. His influence on contemporary Jewish life and thought is just beginning to be felt. Lévinas was an active participant in Jewish-Christian dialogue.

Lévinas's approach is complex and can serve as an example of having all three positions in a theology of other religions having typologies of inclusivist, universalist, and exclusivist. His writings contain universal statements that all share a common approach: inclusivist statements actually paraphrasing Rahner's concept of Jews as anonymous Christians in which Lévinas considers Christians as the anonymous Jews, and he has particularist statements, some sharply polemical.

Lévinas would not claim to be a theologian or even an ethicist; rather he is representing what he calls first philosophy. Our responsibilities are derived from the imperative of serving others in a non-reciprocal and unconditional way, rather than from concern for the self. His approach attempts to truly confront the other religion by taking responsibility for the Other and starts beyond the metaphysics of all prior textual positions and beyond all faith and dogmatic positions, even universal positions.

> To approach the Other in discourse is to welcome his expression, in which at each instant he overflows the idea a thought would carry away from it. It is therefore to

receive from the Other beyond the capacity of the I, which means exactly: to have the idea of infinity. But this also means: to be taught.[48]

Lévinas credits the post-Vatican II church with emphasizing the need to ethically confront the Other and empty oneself before the encounter. He is proud that the Church's rejection of supersessionalism means confronting Others. Yet, Lévinas still believes that Judaism remains the more noble religion because of its emphasis on action:

> I had a very positive reaction to Nostra Aetate, the degree of the Second Vatican Council. To me it is a logical consequence and proof of the fact that an attempt has been made to overcome certain things from the past. I am pleased to accept the parallelism of the theory of kenosis, and in the idea of an omni-human universality and a "for all men." I have understood Christianity in its "to live and die for all men." The authentically human is the being-Jewish in all men (may you not be shocked by this!) and its reflection in the singular and the particular. The Christians attach great importance to what they call faith, mystery, sacrament. Here is an anecdote on that subject . . . What matters is not "faith," but "doing." Doing, which means moral behavior, of course, but also the performance of ritual. Moreover, are believing and doing different things? What does believing mean? What is faith made of? Words, ideas? Convictions? What do we believe with? With the whole body! With all my bones (Psalm 35:10)! . . . "Doing good is the act of belief itself."[49]

Lévinas argues that anyone who accepts responsibility is to be considered a Jew, albeit an anonymous Jew acting as one through their own religious faith, the being-Jewish quality in all men. One discovers in the other person a trace of the divine transcendence that cannot be located in rational discourse, but only through the ethical encounter available to all humanity. Since Lévinas believes that all universal responsibilities can only be acted upon with particularity, his universalism of ethics is presented through the rhetoric of an inclusivist position, while he is at heart a universalist. Lévinas will not let one reduce this ethical universal to a Divine universal that does violence to the diversity of actual ethical alterity, the radical alien otherness of the one encountered.

He defends Jewish particularism as the unique sign of Jewish ethical duties as what he calls "first philosophy." Lévinas praises the best of other religions as hidden Judaism and offers criticism where they get things wrong. Based on the need for an ethic of responsibility, Lévinas's writings contain a critique of Christianity particularly on the grounds that, in two thousand years, it did not prevent Europe from ending six million innocent lives in the cruelest manner imaginable. Lévinas criticized Christian love and charity because of their complicity in violence against a third party.

> [Christianity] both overestimates and underestimates the weight of the reality it wishes to ameliorate. As a result, it has been quite conservative, politically, making concessions in one realm, the earthly, that it has not always considered of decisive importance. But by rendering unto Caesar what is Caesar's, it reassures Caesar, while setting its sights on a utopia.[50]

Lévinas formulates many religious ideas with direct contrasts to Christianity. He even develops a concept of the "suffering of suffering," that transcends ordinary suffering through a withdrawal of interestedness, to describe the ultimate in taking the responsibility upon oneself to suffer for the other. In this suffering, one takes responsibility for the other and thus achieves the ethical and the human. Lévinas in several of his essays, especially those that speak of Christianity, connects this concept of "the suffering of suffering" to the term *kenosis* (Phil. 2:7), where St. Paul says that Christ "made himself nothing" or "emptied himself." He finds the concept of the "passion of the Jews" in Rabbinic Judaism. While some involved in interfaith dialogue may think *kenosis* is a key to connecting Emmanuel Lévinas to Jewish-Christian relations, he himself notes that his Jewish readers are perturbed by the terminology and analogy and they do not relate to the idea.[51]

Lévinas's approach is based on responding to the Other, yet he remains intellectually in the act of self-judgment of other approaches like Rosenzweig. One cannot understand his approach to interreligious dialogue without considering Lévinas's constant returns to the particular of Jewish texts, and Jewish historical experience as an inclusivist understanding of Christianity nor should one evade his negative reactions to aspects of Christianity.

Conclusion

Rabbi Rene Samuel Sirat (b. 1930), former Chief Rabbi of France, stated that the apprehension about interfaith dialogue "was at the very dawning of interreligious dialogue and we had good reason to be concerned about all possible mishaps. However, the situation is not the same today. The friendship between Jews and Christians has known a greater flourishing in the last fifty years than during the previous millennium."[52]

For many there is a stopping at the moment of irreconcilable differences as long as we get along. The idea of a theological moratorium between faiths was formulated by Elie Wiesel and anachronistically projected back onto Martin Buber:

> "My good friends, what is the difference between you and me? Both of us, all of us believe, because we are religious, in the coming of the Messiah. You believe that the Messiah came, went back, and that you are waiting for Him for the second coming. We Jews believe He hasn't come yet, but He will come. In other words, we are waiting. You for the second coming, we for the first coming. Let's wait together." After a pause, he said, "And when He will come, we will ask Him, have you been here before?" Said Buber, "I hope I will be behind Him and I will whisper in His ear, please do not answer."[53]

For some this story ignores truth claims and for others it seems too polarizing, both irreconcilable and pluralistic at the same time. I should emphasize that all the thinkers discussed in the chapter still emphasize the irreconcilable differences between Christianity and Judaism. Buber himself would have assumed that all who meet God in the ineffability of the moment are the same, and so no question was needed. On the other hand a thinker such as Rosenzweig thought that a messiah as a son of God is fundamentally different than one who is not, and so would have possibility asked: "Are you the son of God?" or "Are you the second person of the Trinity?"

This chapter has shown the rapid progression from the defensiveness of Baeck and Buber to the new era of dialogue proclaimed by Schoeps and its critique by Wurzburger, Weiss-Rosmarin, and Berkovits, Ashkenazi and Lévinas are reminders to American readers of the unique European mixture of dialogue and reproach. The following chapter will deal with those thinkers who affirm a common covenant between the two faiths as well as those who reject the very notion. And the fifth chapter will address those thinkers who want to deal with the commonalities and differences.

4

Christianity: Covenants and Dialogue

This chapter will tell two interwoven stories: an American story of the acceptance of Judaism by American Christians as part of a Judeo-Christian covenant and how Jews debated whether to acknowledge and enter the dialogue by focusing on the theological concept of covenant. American Judaism adopted a language of covenant when discussing their faith as a means of showing its relationship to Christianity. This was set against the historical backdrop of Jewish-Christian dialogue first with mainline Protestants, then Catholics, and finally with Evangelicals.

The starting question is obvious: is there a special relationship between Judaism and Christianity based on a common Biblical covenant? Judaism traditionally assumed that only the Jewish people had a covenant. Christians were generally not singled out by Judaism for a special relationship. Rather, Christianity was linked with Islam in which both religions continued Jewish monotheism or they were included in the universal category of God's concern for all humanity. Since Judaism does not view salvation as only attainable through Judaism and does acknowledge the potential for piety among other nations, there was hardly a need to envision the relationship of others to the Biblical covenant.

In the 1950s, American Jews started to rethink their positions about the dominant religion of the United States: Christianity. In order to build commonality, they created a covenant between Judaism and Christianity based on the prevalent Protestant thought of the era, a civil religion of "one nation under God." In the 1970s and 1980s, the covenant was based around a post-Holocaust sense of individual responsibility. Later, in the 1980s, Jews responded to *Nostra Aetate* and the change in Catholic thought by referring to a common covenant, but still spoke the language of Protestant thought. Now, some American Jews are speaking the language of Christian Zionism in which there is a double covenant until the final messianic battles.

The seemingly eternal category of approaching other religion as sharing a Biblical covenant with Judaism is, for Jews, the most temporally bound. These discussions about covenant shift between seeing one covenant or two covenants that bind together Judaism and Christianity. Sometimes, they present a plurality of many covenants. Many popular authors confuse the ability to have dialogue and friendly encounters with the theological language of covenants.

This chapter will begin with the basic definitions of covenant and then trace the use of the term from those seeking to create commonality such as Agus and Herberg to Soloveitchik's rejection of such approaches. Tannenbaum and Heschel are included for their role in dialogue, but they avoided the covenant language. The chapter will then offer the single covenant approach of Wyschogrod, followed by the pluralistic approach of Greenberg, and the new dual covenant of Jews approaching Christian Zionism. We will conclude on the role of covenant language in Judaism.

- Definitions of Covenant: Jewish, Presbyterian, and Catholic
- Jacob Agus and Will Herberg—Judeo-Christian common faith
- Marc Tannenbaum—Mutual Understanding and Shared Vision
- Abraham Joshua Heschel—A Universal Commonality and medieval inclusivism
- Rabbi Moshe Feinstein—Dialogue is a plot for conversion of the Jews
- Rabbi J. B. Soloveitchik—Judeo-Christian secular realm, but rejects any commonality or connection between Judaism and other religions
- Michael Wyschogrod—One covenant
- Rabbi Irving (Yitz) Greenberg—Many Covenants
- Rabbis Yechiel Eckstein and Shlomo Riskin—Two covenants based on Christian Zionism

Biblical Covenant—Jewish Perspective

In the Bible, a covenant (*berit*) is an obligation of two parties in a structured relationship, including individuals, states, kings, and husband-wife.[1] The covenant with Noah (Genesis 9:13–15) is between all of humanity and God. In contrast, the covenant with Abraham, in the Jewish understanding of the Bible, is a particularistic covenant for the children of Israel, which culminates in the covenant at Sinai (Exodus 19:8), a covenant of law, land, and personhood.

The Abrahamic covenant binds the descendants of Abraham as the people of the one and only God, elaborated upon on Mount Sinai when, before the giving of the Law, Israel pledged itself to keep His covenant (Ex. xix. 8). The content of the covenant mainly concerns observance of the commandments and the bond to the land of Canaan. In the Jewish reading of the Bible, covenant became synonymous in Judaism with the Law (Isa. lvi. 6 *et seq.*; Ps. xxv. 10, 14; 1.16; I Kings xi. 11), later defined as adherence to the Oral Law. In fact, the Oral Law portrays Abraham as already fulfilling rabbinic ordinances and studying Torah.

In the Jewish understanding, the covenants discussed by the prophets are linked to circumcision, the Sabbath, and the study of the Oral law. Judaism knows of no other covenant than the Sinai covenant as a continuation of Abraham; all later covenants hearken back to Sinai. Even when Jeremiah spoke of "the new covenant," which the Lord "will make with the house of Israel and the house of Judah" (Jer. xxxi. 31), the Jews explain this verse contextually as applying to fulfilling the law based on the next passage where Jeremiah explained his words by saying that "I will put my law in their inward parts, and write it in their hearts" (*ib.* xxxi. 33; compare xxxiii. 40). In Jewish readings of this covenant, no matter how much Jews stray from God, He never divorces his people but rather continues to reoffer himself. If one violates the covenant then Deuteronomy offers curses, as does Jeremiah 20:2–4 and 34:18, while Hosea, Jeremiah, and Ezekiel point out that the relationship to God is like the loyalty of marriage after unfaithfulness.

Solomon Schechter offers an overview of the rabbinic idea of covenant in his work, *Aspects of Jewish Theology*, which was specifically designed to translate Jewish concepts into Anglican theological language. He points out that for the rabbis, covenant is about a special relationship that includes affirming God's kingship on a daily basis through recitation of the *shema* (doxology of faith in one God) and *amidah* (standing in silent prayer), a covenant of the merit of the patriarchs that assures Israel that it will be forgiven for its sins. It also offers God's secrets to those who fear him. In Rabbinic thought, covenant is tied to the idea of a chosen people, not the availability of God or salvation. God is available to all other people who are not Jews, without a special covenant or revelation.[2]

Presbyterian and Catholic Views of Covenant

Since modern Jewish thought of the twentieth century has been deeply influenced by trends in Christian theology, the term "covenant" entered modern Jewish thought not entirely consistent with the aforementioned Biblical and Rabbinic interpretations. In order to clarify the meaning of the term, I will present the two main usages of the term in American theology: Reformed (Presbyterian) and Catholic.

Reformed theology often is called "covenant theology" since Calvin's writings stressed a biblical fact of God's *covenant*, God's initiative in making a promise, as being that which undergirds all of the biblical narrative, and hence all of creation itself. In this approach, God's covenant initiative cannot be stymied; God's promise will not be broken.

The Calvinist-Puritan reading of the Biblical covenant recognizes successive covenants of Scripture; man is given a second chance after the fall for a Covenant of Grace through Christ.[3] Typical Reformed theology sees the covenant beginning with Adam and Eve, moving on to later covenants with Noah, Abram, King David, and so on. The first covenant is the Covenant of Works, made with Adam, and continued in the other *figures*, is binding on all of humanity. The other covenant is the Covenant of Grace, made only with Christ and his church.

Puritans applied this rhetoric to American political commitment. For them, Americans have a covenant with God to build a nation, a covenant of works. In the climate of the 1940s and 1950s, there was a Neo-Orthodox reaction by some politicians and theologians against self-sufficient individualism, or optimistic social gospels. The proponents sought to reintroduce covenant language into the American political and religious spheres. They held that Americans needed to commit to, as individuals, acting as "one nation under God." In this era, the political and the religious elements of covenant were blurred. President-elect Eisenhower gave a speech before the Freedoms Foundation in New York in which he called attention to the foundations of democracy. "Our form of government," he explained, "has no sense unless it is founded in a deeply felt religious faith, and I don't care what it is. With us of course it is the Judeo-Christian concept but it must be a religion that all men are created equal." Good Americans were all supposed to be committed Judeo-Christians.

During this time as well, Reinhold Niebuhr was the foremost Christian "Hebraist" who looked to the Hebrew prophets to provide the essential inspiration for the moral complexity of historical existence. In 1944, he proclaimed that "I have, as a Christian theologian, sought to strengthen the Hebraic-prophetic content of the Christian tradition."[4] This approach created a common Biblical core to both religions.

Anti-fascist affirmation was another basis for shared religious ground for Western values. Annual symposiums starting in 1940 by the "Conference on Science, Philosophy and Religion in Their Relation to the Democratic Way of Life," promulgated these views that were organized jointly by Columbia Teachers College and Louis Finkelstein of the Jewish Theological Seminary. Jews joined as part of the "religions of democracy" along with Protestants and Catholics to offer "a rallying point for Judeo-Christian forces in America against the threat presented to them by the Axis ideology and action." Later, this rhetoric was used to defend democracy against the threat of atheistic communists.

In the 1950s, Jews were becoming part of the American political covenant, but were they part of the Protestant Biblical covenant? If so, was their inclusion just through Adam as a covenant of works or was Judaism included as a religion of God? And, if the latter was true, was there a single covenant for both Christians and Jews or were there now two covenants: one for Christians and one for Jews?

Agus and Herberg followed the latter path of two separate covenants for Jews and Christians; Wyschogrod chose the single covenant path, and Soloveitchik returned to the original Reformed double covenant of works and grace, one covenant of works jointly with humanity and one specifically for Jews. Soloveitchik limited the discussion to a moral political realm (hence his article contained a prologue on the covenant of works given to Adam for all humanity) but precluded all religious commonality. Greenberg chose the approach of multiple covenants of personal commitment, and now under Evangelical influence Eckstein and Riskin have affirmed a double covenant theory grounded directly in the Bible.

Another point essential to understanding the 1950s Neo-Orthodox political language is that under the influence of Niebuhr, they discussed both the role of commitment within covenant and the role of the free choice to accept the covenant through action. We choose our destiny and freely accept the collective vision for society as a covenantal community.

Some Jewish authors heard more of the choice while others chose more of the collective destiny. Soloveitchik takes both elements of Protestant thought, destiny and commitment. Wyschogrod emphasizes the inviolable divine election, while Greenberg stresses the voluntary nature of affirming the covenant. David Novak, discussed in the next chapter, uses the term covenant to reject liberalism and thereby used the term to imply any religiously mandated community. Agus emphasizes liberal individualism, while Herberg discusses maters in terms of communities of ethnic-religious affiliation.

If this variety was not confusing enough, the language of covenant is used differently by Catholics. In the Catholic tradition, covenantal theology is a specific approach, used only by some, such as those influenced by Henri de Lubac.[5] In Catholic Biblical theology, the many biblical covenants (Adam, Noah, Abraham, Moses, David, and New) are taken to be the chief structural framework for salvation history, but the Abrahamic covenant, however, is the central Old Testament covenant that is fulfilled in the New Testament, in accordance with Pauline theology (Galatians 3:6–29). The Old and New Testaments are, in Catholic thought, to be integrally related through the covenantal correspondence between Abraham and Paul. This approach of a single covenant relies on the Pauline idea of Abraham as having only one covenant; available in potential by Judaism and fulfilled in Christianity.[6] However, this approach avoids the texts that point a conflict or rivalry between Judaism and Christianity as to who is the true covenant, or the Pauline texts that traditionally implied that belief in Christ replaces Judaism.

There was a variety of pre-Vatican II Catholic thinkers who attempted to reformulate the relationship between Judaism and Christianity with a continuing role for the Jewish covenant. Franz Mussner and Jacob Jocz each formulated the Pauline texts to provide a double covenant theory, where Catholicism accepts that the Book of Romans is still concerned for the Jews, and accepts that Jews have their own approach to God. (Michael Wyschogrod developed this approach for Jewish thought, see below in this chapter.) In contrast, Cardinal Augustin Bea, an important figure in the writing of *Nostra Aetate*, left the relationship of the two faiths as a mystery.[7]

The preeminent expression of Judeo-Christian Catholicism was the Institute of Judeo-Christian Studies established in 1953 at Seton Hall University under the direction of Monsignor John M. Oesterreicher. Monsignor Oesterreicher presented a single covenant as "oneness of the Old and New covenants" where "Christ the Lord links Christians of all times to the Jews of old [. . .] also to the Jews of today." He used as his motto the line from Pius XI, "Abraham is called our father, spiritually we are all Semites."[8] This approach of a single covenant was the theological position chosen by *Nostra Aetate*, and subsequently continued by Pope John Paul II, and Pope Benedict. Emphatically, Cardinal Ratzinger as a proponent of a single covenant has called the "double covenant" theory close to heresy.

Recent Catholic thinkers, such as John Pawlikowski, director of the Catholic-Jewish Studies Program at Catholic Theological Union, attempted to argue for the double covenant between Judaism and Christianity that has a start as a single promise and develops in two separate directions. For Pawlikowski, we should not confine the discussion to the Bible, but include how the covenant plays out in history, as two religious communities, and as partners in waiting. He argues that after the Holocaust, Christians have an ethical responsibility to create a protected theological category for Judaism as a lived religion and to respect the important Jewish differences from Catholic thinking. A similar position was developed by the influential Anglican writer James Parkes, who sees two different but complimentary revelations through Sinai and Calvary.[9]

In either the one or two covenant approach, any reconnection between the two faiths is put off until the end of days.

Jacob Agus

Rabbi Jacob Agus (1911–1986) was one of the leading thinkers and ideologues of the Conservative movement's liberal wing. He was ordained by the Rabbi Isaac Elchanan Theological Seminary (RIETS) in 1935 and then headed the Rabbinical Assembly committees that permitted Sabbath driving and advocated prayer book change.

Agus adopted the cause of interfaith and interracial relations, dubbing his forays into Jewish/Christian and Jewish/Christian/Muslim relations "dialogue" and "trialogue" respectively. He advocated not a common bridge but rather, he used a vivid metaphor by comparing interfaith work to the "arc in an alternating current—it lights up precisely because of the difference in voltage."[10] The undertaking of dialogue illumines the space of religion in the modern world. We learn to respect the differences and create a society of tolerance.

Agus seems to be the creator of the widely quoted attribution to Franz Rosenzweig of a double-covenant theory between Judaism and Christianity. (For Rosenzweig's actual position, see above in Chapter 3.) Agus sought the pragmatic kernel of truth in Rosenzweig and wanted to avoid the idealist philosophy. The kernel of existentialism, for Agus, teaches about the need for personal bonds. "Truth is the measure of the strength of the bond, which, we feel, exists between us and that other thing."[11] Agus extracted from Rosenzweig's writings the idea of a common bond felt between people, including between Judaism and Christianity. In Agus's American and pragmatic view, the existential dialogue consists of the Jewish recognition of Christianity as another valid path. He did not resonate with or find useful passages where Rosenzweig offered particularistic judgment on Christianity or presented an opposition between the two faiths.

Agus sees commonality of the two religious communities in the Bible. Yet, the Bible for Agus contains man's word created from general human experience and therefore, we should also find a place at the table for the other religions of the world. Even the relationship with Christianity should be seen as an existential affinity, not as a doctrinal or intellectual commonality since the Bible is itself only a figurative capturing of the human experience:

> Rosenzweig's ontology is strange and even forbidding to one trained in Anglo-American thought. It is so Hegelian, in tone if not substance.[12]

> [There is] the pressing and sacred task of extracting the seed from the shell in Rosenzweig's philosophy.[13]

If the Bible is God-given, it follows that both Israel and Christendom, which are based on the Bible, are divinely ordained religious communities; in both these groups there is an eternal "we" which through common prayer for the Kingdom, acquires eternity for its members and also hastens the final redemption of the world [. . .] both are, in a real sense, revealed religions and each one, in itself, is only part of the truth.[14]

In affirming the Divine origin of both Judaism and Christianity, Rosenzweig does not intend to be understood as implying that these religions are true, in toto, and that God has secluded himself from communion with those who stand outside the confines of these faiths. Revelation, it will be remembered is a general human experience and prayer, in all languages, is still lyrical communion with God.

In both Judaism and Christianity, there is an ongoing tension between myth and the living substance of faith. It is not possible for any organized, institutional faith to escape completely the trammels of myth and metaphor, symbol and ritual.[15]

Rosenzweig's view was remarkable, in that, the Christian community was engaged in fulfilling Israel's mission. The people of Israel are like the sun; the Christian community was the effluence of Divine rays permeating the nations with the spirit of monotheism. The boundary line between Judaism and Christianity was not along the plane of intellectual thought, since the divine being could only be caught figuratively or symbolically within the meshes of human reason.[16]

Remarkable indeed are the ways of Providence! Though both Christianity and Judaism are required in the Divine plan, God had set a wall between them, a wall which will not fall until the end of time.[17]

It is a sad commentary on the tragic momentum of human affairs that in the mid-twentieth century people should still wonder whether a genuine symbiosis of Judaism and Christianity is possible.[18]

Agus notes that Rosenzweig based his thought on Halevi and Maimonides, yet Agus felt that theirs was a literalist faith while Rosenzweig "moved with the thought-world of modern Judaism, where diverse religions are so many pathways to the one goal" for whom "deviations from ultimate truth were only distractions."[19] Despite this celebration of diversity, Agus thought that for the Jewish people, Christianity constituted a descent from the lofty reaches of their faith, since it compromised at so many points with the pure faith." Elsewhere, he writes that he prefers to profess the modern approaches of Mendelssohn, Tillich, Dewey, and Tagore, to any classical or medieval text. Hence, Agus sought a modern tolerance beyond particular myth, a universal vision of a good society.[20]

Will Herberg

Will Herberg (1901–1977) was an American Jewish sociologist of religion and Jewish theologian. Herberg started ideologically as a Communist and then became a religious conservative, following the Protestant Neo-Orthodox theology of Niebuhr. He founded the quarterly *Judaism* with Robert Gordis and Milton Konvitz. During the 1960s, he was religion editor of the conservative journal *National Review*, and taught at Drew University. Herberg created a sociological framework for the study of religion in the United States showing how American ethnic culture divided along the lines of Protestant, Catholic, and Jewish. Herberg also believed that societies cannot long survive without being regrafted onto their Judeo-Christian roots.

Herberg was one of the major formulators of the idea of the Jewish-Christian covenant. In the first issue of *Judaism* (1952), he elicited an article by Paul Tillich on the relationship of Judaism and Christianity. In "Is There a Judeo-Christian Tradition?" Tillich argued the affirmative by asserting that the two religions shared faith in an exclusive and righteous God, an understanding of man's historical existence, and the need to wrestle with "a legalistic and utopian interpretation of righteousness."

In his own writings, Herberg combined and adapted Agus's reading of Rosenzweig, as well as the work of "Religions of Democracy" conferences at Teacher's College together with his own sociological data:

> Is it any wonder that Christian theologians speak of Judaism and Christianity as "not, fundamentally, two different religions by one" (Frederick C. Grant) and note with emphasis "the identity of structure at all points and the identity of content in most" of the two faiths (Tillich), or that a Jewish theologian (Finkelstein) refers to Judaism and Christianity as "twin religions" and indeed speaks of them as constituting "one system?"

> The central category of biblical thinking is covenant. "Never imagine that you have rightly grasped a biblical idea," Paul Ramsey has said, "until you have reduced it to a corollary of the ideal of 'covenant.'" And this is supremely true of biblical thinking about salvation. In the biblical view, man has, so to speak, standing with God, and a direct personal relation to him, only by virtue of his membership in the people of God, the redeemed and redeeming community.

> "Israel," says Franz Rosenzweig, "can bring the world to God only through Christianity." Despite all hostility through the ages, Jewish tradition has always "freely acknowledged the divine mission of Christianity" as "Israel's apostle" to the nations. This, if one may venture to put it that way, is Christianity's service for Judaism.

> And so Jew and Christian stand separated yet united. The unity far transcends the separation, for we are united in our common allegiance to the living God and in our common expectation of, and longing for, the One who is to come. Jew and Christian—to recall Tillich's words—stand united until the end of history in the struggle for the Lord of time against the "gods of space."[21]

Catholics, Protestants, and Jews have in common a Jewish-Christian faith that crosses two religions, one Biblical faith, two covenants, and three religions.

Later Reflections of Covenant

The idea of a common covenant in the writings of Herberg was based on the rise of Neo-Orthodox theology in the 1950s. In 1966, Robert Gordis attributed the phrase "Judeo-Christian" to three socio-political factors: (1) the growth of the interfaith movement after World War I; (2) fear of communism during the depression; and (3) the rise of a pluralist ethic after World War II.[22] Gordis was not sanguine about the way the phrase blurred significant theological differences between the faiths and that most Jewish texts retain caveats on Christian belief.

In 1970, Arthur A. Cohen published a collection of twenty years of his articles under the title *The Myth of the Judeo-Christian Tradition* that rejected this common covenant. Cohen asserted that the Judeo-Christian tradition was not a tradition at all; the history of Jewish-Christian relations is fundamentally a history of social and theological antagonism, not of common cause. Yet, Cohen does accept a contemporary Judeo-Christian humanism of those looking for values by those who no longer believe in the premodern versions of their respective faiths. Cohen does not see a post WWII pluralism, rather a commonality of rhetoric, values, and the newfound rapprochement.[23]

For Arthur A. Cohen, Christians are forever linked to Judaism through the New Testament's use of the Old Testament (Hebrew Bible). Jews never felt the need to reverse the connection. Nevertheless, Cohen included inclusivist musings about the connection of the two faiths: "Maimonides and Jehudah Halevi . . . regarded Christianity and Islam as mimetic faiths, compromised in their understanding of God, but clearly preferable to immorality and . . . to the theological chaos of paganism."

Additionally, the writings of the important sociologist Robert N. Bellah (b. 1927) from the late 1960s (which became popular in the 1970s and 1980s) recategorized the entire enterprise away from theology to sociology, and reconceptualized Jewish-Christian covenant thinking to what he called "civil religion." He presented the commonalities attributed to the Judeo-Christian covenant as part of the national values, beliefs, and history that allow nationalism and civic pride. Bellah credited these values more to American history, post-Civil War rhetoric, John Dewey's idea of a common faith, and Jean-Jacques Rousseau's *The Social Contract* than to theology.[24]

Furthermore, within the field of theology, theologians themselves under the influence of existentialism, removed covenant from any specific theological tradition, turning the term covenant into a way to speak of one's personal commitment. The well-known writings of Paul Tillich formulated religion as the human quest for ultimate concern. The Methodist theologian Paul Ramsey (1913–1988), an important ethicist of the 1970s, treated covenant as the choice of an ethical approach to life by connecting to divine love, shown through commitment and responsibility. Ramsey saw as a fundamental notion of Judeo-Christian belief that God makes a covenant with humanity, offering steadfast love and fidelity and asking in return that humans manifest to each other the care that mirrors that divine fidelity. Living in covenant is to ask the meaning of the sanctity of life and respect for the dignity of persons.[25] In contrast, some existential ethicists of the era, not specifically covenant theologians, such as James Gustafson, stressed the uncertainty of all moral decisions and our inability to ever know what God wants from us. The various proponents of an existential covenant each view the covenant as volunteerism; "we all freely choose our covenants." They reject the binding obligation of the Presbyterian and Catholic covenants, even when they continue to use their theological language.

The theologian Paul van Buren (1924–1998), an Episcopalian who was a member of the radical theologians of the 1960s, became an early associate at the Shalom Hartman Institute where he formulated a one covenant theory of Jewish-Christian relations. In his version, both faiths follow a biblical truth as "a way to live, a way to be human, a way to be a community." Both faiths teach the existential truths of the gift of life and the need for responsibility. For Van Buren, there was one covenant offered to Abraham to overcome the evil of mankind by accepting responsibility and the covenant is continuously renewed, as a coformation, at both Sinai and in Christianity.[26]

Based on the prevailing Existentialism, there were several late twentieth-century Jewish versions of covenant theology. We must, however, spend a moment on Borowitz as a paradigm to the discussion at the end of the twentieth century. Borowitz's covenantal theology starts with the Neo-Orthodox version of covenant as obligation and combines it with an existential treatment of revelation as pure love; covenant became a metaphor for a personal relationship with God capturing both the intimate dimension of loving intimacy with God and the social sphere in which duty is actualized. Borowitz's language that combined love and society has influenced the various Jewish pluralistic positions that claim that Judaism affirms multiple covenants since all human beings are made in the image of God, serve one God, and all follow the universalism of the Noahide laws. This has lead to tremendous confusion of the Calvinist ideas of covenant with the openness contained in the inclusivist positions by Rabbis Emden or Seforno. In turn, dialogue with a member of another faith is confused by many with accepting a common covenant. In the existential position, dialogue is the engagement as humans with another human to discuss their respective religions, while covenant is the formulation of one's own theological vision of God's promise.

Entering the Discussion

For most American Jews of Eastern European background, encountering other religions beyond their own ethic enclave started in the 1950s. According to Martin Marty, the chaplains and soldiers who served in the Korean War brought home to America a sense of the commonality of religion: that we all worship one God. This encounter, among other factors, created the ecumenical climate that in 1954 added "under God" to the Pledge of Allegiance. By 1960, this ecumenicism had progressed beyond mutual tolerance into a liberal campaign for the blurring of divisions between Churches and creeds.[27]

The positions of the Jewish protagonists during Vatican II were contextualized not just within the Jewish-Catholic dialogue but also in the climate of American civil society in which trading theological favors was commonplace. All American religions were hailed as sharing a common humanistic core or, as William

Hutchinson points outs, by 1960, ecumenicism meant shared goals, responsibilities, and even the building of chapels to accommodate in the same structure the worship services of Protestants, Catholics, and Jews.[28] The positions of Agus, Herberg, and those confidently entering dialogue with a Judeo-Christian commonality filled the various Jewish newspapers and journals. The great event of Vatican II was theologically shepherded by Marc Tannenbaum and A. J. Heschel, and rejected by Moshe Feinstein and Joseph Soloveitchik, as well as by Eliezer Berkovits (see above in Chapter 3).

Marc Tannenbaum

Marc H. Tannenbaum (1925–1992) was a rabbi devoted to human rights and social justice activist who is best known for building bridges between Judaism and other faith communities. He played a historical role as a vigorous advocate during the Second Vatican Council (1962–1965) on behalf of what eventually emerged as *Nostra Aetate*, the landmark document that overturned a long tradition of hostility toward Jews and Judaism. He worked for the American Jewish Committee (AJC), one of the few Jewish organizations that took the Ecumenical Council seriously, and Tannenbaum was responsible for involving Abraham Joshua Heschel in the Council.

Tannenbaum shows a dedicated mission for Jews and Christians to work together for a better world. The only way to do it is through increased communication, genuine understanding, and a common theological goal based on scripture and vision of a perfected society:[29]

> If Jews and Christians want to consider seriously their mutual relationships, it is not sufficient that they declare to one another generalized sentiments of reciprocal regard. Genuine caring between groups, as between individuals presupposes a willingness to enter into the life situation of the other, and to be present with concern and support at the moment when the other person or group is hurting.

> When in recent weeks some of my colleagues in the rabbinate have expressed bitter disappointment over the "Christian silence" about Israel, I asked them, "When did you speak to a Christian minister about the religious significance of Jerusalem to Judaism?" Invariably the answer was "never" or "not very recently."

> The more recent substitute for religious dialogue that has been vigorously advocated by some Jews, strange to say, is interfaith social action. I know of no proposal more contradictory to traditional, *halachic* Judaism, for in effect, it advocates a separation between religion and life. The late Chief Rabbi Kook of Israel, one of the great sages of traditional Judaism, declared that "man's physical concerns and spiritual aspirations are inseparable. The sacred cannot exist without the profane."

> Rabbis, priests, nuns and ministers do not come together for social action because they are experts in nuclear non-proliferation treaties, or in the administration of economic development programs in Lesotho, or in city planning. What brings them together is a recognition that they share a moral conscience, which in turn derives

from a certain attitude toward Sacred Scriptures and their sacred history, that they all have a certain explanation for man and society that is shaped by messianic visions of a kingdom to come in which justice and righteousness are consummated. Certainly they will carry out their redemptive work more effectively if they have technical competence, but that is not their primary vocation.

Tannenbaum thought that understanding required actual encounters and not just book knowledge. He also thought that commentaries need to be written to remove anti-Semitic statements. Both religions need to see that they have different historical narratives of the past and Christians specifically have to see that Judaism is an ongoing living faith. His own belief was in a universalism through Adam, a belief in common moral tradition through the Noahide laws, and a belief in universal monotheism. Many of these points seem obvious today, but in Tannenbaum's era he was an original and forceful proponent of these ideas.

> The notion that these changes would have taken place if Christians simply studied Jewish books, without a living encounter with Jews in dialogue, is an illusion and fantasy. Vast libraries of Judaica, in all languages, have been available to Christian scholars, clergymen, and teachers for almost 2,000 years. How many significant changes in Christian attitudes toward Jews and Judaism can be attributed to the study of this literature? Indeed, there is plenty of evidence that Christian savants, nurtured on anti-Jewish theological stereotypes, and living in isolation from Jews as persons, read into or read out of Jewish sources texts that confirmed their preconceived bias.

> If one reads church histories and Jewish histories of the same events, it is as though Christians and Jews are being educated in different universes of discourse.

> Unless and until Christian scholars and people develop theological conceptions regarding Judaism and the synagogue that reflect in some way the vital reality of the existence of present-day Judaism, very little else of significance in Jewish-Christian relations will be possible.

> The relationship of the people of Israel to mankind takes as its first and foremost principle the fact that, according to the Torah, all men are descended from one father. All of them, not as races or nation, but as men, are brothers in Adam, and therefore are called bene Adam, sons of Adam . . . A God-fearer was one who kept the Noachian principles, that is the moral principles known to Noah and to pre-Israelite mankind.

> While there is no unanimity in Judaism regarding the ultimate conversion of the Gentiles, there can be no doubt that, theologically speaking, Judaism does expect a redeemed mankind to be strict monotheists—in the Jewish sense.

Heschel

Abraham Joshua Heschel (1907–1972) was a rabbi, academic, and theologian who later became an active participant in the American Civil Rights and antiwar movements. Heschel expressed his own philosophy of religion in two books, *Man is Not Alone* (1951) and *God in Search of Man* (1955). He defined religion as the attempt by humans to understand and answer the deepest questions about life and the universe.

Heschel's now classic essay on interreligious dialogue, "No Religion is an Island," displays his own movement in thinking about other religions. Heschel starts with a religious and social exclusivism of "uniqueness" and isolation seeking to move to a position of social interfaith engagement. He cultivates the John Donne line "no man is an island" into "no religion is an island." The original proclaims that people are not self-sufficient and we rely on other people in society. Heschel uses this to teach that religions are not self-sufficient in the modern world and that, despite rampant indifference to God in the modern age, religion still has something to say if we join together and get the message out there into society. The goal is to reawaken the engaged life of a divine reality in the modern world.

Even though Israel has a unique mystery and teachings, all religions still need to come together as humans outside of our given faiths. Each must seek a living God outside of church teachings or Jewish law. We share an alienation from God and solve it by cultivating a fundamental religious attitude deeper than a specific religion. Notice, that he only sees common "perils and fears" of a world without God, not common religion:

> The supreme issue is today not the *halacha* for the Jew or the Church for the Christian—but the premise underlying both religions, namely, whether there is a *pathos*, a divine reality concerned with the destiny of man which mysteriously impinges upon history; the supreme issue is whether we are alive or dead to the challenge and the expectation of the living God. The crisis engulfs all of us. The misery and fear of alienation from God make Jew and Christian cry together.[30]

> On the other hand, the Community of Israel must always be mindful of the mystery of aloneness and uniqueness of its own being. "There is a people that dwells apart, not reckoned among the nations" (Num. 23:9), says the Gentile prophet Balaam. Is it not safer for us to remain in isolation and to refrain from sharing perplexities and certainties with Christians?

> Our era marks the end of complacency, the end of evasion, the end of self-reliance. Jews and Christians share the perils and the fears; we stand on the brink of the abyss together. Interdependence of political and economic conditions all over the world is a basic fact of our situation. Disorder in a small obscure country in any part of the world evokes anxiety in people all over the world.

> In the dimension of faith, the encounter proceeds in terms of personal witness and example, sharing insights, confessing inadequacy. On the level of doctrine we seek to convey the content of what we believe in, on the level of faith we experience in one another the presence of a person radiant with reflections of a greater presence.

> The theme of these reflections is not a doctrine or an institution called Christianity, but human beings all over the world, both present and past, who worship God as followers of Jesus, and my problem is how I should relate myself to them spiritually. The issue I am called upon to respond to is not the truth of dogma but the faith and the spiritual power of the commitment of Christians.

> In facing the claim and the dogma of the Church, Jews and Christians are strang-
> ers and stand in disagreement with one another. Yet there are levels of existence
> where Jews and Christians meet as sons and brothers. "Alas, in heaven's name, are
> we not your brothers, are we not the sons of one father and are we not the sons
> of one mother?"

> The children did not arise to call the mother blessed; instead, they called the mother
> blind [. . .]A Jew ought to ponder seriously the responsibility involved in Jewish
> history for having been the mother of two world religions. Does not the failure of
> children reflect upon their mother? Do not the sharp deviations from Jewish tradi-
> tion on the part of the early Christians who were Jews indicate some failure of com-
> munication within the spiritual climate of first century Palestine?

There is one God and we should all have faith in that one God, hence the reason
we should concertedly work together: bring God back into the modern world.
Jews and Christians remain strangers, as Rosenzweig presented, yet our commonality does not lead us to redouble our particularism. Rather, we see a family
resemblance in the other on the level of existence. Even though early Christians
rejected Judaism, Heschel remains feeling responsible for their falling away from
Judaism.

Heschel was one of the first in contemporary Jewish thought to speak of the
dignity of the differences between religions and to work together for a better
world. "Parochialism has become untenable." Nevertheless, we can still disagree
and evaluate other religions. He is not a pluralist but rather, follows the well-worn
universalist and inclusivist path. His universalism is of the intrinsic holiness of
humanity and the universal human ability to be called by God. We differ in law
and creed; still we have to know that Christianity brought knowledge of the "God
of Abraham" to the world:

> The religions of the world are no more self-sufficient, no more independent, no
> more isolated than individuals or nations. Energies, experiences and ideas that come
> to life outside the boundaries of a particular religion or all religions continue to
> challenge and to affect every religion . . . Horizons are wider, dangers are greater . . .
> *No religion is an island.* We are all involved with one another.

> On what basis do we people of different religious commitments meet one another?

> First and foremost we meet as human beings who have so much in common . . .
> We disagree in law and creed, in commitments which lie at the very heart of our
> religious existence. We say "No" to one another in some doctrines essential and
> sacred to us . . . We may disagree about the ways of achieving fear and trembling,
> but the fear and trembling are the same . . . Over and above mutual respect we
> must acknowledge the indebtedness to one another. It is our duty to remember
> that it was the Church that brought the knowledge of the God of Abraham to the
> Gentiles.[31]

He affirms both inclusivism and a universal fear and trembling behind all religion.
Heschel uses the universalism of Malachi to say that everyone is worshipping
one God. Yet, he purposely oscillates rhetorically between the unified approaches

of considering other religions as solely "His majesty's loyal opposition" to the particularism of "is not truth exclusive?" Heschel, whose very theological method is to oscillate between positions, actually resolves the two extremes by using the inclusivism of Halevi, Maimonides, and Emden to resolve this contradiction between universalism and exclusivism:

> Does not the all-inclusiveness of God contradict the exclusiveness of any particular religion? The prospect of all men embracing one form of religion remains an eschatological hope. What about here and now? Is it not blasphemous to say: I alone have all the truth and the grace, and all those who differ live in darkness, and are abandoned by the grace of God? . . . It seems that the prophet proclaims that men all over the world, though they confess different conceptions of God, are really worshipping One God, the Father of all men, though they may not be aware of it.

> Religions, I repeat, true to their own convictions, disagree profoundly and are in opposition to one another on matters of doctrine. However, if we accept the prophet's thesis that they all worship one God, even without knowing it, if we accept the principle that the majesty of God transcends the dignity of religion, should we not regard a divergent religion as His Majesty's loyal opposition? However, does not every religion maintain the claim to be true, and is not truth exclusive?

> Leading Jewish authorities, such as Jehuda Halevi and Maimonides, acknowledge Christianity to be *preparatio messianica*, while the Church regarded ancient Judaism to have been a *preparatio evangelica*. Thus, whereas the Christian doctrine has often regarded Judaism as having outlived its usefulness and the Jews as candidates for conversion, the Jewish attitude enables us to acknowledge the presence of a divine plan in the role of Christianity within the history of redemption. Jehuda Halevi, though criticizing Christianity and Islam for retaining relics of ancient idolatry and feast days, "they also revere places sacred to idols," compares Christians and Mohammedans to proselytes who adopted the roots, but not all the branches (or the logical conclusions of the divine commandments).
>
> Rabbi Jacob Emden maintains that heretical Jewish sects such as the Karaites and the Sabbatians belong to the second category whereas Christianity and Islam are in the category of "a community which is for the sake of heaven" and which will "in the end endure."[32]

Heschel still cites Jewish texts that refer to both Christianity and Islam as ancient idolatry or partial truth. He does neither deny nor reject it. He lets the Jewish texts say what they say.

Heschel has few explicit statements about Christianity and its differences with Judaism. "Christianity begins with the basic assumption that man is depraved and sinful—that left to himself he can do nothing. He has to be saved."[33]

> With your permission, I should like to say that it is difficult for a Jew to understand when Christians worship Jesus as the Lord, and this Lordship takes the place of the Lordship of God the creator. It is difficult for a Jew to understand when theology becomes reduced to Christology.[34]

Judaism is the mother of the Christian faith. It has a stake in the destiny of Christianity. Should a mother ignore her child [. . .]? Is it not our duty to help one another in trying to overcome hardness of heart?

None of us pretends to be God's accountant, and His design for history and redemption remains a mystery before which we must stand in awe. It is arrogant to maintain that the Jews' refusal to accept Jesus as the Messiah is due to their stubbornness or blindness as it would be presumptuous for the Jews not to acknowledge the glory and holiness in the lives of countless Christians. "The Lord is near to all who call upon Him, to all who call upon Him in truth" (Ps. 145:18).[35]

Heschel played a large role in the Jewish attitude toward Vatican II. In 1964, he wrote the following to Cardinal Bea about a desire for the conversion of Jews in *Nostra Aetate*:

A message that regards the Jew as a candidate for conversion and proclaims the destiny of Judaism to disappear will be abhorred by Jews all over the world and is bound to foster reciprocal distrust as well as bitterness and resentment.

Heschel called such church desires for the conversion of the Jews, "spiritual fratricide." His message is that his universal vision of a "living God:" motivated him to adopt an approach of social activism:

It is neither to flatter nor to refute one another, but to help one another; to share insight and learning, to cooperate in academic ventures on the highest scholarly level, and what is even more important to search in the wilderness for well-springs of devotion, for treasures of stillness, for the power of love and care for man. What is urgently needed are ways of helping one another in the terrible predicament of here and now by the courage to believe that the word of the Lord endures for ever as well as here and now [. . .] to keep alive the divine spark in our souls, to nurture openness to the spirit of the Psalms, reverence for the words of the prophets, and faithfulness to the Living God.[36]

Heschel's ability to speak from the heart about God was appreciated by many Christians involved in interfaith, and he was a messenger of the Jewish message to the gentiles.[37]

Some interpreted his prophetic voice as a humanist, not taking into account his severe critique of Tillich's view that God is a ground of being as vacuous and that religion is Divine demands not symbols.[38]

Some of his readers assumed that the way to follow Heschel was to embrace the experimental pluralism of Reb Zalman Schachter or the academic pluralism of the study of mysticism. Harold Kasimow argued for two decades that Heschel was a pluralist, and that the Heschelian approach was pluralism.[39] Recently, Kasimow correctly acknowledges that Heschel's approach is more empirical and universal than pluralistic. Heschel, in Kasimow's current reading, has more in common with the Dalai Lama, who accepts all religions but views meditation as the peak of religion as it brings tranquility and happiness. For Heschel, however, prophecy is the peak of religious experience and it brings concern for humanity.

Rabbi Moshe Feinstein

Moshe Feinstein (1895–1986) was the leading rabbinical scholar and authoritative adjudicator of questions related to Jewish law. He was considered by many as the de facto supreme rabbinic authority for Orthodox Jewry of North America. In the Orthodox world, he is widely referred to simply as "Rav Moshe."

Rabbi Feinstein was a firm and consistent critique of any interfaith activity between Jews and Christians. He considered all interfaith dialogue as a stealth form of missionary activity and enticement to sin. Christianity is consistently referred to as idolatry and any interfaith activity is regarded negatively, as if one is turning to idols. Even discussion of common social concerns is deemed a subterfuge for the Christian Satanic activity. Rabbi Feinstein was responsible for a public statement signed by the Orthodox leaders of America, excluding Rabbi Joseph B. Soloveitchik, against interfaith activity:[40]

19 Adar I, 5727–March 1, 1967

To my honored friend, Rabbi Dov Ber Lander
Regarding the matter that you promised to attend the meeting on the 23rd of Adar I where Catholics and Protestants together with Jews from the Synagogue Council of America and Rabbis from the Rabbinical Council of America will meet. Even though you will only speak general words, it is obvious and clear that this is a severe prohibition of appurtenances of idolatry.

For a plague is now spreading in many places because of the new pope (Pope Paul VI) whose only intention is to move all Jews away from their holy and pure faith to accept the Christian Faith. For it is easier to accomplish this through these methods than through hate and murder that previous popes have used. Therefore any dealing with them even on general matters and all [the more so] actual coming close for a meeting is forbidden with the severe prohibition of "coming close to idolatry." There is also a prohibition of "enticing and leading astray."

Even if you and the other rabbis who go there will be careful with your words and you will also not flatter the priests and their faith as do the Reform and Conservative rabbis, who entice and lead others to go astray, many people will learn from them that it is permitted to go to the events such as the lectures of the missionaries.

Furthermore, you should not even send a letter there expressing what you planned on saying for any interaction with them further assists their evil plans. It is also forbidden to participate in any manner in meetings like these for I heard that they want to have in Boston and Rome. Anyone who joins with them will be considered one who entices and leads astray the Jewish people. For this that the Catholic missionaries tried so hard for all these years and had very little success, but through these rabbis who lack knowledge who want to join with them, it is possible that many will apostate. We cannot justify the one who entices by saying this was not his intention; he is guilty of a capital offense in this act and all that consequences.

Therefore, do not be concerned with not keeping your promise to attend and speak. For on the contrary, perhaps through this that you do not go on account of the prohibition, perhaps others will not go and you will bring merit to the community.

Your Friend, Moshe Feinstein.

Rabbi Feinstein wrote a letter directly to Rabbi Soloveitchik three weeks later on March 21, 1967 calling on his friend to join him in a public ban on the ecumenical meetings with the Catholics since they are a plot for the conversion of the Jews. Feinstein even considers a meeting for social concerns is forbidden because the young rabbis such as Bernard Lander will be enticed to leave Judaism:

> My dear friend, the great renowned Gaon, spreader of Torah Rabbi Yosef Dov Soloveitchik.
>
> Regarding the matter that some young rabbis are trapped in the snare of the Ecumenical Council by the leader of the priests in the Vatican, whose intention is to convert all of the Jews to their faith, heaven forbid. The Cardinals and the Bishops were commanded to arrange committee meetings and conventions between priests and rabbis in every place. The action of Satan was successful for some rabbis joined with a permissive ruling as long as they do not speak of faith but only of societal concerns. However, the priests have a different supposition in that for them almost all matters are faith based. Their true intention is to eventually reach issues of faith, therefore it is obvious that that actual coming together even for "general matters" is forbidden at all times and periods. Now since this has come from the evil counsel of the Pope, it is certainly forbidden. We see the newspapers are boasting the immanent coming to a reconciliation of doctrine and faith as well as praying together.

Joseph B. Soloveitchik

Joseph B. Soloveitchik (1903–1993) was an American Orthodox rabbi, Talmudist, and Jewish philosopher. He is regarded as a seminal figure for many Modern Orthodox Jews and was known familiarly simply as "The *Rav*" (the rabbi) by his followers worldwide.

Soloveitchik demanded the acceptance of each religion as separate theologically, historically, and existentially. He decried any common core theory or the reduction of religion to the lowest common denominator. R. Soloveitchik's position did, however, allow the discussion of "communication among the various faith communities" in "the public world of humanitarian and cultural endeavors," on topics that "revolve about the religious spiritual aspects of our civilization." R. Soloveitchik speaks of "universal religious problems [. . .] and discussion within the framework of our religious outlooks and terminology [. . .] As men of God, our thoughts, feelings, perceptions, and terminologies bear the imprint of a religious world outlook."[41] His position served to reject the irenic trends and to limit dialogue, but also to allow common ground on social issues and universal religious themes.

Rabbi Soloveitchik's essay "Confrontation" written in response to the Catholic-Jewish rapprochement initiated under the aegis of Vatican II warns his followers against dialogue and presents the futility of developing a theology of other religions. His essay is complex and makes several points:

- Faith is private
- Double confrontation—universal secular and particular

- Judeo-Christian Tradition—exists on the secular plane
- No Covenantal Connection
- No Theological Dialogue
- Jewish Particularity as the tension of Jacob and Esau
- No Theology of Other Religions since faith cannot be communicated

The Protestant theological movement of the 1920s, identified with Emil Brunner and Karl Barth, protested against identifying Christianity with ethical social realm, and, under existentialist influence, said that faith was paradoxical and non-communicable. They created a dichotomy between faith as private compared to culture and human activity as public. Hence dialectic theologians were against natural theology, against the irenic trends of ecumenical theology, and against identifying religion with cognitive knowledge. For dialectic thinkers, the universal human quest for God is not part of revealed religion. Soloveitchik was directly influenced by their thought, especially the rejection of natural theology and considering faith as private.

Soloveitchik bases his theological analysis of interfaith dialogue on the theology of Karl Barth, who stated categorically that someone who does not share one's faith could not understand Christian statements. In fact, the entire section of R. Soloveitchik's essay on interfaith dialogue is indebted to Barth's *Church Dogmatics* 1/2 [§ 17]. Soloveitchik follows many of Barth's ideas, stating that this inner faith rejects the cultural elements of religion and cannot be expressed using culture's tools.[42]

> The word of faith reflects the intimate, the private, the paradoxically inexpressible cravings of the individual for and his linking up with his Maker. It reflects the numinous character and the strangeness of the act of faith of a particular community which is totally incomprehensible to the man of a different faith community.

Soloveitchik presents a theory of double confrontation, in which one has both universal connection to God and then specifically Jewish obligations. The first redeems mankind from a nasty brutish secular existence into a dignified existence, and the second creates the Jewish covenantal community:

> We believe we are the bearers of a double charismatic load, that of the dignity of man, and that of the sanctity of the covenantal community. In this difficult role, we are summoned by God, who revealed himself at both the level of universal creation and that of the private covenant, to undertake a double mission—the universal human and the exclusive covenantal confrontation.[43]

> We do not equate commandments ritual—ethos with another—each is unique especially since ours is *halakhah*.

> We are called upon to tell the community not only the story it already knows—but also what is still unknown to it, namely, our otherness as a metaphysical covenantal community.[44]

For Soloveitchik Judaism mandates universal concerns for human dignity through knowledge, philosophy, science, and the building of society, while the second obligation is the covenantal obligation of *halakhah* (Jewish law), metaphysical uniqueness, and narrative separatism. He offers an updated version of the distinction of a covenant of works and a covenant of faith.

Yet, Soloveitchik does indeed acknowledge a Judeo-Christian tradition, however, he considers moral behavior that stems from belief in the God of Biblical culture, as part of the first covenant, outside of faith commitment. Notably, R. Soloveitchik couched the lines between the universal and particular themselves in a universal manner, even a religious universal. Many readers struggle to understand that for R. Soloveitchik the philosophic writings of Tillich, Barth, and Kierkegaard describe the universal, man's ultimate concern. In this aspect, R. Soloveitchik's thought itself was embedded in a specific mid-twentieth century understanding of religion as constituting a universal human condition. This intellectual climate assumed that there was a natural religious universalism as part of the human condition, similar to the quest for human dignity and freedom.

Soloveitchik's classic 1944 essay, "Halakhic Man," finds the Hebraic spirit of Niebuhr in the *halakhah*. Soloveitchik offers a Judaism that is this-worldly and has an ethical commitment to building a better society in America. But this activity does not touch the inner core of Jewish faith:

> It is quite legitimate to speak of a Judeo-Christian tradition . . . However, when we shift the focus from the dimension of culture to that of faith—where total unconditional commitment and involvement are necessary—the whole idea of a tradition of faiths and the continuum of revealed doctrines [. . .] is utterly absurd.[45]

Agus and Herberg's social activity would be secular for Soloveitchik as social mandates as part of American ideals are outside of the *halakhah*. Yet, R. Soloveitchik remains ready to confront the moral issues of the 1960s. "We are ready to enter into dialogue on such topics as war and peace, poverty, freedom, man's moral values . . . civil rights, etc., which revolve about the religious spiritual aspects of our civilization."[46]

Soloveitchik rejects many of the earlier medieval Jewish approaches of any inclusivist or universal connection between religions when he writes:

> First, we must state, in unequivocal terms, the following. We are a totally independent faith community. We do not revolve as a satellite in any orbit. Nor are we related to any other faith community as "brethren" even though "separated."[47]

For Soloveitchik, any relationship is in the realm of culture and our universal religious elements. But we have no theological relationship to another faith as brethren.

Soloveitchik meets the modern world as secular and hence denuded of the theological issues presented above:

> The confrontation should occur not at a theological, but at a mundane level. There all of us speak the mundane language of modern man. As a matter of fact, our common interests lie not in the realm of faith, but in that of the secular orders.[48]

Soloveitchik's second point of the non-communicability of faith is not about the cultural realms of the academic, phenomenological, or cognitive discussions. It is well known that Soloveitchik freely cited Kierkegaard, Otto, and Barth for his Jewish edifice. Cognitive understanding of another religion can be studied and communicated, however the non-cognitive elements are seen as faith and therefore off limits. Faith concerns the existential commitment and for Jews, that includes the sense of *halakhic* confrontation:

> However, if the debate should revolve around matters of faith, then one of the con-
> fronters will be impelled to avail himself of the language of the opponent. This in
> itself would mean surrender of individuality and distinctiveness.[49]

Religious discussion would mean the giving up of the individuality of Judaism. His insistence that Jews can only discuss other religions based on mundane existence, even when they use common cultural sources is in contrast to the natural theology and the sanctified theological reflections of the inclusivist and universalist traditions of prior centuries.

Soloveitchik concludes his essay using a dualistic *Midrash* of how Jacob and Esau can never meet spiritually, a metaphysical destiny in opposition to the other religions. The Jews, while their religious side remains non-communicable, ought to be part of secular society. "Yes—civic, cultural welfare, enrich society with creative talents but not our soul, personality, metaphysical destiny, spiritual future."[50]

Soloveitchik's two-part position may seem structurally similar to Rabbi Ovadiah Seforno's humanistic position in which Seforno affirms a universal dignity of man as well as a second higher special Jewish covenant of Torah. Yet, for Soloveitchik, Judaism has a qualitative difference, while for Seforno the difference between universal human dignity and Judaism is only quantitative. Another difference lies in the publicity of faith. Seforno believes a universal quality lies in connection to God, able to be discussed with various faiths; Soloveitchik, on the other hand, sees faith as private, which emphasizes difference, exclusivity, and uniqueness. (For more on Seforno, see my *Judaism and Other Religions*.)

Many criticize Soloveitchik's position regarding religious dialogue, however, I only present, and want to deal with, his meta-statements about a theology of other religions, not his views on dialogue.[51]

For the purposes of this work, the major point is the need to separate Soloveitchik's view of dialogue from his views of other religions. One can accept Soloveitchik's statement that one should not engage in dialogue, but that does not mean that Judaism, or Jewish texts, do not have statements of other religions. Absolute separation of religions is not in continuity with the traditional Jewish positions of universalism and inclusivism, as there are rabbinic views of other religions that are useful for understanding the self and for encouraging others.

The interpretation of the R. Soloveitchik's document is best seen in an essay by R. Walter Wurzburger written to the Synagogue Council of America to interpret the doctrines of his teacher. There he acknowledges that according to

R. Soloveitchik; one can discuss social issues based on the religious secular order of Judeo-Christian ethics, and he also allows academics discussions of faith. The realm that is off limits is the presentation of our faith commitments.[52]

Wurzburger calls for the need to be open to the word through involvement in the broader concerns of mankind as a religious imperative. He believes that Jewish-Christian social activities are working together for a common socio-religious message (but not common faith):

> In view of the charge of 'moral isolationism' that has so often been hurled against Orthodoxy, I wish to emphasize that I welcome opportunities for inter-religious co-operation on matters where joint activity is feasible (7).

> Far from urging withdrawal into sheltering walls of a spiritual or psychological ghetto, we maintain that under present conditions involvement of the Jewish community in the social, political, and economic concerns of mankind represents a religious imperative (8).

As noted by Rabbi Wurzburger, according to R. Soloveitchik, one could offer up for discussion and share biblical anthropologies, our grappling with the universal religious problems, and even accept the Judeo-Christian moral climate as a basis for discussion. What Soloveitchik precludes from dialogue are doctrinal, dogmatic, and faith discussions:

> But it must be stated categorically that, insofar as the religious individual is concerned, activities of this nature are not of purely secular character, but—as Rabbi Soloveitchik pointed out in an important footnote to his article that has apparently been completely glossed over by some of his critics—they constitute a fulfillment of a religiously motivated and sanctioned mandate. When religious communities address themselves to the so-called secular realm, their policies should be founded not upon a purely secular ethic but upon a philosophy that looks upon man as the bearer of the divine image.

> It must be borne in mind that Judaism and Christianity are two distinct faith communities that cannot be brought together under the umbrella of a so-called common Judeo-Christian religious tradition. Our opposition to this term must however not be misconstrued as total indifference to the religious values of Christianity.

As a final caveat to Soloveitchik's position, in the last fifty years, we have also witnessed the great strides of the Catholic Church, moving from persecutor to greatest friend, from offering us eternal damnation to recognition of the state of Israel. Rabbi Soloveitchik witnessed these immense changes, but did not change his own thinking.

Michael Wyschogrod

Michael Wyschogrod (b. 1928) was Professor Emeritus of Philosophy at Baruch College of the City University of New York. He created a theology of an embodied community of Judaism; Judaism is not an idea or belief but a covenant of the flesh. Unique within Orthodoxy, Wyschogrod builds his own theology of Orthodox Judaism on his reading of the Bible. Wyschogrod affirms the importance of dialogue, and disagrees with those who avoid dialogue. He formulates a Jewish understanding of a unique covenant available to Christians.

Wyschogrod accepts Lutheran Scholars Van Rad's and Bruggerman's commentaries of Genesis as in agreement with Jewish interpretation. In this reading, the evil of humanity is overcome by the covenant made with Abraham, a promise of blessing to the world. Wyschogrod formulated a common covenant between the two faiths as a single covenant, similar to the early works by the Christian thinkers Jacob Jocz or Franz Mussner who created a common Jewish-Christian covenant from the Christian side. Wyschogrod's formulation is the opposite of Soloveitchik's opinion of no common covenant or overlapping in faith commitment. The Jewish view is not just an expanse of Bible monotheism, but is also a mystery of their nonelection, a connection of gentiles to the people of Israel as part of the compassion of God.

Wyschogrod uses a Christian understanding of Abraham's promise similar to Galatians, in which the covenantal community that affirms the word of God is redeemed from secular existence. According to Karl Barth, Luther's majestic man living a proper religious life on this earth becomes connected to the idea of the biblical covenant. Common life and the election of the church are combined. "Israel is the people of the Jews which resist its election; the Church is the gathering of Jews and Gentiles called on the ground of its election."[53] Wyschogrod views Jewish particularism as tribal and embodied, and praises Franz Rosenzweig for accepting Jewish particularity. Wyschogrod thinks that Judaism does not preclude a two covenant theory—embodied Jews who keep law and Jesus bringing a new covenant to gentiles.

For Wyschogrod and Barth, Jesus is neither a rabbi nor a liberal; Wyschogrod accepts the possibility of incarnation and Christianity as "the climax of the process that began with the election of Abraham." However, he allegorizes incarnation as showing that we are all in the image of God:

> The philosophical component in Christianity, its deep involvement with Platonic and Aristotelian philosophy and the myriad problems brought about by this involvement, is thus not merely an accident of intellectual history, but rooted in the Christian kerygma itself.

> First, there is the Divine promise to Abraham that through his election, or in him, there shall be blessed the families of the earth (Gen. 12:3). This makes quite clear that the election of Abraham and his seed, while in many ways separating the history of Israel from those of the nations, cannot rest with such a separation.

> My claim is that the Christian teaching of the incarnation of God in Jesus is the intensification of the teaching of the indwelling of God in Israel by concentrating that indwelling in one Jew rather than leaving it diffused in the people of Jesus as a whole.

> Judaism has never elaborated the Noahide covenant as a form of election not unrelated to the election of Israel. It has not, for example, found a place in the synagogue

for the Noachide converts, not as Jews, but as gentiles who love and are obedient to the God of Israel who is also the God of all humankind.

The welfare of all humanity remains God's ultimate goal as evidenced by his remark to Abraham that "by you all the families of the earth shall bless themselves" (Gen. 12:3). But it is worth noting that the first half of the verse just quoted reads "I will bless those who bless you, and him who curses you I will curse." However much the election of Abraham is intended to serve the welfare of all, God seems aware that the very act of election, even if this involves imposing a higher standard of conduct on the elect, will generate resentment and there will be those who will curse Israel. On the other hand, there will be those who will accept God's sovereign choice in love and obedience and they will be blessed.

The wonder is that nations not of the stock of Abraham have come within the orbit of the faith of Israel, experiencing humankind and history with Jewish categories deeply rooted in Jewish experience and sensibility. How can a Jewish theologian not perceive that something wonderful is at work here, something that must in some way be connected with the love of the God of Israel for all his children, Isaac as well as Ishmael, Jacob as well as Esau?

Just as Judaism, as I have argued elsewhere, cannot claim on *a priori* grounds that God could not have become incarnated in a Nazarene carpenter since to do so would be to make of Judaism a philosophic system.[54]

He feels that Jews have excluded gentiles and should have formulated an inclusive active reading of the Noahide laws. Jews should take pride in the success of Christianity as part of Jewish path of redemption. We do not give a "no" to Christianity as in Rosenzweig (or in Pinchas Lapide in the next chapter), but we need to offer a "yes," an openness to the broader promise of Abraham.

Wyschogrod has a palpable, real covenant, not just a theological construct. In many ways, he is a Jewish version of Monsignor Oesterreicher in suggesting that the God of Abraham is available to Jews and Christians. But for Wyschogrod, Jews have a special relationship as God's Chosen to follow the Law of Moses. Nevertheless, Jews should appreciate the Christian triumph over paganism. If we compare Wyschogrod's universal Abraham to S. D. Luzzatto's, the latter offers an ethical universal of loving kindness (*hesed*) in contrast to Wyschogrod's views of Abraham as a covenantal promise of revelation to the gentile.

Wyschogrod was also at the forefront of the Jewish evangelical dialogue because of his solid presentation of biblical-based common covenant. Both interlocutors are against spiritualization of the text and have a literalism about Israel. He sees the way Evangelists speak of Jesus as equivalent to the way Jews use the word God and he sees that even being a Jew, Christian does not preclude keeping the law:

Neither Judaism nor evangelical Christianity is prepared to submit its sacred books to any validation other than self-validation.

The Jewish observer of the Christian scene, particularly of the evangelical Christian scene, finds it difficult to understand why the legislation of the Pentateuch plays such a relatively small part in the evangelical consciousness.

In one sense, the Jewish position is closer to that of Catholicism and its doctrine of tradition than to the purer Biblicism of evangelical theology.

The oral law elaborates and interprets the scriptural text in such a way that in spite of all the importance Judaism attaches to the oral law, it does not eclipse the primacy of the Bible as the Word of God.

Let us take as an example the bond between the Jewish people and the land of Israel. It is quite clear that from the initial election of Israel in Abraham the bond with the land is an essential part of the divine promise to Abraham and his descendants . . . The promised land can be spiritualized and made to refer to a spiritual state which is the reward of all righteous men.

But these less-than-straightforward readings of the text do not recommend themselves to the evangelical mind and, therefore, unless I am badly misinformed, evangelical Christianity has been quite sympathetic to the recent Jewish return to the land of Israel precisely because evangelical ears hear the biblical promises to the people of Israel, the concreteness of which is not dissipated in sophisticated if not sophistical demythologizations but connected with the real world in which the people and land of Israel are existing entities.

The Jewish relationship is with God the Father, who does for Israel everything that God as Jesus does for the Christian.

When the problem presented by Paul—whether or not Gentile converts to Christianity require circumcision and the law was brought to the Jerusalem church, the decision in favor of Paul ensued only after "long debate" (Acts 15:7). Now—and this is the point—if the Jewish members of the Jerusalem church had been of the opinion that the coming of Jesus as the Messiah, circumcision and obedience to the Torah were no longer necessary for Jewish Christians, there could hardly have arisen any controversy as to whether circumcision and obedience to the Torah were demanded of Gentile converts.

Rabbi Yitz Greenberg

Rabbi Irving (Yitz) Greenberg (b. 1933) was a former congregational rabbi and professor of Jewish studies who became founder and president of CLAL (the National Jewish Center for Learning and Leadership) and then finally, was the president of the Jewish Life Network. Greenberg was instrumental in many aspects of Holocaust education and Jewish-Christian dialogue over the last half century. As a full presentation of Greenberg's theories of modernity and autonomy are beyond the scope of this book, this book will be limited to those remarks that specifically pertain to his covenantal theory of Jewish-Christian dialogue.

Greenberg started his intellectual journey with post-Holocaust anger at Christianity and concludes with respect toward the great post-Holocaust contribution he saw in Christians and Christianity. For Greenberg, the Holocaust was a fall of humanism in Western Civilization and Christianity; therefore the need for religion to respond to this fall was found by restoring the image of God, in which each religion seeks to fulfill the biblical covenant of making the world a better place through human action. His theory of dialogue is part of his post-Holocaust theology of a voluntary existential covenant, in which hatred needs to be removed and replaced with love toward the world.

Greenberg's base for his intellectual formulation of covenant was Soloveitchik's use of the 1950s Neo-Orthodox thinkers in his work, *The Lonely Man of Faith*. Soloveitchik, in line with other 1950s thinkers, describes the faith community of God with Abraham, as moving beyond universal dignity to accept greater majesty and glory. Soloveitchik wrote:

> The element of togetherness of God and man is indispensable for the covenantal community . . . the paradoxical experience of freedom, reciprocity, and "equality" in one's personal confrontation with God is basic for the understanding of the covenantal faith community.[55]

Rabbi Yitz Greenberg developed this passage by stressing the aforementioned elements of freedom, reciprocity, and autonomy, calling the individual goal we are striving to achieve "perfection," with *halakhah*, being the path that will lead us to that goal, with covenant being the force that binds us to the path. We are to take personal responsibility, rather than assuming God or some other person will perform the great human task and responsibility that lies ahead of us. We struggle to existentially define our ever-changing relationship with God.

Greenberg generally follows Soloveitchik's *Lonely Man of Faith* over the latter's essay "Confrontation." For Soloveitchik, religion is an existential commitment, absolute and unable to be communicated to others. But Greenberg, who interprets covenant as a personal existentialist decision following Paul Ramsey and James Gustafson, views covenant as personal.

According to Greenberg, the Jewish message has three aspects or stories, as he calls them, and they are shared by Christianity. The first aspect is that the world has a Divine purpose, which is creation; the second aspect is that there is a Divine human partnership, which is covenant; and the third is that human perfection will eventually be achieved, which is redemption.[56] The first two aspects are universalist and the third is an inclusivist perspective. "The covenant is nothing less than God's promise that the goal is worthy and will be realized." The covenant also guarantees that man is given responsibility for making the world a better place and that it will not be done by divine fiat.

To accomplish equating ethical universalism, redemptive inclusivism, and his aforementioned theological pluralism, he allegorizes Christian doctrine, such as the incarnation, into a theory of Jewish social activity (*tikkun olam*), part of the universal drive for creation, partnership, and redemption. For example:

> We can say firmly and respectfully, that the logic behind incarnation and God becoming flesh is the shared value system: Both religions believe that life will win out over death—resurrection is the climax of that process—because it's God's will that the world will be made perfect, and that this will be accomplished by a partnership, a covenant between God and humanity, which expresses itself in many religions and many covenants, including Judaism and Christianity.

This allows him to proclaim a positive and divine mission for Christians based on Jewish ethics. Dividing points such as the divinity of Jesus, incarnation, and resurrection are treated as "signals" that the Jews should not automatically rule out as the form that God uses to communicate to gentiles. While a noble appreciation of the other, the reduction of Christianity to a symbol of covenant and redemption, a form of symbolic and liberal Christianity, lacks the textual strength to allow the real discussion of theology to begin.[57] Yet, he creatively placed Christianity in relationship with Judaism.

Rabbi Greenberg was the clearest exemplar of the interfaith response to Holocaust theology of the 1970s and 1980s, which moved from the Judeo-Christian optimism of the 1950s to a vision of society that needs rebuilding. Greenberg views the Holocaust as the end of the old theological constructs and the requirement for a new revelation.

Several Christian writers, such as John Pawlikowski on the Jewish Christian dialogue, adopted Greenberg's post-Holocaust urgency for Jewish-Christian reconciliation. Due to Greenberg's influence the Holocaust became an orienting event for Jewish-Christian relations that necessitates overcoming the teaching of contempt. Typical of this starting point is Eugene Fisher, the director of Jewish-Catholic relations for the National Conference of Bishops, who wrote in an introduction to a collection of several 1980s thinkers about the Jewish-Christian dialogue asking "what are the implications for the third millennium of the renewed vision of dialogue that is possible just a generation after the light of the crematoria of Auschwitz set in new perspective the human capacity for evil?"[58]

David Rosen

David Rosen, former Grand Rabbi of Ireland, was a member of the Permanent Bilateral Commission of the State of Israel and the Holy See that negotiated the establishment of full diplomatic normalization of relations between the two states. Now he is Director of Interreligious Affairs at American Jewish Committee.

Rosen has given many important speeches; however one of his noteworthy presentations was a recent speech where he notes that the recent decades witnessed a "transformation in the Catholic-Jewish relationship" and that there is "nothing comparable in human history." In the speech Rosen seeks to create a theology of partnership between Christians and Jews in which the two faiths are joined and complementarity.

This leads me to the second challenge, which is to develop a serious theology of partnership between Christians and Jews and an understanding of the other's complementarity. Efforts at doing so have already begun. These have included seeing Judaism and Christianity in a mutually complementary role in which the Jewish focus on the communal covenant with God and the Christian focus on the individual relationship with God, may serve humanity in parallel as well as balance one another. Others have seen the complementary relationship in that we both need to be reminded that the Kingdom of Heaven has not yet fully arrived, and yet at the same time to appreciate that that Kingdom is already rooted in the here and now.

Another view of the mutual complementarity, portrays Judaism as a constant admonition to Christianity regarding the dangers of triumphalism, while Christianity's universalistic character may serve an essential role for Judaism in warning against degeneration into insular isolationism.

Evangelicals and the Land of Israel

The early twenty-first century generation of conservative evangelical leadership—Jerry Falwell, Pat Robertson, John Hagee and others—are Christian Zionists, supportive of the Jewish state as a fulfillment of biblical prophecy. Evangelicals, like many other Americans, identify Israel as a democracy. They also regard Israel as the enemy of their radical Islamic enemy. However, Christian Zionism grows out of a particular theological system called "pre-millennial dispensationalism," which originated in early nineteenth century England. God's covenant with Israel is eternal, exclusive, and will not be abrogated, according to their reading of Genesis. For them, the Bible speaks of two distinct and parallel covenants, one between God and Israel, one between God and the church. ("I will bless those who bless you and curse those who curse you" [Genesis 12:3]) should be interpreted literally—which leads to maximum political, economic, moral, and spiritual support for the modern state of Israel and for all the Jewish people. Judgment will befall nations and individuals according to how they "bless Israel."

The church itself is a "mere parenthesis" in God's plan that will survive until an event called the Rapture (1 Thess. 4:13–17; 5:1–11). At that point, Israel the nation will be restored as the primary instrument of God on earth. The establishment of the state of Israel, the rebuilding of the Third Temple, the rise of the Antichrist, and the buildup of armies poised to attack Israel are among the signs leading to the final eschatological battle and Jesus's return for his thousand-year reign.[59]

Yechiel Eckstein

Yechiel Eckstein (b. 1951), Orthodox rabbi and president of the International Fellowship of Christians and Jews, is actively building bridges with the evangelical world. The magazine *Christianity Today* calls Eckstein "the ultimate kibitzer" and has written that at times, he sounds as though he is tutoring Christian believers in evangelistic methods. "Christians don't convert anyone. That's the Holy Spirit's job [. . .] the mission should be to share the love of God through Christ. Let God work on the individual. The Christian's task is to love as Jesus loved."[60]

Eckstein goes further than most other Jews and sees Christianity as a God-given plan of salvation for gentiles. While based on Yaakov Emden, one sees that this rhetoric has moved to a new American orientation. His language style is full of Christian terminology such as salvation, Holy Spirit, and redemption. In addition, he clearly thinks that Christianity plays a role in the Jewish narrative. "Only when the two cherubs (the Christian and the Jewish) will reach out to one another will we be able to achieve the glorification of God and redemption."

COVENANTS AND DIALOGUE   105

For Eckstein, Jews especially need to understand the logic and meaningfulness of the Christian position. And, Christians need to realize their unbroken relationship to Judaism:

> Do you see the Ten Commandments? They are yours, too. Do you remember that Paul in the Book of Romans, chapter nine, said that by God's grace and love you gentiles were grafted unto the rich olive tree of Israel and are now of the seed of Abraham? That is a profound lesson of the shared tradition of Christians and Jews.

> The Jews will also be convinced that there are three divine powers which are revealed in the same person—as a Father, a Son and a Holy Spirit, as the *New Testament* has clearly shown us . . . Could it be that the Christians are right when they say that man is intrinsically downtrodden because of previous sins?[61]

> I believe it is definitely possible that Jesus the Jew was in some way sent by God to bring salvation to the gentiles and redemption to the world. (207) I still don't believe in Jesus as Christ . . . and view him instead as a Jew who brought salvation to the gentiles, in some respects, that is exactly what I have become . . . a Jew for Jesus."[62]

Eckstein also has a pluralistic streak about the faiths, thinking that "religion is but the raft that enables us to cross the river of life . . . we dare not absolute the raft and imbue it with exclusive truth. To do so is idolatry, which, like Paul Tillich, I understand as misplaced intimacy."[63]

Rabbi Shlomo Riskin

Rabbi Shlomo Riskin (b. 1940) was rabbi of Lincoln Square Synagogue in Manhattan; after his emigration to Israel, he became rabbi of Efrat and chancellor of Ohr Torah Institutes. While he is not a theologian or scholar he, like Eckstein, can serve as a barometer of the inroads of ecumenical thinking about Christianity in many traditional Jewish circles. Riskin's speeches show that segments of his community are begging to sincerely acknowledge the tremendous strides in Jewish-Christian relation along with post-Holocaust sensitivity to Judaism and the State of Israel.

Riskin's double faith approach seems specifically designed to avoid claiming to be in a single covenant with Christianity because of a lingering Soloveitchik-inspired sense of the separate and distinct nature of faith communities. Therefore, Riskin develops his position as "the understanding of Maimonides [. . .] toward the end of his Mishna Torah," to develop a double faith theory similar to David Hartman's early position. There is the covenant with Abraham fulfilled at Sinai for Jews and the Noahide covenant fulfilled in Christianity.

Riskin boldly acknowledges that Judaism dropped its universal message in the exile and we have to give credit to the Christians for maintaining the biblical message:

> My own theological perspective regarding our true partnership with the Christian world emanates from the biblical "Double Covenant" position: God entered into a

first covenant with Noah, a covenant with humanity, comprising the seven Noahide universal laws of morality, based upon the premise. "He who sheds the blood of another will have his bloodshed, since the human being was created in God's image." He entered into a second covenant with Abraham, eventually comprising the 613 commandments of the Bible.

God charged Abraham: "All the families of the earth shall be blessed through you (Genesis 12:3)." Probably during the Roman period of Hadrianic persecutions (circa 136–140 CE), we dropped the ball and ceased to attempt to fulfill this aspect of our mission.

Thankfully, this function was provided by the Christians, who brought to all the Gentiles of the globe the seven Noahide laws of morality, the Ten Commandments and the belief in a God of love, compassion and peace [. . .] Those many Christian denominations who wish to learn from us and strengthen our common beliefs in a God of love, morality and peace ought to be encouraged in their friendship.[64]

Pastor Jack Hayford, the head of the Pentecostal church, moved me to tears when he repeated twice that were Israel to be in need of soldiers, he and his people . . . would fight side by side with us. Pastor John Hagee of San Antonio, Texas and international TV fame has established a "Christian AIPAC" to politically support Israel throughout America. And both of these charismatic theologians have said that they subscribe to a single covenant theory: God entered into a covenant with Israel, upon which the Christians grafted themselves.

His position is a real opening to Christians, yet the theology may be motivated more by fear of Islamic terrorism and the warm embrace of Christian Zionism than from rethinking Judaism.

Riskin's attitude to Islam shares a rhetoric with his new evangelical partners. Since he also thinks "Islamic fundamentalism has turned Allah into Moloch— Satan, and made every mosque which preaches the doctrine of suicide bombing a hell-haven of idolatry."[65] He also paraphrases Franz Rosenzweig's rejection of Islam in his remarks.

Riskin has recently organized conferences for discussing the common covenant between the two faiths. In his paper, "Covenant And Conversion: The United Mission To Redeem The World," his first novel point is his adaptation of Reformed covenant theology for a Jewish purpose. In the Reformed Protestant tradition, there is a series of covenant of the unfolding of God's will. In a short version, the Noahide covenant is a moral requirement with all humanity, the Abrahamic is the covenant of faith and grace, and the covenant of Jesus is the messianic one of grace. In some versions, Deuteronomy is the covenant of blessings and curses before entering the land. Rabbi Riskin postulates three covenants: Noahide as universal, Sinai as Jewish people, and Deuteronomy as universal redemption. In the third covenant, we bring the redemptive universal message to the world. He has transferred some of the aspects of the Jesus covenant to a universalism from Deuteronomy.[66]

Rabbi Riskin pushes for a Jewish drive to seek conversion of Christians to Judaism or more to the point the conversion of Christians in the eschaton. He finds passages in the Bible, Talmud, and Maimonides to support a mission to the gentiles. But in each section, he returns and says there are two opinions, conversion or conversion to the Noahide code. He concludes with a need to teach gentiles Torah since they will be united with us in the eschaton:

> It is generally not recognized that there is yet a third covenant, presented by God before the Jewish people entered the promised land of Israel . . . The Bible states: "These are the words of the Covenant which the Lord commanded Moses to seal with the children of Israel in the land of Moab, aside from (in addition to) the covenant which He sealed with them at Horeb," emphasizing the unique nature of this third covenant (Dt. 28:69). What is the message of this third, additional covenant, especially since our other two covenants have already designated us as an eternal nation and an eternal religion? I submit that this is the Covenant of Universal Redemption, which can only come about if the nations of the world accept fundamental biblical morality. It is the covenant that squarely places upon the Jewish people the responsibility of teaching the moral truths of the Bible to the world.
>
> This universal message of the Third Covenant may likewise be why, immediately after the content of the Third Covenant is delineated, the Bible records, "Not with you (Israelites) alone do I seal this covenant and this imprecation, but with whoever is here, standing with us today before the Lord our God, and also with whoever is not here with us today" (Dt. 29:13–14). The meaning of these words seem to be the inclusion of the gentiles as well as the Israelites: the gentiles who are not with us today will one day stand with us in acceptance of the fundamental laws of morality.
>
> If I am correct in interpreting this Third Covenant to be a covenant for all the nations of the world, the implications of this debate are serious indeed. Are Jews covenantally responsible to teach gentiles only the seven Noahide laws and these twelve moral imprecations, or is the Jewish people duty bound to teach the world all 613 commandments to convert them to Judaism?
>
> Does the Bible and Talmud advocate converting the world to full Judaism, or merely to bring as many people as possible into the third covenant and the Noahide covenant with its seven fundamentals of morality? . . . We are however permitted—and perhaps even encouraged—to teach gentiles the Torah and its commandments, an act that Maimonides saw as part of the commandment for Jews to love God. Finally, Maimonides contended that in the eschaton all will convert because it will be rationally and morally compelling for them to do so.

At the end of his paper, Rabbi Riskin pleads for religious pluralism in which there is one God and the names YHVH, Allah, the Trinity, and Buddha all reflect one reality. All ritual, images, statues, and representations serve the same Divine force. God only cares about morality and the forms of worship are incidental. The rainbow metaphor and its explanation seem like a paraphrase of the famed pluralist John Hick's rainbow of faiths:

> Can we not argue that, although we use different names, symbolic images, rituals, customs and incantations by which we call and worship the Deity, everyone is speaking and praying to the same Divine Force who created and guides our world? Allah is another name for the one God ("El" or "Elohim"), the Trinity is mysteriously considered a unity by Christians, all the physical representations of the Buddha are meant

to express the All in the All that is the god of the Far East. Is it not possible that the real meaning of the credo of Judaism, the Sh'ma, is: "Hear Oh Israel, the Lord (who is known by our different names of different forces and powers), Elohaynu, is (in reality the) One (YHVH of the entire cosmos)." Just as the white of the cloud is refracted into different colors, so the one God of love may be called by different names and different powers, but these all coalesce in the mind of the one praying and in the reality of the situation into the one all-encompassing Lord of the Universe.

If this is the case, as long as humans are moral, they can call God by any name or names they wish since their true intent is the God of the universe. They may even be secular humanists, as long as they do not engage in the abominations of idol worship. The ultimate religious concern is that humans not destroy the world, and this can only be predicated upon the universal acceptance of ethical absolutes, compassionate righteousness and justice, the inviolability of the human being, and his/her right to live in freedom, peace and security.

Riskin concludes with an acceptance of the Pauline understanding of Abraham as the covenant of faith and views Christianity as entirely within the Noahide laws and as reconciled with Judaism. He ends with a call for moderate Muslims to show their morality against Satanic Islamic radicalism:

Christianity sees itself as being grafted onto the Jewish covenant, God's covenant with Abraham. This is legitimate from a biblical and Jewish perspective, since Abraham, by his very name, is a patriarch of a multitude of nations. Christianity worships Abraham's God of compassionate righteousness and justice, and traditional Christianity surely accepts the seven Noahide laws as given by God. The return of the younger faith to its maternal roots was eased by leading theologians from most churches recognizing the permanent legitimacy of the Jewish covenant with God and the possibility of Jewish salvation on the merit of that covenant. The partnership between the daughter and mother religions is particularly important today in the face of the existential threat of Islamist extremism against which all who are committed to a hopeful future must battle—including moderate Muslims. The Bible records a loving reconciliation between Isaac and Ishmael, coming together in bringing their father to his eternal resting place. The God of Abraham as the God of love, compassion, and peace is the antithesis of Satan, who instructs violence against all those who do not accept his cruel prescription for world domination.

Now that the Jewish people have returned to their homeland and to empirical history and now that Christians again recognize the legitimacy of the Jewish covenant, Jews and Christians must march together to bring the faith of morality and peace to a desperate but thirsting world.

This is a major rejection of the Orthodox ban on joint faith statements or theological dialogue. This is thinking about the very issues of covenant and redemption that separate faiths and now, with Rabbi Riskin's help, unite us.

Riskin offers a direct integration of Christian thought with the goal of closing the gap between the two faiths. He combines two lines of thought that are usually kept separate. The first concerns finding Jesus's universal message in Deuteronomy. Similar to Wyschogrod, Riskin's version seems to have origins somewhere in a student of Walter Bruggerman. It is about an actual belief in a

God-given, universal covenant as presented in the words of Scripture. This line of thought as applied to Mt. Gerizim and Mt. Eval is original and works well for both Protestant and Catholic thought. It affirms revelation of the Bible and the special role of covenantal history. The second line of thought is the pluralism of John Hick in which all religions are human responses to the quest for the absolute. This requires nothing more than a theism that can be considered as a ground of reality.

Recently in May 2011, Riskin has reached the culmination of several years of interfaith dialogue by declaring in a new statement that "Judaism must respect Christian faithfulness to their revelation, value their role in divine history, and acknowledge that Christians have entered a relationship with the God of Israel. In our pre-eschaton days, God has more than enough blessings to bestow upon all of His children." He does this, in his own proclamation, "as a catalyst for other orthodox Jews and Jewry worldwide . . ."[67]

Contemporary Catholic Approaches

Much of the interreligious encounter accepts, uses, or offers alternatives to the language of Protestants. Yet, presently it reacts to the writings of Pope Benedict, written when he was Cardinal Ratzinger. *Nostra Aetate*'s repudiation of the teaching of supersessionalism and rejection ended centuries of a theology of contempt and should be applauded.[68]

Nostra Aetate has two elements that remain sharply disjunctive for a Jewish audience. The first is the claim of the Abrahamic element as the common core of Judaism and Christianity, as a branch grafted on a tree, and the second is the idea of one covenant for all religions.

First, Abraham is not Judaism's main source for discussing Christianity or the other religions. Traditional Jewish texts, as discussed in this book, do not use a single view by which to consider Christianity. In fact, they use many including the covenants of Adam, Noah, Abraham, Moses, and Daniel to explore Judaism's relationship to Christianity. The basic rubric by which Jews discuss other religions, when they are inclusivist or universalist, is either as part of a general relationship to God available to all to all humanity, or as part of an acceptance that all of humanity is created in the image of God, usually discussed through Adam or Noah. Sometimes, the Sinai event, the Mosaic prophesies, and the giving of the Torah are all credited as the source of all morality and religion in the world. In the Kabbalah, the Daniel model of different levels of access to divinity is used. Even those Jewish texts that place Abraham as the father of monotheism, Abraham leads to Sinai, personhood, and commandments. The other religions are either "the souls that Abraham made in Harran" whom Abraham brought close to his faith or are his descendents of Ishmael and Esau. Jews should, therefore, not fall into passively using the language of *Nostra Aetate*.

Second, the question arises of whether or not gentiles share a covenant with the Jews. As stated in the beginning of this chapter, in Jewish thought, gentiles are not part of the Abrahamic covenant (except for the approach of Wyschogrod), but God is available to all people through a variety of models. Among the models shown in this book include the Adam model of a natural ability to know God; the Noah model of the seven Noahite laws that build a moral society; the Abraham model of choosing mercy; the Moses model of revelation known by diffusion to the whole world.

Judaism lacks statements in primary texts that exclude other religions from personal piety or salvation. Hence, a new understanding of the covenant is not needed for a Jewish understanding of other religions. Covenant as exclusive access to God is not the Jewish reading of the Bible. Judaism does not have explicit verses limiting access to God only to Jews like one finds in Christianity, such as "no one comes to the father but by me" (John 14:6), and "there is salvation in no one else" (Acts 4:12). When limiting statements do occur in Judaism, they appear in either a specific particularistic thinker or in a restrictive sociological community. Unless one is committed to that specific sectarian sociological configuration or has particular allegiances to that exclusivist author, one has the option in Judaism to choose an inclusivist, pluralist, or even another, less restrictive, particularist response. In Judaism, the universal paradigms of Adam, Noah, and Abraham remain in effect for gentiles. And all moral behavior in the world is considered a continuation of Noah and/or Moses.

None of the above-mentioned Jewish theologies influenced by the American Neo-Orthodox idea of covenant use the word covenant as the word is used in *Nostra Aetate* or the writings of Cardinal Ratzinger. Jewish texts that stress the ethical covenant for man in society, or an existential covenant, are not actually discussing covenant as God's offering or the eschatological fulfillment of God's mission.

In order to continue the clarification of where the theological language differs between Jewish and Catholic traditions, we will consider the influential writings of Cardinal Ratzinger. In Cardinal Ratzinger's 1985 work *Notes on Nostra Aetate*, he comments that both Jews and Christians have love of neighbor, hope for the kingdom of God, and a relationship to the prophets. But Judaism does not define itself by any of these three concepts, as Ratzinger explains them. Judaism is the promise to Abraham to be a chosen people, to thereby inherit the land of Israel, to accept the Sinai covenant of the commandments, to remember the Exodus, and to study the Oral Law. The covenant is the messianic promise to the Davidic dynasty for a restored earthy Kingdom.

Judaism does indeed have love (*hesed*) as mediated with justice (*mishpat*) and righteousness (*zedakah*), shown by the Jewish exegetes in Jeremiah 9:23. They point out that God wants humanity to imitate God, but in Judaism these cardinal virtues are part of the universal need for wisdom and ethics, not a restrictive covenantal gift of love.

In Cardinal Ratzinger's article "Jewish People and Sacred Scripture," he reminds his readers of the election of Israel and the continuing covenant of Noah, Abraham, Sinai, Deuteronomy, David, and then later Qumran. He even notes that the Jewish messianic path is still valid. Yet he leaves out the specific Jewish elements of messianism, the promise of the land and the physical reward of the land. More importantly, for Jews there is no need for an inner reconciliation between the Jewish law and the gift of the spirit. For Jews, God considers the law itself as the covenant.[69]

Conclusions

Time magazine recently listed the reclamation of the Jewish and rabbinic background of Jesus as one of the top ten current ideas changing our world. This rabbinic context for Christianity will create ever new points of connections and respect for Jewish views. However, the idea of a common covenant, or its rejection, remains linked to the ever-changing theological concerns of public religion. A common covenant reflects post-WWII America, *Nostra Aetate*, Holocaust theology, and the rise of the evangelical Christian Zionism. This chapter surveyed the intense protagonists involved in the forging or breaking of a Judeo-Christian covenant and the broad usages made of the term covenant. The next chapter deals with the more recent theological and scholarly attempts at creating commonality.

5

Christianity: Commonalities and New Understandings

Medieval Jewish philosophers saw a commonality between Judaism and Christianity in terms of monotheism and the Biblical God as creator of heaven and earth. This chapter will look at the possibilities of commonality in the contemporary era. For almost two millennia, when Jews spoke of Christians, it was either to extenuate the difference between the two religions or it was to point out that Christianity was incomprehensible.

The British-Jewish historian, Chaim Macoby, draws our attention to how medieval disputations lack understanding or any shared discourse between the religions. Judaism and Christianity generally avoid developing empathy and, not without prior prejudice, affirm that reason cannot bear the other faith. Nevertheless, there is an occasional glimmer in which medieval works such as Joseph Kimhi's *Book of the Covenant* noted the similarity of rabbinic thought to Christian theology. Kimhi could acknowledge that, corresponding to the explanation of the Trinity that he heard from Christians, in Judaism "there is Father and a lower manifestation of spirit."[1] But the agenda of the era was to quickly move back to a polemical mode and show that the rabbinic statement acknowledges nothing about Christian truth. All things depend on attitude; proposition comes later.[2]

R. J. Z. Werblowsky, writing from the historical perspective of religions, notes that there is a built-in asymmetry between the two faiths, in that Christianity must speak of Judaism and Judaism does not need to discuss Christianity. And, that in the scheme of comparative religion, the two religions share two main dogmas: creation and revelation. Creation is beyond human-understanding, the world is not of our making; Revelation, in contrast, places limits on moral choice, the source of values and knowledge from God's will.[3]

In twentieth century dialogue, the emphasis was on earning respect through stating our differences with Christianity, even if there are common ethical and humanistic elements. The approach of reconciliation was to work to have our historical experience heard. This occurred alongside the attempt at creating a common covenant, which has tended to isolate broad covenantal themes rather than deal with specifics.

As moderns living in an era of reconciliation and Globalization, the question remains: how much stock should be put into these differences and similarities? Dabru Emet was an attempt to come to terms with the change. Three of its authors, David Novak, Peter Ochs, and Michael Singer, each have articles in their own names to follow their individual reasoning. Jon Levenson, a sharp critic of Dabru Emet and David Novak, each see difference between the two faiths but debate about the commonality despite differences. The question of whether the glass is half full or half empty remains, which in this case translates to: are they more the same or more different? Levenson downplays the commonality as not very relevant by turning to Scripture and the particular God of history. Novak, on the other hand, treats the commonality of monotheism as sufficient ground to create identity. Peter Och's project of Scriptural Reasoning, and Michael Signer's discussion of Scripture, each offer a non-theological approach to commonality.

Jacob Neusner assumes sharp normative differences between Judaism and Christianity. Pinchas Lapide and Alon Goshen-Gottstein both try to create more commonality by looking at a range of Jewish conceptions of God and refining theological understanding. They will each open up afresh the question of commonality and similarity. The scholars Daniel Boyarin and Moshe Idel offer a bold reformulation of the question from the perspective of the history of thought. This chapter concludes with a brief summary of the new Jewish approaches to Jesus and the apostle Paul as well as some contemporary theological observations.

- The French Statement and the Dabru Emet as documents attempting commonality.
- Novak finds similarities between Judaism and Christianity. Ochs and Signer offer a commonality of common textual study and dialogue.
- Levenson and Neusner emphasize the differences.
- Goshen-Gottstein and Lapide move beyond the medieval thinkers by looking at contemporary theology.
- Boyarin and Idel break new grounds by seeking commonality between rabbinic text and early Christian thought.
- Similar new readings are now done to the New Testament, including Jesus, Paul, and the early Christian community.

The French Statement

In 1968, three years after the Second Vatican Council declaration *Nostra Aetate*, the Catholic bishops of France asked the chief rabbi of France, Jacob Kaplan, for a description of Jewish opinions on Christianity. A committee composed of the renowned philosopher Emmanuel Levinas, Near Eastern Studies specialist, Georges Vajda, and president of the French rabbinate's doctrinal commission and medieval philosophy expert, Charles Touati, assembled the pertinent rabbinic commentaries from over the centuries and produced an outline, making six assertions supported by the works collected.

A formal debate of the outline by the French rabbinical assembly did not occur until 1978. A significant minority of the assembled rabbis had grave reservations about the proposed statement. Seeing that consensus would be impossible, chief rabbi Kaplan withdrew the proposal from consideration. After the publication of the American text, "Dabru Emet: A Jewish Statement on Christians and Christianity" in 2000, Touati, the only surviving member of the drafting committee, saw the historical value of the outline and suggested its release to the general public in 2001.[4]

Among the six principles that comprise the outline, the first principle is original by seeking to undo the damage of the tensions of the early centuries. This first principle was based on a rabbinic text that possibly shows remorse about pushing Christianity away. The second, third, fifth, and sixth principles are based on the classic medieval positions of Halevi, Maimonides, Meiri, and Arama presented in my book *Judaism and Other Religions*. The third principle takes the statement from the fifteenth century thinker Isaac Arama that says "all who are righteous are called Israel" in an expansive way for creating eternal salvation on par with Israel for all righteous gentiles. The fourth principle is concerned about the need to learn from other faiths. The passage from Bahye (eleventh century) about learning from Sufis is widely known but takes on new significance in this context:

1. The rejection of Christianity could have been avoided.[5]
2. The Christians are not idolaters; they adore the God who created the world and they have a certain number of beliefs in common with the Jews.
3. There is Eternal Salvation for Christians.[6]
4. Israel must be inspired by Christians and by Muslims, etc.[7]
5. Christianity and Islam contributed toward the improvement of humanity.
6. Christianity and Islam clear the way for the Messiah.

Dabru Emet

A more recent and more important document "Dabru Emet" (2000)[8] was a Jewish recognition of Christianity. It was to be an overture to Christians, in some ways, to reciprocate the recognition of Judaism by Christians in recent decades. The document was authored by Tikva Frymer-Kensky, David Novak, Peter Ochs, and Michael Signer. The document was issued in a full explanatory version and in a summary version. Listed below are all of the affirmations and then some brief selections from the explanation as needed for our theological discussion here:

Dabru Emet
A Jewish Statement on Christians and Christianity
We believe it is time for Jews to reflect on what Judaism may now say about Christianity. As a first step, we offer eight brief statements about how Jews and Christians may relate to one another.

[1] Jews and Christians worship the same God. Before the rise of Christianity, Jews were the only worshippers of the God of Israel. But Christians also worship the God of Abraham, Isaac, and Jacob; creator of heaven and earth. While Christian worship is not a viable religious choice for Jews, as Jewish theologians we rejoice that, through Christianity, hundreds of millions of people have entered into relationship with the God of Israel.

[2] **Jews and Christians seek authority from the same book—the Bible (what Jews call "Tanakh" and Christians call the "Old Testament").** Turning to it for religious orientation, spiritual enrichment, and communal education, we each take away similar lessons: God created and sustains the universe; God established a covenant with the people Israel, God's revealed word guides Israel to a life of righteousness; and God will ultimately redeem Israel and the whole world. Yet, Jews and Christians interpret the Bible differently on many points. Such differences must always be respected.

[3] **Christians can respect the claim of the Jewish people upon the land of Israel.**

[4] **Jews and Christians accept the moral principles of Torah.** Central to the moral principles of Torah is the inalienable sanctity and dignity of every human being. All of us were created in the image of God.

[5] **Nazism was not a Christian phenomenon.**

[6] **The humanly irreconcilable difference between Jews and Christians will not be settled until God redeems the entire world as promised in Scripture.** Christians know and serve God through Jesus Christ and the Christian tradition. Jews know and serve God through Torah and the Jewish tradition. That difference will not be settled by one community insisting that it has interpreted Scripture more accurately than the other; nor by exercising political power over the other. Jews can respect Christians' faithfulness to their revelation just as we expect Christians to respect our faithfulness to our revelation. Neither Jew nor Christian should be pressed into affirming the teaching of the other community.

[7] **A new relationship between Jews and Christians will not weaken Jewish practice.**

[8] **Jews and Christians must work together for justice and peace.**

The first of the document's principles "Jews and Christians worship the same God" would be accepted by most texts cited in this work. However, almost every traditional position whether universalist, inclusivists, or exclusivists would offer a criteria to judge the applicability of a common approach, or they would provide caveats. They would immediately point out that despite the similarities there are also differences—notably the Passion, Trinity, and Incarnation. The document says, without further delineation, that, "Christian worship is not a viable religious choice for Jews." But that would not be enough detail to correspond to any of the traditional texts. The drafters of the document avoided traditional theology and metaphysics.

Similar to the problem that many scholars have with the lack of clarity in the first statement due to a lack of substantive differences, the second and fourth principles also needed caveats on how we differ on the role of Scripture and even more so how we differ on ethics. The fourth principle has many implicit ideas that needed explication, including: making an equation between Christ and Torah, the differences will not be settled until the eschaton, and that Jews can respect Christian faithfulness to their revelation.

My entire project of my previous book, *Judaism and Other Religions*, and this book, with their huge collection of sources started as a means of providing models of what a more open traditionalist position could look like compared to the "Dabru Emet." Three of the four drafters, Novak, Signer, and Ochs have written articles to elaborate their positions. And its major detractor Levenson has been prolific in his criticism. My goal in this chapter is not to give a summary of the reception of "Dabru Emet" or to present the arguments on both sides. Rather, it is to discuss the commonality of the two faiths in contemporary Jewish thought.

David Novak

David Novak (b. 1941) is a rabbi and the J. Richard and Dorothy Shiff Chair of Jewish Studies at the University of Toronto. His thought and language played a major role in the drafting of the "Dabru Emet." He is a regular writer for journals such as *First Things*, which seek to bring a conservative religious social vision into the public sphere.

Novak, though a student of Heschel, avoids discussion of the experience of God and theology, viewing those as an "ultimate impasse" between the two faiths. Rather, he sees a commonality between Judaism and Christianity in social doctrine and morality. Novak thinks that both share a rejection of relativism and the evils of secularism. He thinks Judaism and Christianity both share the firm ground of producing moral truths and natural social ethics.

Novak rejects the idea of a Judeo-Christian faith or even a shared moral vision, but that they have enough of a "rich commonality" that they usually run in tandem. "This view preserves the truth that the difference of Judaism from Christianity and Christianity from Judaism is still greater than any commonalities the two communities now share." Worshiping the same God as we do, and reading the same Book as we do, it is inevitable that our religious ways of life are often parallel and overlap.[9]

Novak is adamant that Jewish theology cannot be constructed on just aggadah (the narrative and homiletical parts of rabbinic texts) alone, but it needs to be informed by the *halakhah* (the legal and normative parts of the rabbinic texts). Novak thinks that this turn to the *halakhah* is for the sake of authenticity, to avoid the syncretism of civil religion, and for the intrinsic need to submit to a theonomous system. When Novak generally turns to *halakhah*, it is to the spirit of the law rather than to the legal precedents.

In a famous medieval comment by Rabbi Tam in the tosafot commentary of the Talmud, he wrote that a Jew can accept an oath of a Christian because they are allowed to associate (*shituf*) God with other names, such as Jesus. (For the medieval text and its reception see my previous book, *Judaism and Other Religions*.) Novak, however, offers a startling new interpretation. Rabbi Tam's comment is explained as a general thrust within the *halakhah*, which allows a place in Judaism for a Christian conception of God. Novak extended tosafot into a general acceptance of Christianity. Novak reasons that if they trusted a Christian to take an oath even though he associated (*shituf*) something else with God then there must have been implicit trust based on a common heritage of a biblical God. In a similar broad manner, Novak claims continuity with Maimonides in that one can acknowledge the contributions of Christianity, and continuity with the Meiri by explaining the latter's "people of religion" with a moral code, as the criteria for accepting another faith. Novak states that Meiri would accept contemporary Catholic moral doctrine as a covenant. Novak uses the biblical term covenant in a generic manner to refer to a community that has a moral mandate from God through the Bible, and therefore since both Jews and Christians acknowledge their moral mandates from God they are in moral covenant with each other.

> Relativism is especially dangerous to the dialogue because it denies that some things are true all the time everywhere for everyone.

> But it is only in the thorough theological renunciation of supersessionalism and counter-supersessionalism that Jewish and Christian scholars can exchange this type of textual and historical information in a way that is neither adversarial nor capitulating.

> At the ultimate level, no matter how worthy they deem dialogue to be, Jews and Christians have to recognize that their truth claims are not only different, they are mutually exclusive . . . The recognition that the ultimate claims of Judaism and Christianity are mutually exclusive need be the basis of hostile disputations only when it is assumed that Judaism and Christianity have no commonalities at all.[10]

To find a place within Judaism for a Christian covenantal mandate, Novak uses the Seven Noahide laws as general moral code provided by the rabbis for gentiles. Novak rejects the approaches that treat these laws as *halakhah* or a separate religion for gentiles; rather, he creates a concept of the seven laws as the theological foundation for Christian normativeness. (There is precedent for this in Meiri, Meir Simchah of Dvinsk, S. R. Hirsch, and Chaim Hirschenson, see my prior book.) He also turns general statements about gentiles into a privileged covenant with Christians. In fact, he explains the inclusivist positions of Halevi and Maimonides—as teaching respect for other covenants. Where medieval texts speak of theological realism or nominalism, meaning that we share a common monotheism, Novak renders these texts as referring to moral nominalism, we share a common ethos. The requirement in Jewish texts that holds Christians to a moral standard is read as a covenantal affirmation of Catholic social thought.

> To look at Judaism and Christianity as covenantal religions is to see that the relationship with God of the individual Jew and the individual Christian is always within covenanted community.

> From rabbinic times on, Jews have developed a rubric for dealing with the issue of gentile normativeness. That rubric is the concept of the "seven commandments of

the children of Noah" . . . Some have seen these as a code unto itself and others as separate status from Christianity . . . Nevertheless, most Jewish thinkers have used these concepts more heuristically than descriptively, that is, they are used to discover what is the "condition sine qua non for a community of gentiles with whom Jews can interact out of genuine respect . . . No human community could live by Noahide law alone, but no human community who does not affirm it is worthy of the loyalty of human created in the image of God.

In order to constitute properly a Jewish appreciation of Christian normativeness, it must be emphasized at the outset what the political context of that normativeness is. [. . .] The acceptance of the Noahide law is, then, the acceptance of natural law . . . The humanely inhabited world is the most general political context of a Noahide law, including some basic recognition of God as sovereign.

Both Jews and Christians can agree that Christianity has only approximated part of the law of the Torah for herself. That part appropriated has been the moral law of the Torah in general—including basic obligations of love and respect first to God and then to fellow humans.[11]

Novak feels that Christians will identify with his vision. Novak does not want to offer "an understanding of the other community that the other community could not accept about itself." He grants revelation to gentiles and a special revelation to the Church. He does not deal with Jesus, incarnation, the Trinity, or the different functions of law in the two religions, since it would not be productive to discuss topics in which the two faiths differ. For Novak, the limits of theological knowledge are issues concerning God's essence, as well as all metaphysical. Even though Judaism and Christianity cannot compare theology, nevertheless they share in common a social ethics that in our contemporary world translates into a shared need to fight against same sex marriage in the common sphere.[12]

Jon Levenson

Jon D. Levenson (b. 1949), the Albert A. List Professor of Jewish Studies at Harvard is a biblical theologian emphasizing the rival interpretations of the traditions. For Jews, the Bible is to be read through the lenses of rabbinic understanding, conflicts in interpretation between religions are eternally recorded in the history of interpretation. He focuses on the differences despite the commonalities, and God is only known through particular interpretations. Levenson downplays the creation of common core monotheism and instead advocates a public role for pointing out divergences between religions. With Levenson's emphasis on difference despite commonality, "Dabru Emet" finds its academic critique.[13]

Levenson treats the biblical narrative as primary and the God of the Bible is a specifically Jewish God. Levenson thinks that the divine name *Hashem* should be translated as the Jewish kingly patron and suzerain, a god as political dominator of empire and history rather than in terms of any theological monotheism. For Levenson, "meaning can be disclosed in history." History is the area in which Israel has met, and comes to know the deity who has become her suzerain. A Jewish understanding of covenant is this vassalage relationship; it is not any of the Christian or nebulous versions discussed in the last chapter. He sees the Talmud as continuing these particularistic ideas by way of "covenantal renewal," a privileged love of God, and the scrupulous keeping of his commandments.[14]

Even though there is a commonality of shared scripture, for Levenson the important upshot of this commonality is a perpetual sibling rivalry. Judaism and Christianity have a commonality of exclusivism and the battle for who is the true Israel is forever in our texts:

> Radically transformed but never uprooted, the sacrifice of the first-born son constitutes a strange and usually overlooked bond between Judaism and Christianity and thus a major but unexpected focus for Jewish-Christian dialogue . . . The bond between Jewry and the Church that the beloved son constitutes is, however, enormously problematic. For the long standing claim of the Church that it supersedes the Jews in large measure continues the old narrative pattern in which a late-born son dislodges his first born brothers, with varying degrees of success. Nowhere does Christianity betray its indebtedness to Judaism more than in its supersessionalism.[15]

> "The language of sonship common to these two parables, the one Jewish and the other Christian, discloses a critical insight about the relationship of the two traditions. That relationship, usually characterized as one of parent and child, is better seen as a rivalry of two siblings for their father's unique blessing."[16]

> "In their different ways, both the Shemoneh Esreh and the mass have roots in the sacrificial ordinances of the Torah and a substantial debt to post-biblical Jewish exegesis of the story of the binding of Isaac. The indisputable differences between the two great liturgical practices should not be allowed to obscure their profound commonalities."[17]

> In light of the universalistic dimension of that legacy (e.g., Genesis 9:1–17), it is not surprising that both Judaism and Christianity have proven able to affirm the spiritual dignity of those who stand outside their own communities. But the two traditions lose definition and fade when that universalistic affirmation overwhelms the ancient, protean, and strangely resilient story of the death and resurrection of the beloved son."[18]

Levenson acknowledges biblical universalism but feels that the overriding element is the antagonism. Levenson is an anti-pluralist who does not like unqualified statements of commonality. His approach does not listen for multiple voices in a text, of a tension between a universalism in Genesis 9, and a particular covenant in Genesis 12. Rather, he creates his own rabbinic reading that harmonizes the texts in a reading in which everything needs to be seen through the particular vassalage covenant at Sinai, where the descendants of Abraham accept the commandments.

Yet, Levenson acknowledges that: "The charge that the two other religions have seriously misidentified the God of Abraham—is not necessarily the same as the claim that they worship another God." Levenson downplays the universalism of the medieval tradition or the creation of any universals. For him, Judaism is known through literary narrative and if narratives differ then the object under discussion differs. Following the broad critiques of natural theology, and even quoting Harold Bloom about the literary nature of God in the Bible, he concludes:

> An argument can be mounted that since monotheism means that there is only one God, no monotheist can ever accuse anyone—certainly not another monotheist— of worshiping another god, only (at most) of improperly identifying the one God that both seek to serve. This is all the more the case with the three religious traditions that claim to worship the God of Abraham, since these exhibit complex patterns of dependence and reciprocal influence. The charge that the two other traditions have seriously misidentified the God of Abraham—a charge made by each in various ways and times—is not necessarily the same as the claim that they worship another god.

> To the extent that God is characterized by attributes such as uniqueness, omnipotence, foreknowledge, justice, mercy and the revelation of his will in prophecy and scripture, then Jews, Christians and Muslims can easily detect the selfsame God in the LORD of Judaism, in the triune God of the church, and in Allah (which is simply the word for "God" used by Arabic speakers in all three traditions). There is a problem with such reliance on attributes, however, for it actually describes a Supreme Being who is closer to the God of the philosophers than to the God of Abraham, Ishmael, Isaac and Jacob. To state the point differently, to the extent that the one God of the universe is rendered through narratives such as those in the scriptures and not through abstract attributes. The claim that we worship "the same God cannot appear, if not false, then certainly simplistic and one-sided."[19]

Levenson envisions a fixed God of the Bible without a difference between texts and theologies. God is known from the Biblical story, in that: "their monotheism had to do with questions of service and loyalty and was not an ontological monism"; the number of deities was not usually the issue. "Their liturgies are replete with recollections, re-presentations, and reenactments of their God's interventions into history; hence the Christian story will always be a different God since their Biblical story always includes the *New Testament*. Furthermore, the Jewish story is always filtered through the Oral Torah.

Levenson does not favor the approach of "Dabru Emet," in which he critically refers to as: "Aren't we all saying the same thing?" A theological approach, which consists of conflict resolution and diplomatic negotiations, rather than confronting misunderstandings of the other's positions. Therefore, when discussing Christianity, Jews need to emphasize how Judaism does not accept the Trinity or incarnation:

> It insists in the importance of the theological core of each tradition and requires both partners to reckon with the full import of the other's theology, even when it not only contradicts but also critiques one's own. In this model, the differences, no less than the commonalities, must be brought to the fore, for without them the full truth of the individual religious traditions and the relationship between them will remain concealed.

Levenson notes that Protestant theologian Wolfhart Pannenberg (b. 1928) saw Dabru Emet as a repudiation of association (*shituf*), rather than their claim to continuity. Levenson stated that clarity would have been better achieved by either accepting the traditional opinion viewing Christians as a defective theology of association (*shituf*) or to openly reject association and accept the commonality of the Jewish and Christian God.[20] Levenson thinks that it is correct to focus on narrative without an overreaching metaphysics or theology. He dismisses value accorded to the medieval inclusivist positions, since the focus on the common monotheism, does not take into account the God of history whose deeds are shown in the biblical narrative. Furthermore, for him, words have clear meanings, without the metaphysics or metaphor of the theologians.[21] Without philosophic universals or cultural convergences, texts remain bound in their concrete differences.

However, the God of the literary critics is not the God of the medieval authorities; nor are medieval thinkers simplistic. For medieval, theologians, the Bible is both theological and philosophic. The medieval Jewish philosophers would therefore consider Levenson's position, as tinged with anthropomorphisms and having a plebian, and thus mistaken, view of the God of Abraham. Theological statements about God require philosophic qualification, especially with regards to metaphysical and doctrinal formulations and philosophers think that statements require interpretation.

On the other hand, Levenson thinks that Jews create a greater than necessary break between a rational this-worldly Judaism and an irrational other-worldly resurrected centered approach of Christianity. In his reading of the Bible, God is in battle against evil and death. God's creation of the world is a blatant rejection of any religion that places evil or sin within the divine realm or creates a God indifferent to the human condition.

> *Creation and the Persistence of Evil, the Death and Resurrection of the Beloved Son, and now Resurrection* and *the Restoration of Israel*—are actually the same book written about different material . . . Chaos and evil (really, the same thing) were thought to be in league with and leading to death. This is a worldview that sees these forces arrayed against God and God's wishes, as extremely powerful and able to triumph for a long time. This, then, rightly raises the question of whether God will ever triumph over them. The texts I discuss envision just such a triumph.

> One reason that it's useful for many modern Jews to say that Judaism doesn't have, and never had, a belief in the resurrection of the dead is that it enables them to differentiate Judaism from Christianity. Because Christianity is so focused on the resurrection of Jesus as the conclusive evidence of a more general resurrection to come, one can make Judaism out to be more scientific than Christianity by claiming, inaccurately, that Judaism has no notion of resurrection. There's a stereotype that Judaism is more "this-worldly," naturalistic, and ethical, whereas Christianity is "otherworldly" and superstitious.[22]

Christianity in Jewish Terms: Peter Ochs

Many of those involved in the authorship and signing of "Dabru Emet" then produced a volume consisting of a collection of essays nobly attempting to place

Christianity in Jewish terms in order to remove the sense of difference and otherness. Peter Ochs (b. 1950), the Edgar M. Bronfman professor of Modern Judaic Studies at University of Virginia, and one of the signers on "Dabru Emet" was involved in all aspects of this approach. From his own definition:

> For the past hundreds of years, when Jews have been taught about Christian beliefs, it has been primarily in non-Jewish terms [. . .] we believe it is time for Jews to learn about Christianity in Jewish terms, to rediscover the basic categories of rabbinic Judaism and to hear what the basic categories of Christian belief sound like when they are taught in terms of this rabbinic Judaism. To hear Christianity in our terms is truly to understand it, perhaps for the first time [. . .] What is the significance for my Judaism for my understanding of Christianity?[23]

The book suggests that the effort to explain Christianity to Jews will take years. It also rejects any form of disputation and proselytizing while, at the same time, it seeks to avoid syncretism and relativism.

Yet, the book is still troubled by the vast differences between revelation at Sinai and revelation through the incarnation of Jesus. The Jews involved still feel that the Trinity and Incarnation is not a Jewish story, and appears to many Jews as incomprehensible. Peter Ochs offers guidelines for understanding *Christianity in Jewish Terms* as four moments of recognition of the other. (1) First, the two faiths are shown to overlap and have common elements; (2) Then from a Jewish perspective, we have to recognize that Christianity adds new elements to the biblical story and to the religion of the Bible; (3) Jews need to reject the elements foreign to Judaism; (4) What is the legitimacy of those elements for non-Jews? Ochs considers the Suffering of Jesus, Trinity, and Incarnation.

> In Jewish terms, the Christian claim that Jesus is the suffering servant means that Christians believe, on one level, that the end of days has come and that the messiah who takes on Israel's burden is Jesus. On a second level, this Christian claim means they believe that the messiah not only receives but also fully embodies God's Torah for redeeming all human suffering. On a third level, the Christian claim means they believe that full embodiment of God's word is itself an identity of God.[24]

Ochs, in one of his own articles, points out that there are elements of Christian doctrine that are not part of the Jewish reading of the text, and that some Christian readings of the Bible are against the Jewish logic of the text:

> The Christian doctrines of the Incarnation and the Trinity present two main challenges to traditional Jewish study. One challenge is that the narrative of God's incarnation in one Jew belongs to a history that Jews do not share and cannot accept in their story. In this case, the Christian doctrine of the Incarnation appears comprehensible but simply wrong: the event did not occur. A second challenge is that the doctrine of God's having three identities appears incomprehensible: the Jewish biblical record does not speak of God in a way that allows us to characterize His nature as a relation among Father, Son, and Holy Spirit. From this perspective, Trinitarian doctrine, like the Kabbalah, appears incomprehensible and alien even before it appears wrong. . . . Jews are called to do more than throw up our hands in the face of Christian doctrines; we must, instead, find a way to reason Jewishly about them.[25]

If there is such a great difference between the faiths, where is the commonality? Ochs acknowledges that there is an overlap of doctrines between Judaism and Christianity (or Islam), but that Christians add certain claims, which in turn are not accepted by Jews. Ochs asks: Is it legitimate for non-Jews to make these additions, meaning can Jews create a space for Christians to add to those doctrines that they have in common? Ochs states that the Trinity of the New Testament is unlike the biblical God of the Hebrew Bible but Jews can at least find similar attributes of justice and mercy, logos, and holy spirit. In addition, both faiths have similar actions performed by God. In rabbinic literature, the concepts of *ruah hakodesh* and *shekhinah* offer the possibility of a theological bridge to the Christian concepts.

In the end, Ochs's essay still points to a gap between the Jewish emphasis on God's simplicity, necessity, and lack of composition and the Christian's belief in persons within God, and a sharp differentiation of the Father from the Son and the Holy Spirit. And, more importantly, Ochs does not take into account the differences that flow from the Christian story of the New Testament, the passion narrative.

Ochs writes that, in a post-Holocaust world, to cling to one's tradition alone is presumptuous and a dialogical understanding of one's tradition is necessary:

> A new obligation for Jews may be to support Christian communities that enhance Israel's mission. If these guidelines are presumptuous, we must remember that living still in the shadow of the Shoah, we have unusual obligations to work against corrosive influences of supersessionalism.

> To evaluate Christianity from the perspective of received Jewish tradition alone, would be to offer a reversed form of Jewish supersessionalism: treating the words of Christian doctrine as if they could be understood and judged independently of how they are actually lived and interpreted in a given community. On the other hand, to evaluate Christianity only from the perspective of some new encounter between Jews and Christians would be to abdicate responsibility to offer a specifically Jewish judgment.

> There needs to be mediation between new encounters and received Jewish opinion. Therefore there is a need for Jewish skepticism to mediate the tradition.[26]

Tradition and new encounters need to relate one to another in dialogue. Ochs chooses to be biblical centered as a means of creating a fluid tradition that emphasizes the plain sense of the words, without eternal verities. "By stressing biblical sources, I do not mean to suggest that there is no place for philosophy in Judaism or Christianity" but "philosophy began with the scriptural word and the questions it raised."[27] One studies texts in a way that stresses openness, ethical responsibility, and hospitality.

What about the eternal truths of God and theology? Ochs puts them entirely out of reach by asking the dialogue partners to focus on those aspects of God that are infinite and therefore indefinable, this way Ochs claims to be able to bring both believer and skeptic to the table.

Ochs himself presents a dynamic Torah, whose meaning only unfolds over time and that the text itself has to suffer many limited interpretations, which in turn the Jews themselves have to bear:

> The Torah is not fully disclosed to Israel all at once, but only through the entire history of Israel's reception and retransmission of the divine word. The infinite word suffers being delivered to a finite people, among whom its meaning and identity is fully disclosed only at the end of its infinite history with them.

It takes greater humility to accept ("suffer") the wisdoms one has inherited from age-old traditions, except where those traditions have proved themselves wrong or unjust or oppressive.[28]

In order to understand Ochs, one must look at a process called Scriptural Reasoning. In the 1960s, there was a trend toward seeking Jewish-Christian dialogue through common prayer and shared pulpits. In the last decade, there has been a new trend in dialogue toward jointly studying texts, called Scriptural Reasoning. The founding group was called Societies for Scriptural Reasoning and was based in England. It included David F. Ford, Daniel W. Hardy, and the Jewish author Peter Ochs. A similar approach has been the method at the annual interfaith conferences at the Shalom Hartman's Institute since the 1980s, where they studied their respective religious texts in the presence of the other. Ochs is a regular attendee at the Hartman's Institute events.

> What is SR [Scriptural Reasoning] in practice? Jews, Christians and Muslims (roughly equal numbers of each) gather to read passages from three scriptures that are usually thematically related. Sessions are not held in a synagogue, church or mosque. Instead, SR, invoking the shared "tent of meeting" imagery of Genesis 28, seeks out a neutral space.

> In a typical gathering, a member of one faith will make a few introductory comments about a scripture passage, and then the entire group attempts to understand what the passage is teaching and how it ought be applied today. Slow, patient work is done to unpack how a faith tradition has interpreted the passage. The same is then done with texts from the other two scriptures. At the end the three texts are brought into dialogue with each other. Many questions ensue, not only from representatives of other faiths but also among members of one faith who may disagree over the interpretation of their scripture. A member of a different faith may bring the strongest insight into a scripture that is not his or her own . . . The SR movement is a far cry from a search for lowest-common-denominator faith, for an all-roads-lead-to-the-same-place consensus. It insists that believers go deeper into their own tradition. At the same time, it insists that each participant engage with those of other faiths.[29]

This approach seeks to create common ground through shared understanding of sacred texts and commonality on methods and insights of the faiths. It avoids the academic, the historical, or the theological in favor of dialogue and learning how the other faith thinks. It becomes a method of dialogue that does not require the advanced preparation of presented position papers, yet at the same time, it can

produce high-level results. At its best, the testimonials call the method "the practice of humanity and the extension of self to other." One learns by sharing one's
textual concerns with members of other faiths treated as friends.

Meir Sendor, a pulpit rabbi and scholar, criticizes the book and the entire project
as the violence of the neutral produced through quick equivalents based syncretism,
selectivity, and neutralization. Sendor finds the book, *Christianity in Jewish Terms*
working in a vague abstract way in which Divine immanence is seen as the same as
incarnation. Sendor reminds us that finding a way to close the gap does not deal with
the complexity of the liturgical, theological, moral, and political implications.[30]

James Aitken, a protestant minister, challenges the "Dabru Emet" project and
claimed that there are irreconcilable differences between the faiths since the New
Testament is more important for Christians than Hebrew Bible. Dialogue cannot
only be done according Aiken with the Hebrew Scripture; we cannot bypass the
New Testament and Jesus.

> An honest appreciation of Christianity would have been preferred, one in which
> the Trinity, one of the elements in Christianity that Jews often express as being the
> hardest to accept or to recognize as monotheistic, should be given full weight. The
> need for Jews to say that they may not understand Christianity, they may not be able
> to accept the divinity of Jesus, but that they understand that Christians believe in
> it, and that the Christian belief in the trinity is a wrestling with the complexity of
> revelation, while holding onto a monotheistic belief.

Michael Signer

Another important member of the group that created "Dabru Emet" is Michael
A. Signer (d. 2008), rabbi and the former Abrams professor in the Department of
Theology at the University of Notre Dame. Signor avoids formal theology or comparisons between faiths. When faiths meet, they have "Conversational relationship
to the text, the world of life, and the community that is created out of the text
and life-world." The very text of the Bible is polyphony, and our engagement with
it brings out the potentials for the current situation. Israel faces its creator, and
then it faces other peoples; "The Jewish people discerns their message reflected in
another people which also cherishes their scripture."

When asked, do Jews share a covenant with Christians or are there two separate covenants, Signer answers that he does not use the fixed theological idea of
covenant, rather he assumes a biblical commonality and that together there is
reciprocal scriptural comparison from the divergent traditions that reflect "the
complex nature of divine revelation. Signer asks: "Do we read the same book? The
comfortable response would be "no." But then he seeks to move us beyond comfort
by affirming that we do indeed share scripture. Our commonality is that both religions are engaged in a quest for meaning using the Bible as their starting point.

> Both Jews and Christians seek out meaning with God's word for their lives in scrip-
> ture. The word for "seeking" in Hebrew is *darash*. To seek meaning is not a casual
> or cursory reading. . . . In our search for religious meaning; we want to bring our

lives to the text and the text into our lives. The search for meaning is not new to our generation. It reaches back to the origins of Judaism and Christianity.

When the study of scripture is viewed in this binocular fashion—through the eyes of both traditions—we can observe both the similarities and differences between Jews and Christians.[31]

We need to study texts in the presence of the other. Interpreting the Hebrew Scripture as the foundation for Judeo-Christian dialogue will enable Jews to recognize Christianity as a profound exploration (*derash*) of the way God operates in humanity:

It is precisely the inability to grasp the whole Scripture, meaning that can create a spirit of collaboration between two communities, and so even here there is promise. No single tradition can or ought to dominate the other. The ability to share our readings of "spirit" or *darash* may be the model for a future reconciliation that recognizes both our profound differences and the imperative to become partners in understanding the divine word to be a blessing for the entire world.[32]

According to Signer, Jesus had a solid Biblical foundation so the Hebrew sense of the Bible is not in vain. We can come together based on Scripture, however Signer reminds us that there is a fundamental interpretive difference between the two religions.

Jacob Neusner

Jacob Neusner (b. 1932) is an American academic scholar of classical Judaism and the author of nearly one thousand books. Neusner's position is that dialogue and comparisons should only be done between the normative versions of both faiths and this normative version is known through academic scholarship. Neusner's focus is not on the variety of theological and historical contexts but from his sense of a theoretical core and in emphasizing that both sides ask very different theological questions. The two faiths share monotheism, creation, and some scripture but the integration into each system is very different; commonalities of religions can gloss over differences. Neusner has a consciousness that Judaism is completely distinct from the new faith that arose around it.[33]

In his book, *A Rabbi Talks with Jesus*, Neusner makes a sharp distinction between the message of Jesus and his Jewish milieu. "For a long time, Jews have praised Jesus as a rabbi, a Jew like us really; but to Christian faith in Jesus Christ, that affirmation is monumentally irrelevant" (xii). For Christians, Jesus is the incarnation of God the Father. There is a need to engage in dialogue concerning the Jesus of Christianity, not the Christianity of scholarship. A dialogue in which the Judaic partner speaks of a merely human Christ, and the Christian partner dismisses the supernatural people of "Israel after the flesh . . . improves not at all of the matching monologues of earlier centuries." Within dialogue, Neusner is against any attempt at situating Jesus as Rabbi Jesus and he is equally against any non-Rabbinic versions of Judaism.[34]

An exchange between Professor Jacob Neusner and then Cardinal Ratzinger in 1994 is illustrative. In *A Rabbi Talks with Jesus,* Neusner says that, had he been present for the Sermon on the Mount, he would not have followed Jesus because it went against Jewish teachings. Nevertheless, Cardinal Ratzinger sent him a blurb for the book jacket, despite its rejection of Christian teachings:

> The absolute honesty, the precision of analysis, the union of respect for the other party with carefully grounded loyalty to one's own position characterize the book and make it a challenge especially to Christians, who will have to ponder the analysis of the conflict between Moses and Jesus.

Rabbi Neusner said Cardinal Ratzinger's unflinching conviction in his own faith is precisely what makes the cardinal such a valuable interlocutor—because he can appreciate Jewish leaders' staunch belief in the truth of their own religion.[35] Neusner's vision of the huge abyss between the two religions has recently become Vatican policy in a 2011 speech given by Cardinal Koch, the newly appointed liaison between the Holy See and the Jewish people.[36] Neusner thinks that we should compare Jewish normative positions with Christian normative positions at their points of self-definition. For example, we should compare the two faiths in the fourth century when Judaism was forced to review itself in the context of a triumphant Christianity. The definition of issues long discussed in Judaism—the meaning of history, the coming of the Messiah, and the political identity of Israel—became of immediate and urgent concern to both parties. Neusner finds that both religious groups turned to the same corpus of Hebrew scripture to examine the same fundamental issues but reached opposite opinions. Eusebius and Genesis Rabbah both address the issue of history, Chrysostom and the Talmud the issue of the Messiah, and Aphrahat and Leviticus Rabbah the issue of Israel.

In later works, Neusner compare what he defines as the system of Judaism to the non-commensurate system of Christianity. He emphasizes that Judaism as a religious system defines itself as the community of Torah. This Torah is a dual-Torah with two connected parts, the written Torah and the Oral Torah. Judaism engages with God by studying the Torah, the rational model of the world, and by following the precepts of the Torah, the revealed God's will on all aspects of ritual, family, and economic life. Neusner sharply contrasts this to the Christian Kingdom of God as an imminent eschatological promise of Jesus. Christians engage with God by means of baptism, communion, and Eucharist. The Bible for Christians is for inspiration and instruction (2 Tim 3:16) but the words are not God's wisdom itself as in Judaism. And in Neusner's understanding, Israel is not concerned with salvation, while Christians focus on a needed savior and redeemer.

In a recent public address, Neusner does indeed offer commonality and he gives his developed thought that one can create a commonality between faiths. There is commonality in theology and scripture:

> First, the three monotheisms share elements of a common theology. They think of God within a common pattern and confront the same issues of theology and

COMMONALITIES AND NEW UNDERSTANDINGS

philosophy. They therefore may expect to communicate with one another. Why do I claim they share an agendum? All three affirm that God is one and unique. So they worship the same God.

All three concur that God rewards virtue and punishes sin and governs the fate of all humanity. All three believe that God has sent prophets to humanity and all three are religions centered on revealed books, the Torah, the Bible and the Quran. So they share elements of a common structure and as a matter of fact a common morality.

Second, all three share a common heritage of narrative contained in Scripture. They are not strangers to one another . . . Islam recapitulates the narrative of Christianity and Judaism, and Christianity that of Judaism . . . Specifically, they tell stories of the same type, and some of the stories that they tell turn out to go over much the same ground.

That leads directly to the third and most important link among the monotheisms: Christianity sees itself in continuity with Judaism, and Islam undertakes to continue Christianity and Judaism. Moses is prophet in not only Judaism but also Christianity and Islam. Abraham and Sarah are father and mother in Christianity and Judaism.

But while they disagree on fundamentals, they concur on details . . . These topics show us similarity and difference. The interior logic of monotheism raises for the three religions a common set of questions. But then each religion tells the story in its way, and the respective narratives—in character, components, and coherence—shape the distinctive responses spelled out here.[37]

In other texts, however, Neusner does not think that Jews and Christians share scripture, he seems to have changed his mind.[38]

There are those who criticize Neusner for creating a radically de-Judaized Christianity of the Church fathers and a Judaism that has not acquired any form of content from Christianity. Neusner sees an unspoken agreement to avoid issues that go to the heart of each other's beliefs. In this, Neusner is similar to Joseph Soloveitchik in that he believes that religions cannot communicate in their public face, privately we can share; both sides are monologues and neither could make sense of the other. Neusner, on the other hand, encourages the role of the academy in creating comparative religion comparisons of the humanistic dialogic encounter. We can see the "poetry of the other, the yearning for God conveyed by the other. It is not looking for parallels but learning to have empathy dialogue is condescending, disingenuous, and, in the end, self-serving" while the academic classroom is serious, sympathetic, and unapologetic.[39]

Many think Neusner does not understand the changes of Nostra Aetate. As A. Roy Eckardt complains, "Why is he silent upon every major figure and institution on both sides that have made the dialogue a living reality?" To give but one example, he identifies as the integral and abiding Christian position that of the fourth century in which "Israel today does not continue the Israel of old." The opposite is the case among hosts of Christian thinkers for whom Jewish people remain the people of God. "To read this book is like standing with someone in the sunlight and hearing the other lament, 'What a pity that the sun is not shining.'"[40]

Pinchas Lapide

Pinchas Lapide (1922–1997) was an Orthodox Jew, a theologian, a specialist in New Testament studies, and senior lecturer at Bar-Ilan University. After serving in the British Army during World War II, he emigrated to Israel where he entered government service as deputy editor of the Government Press Bureau and was later appointed Israel's consul to Milan from 1951–1969. Lapide gained renown by defending the wartime activities of Pope Pius XII and engaging in explicit theological dialogue with the best Christian theologians of the 1960s such as Jurgen Moltmann, Karl Rahner, and Hans Kung.

Lapide is not often cited today because his works are seen as too willing to acquiesce to the theological positions of his Catholic interlocutors. Yet, he was one of the few Jewish thinkers that did directly overcome the stereotypes of what Christian theology teaches and actually engage in contemporary theology.

Early in his career, Lapide follows the nationalist approach to Jesus as Jewish presented by Joseph Klausner and David Flusser, and clearly advocates that Jesus was Jewish and a historical figure, who preformed miracles, and was resurrected. He accepts Jesus as one of several sons of God but not as "an only begotten son of God." Similarly, in regards to resurrection, Lapide remarks, "I accept the resurrection of Jesus not as an invention of the community of disciples, but as a historical event." The dual covenant theorist Jacob Agus writes that Lapide is unique among modern Jews in that he accepts resurrection as a historic occurrence, and that Lapide thinks the miracle galvanized the early Christian community to be God-willed. Personally, Agus did not accept miracles and considered all scripture as myth.[41]

For Lapide, it is Christianity's claims about the Messiah rather than claims about the resurrection that is the key divide between Christianity and Judaism. But, he also follows this approach and completely separates Jesus from Christianity and from Paul. Lapide argues that Jesus did not introduce himself to his people as the Messiah, that the Jews did not reject Jesus, and that Jesus did not reject his people. He goes out of his way to paint Jesus as an Orthodox Jew, and rejects what he refers to as the de-Judaized Jesus of Geiger and other Reform positions. At this point, Lapide has created a speculative Jesus that bears little resemblance to history or theology.[42]

Lapide moved from this nationalist interest in Jesus to theology.[43] By engaging in conversation with the Jurgen Moltmann (b. 1926), a German Protestant theologian who was significant in reformulating eschatology as a hope and an existential anticipation and away from an apocalyptic era, Lapide follows suit and reads the biblical verses about a messianic humanism as a contemporary hope.

> "Then, however, I will give pure lips unto the nations so that they all may call upon the name of the Lord and serve the Lord with one accord." Pure lips, in a rabbinic exegesis, means that all of the nations without exception already for a long time have sought the One God, although they have often made use of strange circumlocutions in order to name God. For indeed all human beings are fundamentally, as many Talmud masters along with Karl Rahner believe, "anonymous monotheists," whose service of God only needs a conceptual clarification.[44]

He also interprets the biblical verses about acknowledging that other religions serve God as "anonymous monotheists" similar to Rahner's anonymous Christians.

Lapide is willing to actually compare theologies of God and think about the important topic of inter-divine structures of God. He makes an anti-Trinity distinction between tritheism, Trinity, and triadic. Judaism clearly rejects the position of three gods, tritheism, and it rejects three persons in one God, the Trinity, but it accepts three aspects to one God. He finds the latter position in many medieval Jewish theories of the divine glory (*kavod*). Lapide is willing to entertain exploring the gap between the Jewish triadic Divine and the Christian trinity. The tenth century Jewish thinker Saadyah considered the Trinity as divine attributes not as separate entities and therefore Lapide concludes that there are "many triadic (in no way Trinitarian) traces which are to be found in Judaism."[45] According to Lapide, Judaism does not accept the infinite Divine in the finite, but does have a triadic religion of three patriarchs, three parts of the *kedusha*, creator, redeemer, and spirit, and a Kabbalistic view of three Divine names: Eh-yeh, Tetragrammaton, and *El-Shaddai*. Lapide thinks all these divisions melt into a single unity, without the need for unification or metaphysics:

> One God is against Christianity "the Lord cannot be viewed as something put together which would be divisible into various properties or attributes. . . ." It is difficult for me to grasp the notion that God divides himself. All distinctions . . . "melt into a unity in the faith world of Judaism. . . ." But because of God's incomprehensibility I am still not prepared to divide God into two or into three or into ten so as to make God more easily presented. . . . The cabalists have a ten-level theology. That strikes normal Jews like myself as illogical, and precisely therefore, perhaps, it also belongs in the faith world of Israel.[46]

Lapide is willing to entertain the modality model of the Trinity, presented by Karl Barth, where the three parts are of three modes, close to medieval attributes of the revealer, the revelation, and the being revealed. Karl Rahner wrote that, despite confessions of the Trinity most Christians are living as monotheists, if the Trinity were to be removed, the great majority of religious writing could remain unchanged. Rahner treated the Trinity as separate persons. He once asked Lapide why he did not become a Christian if he, as a Jew, can already accept Jesus as the resurrected son of God. Lapide answered to him, the term son of god is a Jewish term from Daniel and does not mean the same thing as the Trinity. More than that, "neither of us can logically prove the fundamentals of our religion."[47]

Lapide is universalist, theocentric with God as father caring for all people and embracing many paths. There are many ways to serve the one God.

> For me, Christianity is a God-willed way of salvation. We Jews and Christians are and remain children of the One Divine Father, and our things held in common outweigh by far our legitimate differences.

> I believe in a plurality of ways of believing in the One God, and I am convinced that God is large enough that several paths of salvation could lead to God, of which Judaism and Christianity are only two.[48]

I can scarcely imagine that the grace of God . . . depends on whether the individual Jews believes in him or not. It often strikes me that God also has a heart for atheists who seek him unconsciously. God's work appears to me so universal. As the psalmist says: The Lord is good to all and his compassion is over all that he has made (Psalms 145:9).

To whom then will you liken God, or likeness compare with him? (Isaiah 40:18) It often appears almost as if Wittgenstein was right when he said, that about which we do not know, we should keep silent.[49]

Lapide says that we have limits about speaking about the mysteries of God, which Rahner rejects.

Lapide believes in the possibility of resurrection and son of God but not in the "only begotten Son of God." There are themes in the Bible and Second Temple literature that have similarities but none with the same significance. It is possible to accept a resurrection but not as an "eschatological watershed." Jorgen Moltmann accepts Lapide's explanation that the Jewish "No!" is not hard-heartedness or blindness but because Jews are not able to believe in the way of Jesus Christ. Lapide states that if all Jews had accepted Jesus then his message would have remained intra-Jewish. And would have never been brought to the wider world. For Lapide, the Jewish reply of "No!" to Jesus is important. In contrast, Rahner is still expecting an eventual yes—to be given by Jews to Jesus's message.

"I believe that the Christ event leads to a way of salvation which God has opened up in order to bring the gentile world into the community of God's Israel. . . . For if there had been no large Jewish: No! . . . the entire church would have remained intra-Jewish . . . we did not need it. Since Sinai we have known the way to the Father. You on the other hand were very much in need of it.[50]

Paganism was defeated, but it was the two daughter faiths—Christianity and Islam—not Judaism, which reaped the harvest of Israel's victory, Judaism was confined within the bounds of Jewry . . . Christianity and Islam were new pronouncements, new revelations of the religion of Israel, addressed now to gentiles . . . Detachment of the religion of Israel from the nation Israel was a precondition of its acceptance beyond Israel.[51]

Jesus was closer to Jewish monotheism and unrelated to Zeus or any god of pagan provenance.[52]

The extraordinary phenomenon was not Jewish rejection, but gentile acceptance of Jesus and Muhammad. "The transgression of Israel is transitory. God hardened the heart of Israel in order to redeem the gentiles . . ."[53]

Lapide shows that Judaism is a relationship with God and not a mechanical checklist manipulating God. (In this he is similar to Buber). Foreshadowing current works on the new Paul, Lapide claims that he was not an apostate or antinomian. Rather, Paul had the "incandescence of Hebraic emuna," in which he had the exalted vision to bring everyone to one God. "In my opinion Paul's primary concern was the unification of that division of humanity which he as a Jew had learned to consider almost a law of nature: Jews and Gentiles." Lapide blames the dichotomy between the faiths on Augustine and the Augustinianism monk Luther who created a dichotomy of faith and works and then demanded faith alone—Judaism is outdated as works.

> When Paul says that neither Jew nor Gentile can achieve salvation by fulfilling the commandments or performing the deeds of the Torah, he is kicking doors that are already wide open to all biblically knowledgeable Jews . . . To see Judaism as achievement oriented, as reckoning accounts with God instead of counting on God; indeed to debase divine instruction by equating it with the narrow minded word nomos—all of this is an absurd character which finds its source in Paul.

> If I contemplate the Incarnation in this way, it is basically neither idolatry nor deification of the creature and not at all an attempt to seize hold of God, as some Jews maintain, but in the final analysis only a further development or the taking to its logical conclusion of that Hebrew doctrine of salvation that understands the loving bestowal of God in his humanity as the basic dynamic of all world history.

> The God of Israel, who is also my God, does not transform himself into a human being. There is no change or becoming or transformation despite "normal linguistic usage."[54]

Lapide was criticized in his time for being too accommodating to Christianity and rejecting the historical claims of Judaism as being in contradiction to Christianity.[55] In other words, most participants of the Jewish-Christian dialogue wanted the differences between the two faiths to be accentuated and discussed in terms of Jewish historical memory. They wanted reconciliation by the Christian acceptance of Judaism and the understanding of anti-Semitism and the Holocaust. What they did not want was a comparison of the faith, especially one so eager to close the gap between the religions.

Alon Goshen-Gottstein

Alon Goshen-Gottstein is a rabbi, academic, and the head of the Elijah School for the Study of Wisdom in World Religions and the World Council of Religious Leaders, a major international organization bringing together leaders of world religions.

Alon Goshen-Gottstein asserts that the entry of Orthodox Jews into the Jewish-Christian dialogue, especially in Israel, "has expanded the boundaries of the conversation and introduced new dimensions." Goshen-Gottstein advocates bringing to the discussion the wide range of Jewish theological works found in both the traditional study hall and in the academic library. Furthermore, interest in mystical, pietistic, and metaphysical texts read specifically help in closing the gap between the presentations of other faiths and those of Judaism.

Goshen-Gottstein seeks to close the spiritual gap between faiths through careful comparison. Whereas selective texts can be used to show vast differences between faiths, he seeks to find the Jewish texts that closest approximate the other faith, or even asks whether the language of the other faith can be used in a Jewish context. For example, he considers the case of the Christian concept of incarnation. He looks for commonality with Judaism:

> Various senses of incarnation in Judaism are presented. First, a weak sense of the incarnation is found in a variety of early rabbinic materials. Then, a stronger sense of incarnation, relating to God's incarnation, is examined. It is suggested that resources exist within Kabbalistic and Hasidic Judaism that, at the very least, make it possible to speak of such incarnation. While obvious differences between Christian and Jewish understandings cannot be fully bridged, these texts suggest that the gap may be narrowed. Thus, Christian religious language is not completely senseless in a Jewish context. Finally, the essay poses some questions to the Christian reader regarding the negative implications of the doctrine of the incarnation for Jewish-Christian relations.[56]

He starts with the empirical and existential but then moves to a textual understanding of the position of the other faith and a new self-understanding.

> First, to correct imbalances that stem from a false perception of the other or from excluding the other from one's horizons; and second, the encounter with the other furnishes us with new ways of perceiving and presenting our religious convictions. Ultimately, the encounter with the other fashions our own self-perception, as well as our religious understanding.

> "Listening is the first step in understanding." Incarnation—

> We must, therefore, be aware of the type of Judaism we present and of the conscious choices we must make in order to make our creative theological moves.
> Most presentations of Judaism, founded upon the articulations of Judaism in the great polemics of the Middle Ages, dismiss the idea out of hand, as having no meaning.

> The confusion of historical and theological method is a major obstacle in the present context . . . While such statements ought, methodologically, to be founded upon purely historical study, such study is hopelessly informed by a theological perspective that totally breaks down the kind of methodological rigor that would be necessary to establish the desired historical truths.

After surveying the various reasons for why Jews could not relate to the incarnation, he too surveys prior attempts to create commonality through incarnation of God in the body of the people of Israel, or man as the image of god, or the names of god, and finds that the closest parallel is those who worship the Hasidic saint, *zaddik*. Goshen-Gottstein ponders how far the analogy can be perused. In the process, he discovers the boundaries. Yet the commonality was discovered by putting away the theological preconception of difference, letting oneself be open to the historical data, and then returning with a new theological position that has a sharper perspective of where the differences actually lie. Maybe Incarnation is a way of saying that God loves humanity, that there is presence and closeness of

God, that God shows humility in these interactions, and that God wants to be of extreme value to humanity.

> One might say that the person is divine, but one would never say that the person is God. This, it seems to me, is a chasm over which it is hard to build a bridge. The problem is primarily theological, but it has serious moral consequences as well. . . . However, is there a threshold that Judaism(s) will not cross? . . . I have allowed the Christian tradition, throughout our discussion, to pose questions to the Jewish tradition, and I have attempted to respond to the challenge by bringing out those elements found within the Jewish tradition that might allow for bridge-building.

> I gradually came to entertain the possibility that the incarnation poses more of a threat—or challenge—to the Jewish sensibilities than the Trinity, which is often portrayed as the core of the Jewish objection to Christian theology. . . . By contrast, the incarnation touches a deep nerve in the Jewish awareness, concerned with the preservation of boundaries between the human and God.

There are three separate levels: the level of commonality, the ability to translate, and the difference; one should not collapse one into the other. We look at the historical accounts to find similarities, which can help to overcome current theological blinders, we learn to give a charitable and sympathetic reading to the other religion by translating as best as we can their terms into ours, and then we look at the insurmountable theological differences that remain. These differences should, according to Goshen-Gottstein, still be seen with empathy for the psychological drive toward these theological positions. In some ways, this approach is similar to the empirical approaches in comparing religions and the documented ability for spiritual adepts to compare methods:

> Can the two traditions speak in a meaningful way about the common image of God the Father, and can religious reflection of one tradition serve as inspiration to members of the other tradition?[57]

> For Judaism, both ancient and later, "Father" never ceases to be a metaphor. It thus belongs to the arena of religious language, as do all expressions that describe God. It teaches us about God and about the suitable approach to God, yet it does not truly describe God. . . . It is at this point that a great divide exists between a Jewish understanding and a Christian understanding of the meaning of "Father" as applied to God. . . . From a Christian perspective, God's paternity is anything but optional. . . . In one sense, the Christian understanding is simply a case of taking religious language more seriously.

> From the perspective of the first level, Judaism and Christianity share a common language, grounded in common scriptures. The very use of common religious language lends a commonality to the two religions. Moving to the second level, if Jesus had a realization of God to share with his Jewish audience, this was an experiential deepening of their own traditional understanding and obviously did not stand in conflict with it.

> However, the hallmark of Christian faith is precisely the third level of meaning, whereby God the Father is understood initially and primarily as the Father of Jesus

Christ. Here one must recognize a fundamental divide between the Jewish and Christian understanding of divine fatherhood.

Part of the task of encounter is to examine where and how the two religions' perceptions of God differ, a task part theological, part academic, and part phenomenological. Just as the Jewish, Christian, and Muslim traditions have been enriched by centuries of theologians, philosophers, and mystics, each adding to the tradition's perception of the Divine, so too can encounter open the possibilities of further enriching our access to holiness and to a theological attempt to understand religion, of which philosophy has traditionally been a part.

When asked to engage in the process of Scriptural Reasoning where one speaks about one's contemporary horizons, Goshen-Gottstein demurred and claimed the inability to have the naiveté of scriptural reasoning that seeks to interpret texts outside of the history of interpretation.

> I may be able to "think of" the Song of Songs, through the lens of the Rabbis, Maimonides, the Zohar or Rav Kook. . . . It will not be the Song of Songs that has functioned as a spiritual structuring force but what has been made of it through the history of interpretation. Perhaps I am too deeply influenced by the history of interpretation.[58]

This book shares many of Rabbi Goshen-Gottstein's sentiments of starting with rabbinic texts and their interpretive history as a definition of Judaism. I too find it difficult to speak of the meaning of the biblical text outside of the interpretive traditions.

The Quest for the Historic and Jewish Jesus

From the 1950s through the 1980s, the precedent for a positive theology of Jewish-Christian relations was the appreciative Jewish views of Jesus among modern thinkers, such as Joseph Salvador, Abraham Geiger, Claude Montefiore, Martin Buber, and others. Their willingness to discuss Christianity and their use of Jesus as a positive role model for Judaism serves as a paradigm of openness. The quest for the historical Jesus and the quest to return Jesus to a Jewish context become the focus of a positive theological attempt by Christianity rather than the actual doctrines of any Christian denomination. To return Jesus to a Jewish context becomes a reversal of Christianity's own perception. Prior to continuing the discussion on the difference between theologies of other religions and a theology of Christianity, these quests must be properly explained.

In the first phase of the quest for the historical Jesus, from the eighteenth into the end of the nineteenth century, the goal was to separate the myth and miracles in the New Testament from the actual historical event. Ernest Renan, Albert Schweitzer, and Rudolf Bultmann created some of the more famous ethical and rational portrayals of Jesus. The aforementioned Jewish authors Salvador, Abraham Geiger, Montefiore, and Buber sought a Jesus that represented, in the Jewish context, the ideal Jew who, in their opinion, correctly grasped the ideal of liberal Judaism (i.e., that Judaism was not legalism). Salvador specifically believes

Jesus sought a pure Judaism but "his struggle with Pharisaism was never crowned by a decisive victory."[59] However, with the Apostle Paul and the Gospel of John "all the errors of polytheism are hallowed."[60] For Geiger, Jesus was the ideal Jew, expressed truly by Hillel, the sage. Montefiore treats Jesus as a role model for a proper return to the prophets. Buber speaks of "my brother Jesus," who taught the authentic Jewish message later found in Hasidism.[61] For all authors, Paul is the one who deviated from Jesus's teaching to found Christianity. All essentially ignore Incarnation, Resurrection, and Trinity.[62]

A nationalistic Jewish approach was offered by Joseph Klausner who reclaimed Jesus as part of the national Zionist endeavor. Klausner was so successful that Israeli culture today naturally thinks of Jesus as part of the rabbinic era and places the blame for Christianity on the shoulders of Paul. For the Jewish community, which had a tradition of never pronouncing Jesus's name (referring to him as "that man," *otoha 'ish*) and which considered the very act of reading the New Testament idolatrous, the production of books in Hebrew about Jesus and Paul was a radical step.[63]

In the second phase of the quest for the historical Jesus starting in the late 1950s, both Jewish and Christian scholars sought the Jewish context for early Christianity. The method was a comparison of Christian and rabbinic sources through an attempt to move away from theology and toward history of texts. Asher Finkel, David Flusser, and E. P. Sanders reclaim a Jewish context for Jesus's statements. Unlike their predecessors, they sought the first-century Jewish context for Jesus and do not seek a Jesus as an ideal representation of Judaism.[64]

In the third phase of this quest, there is a separation of statements deemed authentic from those seen as later additions. There is an integration of archeology and material history of the era, knowledge of ancient synagogues and Greek inscriptions, and, most importantly, the writings from Qumran. Jesus now emerges from the Jewish context as divergent images: a revolutionary, a teacher of wisdom, or even a pneumatic. At this point, there is a sharp separation of the naturalistic Jesus imagined by the academy from the sensibilities of religious communities. One even sees book reviews blaming contemporary Church leaders for not accepting the latest scholarly image of a naturalistic historically reconstructed Jesus.[65]

Géza Vermès, who wrote one of the leading selling books on the topic, ends the introduction to his *Jesus the Jew* suggesting that if we can recognize that "this man, distorted by Christian and Jewish myth alike, was in fact neither the Christ of the Church, nor the apostate and bogeyman of Jewish popular tradition, some small beginning may have been made in the repayment to him of a debt long overdue."[66]

John P. Meier's multivolume series, *A Marginal Jew: Rethinking the Historical Jesus*, holds that "the historic Jesus was the halakhic Jesus." The debate stories are about the proper interpretation of the law and not about the basic requirement to keep the law. The law is God's gift to his people. One must not confuse the historical Jesus with Christology.

Amy-Jill Levine, professor of New Testament at Vanderbilt University Divinity School, offers a Jewish summary of the new scholarship that treats Jesus as a Jew who lived in a Jewish context while practicing Judaism. Jesus was "a Jew speaking to Jews," and Christianity was a Jewish movement that ultimately swept the world in its influence and authority. However, according to Levine, with this expansion came an insidious anti-Jewish sentiment, fed by some New Testament texts that were wrongly understood. Levine considers the errors of both the Church and the Academy in drawing conclusions about presumed monolithic Judaism, supposing that whatever Jesus seemed to oppose must have been normative in Judaism of his day. Moreover, she shows that the New Testament does not describe Judaism of its day both accurately and exhaustively.[67]

Most of these early studies on the life of Jesus in the first phase were theologically inclusivist, seeing ideal Jewish traits in aspects of Christianity. The scholars of the second phase were non-theological, and the third phase consists of historians not theologians. However, it is important to note the tenacity for some of the writers involved in the Jewish-Christian dialogue to hold on to the views of Jesus from the first phase of the quest; they make claims to historical scholarship, but they themselves have not moved onto the third phrase.

A recent volume, entitled *Jesus through Jewish Eyes*, shows that many twenty-first century Jews who approach other religions still accept the Buberian perspective. Jesus is portrayed as a teacher, a healer, a proto-Hasid, a God-intoxicated Jew, "a flower of Judaism," and a perrenialist mystic. Herbert Bronstein writes, "I think of Jesus in the same way as I do of Hillel and Akiba, of Jeremiah, Siddhartha Gautama (the Buddha), certain Confucian, Taoist and Hindu sages—all of them teachers—whose message was identification in the spirit of love and service with an Ultimate beyond oneself.[68]

The New Thinking about the New Testament

From St. Augustine to Martin Luther, St. Paul was seen by most Christian interpreters as teaching a radical opposition of the law and the spirit. The Mosaic Law was considered pride, restrictive in salvation, and was no longer needed in the messianic era. Biblical scholarship is beyond the scope of this book, however the Anglican E. P. Sanders revolutionized the study of Paul with the "New Perspective on Paul" showing that Paul's problem with Judaism was that it was connected to Christ, not that there was a problem with the practice of Judaism.[69] In the last decade, there has been many further changes beyond the "New Perspective" to what is now called the "New Paradigm." There are many new Christian readings of Paul, Luke-Acts, the Johannie Community, Hebrews, and Church fathers that take account of Second Temple Judaism and remove much of the assumed anti-Judaism. (After this volume was already submitted, there was a major publishing event of a multi-author Jewish commentary on the New Testament. It will substantially reclaim the Jewish context for the New Testament.) This all too short introduction is needed as a preface for understanding the next authors.[70]

Daniel Boyarin

Daniel Boyarin (b. 1946) is the professor of Talmudic Culture at the University of California, Berkeley. His ongoing work is influential on the current generation of scholars and is only now beginning to filter down to the clergy level.[71]

Boyarin has written on early Jewish-Christian relations and emphasizes that in the early centuries, there was no clear border between the two faiths. Both groups were figuring out their identity based on and in contrast to the other group. Christians produced Jews and Jews produced Christians. One of his earlier books, *A Radical Jew: Paul and the Politics of Identity*, was part of the new wave of Pauline scholarship showing that Paul did not reject Judaism but he rather sought to create a universal religion for the gentiles. In his work *Borderlines,* Daniel Boyarin suggests that the during early period following the destruction of the Temple, the divide between Jewish and Christian was based on the Christian use of originally Jewish eschatology and theology themes that became incompatible with rabbinism. Commonalities between the two faiths include messianism, martyrdom, and logos. Polemics created the nascent borders, yet it was intellectual "smugglers who transported discourses . . . in both directions across the abstract frontier of the two groups."

Whereas Neusner contrasts the two faiths based on their fourth or sixth century differences, Boyarin compares the two based on their second and third century commonalities.[72]

> We might think of Christianity and Judaism in the second and third centuries as points on a continuum [. . .] Not tree and branches, families, parent and daughter differentiation but a wave theory in which identity is hybrid [. . .] The issue is not Jesus but more salient points of cultural construction such as logos theory. . . . By the [4th century,] we have Rabbinic Jews, Christians, and heretics on both sides.

Logos theology was widespread within Judaism that preceded the rabbis.[73] Boyarin focuses not on Jesus or the incarnation, immediate obvious differences, rather on the shared visions of logos and messianism.

Much of the fluid location of division centers on what Boyarin calls Jewish Binitarianism in which there is a lower entity below God that still bears many of the elements of God or is God's manifestation on earth. Second Temple literature is replete with forms of bitheism, including the philonic logos and the Ezekiel traditions of an Angel of God in the image of a man appearing on the throne. Even rabbinic liturgical terminology, such as the Alenu hymn, speaks of "The Lord of All" as distinct from the "Creator of Bereshit." For Jews, the two powers are one and a person does not worship one without the other. Most Jews are no longer aware of this bitheism and the rabbinic polemics against considering them two entities. Boyarin based his work on that of Barnard professor Alan Segal (d. 2011) who suggested the early rabbinic rejection of "Two Powers in Heaven" was against Christianity.[74] According to Boyarin, debates against Gnostics became a polemic against Christians, it is treating the logos as God, as a power in heaven; our image of God is good, the Christian image is not.[75]

Boyarin thinks that many of the theological concepts, which earlier scholarship, such as Rudolf Bultmann, had credited to a Hellenistic break from Judaism are actually antecedent to rabbinic Judaism as part of Second Temple Judaism. Bultmann in the 1920s declared that the wisdom traditions of the logos were not a living force in Judaism. For Boyarin, the logos is ever present as the site of God's presence in the world in the *targumim* (translation), in Philo of Alexandria Ben Sira, and then later in the *midrashim*.[76]

Boyarin uses this text from the rabbinic work *Mekhilta* to illustrate his points. The text states that we are not to confuse the different images of God as two separate beings. Sometimes God appears as a warrior and sometimes as an old man, yet Peur and Senex are one God. The God of creation is the same as the God of eschatology. There is no need to say that they are separate Gods and separate persons of one God:

> I am the Lord your God (Exodus 20:2). Why is it said? For this reason. At the sea He appeared to them as a mighty hero doing battle, as it is said The Lord is a man of war (Exodus 15:3). At Sinai He appeared to them as an old man full of mercy.... Scripture, therefore, would not let the nations of the world have an excuse for saying that there are Two Powers, but declares: I am the Lord your God. I am He (ani hu) who was in Egypt and I am He who was at the sea. I am He who was at Sinai. I am He who was in the past and I will be in the future. I am He who is in this world and I am He who will be in the world to come. As it is said, See, then, that I, I am He; there is no god beside Me. I deal death and give life ... (Deuteronomy 32:39). And it says, Till you grow old, I will still be the same (Isaiah 46:4). And it says, Thus said the Lord, the King of Israel, their Redeemer, the Lord of Hosts: I am the first, and I am the last (Isaiah 44:6). And it says, Who has wrought and achieved this? He who announced the generations from the start. I, the Lord, who was first and will be with the last, I am he (Isaiah 41:4).[77]

In this text, we are introduced to the rabbinic idea that God has a lower throne on which sits the Metatron, a lower form of the divine. The Metatron is even the protagonist in biblical verses, which seem to refer to God. At the same time, the rabbis held that one should only worship God, not his manifestations. If one worships the lower manifestations then one is a sectarian. According to Boyarin, this sectarian polemic was transferred to become a polemic against Christian theology and a rabbinic avoidance of discussing bitheism.

> Once a Min [a heretic or sectarian] said to Rav Idit: It is written, Then He said to Moses, Come up to the Lord [...] (Exodus 24:1). But surely it should have stated, Come up to Me! It was Metatron [who said that], he replied, whose name is similar to that of his Master, for it is written, [I am sending an angel before you to guard you on the way and to bring you to the place that I have made ready. Pay heed to him and obey him. Do not defy him ...] since My Name is in him (Exodus 23:20–21). But if so, [the Min retorted,] we should worship him! Rav Idit replied however, that the same passage says: Do not defy him, i.e., do not exchange Me for him.... According to our beliefs, we would not accept him [Metatron] even as a messenger.[78]

Metatron traditions were common among the Hellenistic Jews of antiquity, and Metatron is often represented as a Son of God in these traditions.[79] In Boyarin's view, this was a deliberate reaction to Christian Logos theology, which adopted those parts of the Jewish traditions that were eliminated by the early Mishnaic rabbis. "Metatron is given a status that is quite unique, and the strong affinity between his status and that of God [. . .] of the intimate affinity between the two powers in high."[80]

This rejection of a "second power" by rabbinic Jews, which Boyarin sees as mainly a pre-rabbinic formulation of Philo's Logos (sometimes represented by Metatron), is what begins a "heresiological" process in Christianity and Judaism. The Church Fathers affirm Christ as God's incarnated creative Logos and most Jewish texts reject logos speculations. The disbelief in two separate powers is what Christians call the heresies of sabellianism, Modalism, Monarchism; they are the line between inside and outside the church.[81]

Daniel Boyarin states Judaism as rejecting the Trinity in favor of its own bithe-ism and Metatron theories. The Jewish position is known in Christian theology as the heresy of Modalism, (modalistic monarchianism, or modal monarchism), the nontrinitarian that the Heavenly Father, the Resurrected Son, and the Holy Spirit are different *modes* or *aspects* of one God, as perceived by *the believer*, rather than being three distinct persons in *God Himself*. It is important to note that recent Christology by both Catholics and Protestants is closer to monarchism than to the fourth century formulations. Karl Rahner, Karl Barth, and Roger Haight would each be closer to appositions, which could be compared to Jewish theology; Pinchas Lapide successfully brought this out in his discussion with Rahner. Barth starts by identifying God as being "One" and then develops from there into the doctrine of the three "modes of being." In contrast, modern Christologies of Moltmann, and von Balthasar are closer to Kabbalistic distinctions between the three aspects of Divinity *Eyn Sof*, the *sefirot* around *teferet*, and the immanent *Shekhinah*. Hence, the current dividing line is the concept of person as relates to God and the Incarnation of the infinite in the finite. Moltmann himself finds affinity between his position and those of Heschel.

In his recent book *The Jewish Gospel: The Story of the Jewish Christ*, Boyarin draws the full conclusions of his prior work *Border Lines*. The ideas of a complex godhead (a God with two or three persons) have their origins in the Judaism of Jesus's time and before him. Also many, perhaps most, Jews were expecting a Redeemer who was a divine being in the shape of a man, known as the Son of Man. Most people believe that the Gospels (especially Mark) tell us that Jesus abrogated and set aside the Torah, Boyarin proposes that the Jesus of Mark defended the Torah, and that Jesus, himself, was portrayed as keeping the Sabbath and the kosher rules. Finally, the suffering and dying of Jesus did not cause a break with traditional Judaism because the idea of a suffering and even dying Messiah was not foreign to Judaism even beyond the Jesus movement. Boyarin calls on Jews to stop vilifying Christian ideas about God as simply a collection of "unJew-ish," perhaps pagan, and in any case bizarre fantasies.[82]

Moshe Idel and Peter Schaffer

Moshe Idel (b. 1947), the Hebrew University professor of Jewish Mysticism, pub-lished a book, *Ben: Sonship and Jewish Mysticism*, where he deals with many of the same texts as Boyarin and which contains many of the texts useful for a comparison of early Judaism and early Christianity. Idel deals with ideas including: The Son of God, Divination of the Righteous, and figures sitting on the Divine Throne.[83]

Nevertheless, Idel does not find fluid borders or border crossings. Jews accept binitarianism but do not worship the lower form, or ask mercy from it. Those who have two forces do. Idel argues that Boyarin's argument would be more convincing if the Church Fathers had affirmed the Logos as distinct and separate from God, but rather they created a Trinitarian system in which one cannot exist without the other, and therefore maintain one power in heaven. Trinitarian thought does *not* take the place of Metatron represented in traditions of antiquity. The "Metatron may indeed be the figure in non-Christian myth that is most closely related to Jesus, but Christians don't worship Metatron; they worship Jesus, Idel views Metatron's "Two Powers" as not being important enough of a concern for the rabbis to spend much time thinking about.[84] "Thus much more drastic and efficient forms of censorship were applied to less dangerous topics found in pre-rabbinic Jewish culture than were applied to the possible status of Metatron as a kind of Son of God [or second power]."[85]

Explicit in the Nicene creed's affirmation of Logos theology is exactly what is missing from rabbinism and is the basis of Idel's assessment. "Rabbinism never attained a degree of orthodoxy even remotely similar to the dogmatic formulations which permeate Christianity through the centuries, but loose forms of theological thought remained part and parcel of Rabbinism in the medieval period."[86] Idel sees the early rabbis' main project as "the elaboration of ritual as a shared worship, much more so than building theologies of philosophies."[87]

Another scholar Peter Schäfer (b. 1943) of Princeton University focuses on the connections between Mary and the *Shekhinah* as described in the early form of Kabbalah found in the Book of Bahir, a text from twelfth century Provence. He points out that both female figures perform a role of mediation between God and humans, and that both express God's desire to reach out to the world of humanity. In addition, Schäfer draws his reader's attention to the temporal correspondence between the rise of the cult of Mary in Western Europe and the emergence of the *Shekhinah* in Jewish theology. Veneration of Mary develops in the tenth through the twelfth centuries, and the *Shekhinah* appears as a feminine aspect of God in the twelfth Bahir. Schäfer also demonstrates that Christian religious processions, external Church art, and public sermons would have been easily visible to Jews in this region. Schäfer suggests that such an influence is "a continual and dynamic interplay of active and constantly changing partners. Thus conceived, historical influence is a creative and mutual process that affects both partners."[88] Schäfer's book privileges the idea of divine Wisdom in a way that other scholars do not. Arthur Green suggests that the key point of connection between the *Shekhinah* and Mary may be the identification of Mary with the Christian Ecclesia, and the *Shekhinah* with the Community of Israel, rather than the figure of divine Wisdom.[89]

Summary of the New Field

Jacob Neusner finds Judaism and Christianity dissimilar based on their fourth century canonic texts. Daniel Boyarin believes that Judaism and Christianity were originally similar and connected in the second and third centuries. Moshe Idel, on the other hand, maintains that the two faiths are similar but are neither connected nor dependent on each other. There is no essence of early Judaism; one can find positions similar to those chosen by Christianity in Judaism, albeit even if not mainstream.

In contrast, Martin Buber and Leo Baeck found the two faiths to be greatly dissimilar and disconnected and that currently, we [only] have dialogue due to modernity. Buber could appreciate Jesus as a Jew who did not accept any of the theology later associated with Christianity. Paul, according to Buber, was the beginning of this different faith. Trude Weiss-Rosmarin and Eliezer Berkovits find the two faiths to be not only dissimilar but opposite and contradictory. Mid-twentieth century scholarship, such as that of E. E. Urbach, took all the bitheism concepts and ideas such as logos, *mamra*, *Shekhinah*, *gevurah* as metaphors, not metaphysics, which precluded the possibility of the readings of Boyarin or Idel.

Alon Goshen-Gottstein and Pinchas Lapide show that, based on Jewish meta-physical texts, the metaphysical Trinity is not as much a problem as the incarnation or the Trinity as three persons. The differences now lay in the realm that Lapide is willing to accept that is, Christians have the same God as the Jews; however, they do not have the special status or unique revelation from "God of Israel." Even a Jewish theology, which granted prophecy to all nations, would not grant Christians the revelation of new covenant or to treat the New Testament as God's word.

To place these changes in perspective, Pope Benedict in his recent work, *Jesus of Nazareth*, views Christianity as a natural outgrowth of Judaism, respecting ritual, law, priesthood, monarchy. He firmly rejects the older quest for Hellenistic sources for Christian theology by crediting Catholicism to Hebraic thinking and he rejects the distinction and dichotomy of Christian faith compared to the lesser value given to Hebraic works; Christianity is an outgrowth of Judaic ritual and priesthood. Benedict accepts Jesus, the Apostles, and Paul as Jews practicing Judaism within a Jewish context. His new reading of Jesus is based on the histo-rian John P. Meier's multivolume series, *A Marginal Jew: Rethinking the Historical Jesus* that holds that "the historic Jesus was the halakhic Jesus."[90]

Benedict places the dividing line between the two faiths by saying that the Jews did not accept Jesus as Divine, which Jesus, now in a new covenant, fills the role of Torah. To further divide Christianity and Judaism, Benedict suggests the Jews are awaiting an earthly messiah whereas the Christians accept a messiah of the divinity in Jesus. However, according to Benedict the Jewish answer of "No!" to the early Church serves a fortunate purpose of allowing the Church to move its mission to the gentile communities. Carlo Cardinal Martini S. J., the former Archbishop of Milan, expresses similar sentiments when he writes that, "Without a sincere feeling for the Jewish world and a direct experience of it, one cannot fully understand Christianity. Jesus is fully Jewish, the apostles are Jewish, and one can-not doubt their attachment to the tradition of their forefathers."[91]

Conclusion

This book does not find resonance with either the approach that sees no com-monality nor with the approach does that finds commonality without caveats.

One can assume that Judaism and Christianity share the God of monotheism, but the question becomes the caveats and the value in the commonality. Jews are usually stopped in their tracks by the concept of the Trinity since they have traditionally understood their proximal other as a repudiation of monotheism, or at best, a defective form acceptable for gentiles. Jewish understanding of the Trinity varies between tritheism and Arien lower entity.

Yet, Jewish texts have a variety of Logos theories and lower images of the Divine glory that are arranged as a lower hypostasis, never as a logic of the Trinity. Here is a text from Profiat Duran, a fifteenth century philosopher and grammarian, who treats the Trinity as divine attributes:

> They all agree that their assumption of a Trinity refers only to the attributes, which they call Persons. These attributes are distinct, not just conceptually, but *in actu*. There is one subject, the suposit, which is the divine essence which is one in utmost simplicity. Further, while the whole God became incarnate, only the attribute of the Son became incarnate. Nevertheless, they think that they can combine absolute unity and absolute simplicity. . . . They maintain that the Trinity is wisdom, power, and will (74).

But we are past just pointing out the Trinity can be explained in Jewish thought as modalities; we need a Jewish theology to discuss contemporary issues of Christology, ecclesiology, and eschatology.

6

Islam: Scripture, Prophecy, and Piety

This chapter discusses the theological similarities and differences between Judaism and Islam as represented in traditional Jewish works. Even though Jewish scholarship of the early twentieth century presented a vision of a Judeo-Islamic tradition with a linked social and cultural history, scholars have not explored theological connections between the two faiths. Therefore, in this chapter, I seek to compare theology rather than history. No attempt will be made to give a historical account of the relationship of the two faiths since there are already several good books on the subject.

First I will briefly discuss the role of Jews and Judaism in early Islam, including the relationship of Judaism to the Arabs, the representation of Jews in the Koran, and the textual treatment of Ishmael, who is represented as the genealogical link between Judaism and Islam. The texts discussed will be those that lead to the theological understanding of Islam. Especially important are the midrashim and apocalyptic tracts such as *Pirkei de-Rabbi Eliezar* and the *Secrets of Rabbi Shimon bar Yohai,* which offer both typological and apocalyptic perspectives on the new world order of Islam.

Next, I will turn to the medieval era of cosmopolitan synthesis—Islam's humanistic age under the Ummayads and Abbasids—during which the Jewish religion adopted Islamic forms to create moments of true synthesis between Judaism and Islam, especially in the realms of philosophy, theology, poetry, linguistics, jurisprudence, science, and literature. During this era, theological similarities and differences between the two faiths were formulated. While this section will include some discussion of theological similarities, like monotheism, it will focus on the basic difference between the two faiths rooted in the different revelations of Moses and Mohammed because the lack of a shared scripture has been crucial in underwriting the subsequent charges of falsification and misrepresentation on both sides. This section will examine Sa'adiah, Halevi, Maimonides, Aderet, and Ibn Kammuna. As needed, context for the Jewish texts will be provided by turning to the Muslim works.

The chapter will then consider the mix of law, kabbalah, and legend that informs the popular and legal understandings of Islam within Judaism. These features inform a range of Jewish attitudes toward Islam. Some Jews see Islam as so close to Judaism that they will pray with Muslims and attend mosques, while others see Islam as inherently idolatrous. We will conclude with a unique Jewish Fatwa defending Judaism, and some poems reflecting the Jewish debate about Sufism.

- Early Islam
- *Pirke de-Rabbi Eliezer* and *Secrets of Rabbi Shimon bar Yochai*
- Cosmopolitan Synthesis
- Sa'adiah, Halevi, Maimonides, Aderet, and Ibn Kammuna
- Law
- Exclusivism
- Fatwa and Sufi materials

Early Islam

Even though Muhammad lived after the close of the rabbinic period, there are rabbinic texts that play a role in the later Jewish encounter with Islam: some texts describe the pre-Islamic Arabs, some treat the biblical figure of Ishmael as an opposing typology to Isaac, and finally some rabbinic texts written or edited after the rise of Islam shape Jewish perceptions of Judeo-Islamic history.

The rabbinic texts are intimately aware of the pre-Islamic pagan Arab tribes, which they connect with the clans in the genealogies of Genesis and the people mentioned in *Nehemiah* (2:19; 4:7). In rabbinic texts, Arabs are depicted guiding caravans through the desert and leading a Bedouin lifestyle. The Talmud notes that the Arabs are circumcised, that their women wear veils in public, and that they domesticate camels in addition to horses (*Yevamot* 71a). It also contains some xenophobic portrayals of Arabs as untrustworthy, licentious, and larcenous.[1] Within the rabbinic texts broadly speaking, pre-Islamic Arabs are considered idolatrous. For example in the Talmud, Abraham's angelic visitors chide him saying "Do you suspect us of being Arabs who worship the dust on their feet?" (*Baba Metzia* 86b based on Genesis 18:3.)[2]

Islam is linked to the genealogy of Abraham through the rabbinic texts. Isaac is considered the true heir of Abraham; while the descendents of Abraham's other son, Ishmael, are depicted in rabbinic texts as nomadic hunters who inhabit a wide swath of the Middle East; sometimes they are also called Hagarites. Though there is no direct reference to Islam, later Jewish texts associated these peoples with ethnic representations of the Islamic conquest. Through this association, later texts connected to Islam the negative image of Ishmael in the rabbinic sources. Ishmael, as the negative counterpart of Isaac, is associated with the unrighteous descendents of Abraham, as opposed to the chosen descendants of Isaac. In Job, "the Ishmaelites" are portrayed as thieves: "The tents of the robbers prosper, and they that provoke God are secure since God brought them with His hand" (Job 12). He is depicted as violating the three cardinal sins of idolatry, sexual immorality, and murder (Genesis Rabbah 53, PT Sotah 6:6).

There is no explicit connection in Jewish texts between the Ishmaelites and Arabs until the first century BCE.

> And he [Abraham] gave to Ishmael and to his sons, and to the sons of Keturah, gifts, and he sent them away from Isaac, his son, and he gave everything to Isaac, his son. And Ishamel and his sons, and the sons of Keturah and their sons went together and they dwelt from Paran to the entrance to Babylon in all the land, which faces east opposite the desert. And these mixed with each other, and they are called Arabs and Ishmaelites (Jubilees 20:11–13).

Other sources that connect Arabs and Ishmael include Josephus, who notes that the Arabs circumcise at thirteen because of Ishmael,[3] and the Talmud, which mentions that Ishmael covers the face up to the lip (BT MQ 24a).

The traditional Muslim perspective, which also connects Ishmael to the pre-Muslim Arabs, has viewed Jewish accounts from the book of *Genesis*, which fail to support this connection, as corruptions of the original revelation (see below). Yet the citations above show that outside of *Genesis*, based on Jewish homiletic of the rabbinic texts, we find many acknowledgments of this connection.

Furthermore, the negative portrayal of Ishmael and the Ishamaelites that we sometimes find in Jewish texts actually did not arise until the rise of Islam. On the contrary, legend and midrash recount that when the Hebrews were exiled by Nebuchadnezzar and the Ishmaelite tribes of Arabia did not give water, the Arabs were viewed as innocent of any wrongdoing (PT Taanit 4:5; *Genesis Rabbah* 53:14). This is just one example of a broader trend. Before Islam, Ishmael was typically portrayed as either neutral or positive, with very few negative references. After the rise of Islam he is portrayed negatively with much more frequency and intensity.

Islam

The rise of Islam itself is mentioned in various rabbinic works that were edited in the seventh, eighth, and ninth centuries.[4] Since these texts contain no clear distinction between the rabbinic material and the additions of later editors, many later statements became canonical as rabbinical statements. The late haggadic works *Pesikta Rabbati* and *Pirkei de-Rabbi Eliezer* demonstrate knowledge of the Arab-Muslim conquest, and the later work even devotes a chapter to the fifteen subsequent changes in society.

Pirke de-Rrabbi Eliezer

Pirke de-Rabbi Eliezer, compiled between the eighth and tenth centuries, is a midrash on the biblical narrative with many parallels to both Koran and Hadith. In the early twentieth century, these parallels were mistakenly used to show the Jewish origins of Koranic stories. Currently, however, the stories are treated as either dependent on Islamic sources or derived from common antecedents.[5]

Furthermore, some chapters seem similar, or at least share common sources with the tenth century Persian historian al-Tabari's, *On Prophets and Patriarchs*. Despite probable Islamic sources, *Pirke de-Rabbi Eliezer* does depict certain events of Islamic province, such as Abraham's visit to Ishmael, with a contrarian anti-Ishmael valence.[6]

Pirke de-Rabbi Eliezer portrays the social and economic changes that occurred with the rise of Islam in the land of Israel—the land was surveyed, the cities were repaired, the Dome of the Rock was built. Despite these advances, the early years of Islam in Israel are depicted as a period of lawlessness. These rapid social changes led to an acute messianism, aided in no small part by the Islamic millenarianism of the time.[7] Looking forward to the end of time, *Pirke de-Rabbi Eliezer* foresees a great battle between Islam and Christendom, followed by the messianic era.

> R. Ishmael said: The Ishmaelites will do fifteen things in the Land (of Israel) at the End of Days, to wit: They will measure the Land with ropes, and make cemeteries (places for) the lodging of flocks and (for) trash-heaps, and they will measure from them and by them on the mountains. Deceit will increase, truth will be hidden, law will be distant from Israel, and transgressions will proliferate in Israel. The ruling kingdom will withdraw coinage. They will confuse scarlet-dye and worm, and paper and pen will decay. They will refurbish the destroyed cities and clear the roads. They will plant "gardens and orchards" (*Ecclesiastes* 2:5), and repair the holes in the walls of the Temple. They will build a structure at (the site of the) sanctuary. Two brothers will arise over them as leaders. In their days the Branch, the son of David, will arise, as scripture says: "and in the time of those kings the God of Heaven will establish a kingdom, etc." (Dan 2:44).[8]
>
> R. Ishmael also said: The Ishmaelites will fight three great battles on the earth at the End of Days, as scripture affirms: "for they fled from swords" (Isa 21:15); the expression "swords" refers to "battles." One (will be) in the forest—"from the drawn sword" (ibid.); one (will be) on the sea—"from the drawn bow" (ibid.); and one (will be) at the great city of Rome, which (will be) more fierce than the (preceding) two, as scripture states: "from the ferocity of battle" (ibid.). From there (i.e., Rome) the son of David will sprout up, and he will come to the Land of Israel and behold the destruction of both these and those, as scripture states: "Who is this *who comes from Edom*, red of garment from Bosra, this one majestic in his clothing etc." (Isa 63:1).

The Secrets of Rabbi Shimon bar Yohai

An early eyewitness account to the Arabic conquest, *The Secrets of Rabbi Shimon bar Yohai*, connects the conquest to an acute era of apocalyptic wars. The text praises Islam for saving Jews from the hands of the Christians: "The Holy one will bring the kingdom of Ishmael to save you from evil. According to His will, He will raise over them a prophet. They will conquer the land and restore it to greatness. There will be a great fight between them and Esau." These accounts do not directly discuss the Islamic religion but they do convey a sense that the kingdom of Ishmael will defeat the evil empire of Edom-Christianity. This text foresees a post-apocalyptic era in which the temple is rebuilt, and in which Islam reigns benevolently over Jews. Finally, the messiah will come to destroy Edom (a symbol for Christianity).

In the text, the angel Metatron comes to offer these good tidings of comfort to rabbi Shimon.

> He began to sit and expound (the passage) "and he beheld the Kenite" (Num 24:21). When he perceived that the kingdom of Ishmael would come (and exercise dominion over Israel), he exclaimed: "Is it not sufficient what the wicked kingdom of Edom has done to us that we should also (suffer the dominion of) the kingdom of Ishmael!?" Immediately Metatron the prince of the Presence answered him and said: "Do not be afraid, mortal, for the Holy One, blessed be He, is bringing about the kingdom of Ishmael only for the purpose of delivering you from that wicked one (i.e., Edom). He shall raise up over them a prophet in accordance with His will, and He will subdue the land for them; and they shall come and restore it with grandeur. Great enmity will exist between them and the children of Esau."

> They (Ishmael) are a deliverance for Israel like the deliverance (associated with) the "one mounted upon an ass" (Zech 9:9).

> The second king who will arise from Ishmael will be a friend of Israel. He will repair their breaches and (fix) the breaches of the Temple and shape Mt. Moriah and make the whole of it a level plain. He will build for himself there a place for prayer upon the site of the "foundation stone," as Scripture says: "and set your nest on the rock" (Num 24:21). He will wage war with the children of Esau and slaughter their troops and capture a large number of them, and (eventually) he will die in peace and with great honor.

A later version of the text from the crusader era called *The Prayer of Rabbi Shimon* shows contempt for both Islam and Christianity. In this version, Islam saves the Jews only after they are persecuted by the Islamic Ishmaelites. Muhammad is portrayed in derogatory terms and the Christians are portrayed as ruthless slaughterers who engage in child sacrifice. Jews will have to unite against both groups; God will personally bring back the lost tribes to fight the final messianic battle.[9]

> For during the final period of its rule, it will effect a great slaughter beyond measure among Israel and decree harsh edicts against Israel and announce (that) "anyone who reads Torah will be pierced by the sword." A portion of Israel will turn to their (i.e., Ishmael's) laws. At that time the kingdom of the Kenites will come to Jerusalem, subdue it, and kill more than thirty thousand within it. Due to the pressure with which they constrain Israel, the Holy One, blessed be He, will send (more) Ishmaelites against them, and they will make war with them in order to deliver Israel from their grasp. A demented, demon-possessed man—one who speaks lies about the Holy One, blessed be He—will arise and subdue the land, and there will be enmity between them (the Ishmaelites) and the children of Esau.

> I turned to Metatron and said to him, "Are the Ishmaelites a deliverance for Israel?"

> The Romans will go forth against Jerusalem and make war with the Ishmaelites. The land will be subdued by them. They will enter it (i.e., Jerusalem) and slaughter

many Ishmaelites and cast down numerous corpses in it. Each day they will sacrifice children to Jesus. At that time Israel (too) will suffer much distress, and at that moment the Lord will arouse the tribes of Israel and they will come to Jerusalem, the holy city.

Cosmopolitan Era

Islam and Judaism were intertwined historically and culturally from the rise of Islam and onward. Jews lived in the very heart of the Arabic peninsula from whence Islam grew. Jews spoke Arabic and Arabian Jews saw themselves as Arabs. After the Islamic conquest and the rise of the Caliphate, Jews lived in the center of the caliphate. The rabbinic center followed the caliphate as it shifted throughout the Islamic empire, first moving to Ummayad Baghdad, continuing though the Abbasid dynasty, then finally moving west together with the Umamyad dynasty into Spain. Jews were diffused throughout the empire. In the thirteenth century, Jews lived in the heart of Fatimid Egypt; in the sixteenth century they formed an important part of the Ottoman Empire; and for a millennium Jews lived among the North African dynasties. There are still unexplored histories waiting to be written about Jewish life in diverse Muslim lands, including Persia and Central Asia.

Muslims, however, took little particular interest in their non-Muslim subjects. Jews were tolerated as people of the book under the *dhimmi* laws and were included within the national entity (*ummah*).[10] In theory, there was never a greater similarity between Judaism and its host culture. Jews generally looked, talked, ate, and dressed as their Muslim neighbors did. For example, Jewish women wore burkas and veils. Jews would not have considered the culture in which they lived as Islamic and, therefore, other to their own. This history prompted Fritz Goitein to write, "Islam is of the very flesh and bone of Judaism."

Yet, in the 1000 years in which the majority of Jews lived under Islam, there were both good and bad periods, and the experience of Jews certainly differed country to country. Differences were sometimes rooted in different interpretation of Islamic law. There are both lenient and strict opinions in Islamic law toward Jews. Some Islamic caliphs listened to the Islamic jurists and others almost completely ignored the dhimmi laws. The variance of practice was based on many factors including: economic and political expediency.[11] The demographic makeup of a region also affected Islamic policy toward Jews. Furthermore, Ismaeli and Shiite countries, which approached Islamic law with greater leeway, showed greater latitude in their approach to Jews.

Given the varied realities of Jewish life under Islam, varied historical perspectives have arisen to describe it. Professional historians tend to stress the times of cultural synthesis and the moderate quality to Jewish life under Islam. Amateur historians tend to see more bad than good, and they emphasize periods of oppression, anti-Judaism polemics, and anti-Jewish violence.[12,13]

Despite these different views, the reality is that Jewish life was deeply embedded within Islamic culture, irrespective of the high and low points in the relationship between the two faiths; and in general, Jewish life flourished under Islam much more than under Christianity.[14] Moreover, many Jews traveled among Islamic communities and they experienced the diversity of Islam, which included Arabs, Berbers, Persians, Mongols, and Turks. A single figure such as Maimonides lived under diverse Islamic societies Almohads, Almoravids, and Fatimids; with two of them an era of cultural synthesis and one of them a regime of repression.

Thereby, Jews were comfortable enough with Islam that many aspects of medieval Jewish culture were articulated, defined, and systematized under Islam. The scholarship of the Islamic Renaissance was read and absorbed by Jews, leading them to formulate Judaism in response to Arabic culture. For instance, knowledge of Arabic linguistics allowed Jews to refine Hebrew as a sister language. Jews followed Arabic and Persian models of poetry, and Jewish law was influenced by Islamic courts and Islamic jurisprudence. In addition, Jews assiduously studied Arabic mathematics, astronomy, and medicine. A remarkable indication of the depth of this penetration of Arabic language and culture is the adoption of Islamic terminology to designate even the most sacred notions of the Jewish faith, a fact that has practically no parallel among Ashkenazi Jewry prior to the modern era. For example, the Hebrew Bible would be referred to as the Koran, the halakhah as the sharia, and Moses as *rasul Allah* "the Apostle of Allah."[15]

Starting in the last half of the twelfth century, when Jews lived in the Mediterranean countries reconquered by the Christians, the translation of Arabic classics into Hebrew rapidly increased. Jews always had been avid readers of Arabic, and now the translations into Hebrew for Jewish audiences in Christian Spain, France, and Italy, transformed the Arabic texts into part of the Jewish canon. Jews regularly read works of Muslim theologians and would translate them into Hebrew for their coreligionists who were not fortunate enough to know Arabic. This contrasts remarkably with the medieval Jewish view of Christian texts; in Northern Europe Jews did not read Christian texts and even the Roman alphabet was eschewed as gentile and Christian.

Though Muslim theologians were the intellectual guides for Jewish thinkers, they also remained their competitors. Jews of this period, therefore, refrained from discussing or portraying Muslims at all. The translated works were denuded of Jewish-Muslim differences, although the Islamic texts were known and assumed to be known by Jewish writers. Many authors had to grapple with whether to reproduce the citations from the Koran in Arabic works, or to paraphrase them as known wisdom or substitute biblical verses.[16] Since the authors still worked in an Arabic literary world, many did not have a clear sense of what was culturally Muslim and what was Jewish.[17] For instance, Moses ibn Ezra uses passages from the Koran as examples of literary poetics.

One Islamic theological work that had a wide circulation in Hebrew, almost as wide as many Jewish works, was the writing of Al-Ghazzali with his unique mixture of jurisprudence, Kalam, Falasifa, and Sufi piety. Al-Ghazzali's *Balance of Human Action* (*Mizan al-amal*) was translated into Hebrew by Abraham ibn Hasdai as *Meozne Zedek*. The text provides an important window into the process of cultural translation. In the Hebrew version, Koranic proof texts were replaced with biblical verses. While the translation maintains a deep respect for Muslim wisdom, it regards it as universal philosophy and removes it from its cultural and religious context.[18] That is, Al-Ghazzali functioned the way Kant, Kierkegaard, and Dewey functioned for modern Jews.

> Although [al-Ghazzali] was a great sage who inclined toward philosophy, he would support his demonstrations with . . . texts of their faith and the stories that are among their wise men. It is from the weakness of their books and the feebleness of their writings that they bring proofs for their claims, to strengthen and support their opinions. A fortiori those whose words are smelted from gold, sweeter than honey, built and founded upon the line of truth, their source a spring of living water, their proofs are more limpid and pure, stronger and more truthful. Therefore I decided to supply, according to my ability, words similar to the original from our holy books so that I will go in the path of the author and not depart from his course, and not veer to the right or the left.[19]

Jonathan Dechter compares the texts where the Koran is removed and replaced with the Bible to cases where the Koran is presented as the works of the universal sages. Dechter cites the Hebrew poet and translator Yehudah Al-Harizi (d. 1225) quotes the first Sura of the Koran as the words of a sage, rather than Muhammad. Al-Harizi changes the text by adding the word father to first Sura.[20]

> A Sage used to insert the following into his prayers, saying: "God, the One the Father (!), the Merciful, King of Judgment Day, you we worship and in you we take refuge. Show us the straight path (ba-derekh ha-yesharah), the path of those upon whom you have shown compassion, not that of those upon whom you have shown anger—they are the confounded ones.[21]

Al-Harizi also quotes Q 57:26, "All excellence is in the hand of God; he gives it to who he will," which in the original discusses the excellence of the Muslims, to demonstrate that God gave the excellence of eloquence to the Jews.

In addition to relying on Muslim theology itself to provide universal philosophical wisdom, Jewish philosophy also built upon the Islamic reception of Plato and Aristotle as well as the medieval synthesis by the great Islamic philosophers and theologians. It is important to note that Jewish theologians formulated their theology of Judaism using the categories of the Muslim theologians, the Muatazilites and the Falasifa, especially Ghazzalli, Ibn Sina, and Farabi. Furthermore, Jewish thinkers including Yehudah Halevi, Maimonides, Aderet, and Ibn Kammuna also relied heavily on the Muslim thinker Ibn Hazm's summary of the Islamic criticisms of Judaism as they distinguished Judaism from Islam for themselves. Therefore, before proceeding with the Jewish theologian's views of Islam, we will first briefly consider the Islamic views of Judaism that influenced them.

Theological Differences

Both Judaism and Islam have historically recognized fundamental commonalities between the two faiths, their shared monotheism in particular. Maimonides's son, Rabbi Abraham, praised Islam because "Muslims are monotheists who abhor idolatry."[22] Furthermore, the two faiths share a common conception of revelation and prophecy as the basis for religion, and both employed and reshaped common ideas of Second Temple Judaism(s). They also share the vast amount of Jewish traditions contained in Islam (*Israliyat*).

On the other hand, the two faiths have also historically acknowledged fundamental differences. While Islam positions itself as the final seal of the prophets, medieval Jews sought to construe Islam as derivative of Judaism, denying Muhammad's prophecy. Muslims, in turn, sought to play down the Sinai revelation and to generally minimize the direct influence of Jewish materials upon Islam. In addition, Jews saw Islam as a religion of violence, as an abnegation of Torah, and as a version of ignorance.

While this book is on Judaism's view of Islam, it is important to note that Islam's view of Judaism served as background for the Jewish authors. Since Islam is not my area of expertise, I will be following the accounts given by Camilla Adnag and Jacques Waardenburg.

The early Mecca *Sirra* have little to say against contemporary Jews. In contrast the later Medinah *Sirra* portray Jews as unreliable and treacherous, and accuse them of altering scripture and ignoring God's word. The early texts from the Mecca period treat Judaism as part of Muhammad's nation. The Koran is very explicit when it says "there is no compulsion in religion," (Quran 2:256). Elsewhere the Koran exhorts Jews to live by the laws revealed to them in the Torah (5:43).

The Medina texts charge the Jews with a number of wrongs, including corrupting scripture, following incorrect doctrines, and engaging in needless rites. With regard to corrupting scripture, Jews are charged with abrogation (*naskh*), falsification (*tahrif*), and unreliable transmission (*tawatur*) (4:160). Jews are also depicted as marked for punishment by God. God acted toward the Jews with good deeds: "In his grace, God, through Moses, gave the children of Israel their scripture and saved them from Pharaoh but the Jews showed nothing but ingratitude. The Jews questioned and murmured against Moses and they wrongfully followed incorrect dietary laws."[23] The punishment for the former sin was poverty; for the latter Jews were condemned to follow the Kosher dietary laws. Other sins of the Jews recorded in the Koran include driving people from their homes, charging interest, and stealing through deception.[24] Camilla Adang, in her fine work on *Muslim Attitudes Toward Judaism*, opines that though the Islamic attitude stops well short of deicide, it nevertheless presents a social and theological problem.[25] Ignatz Goldziher, the great Jewish lover of Islam, wrote in 1878 that the polemic against Judaism started in the Koran itself.

Different narratives of revelation between the two faiths motivated Islam's charges that the Jews had tampered with the Bible, perhaps the most serious negative depiction of the Jews in the Koran. The charge of abrogation claims that the Jews used the revelation of Moses to replace the truer, earlier revelation of Abraham. In a Muslim reading, the revelation of Moses needlessly annulled the revelation of Abraham and Jacob. Muslims privilege the revelations of Abraham along with those of Muhammad, while Jewish theologians claim that Moses's is the true revelation and say that it is impossible for God to change his mind and give new revelations. This tension between the two faiths grew and in later centuries the abrogation charge was changed to a charge of deliberate falsification (*tahrif*).

The charge of misunderstanding is based on an Islamic view that the Jews simply did not have a reliable tradition of the revelation. Those who charge misunderstanding accept the Bible and quote the Bible, whereas those accepting the charge of falsification do not trust the Bible enough to quote it. In general, Muslims did not see the Bible as revelation and prophecy, but as a dubious record written long after the original revelation. There is significant literature on the relationship of the Bible and Islam beyond our interfaith scope.[26]

In the Islamic telling of the event at Sinai, the laws of Sinai were either needlessly self-imposed by the Jews as a falsification of the original revelation or they were given by God as a punishment. Brannon Wheeler quotes Abu al-Qasam Zamakhshari (twelfth century theologian and exegete) who wrote that the Jews were punished with dietary restriction; Jews writing later repackaged this punishment as revelation. In this case, the Jews did not deliberately falsify, but misunderstood and therefore misrepresented the significance of Moses at Sinai. In the Kalam, there are further charges against Judaism. These texts charge that Jews have removed biblical references to the resurrection of the dead, and enumerate other misleading mistakes, for example, substituting Isaac for Ishmael and including Isaiah and Jeremiah, whom the Koran omits. A greater charge is that Jews misread the revelation of God as a private revelation, limited to the chosen people, rather than as revelation for the entire world. Ali Ibn Rabban Al-Tabiri (ninth century) stated that the world needed a new revelation that superseded the revelation of the Jews. The Torah, which describes and addresses one nation, cannot lay claim to universal validity. It is therefore viewed by some Islamic texts as a source of curses and injustices, while Koran provides forgiveness and mercy. Finally, Islam rejects the anthropomorphic representation of God found in the Bible and Talmud, for example the representation of God resting on the Sabbath; Muslims deny that God needs to rest.[27]

The major Islamic theological critique of Judaism, which incorporated many of the prior critiques, was written by Ibn Hazm (Cordova, 994–1064 CE), a Muslim theologian, jurist, and literary historian. He was famous for the *Fisal* (Detailed Critical Examination), in which he offers a critical survey of different systems of philosophical thought in relation to religious beliefs among the skeptics, Peripatetics, Brahmans, Zoroastrians and other dualists, Jews, and Christians. Ibn Hazam used the examination of these religions to establish the preeminence of Islam.[28]

Ibn Hazm shifted earlier polemics against Jews in two respects. First, he revised the narrative of Islam's supersession of Judaism; rather than Islam rising to preeminence after the Jews lost the covenant through sin, Ibn Hazm claims that the Jews never really had a covenant and were always idol worshipers who did not follow Abraham. He argues that from the Golden calf to Menasheh and Jehoiakim the Jews were as bad as the pre-Islamic Arabs. Ibn Hazm stated that the common Israelite had no knowledge of Torah and speculated that they collectively possessed only one manuscript of the Torah, which was hidden away and not taught in public. According to Ibn Hazm's reading of biblical history, there were seven periods of mass apostasy by the Israelites, some up to forty years, leading to an almost complete loss of the tradition (223).

Second, Ibn Hazm shifted the discussion from saying Jews misunderstood their revelation to say that the Jews falsified their revelation. Following earlier texts, Ibn Hazm finds the Hebrew Bible filled with anthropomorphisms.

> In a book of the Jews entitles the *Shiur Qoma* . . . it is said that the length of the Creator's forehead measured from its upper part to its nose, is 5000 cubits. May God preserve us from ascribing shape, size, limits, and boundaries to Him. . . .

> In another book of the Talmud . . . it is written that on the head of the creator there is a crown in which are 1000 quintars of gold and that on the finger there is a ring from which the sun and the stars radiate and that the angel who ministers to the crown is called Sandelphon ... smaller god ... cries slowly while plucking his hairs: woe unto me, I have destroyed my house and made my sons and daughters orphans.

He is shocked by the Talmudic image of God weeping among the ruins of the Temple. As a result of these passages Ibn Hazm concludes that the sayings of the rabbis show their depravity and that the Talmud is a compilation of old wives tales. However, of the charges against Judaism this was the easiest to respond to since Saadyah, Bahye, Maimonides, and others removed the anthropomorphism from Judaism.

Medieval Jewish Positions

We will now consider Jewish statements about Islam from Saadyah, Yehudah Halevi, Maimonides, Aderet, and Ibn Kammuna with an excursus on the Islamic presentation of Judaism to which the above authors were responding in their writings.

Sa'adiah

Sa'adiah Gaon (882–942) was a leading rabbi and early medieval Jewish philosopher whose *Book of Beliefs and Opinions* set the parameters for the tradition of Jewish philosophy, differentiating Judaism from Christian and Islamic thought. Sa'adiah knew the Islamic tradition well, especially Arabic poetics and Kalam theology. Many of Sa'adiah's arguments were already fully developed in the writings of the Karites such as Qirqisani.

Sa'adiah as a theological defender of the truth of Judaism, which for him was based on Mosaic prophecy, had to preclude the acceptance of Muhammad's prophecy. In his theological differentiation of the two faiths Sa'adiah defines prophecy within the Jewish faith as a metaconscious state predicated on the prophet's prior intellectual and moral perfection. Sa'adiah points out that, in contrast, Islam's prophet Muhammad was illiterate and the Koran, understood as

God's speech, is seen as outside and above human logic; since Muhammad did not achieve prophecy through perfection, Muslims must believe in the miraculousness of the event.

Sa'adiah emphasized the role of logic in prophecy in a variety of ways. He wrote that the Jews did not believe in Moses due to miracles alone, but rather because the message of Moses was intellectually sound and Moses could prove its truth. Sa'adiah also minimized the miracles of Islam by distinguishing between true miracles and magic. Real prophets perform miracles, while false prophets, like Muhammad, deceive with magic or natural events that appear as miracles. Sa'adiah also argued that Judaism was an authenticated tradition in that many people witnessed the prophecy of Moses. He emphasized the importance of witnesses over the prevalence of the tradition and the authority of its source for authenticating the tradition, thereby casting suspicions on the authenticity of Mohammed's revelation. Finally, Sa'adiah goes out of his way to translate every proper noun in the Bible in order to show that Jews have a better tradition.[29]

These arguments will be continued and refined by Yehudah Halevi and Mamonides. The former emphasizes the reliable tradition argument, and the latter emphasizes the inability of a nonintellectual to receive prophecy.[30]

Kuzari

Yehuda Halevi (c. 1075–1141), a twelfth-century heir to Spanish philosophical and poetic traditions, wrote a defense of Judaism called *Treatise in Defense of a Despised Tradition*, popularly known as *The Kuzari*. The opening of Halevi's book is written in the form of a fictitious dialogue between a Jew, Muslim, and Christian, each attempting to convince a pagan king about the truth of his religion.

Halevi's book is embedded in Islamic culture and both borrow from and respond to the world of Islamic religious thought, piety, Sufism, and Kalam. He uses many of the theological arguments of the Islamic thinker Al-Ghazzali against materialists and philosophers, and is also acutely aware of the Islamic science of the law, especially where it presents Judaism as a reliable tradition (*silsila*). In particular, Halevi grapples with Sufis' piety, preferring a pietistic heart over external practices of asceticism and seclusion. He also views the Kalam theology of Muatazilites as the most compatible with Judaism since it mediates between the emphasis on predestined Divine will of the Asherite form of Kalam and the naturalism of the Falasifa philosophers.

Halevi presents Islam as the monotheistic religion of an eternal God, and credits Islam with removing anthropomorphism from religion. On the other hand, Halevi rejects the claim that the Koran is a special speech of God, which cannot be judged by human standards, and also rejects the notion that Islam has superseded all other religions. In addition, he is uncomfortable with Islam's corporeal image of the afterlife.

Halevi places these reservations about Islam in the mouth of the pagan King, who dismisses the special status of the Koran and is skeptical toward its revelation.

Speaking for Halevi, the King asks: How can we know that revelation is real and not a figment of the imagination or magical thinking? To ensure against these doubts, revelation must be public and subject to scrutiny.

> He then invited one of the Doctors of Islām, and questioned him regarding his doctrine and observance. The Doctor said: We acknowledge the unity and eternity of God, and that all men are derived from Adam-Noah. We absolutely reject embodiment, and if any element of this appears in the Writ, we explain it as a metaphor and allegory. At the same time we maintain that our Book is the Speech of God, being a miracle which we are bound to accept for its own sake, since no one is able to bring anything similar to it, or to one of its verses. Our prophet is the Seal of the prophets, who abrogated every previous law, and invited all nations to embrace Islām. The reward of the pious consists in the return of his spirit to his body in paradise and bliss, where he never ceases to enjoy eating, drinking, woman's love, and anything he may desire. The requital of the disobedient consists in being condemned to the fire of hell, and his punishment knows no end.
>
> Although your book may be a miracle, as long as it is written in Arabic, a non-Arab, as I am, cannot perceive its miraculous character; and even if it were read to me, I could not distinguish between it and any other book written in the Arabic language.
>
> Al Khazari: Exactly so; but the human mind cannot believe that God has intercourse with man, except by a miracle which changes the nature of things. He then recognizes that to do so He alone is capable who created them from nought. It must also have taken place in the presence of great multitudes, who saw it distinctly, and did not learn it from reports and traditions. Even then they must examine the matter carefully and repeatedly, so that no suspicion of imagination or magic can enter their minds. Then it is possible that the mind may grasp this extraordinary matter, viz. that the Creator of this world and the next, of the heavens and lights, should hold intercourse with this contemptible piece of clay, I mean man, speak to him, and fulfill his wishes and desires.
>
> The Doctor: Is not our Book full of the stories of Moses and the Children of Israel? No one can deny what He did to Pharaoh, how He divided the sea, saved those who enjoyed.

Halevi seeks to undercut Muslim supersessionalism, which claims Muhammad was most trustworthy since he was the last of the prophets. Halevi claims instead that the original recipients of knowledge are most reliable, rather than the most recent. He points out that the Koran presents biblical stories that were first given to Israel.[31]

Halevi's major defense of Judaism is to assert its chosenness. While Islam follows the universal God of Adam, Jews have a special relationship with God, who created a covenant with the Jewish patriarchs. The Torah, given to Jews by the patriarchs, and later Moses, is not just a revealed book but an entire realm of revealed religion reserved for the Jewish people. Moses's addition to the original law of Adam and Noah was crucial for the Jewish people to reach their perfection. Most importantly, Halevi notes, the Jews are the one special people who observed the biblical miracles and are thereby more reliable than later prophets.

> The Rabbi replied: I believe in the God of Abraham, Isaac and Israel, who led the children of Israel out of Egypt with signs and miracles; who fed them in the desert and gave them the land, after having made them traverse the sea and the Jordan in a miraculous way; who sent Moses with His law, and subsequently thousands of prophets, who confirmed His law by promises to the observant, and threats to the disobedient. Our belief is comprised in the Tōrāh—a very large domain.

> The Rabbi: Up to this time they had only a few laws which they had inherited from Adam and Noah. These laws were not abrogated by Moses, but rather increased by him.[32]

Maimonides

Moses Maimonides (1138–1204), the great codifier and systematizer of medieval Jewish law and theology, presents several highly influential statements about Islam almost as side notes to his grand vision.

Most of Maimonides's statements are found in a letter that he had written for the comfort of Jews facing forced conversions in Yemen. The letter is a complex historical document combining Maimonides's true opinions with comfort, polemic, and historical and theological explanations of Islam. Maimonides portrays Muhammad as a madman, who could not have had a true revelation since he was not intellectually prepared. Muhammad, according to Maimonides, presented himself as a false messiah and gathered renegade and foolish followers. Then, Maimonides says, the so-called prophet fabricated a one-dimensional religion without esoteric meaning, which could not perfect society or produce an ideal state.[33]

> After him arose the Madman who emulated his precursor since he paved the way for him. But he added the further objective of procuring rule and submission, and he invented his well known religion.

> But only a simpleton who lacks knowledge of both would liken divine institutions to human practices.

> A person ignorant of the secret meaning of Scripture and the deeper significance of the Law, would be led to believe that our religion has something in common with another if he makes a comparison between the two. For he will note that in the Torah there are prohibitions and commandments, just as in other religions there are permitted and interdicted acts. Both contain a system of religious observances, positive and negative precepts, sanctioned by reward and punishment.

> If he could only fathom the inner intent of the law, then he would realize that the essence of the true divine religion lies in the deeper meaning of its positive and negative precepts, every one of which will aid man in his striving after perfection, and remove every impediment to the attainment of excellence.

> These commands will enable the throng and the elite to acquire moral and intellectual qualities, each according to his ability. Thus the godly community becomes

pre-eminent, reaching a two-fold perfection. By the first perfection I mean, man's spending his life in this world under the most agreeable and congenial conditions. The second perfection would constitute the achievement of intellectual objectives, each in accordance with his native powers.

The tenets of the other religions which resemble those of Scripture have no deeper meaning, but are superficial imitations, copied from and patterned after it. . . . However; their counterfeiting is an open secret to the learned. Consequently they became objects of derision and ridicule just as one laughs and smiles at an ape when it imitates the actions of men.

The Muslim philosopher, Farabi, taught that the purpose of religion and political leaders is to create a virtuous city that administers justice and allows the development of its citizens. Maimonides thinks that Islam does not fulfill this requirement of creating a just society, while Judaism does. It is significant to note that Maimonides does not allow comparison between Jewish and Islamic law despite the inherent closeness of the two legal systems. It is also worth noting Maimonides's dehumanizing talk—comparing Muslims to apes.

Maimonides concedes for polemical reasons that the Bible did indeed refer to Muhammad, but emphasizes that the reference to Muhammad in the book of *Daniel* is a critique. Islam is predicted in the Bible as one of the four evil kingdoms ruling the world.

Thus Daniel in his description of the rise of the Arabic kingdom after the fall of the Roman Empire, alluded to the appearance of the Madman and his victories over the Roman, Persian, and Byzantine Empires in the vision concerning a horn which grew, became long and strong . . . "I considered the horns, and, behold, there came among them another horn, a little one, before which three of the first horns were plucked up by the roots; and, behold, in this horn were eyes like the eyes of a man, and a mouth speaking great things." (Daniel 7:8).

In your letter you mention that the apostle has spurred on a number of people to believe that several verses in Scripture allude to the Madman, such as "bimeod meod"(Genesis 17:20), "he shined forth from Mount Paran" (Deuteronomy 33:1), "a prophet from the midst of thee" (Deuteronomy 18:15), and the promise to Ishmael "I will make him a great nation" (Genesis 17:20) . . . Neither the untutored multitude nor the apostates themselves who delude others with them, believe in them or entertain any illusions about them.

But the Muslims themselves put no faith in their own arguments; they neither accept nor cite them, because they are manifestly so fallacious. Inasmuch as the Muslims could not find a single proof in the entire Bible nor a reference or possible allusion to their prophet which they could utilize, they were compelled to accuse us saying, "You have altered the text of the Torah, and expunged every trace of the name of Mohammed there from." They could find nothing stronger than this ignominious argument the falsity of which is easily demonstrated to one and all by the following facts.

First, Scripture was translated into Syriac, Greek, Persian and Latin hundreds of years before the appearance of Mohammed. Secondly, there is a uniform tradition as to the text of the Bible both in the East and the West, with the result that no differences in the text exist at all . . . The motive for their accusation lies therefore, in the absence of any allusion to Mohammed in the Torah . . . The phrase "a great nation"—phrase "bimeod meod," is A.H.M.D. and not M.H.M.D.

Maimonides asserts that the Jewish religion is based on the revelations of Moses and Sinai—not on the revelation to Abraham. Maimonides also rejects the notion that other prophets were needed to complete Moses's prophecy. Though later prophets served important social functions, they simply continued the Message of Sinai. Jewish revelation exhibits neither misunderstandings nor willful changes of Mosaic prophecy; nothing of Moses's Law is to be abrogated or superseded. The memory of the Sinai event is central for Jews as the source of religion.

> God is one in a unique sense of the term, and Moses is His prophet and spokesman, and the greatest and most perfect of the seers. To him was vouchsafed by God what has never been vouchsafed to any prophet before him, nor will it be in the future. The entire Torah was divinely revealed to Moses of whom it was said, "with him do I speak mouth to mouth." (Numbers 12:8). It will neither be abrogated nor superseded, neither supplemented nor abridged. Never shall it be supplanted by another divine revelation containing positive and negative duties. Keep well in mind the Revelation on Sinai in accordance with the divine precept to perpetuate the memory of this occasion and not to allow it to fall into oblivion. Furthermore we were enjoined to impress this event upon the minds of our children, as it is written, "Only take heed to thyself, and keep thy soul diligently, lest thou forget the things which thine eyes saw, and lest they depart from thy heart all the days of thy life; but make them known unto thy children and thy children's children." (Deuteronomy 4:9).

> Our disbelief in the prophecy of Omar and Zeid is not due to the fact that they are non-Jews,

> For Job, Zophar, Bildad, Eliphaz, and Elihu are all considered prophets and are non-Jews. On the other hand, although Hananiah, the son of Azur was a Jew, he was deemed an accursed and false prophet. Whether one should yield credence to a prophet or not depends upon the nature of his doctrines, and not upon his race, Scripture prohibits us from making any amendments to the Law or eliminating anything, for we read "Thou shalt not add thereto, nor diminish from it" (Deuteronomy 13:1).

There is an opening here to allow gentile prophets if they meet the intellectual requirements of a prophet. However, Omar and Zeid, companions of Muhammad, are rejected by Jews not because they are non-Jews but because they do not meet the requirements of prophecy.

> Transcendent wisdom is a sine qua non for inspiration. It is an article of our faith that the gift of prophecy is vouchsafed only to the wise, the strong, and the rich. Strong is defined as the ability to control one's passions. Rich signifies wealthy in knowledge. Now if we dare not put trust in a man's pretensions to prophecy, if he does not excel in wisdom, how much less must we take seriously the claims of an ignoramus to be the Messiah.

Other scholars have elaborated Maimondes's view that Muhammad could have not been a true prophet. Moses ben Joshua of Narbonne (died after 1362) was a Catalonian physician and philosopher who wrote an important commentary on Maimonides's *Guide of the Perplexed*. Narboni emphasizes Maimonides's view that one's intellect is not ready for prophecy at any time but needs to be purified to receive prophecy from the active intellect. Narboni connects this need for perfection to the Maimonidean understanding of Exodus 20:18–19 in which the masses who did not have developed intellects only heard lightening and thunder at Mt. Sinai, since it is impossible for undeveloped intellects to receive prophecy. For Narboni, Maimonides's principles are valid, and just as the masses at Sinai could not receive prophecy, neither could Muhammad have received prophecy.[34]

> Now how is it that a verse from their Law accords with the secrets of reality? And how is it that statements from that Law offer instruction in the divine secrets? No one who has understood what our Master Moses [Maimonides], peace be upon him, explained in his book the Guide concerning his division of the religions will be amazed by this.

> "This has also happened with regard to the prophetic perfection. For we find people who laid a claim to prophecy and said things with regard to which there had never been any time a prophetic revelation coming from God." (Guide 2:40)
> (Narboni links the references in Maimonides about sexual indulgence with Muhammad).

> This would be like those who plagiarize our perfect Law or the prophecy of Abraham, who fulfilled the Torah in its entirety and who commanded it to his children in the form of a testament. Then arose a man (i.e. Muhammad) who claimed credit for his prophecy of that testament, calling it a Law.[35]

A sixteenth century Yemenite poet, Zekhariyah al-Dâhiri, was inspired by Maimonides's position to compose a fictional disputation between a Muslim and a Jew. The Jew explains that in His wisdom, God sent Muhammad to uproot idolatry from their minds. However, the Muslim prophet added to his prophecy false notions and a few confused precepts. Yet, the spiritual development of humanity is analogous to that of an infant who is introduced to solids only after having been weaned from its mother's milk.

> The sage (Maimonides) stated that Muhammad's appearance was only to prepare the path of the Messiah. Indeed when Israel's savior will come you will say to our ears "our forefathers have inherited naught but falsehood" (Jer. 16: 19). Do not then imagine that your creed is perfect and your religion complete, nor that your worldly triumph is a proof, . . . for truth will triumph with the return of prophecy to Zion. He who says otherwise speaks falsehood, for prophecy is the exclusive prerogative of the Land of Israel and is not to be found amongst Se'ir and Ishmael. Indeed, a prerequisite of prophecy is to be endowed with wondrous knowledge, unlike the raving prophet (Muhammad) who, moreover, each day would deflower a different maiden. Only when man is sanctified and possessed of a 'new heart' can the Divine Presence rest upon him."[36]

Solomon ben Abraham Aderet

Solomon ben Abraham Aderet (known as Rashba 1235–1310) was a Catalonian Talmudist and legal authority under the Christian king of Aragon, responsible for the creation of a working Jewish civil law. Aderet is noteworthy in this context for having written one of the few full length treatises against the Islamic critiques of Judaism. In this context, I seek only to offer the flavor and outline of this important work.

According to Aderet, Muslims posit that Jews and Jewish texts do not contain the correct versions of the biblical stories.[37] Their claim is that Jews do not have continuity with the biblical prophets and therefore have no reliable tradition from them because when Jews sinned with the Golden Calf and innumerable times in the era of the Kings of Judah and Israel, they also forgot the biblical message and did not preserve the correct text. The Book of Kings explicitly describes how the Jews went after idols, forgot the Torah, and Josiah had to restore the Torah. In this Muslim reading, the Jews are not much different in their idolatry than the pagan Arab tribes.

> The madman said that the Torah was never in the hands of the Jews, only in the hands of the priests, as leader, and it was not given to anyone but him. For more than a thousand years it was like this and it became mistaken over time from their lack of religion, the denial of kings and their desire for the worship of statues, and their building of palaces for them and their killing of people of faith, and the loss of prophets and the killing and the destruction of them from the first to the last. In their worship of statues, they placed aside the religion of the Torah completely until there was only one priest left.

For Aderet, Muslims claim that much of the Jewish religion was lost before Josiah's restoration, when Menashe removed God's name from the text and when Jehoiakim entirely burned the Torah. After the Torah was lost from the Jews during the reign of these monarchs "it was returned to them after the destruction of their kingdom, by one of the scribes called Ezra." In the Muslim tradition, the Hebrew Bible was the product of Ezra, who is portrayed as a loyal scribe in most early Islamic literature and as a deceitful forger by the Muslim polemist Ibn Hazm.[38]

Aderet vehemently denies all these claims against the Jewish tradition and categorically states that the Jewish people since Sinai have had continuous knowledge of the Torah. He totally rejects the notions that only a few priests had copies of the Torah, rather he says, "this is a great mistake since the Torah was given to all." When Moses wrote the Book of the Torah, he gave it to the Priests, Levites, and elders of the people who in turn taught the Torah to all the children of Israel. "It was commanded to write the Torah on stones in order for those stones to last forever and all those who come will learn." In addition, the Torah was known to non-Jews through the translations of the covenant carved in stone at the mountains of Gerezim and Eval. "It was commanded that even the other nations would know the Torah, available written in 70 languages (Sotah 32a)." Aderet considers the inference from Jehoiakim blatantly false and asserts that "not even one letter from the Torah was lost or destroyed."[39]

In place of Muhammad, Aderet situates Noah as the direct prophet to the gentiles. The Mosaic prophecy was special for the Jews and was directly given to the people in order that it should not be doubted and to prevent future imposters.

> Contemplate that there are two Torahs—the Torah of Noah and the Torah of Moses. God did not want them received by our prophet but from a prophet of the other nations. This is to teach two major principles.

> First, that one who is obligated in the way of the Torah is not to have any doubts about acceptance or to suspect the one from whom he received it that he deceived from his heart or he confused it slightly.

> Second: in order to prevent a future mistake in religion. It will make sure that in the future someone cannot claim that God gave by his hand at present [a Torah] like the giving of the original Torah. A prophet cannot collect all the contents of the original Torah in one time and claim that he received a revelation from the Almighty, because in the original [Torah] God placed his spirit on them and they prophecized. No one who comes after the giving of the Torah can uproot it because we can demand [to the new prophet] to reveal it to us now and we will accept as prophecy only what was taught to us in the original giving of the Torah at Mt Sinai.

Aderet answered many of the other specific theological charges against Judaism. Following Maimonides, Aderet writes that the revelation was a hearing of the mind not of the senses, so prophecy cannot rest on an illiterate.

> In Babylon there were other sages and prophets besides Ezra, such as Daniel and his friends, Mordechai, Zerubavel, and Haggai Zechariah, and Malakhi. They were true prophets and their prophecy is not denied by any of the other religions. There was also in their midst a great community of great Sages that knew the entire Torah. If so, how can you say it was forgotten and restored by Ezra alone? Know, that our holy Torah is called "the Torah of the Lord is complete" (Psalm 19:8) something complete is not lacking in any way or having extra.[40]

Turning to other critiques of Ibn Hazam, Aderet acknowledges that prayer was instituted in place of sacrifice, but only because sacrifice cannot be done according to the original intent of Mosaic law. He further argues that the laws of the Bible are God's intention and therefore that the prohibition against eating the sciatic nerve is not punishment from God nor are the other dietary restrictions. Instead these are God's original will. Finally, Aderet responds to the perceived discrepancy between the Bible and the Talmud. He first argues that the Talmud is not a substitute for the Bible, and then explains the value of the Oral law. "We do not follow Talmud instead of Bible. The Bible is a book of wisdom that has much hidden within it—just like the works of the philosophers that have later commentaries which present the depths of the original." Since the text of the Torah is filled with wisdom and multiple meanings, it is given to readings beyond the surface.[41]

Ibn Kammuna

Said ibn Mansur Ibn Kammuna (Baghdad, d. 1284) was a Jewish thirteenth-century eye doctor and philosopher. As a resident of Mongol Baghdad, which did not have an established religion, he was free to criticize other religions. Though his philosophic works were so important in their own time, they have fallen into obscurity over the centuries. The publication of his book originally caused rioting in Baghdad, forcing Ibn Kammuna to flee that city in secret; this was recorded by the thirteenth century historian Ibn al-Fuwati. "In this year 1284 it became known in Baghdad that the Jew Ibn Kammuna had written a volume in which he displayed impudence in the discussion of the prophecies."[42]

Ibn Kammuna wrote an examination of the three monotheistic religions, titled *Examination of the Three Faiths*, from the perspective of a somewhat lapsed Jew skeptical toward all three faiths but still accepting of theism, prophecy, and following God's will. The fundamental premise of the treatise is that there is a single theory of prophecy accepted by Jews, Christians, and Muslims alike, and which, more-over, meets the truth standards of philosophy. Ibn Kammuna freely uses Ibn Sina (d.1037), al-Ghazali (d. 1111), Maimonides, Al-Razi (d. 1209) as a foundation.

Ibn Kammuna is unique in his emphasis on the mutual ignorance that exists between Jews and Muslims, despite their cultural proximity.

> The Jews may say: if the contacts of non-Jews with us were as close as our contacts with Muslims, this necessarily would be known concerning our faith. But the contact of Muslims with Jews does not necessitate a Muslim inquiry into what the Jews assert, especially since the Jews are prevented from declaring their creed, and their books are in a tongue the Muslims do not understand. The contact of a minority with a majority affects the majority and the minority differently. Thus, when a linguistic minority is in contact with a linguistic majority, the minority learns the language of the majority whilst the majority does not learn the language of the minority or, at best, learns it much later. Moreover, despite numerous contacts of the bulk of the Jews with the Muslims, many Jews still do not know the basic Islamic tenets known by the rank and file Muslims, let alone the elite. It is even more natural that a similar situation should obtain on the Muslim side, or, at the very least, that both sides should be equal [in mutual ignorance].

> It is possible that Muhammad had read or heard the books of earlier prophets and had selected and compiled what was best in them; or that, attentive to the words of men, he studied them, chose and collected the more remarkable expressions and fine points and thus produced the Koran.[43]

Yet Ibn Kammuna, himself, did study Islam and was not swayed by Muhammad's prophecy. Like many before and after him, he considered the Jewish material as the source of the Koran. Discrepancies between the two texts exist because "the quotations from the Torah and other scriptures were translated into Arabic inexactly and were considerably distorted." In this way, Ibn Kammuna reverses the Islamic argument against the reliability of Jewish revelation, stating that the "verses of Koran have not been accurately transmitted." He notes that since the Koran was only known to a few people in Muhammad's lifetime, error may have crept in; certainly, collusion is also possible. Using inter-Islamic debates against Islam as a whole, he states that there is no evidence for the miraculous in the language of Koran. He cites Islamic debates over words, order, additions, deletions, and even contradictions to challenge the reliability of the Koranic tradition.[44]

Ibn Kammuna notes that despite the monotheism of Islam, Muslim practice maintains traces of ancient paganism. He takes exception to thinking that the only right religious acts are those commanded by God through Islam, observing that both Farabi and Maimonides taught that religion sought to create a just society, yet Islam has not had the wisdom to succeed. He challenges Islam's claims of creating the perfect man, writing that that people convert to Islam for ulterior motives. He regards the Prophet Muhammad as "unoriginal" and "imperfect."

> It has been said, however, that the Black Stone was one of the idols that was in the Ka'ba, but that, unlike the other idols, it was not removed. Muslims to this day seek closeness to God through kissing and touching the Black Stone, which is a kind of worship. The idolaters do not believe idols create heaven and earth; no sensible person does. But they do feel that idol worship brings one closer to God . . .

> Submission to God is enjoined upon man in the other faiths, also, *If* it is said that what non-Muslims do in their prayer, fasting, and other specific rites is *no* worship, for worship is that which is done in accordance with God's commands and is not abrogated by another religion, and that which the non-Muslims do does not come under this category.

> Further, how can Muhammad be called the most perfect man in practical wisdom when Muslim kings, in carrying out government and maintaining law and order in the polity, are compelled to violate the religious law in stipulations on punishment and retaliation, and so on? . . . This is no secret to anyone acquainted with Muslim jurisprudence and with the evil and corruption people sink into.

> We will not concede that Muhammad added to the knowledge of God and of obedience to him anything more than what was found in the earlier religions.

> There is no proof that Muhammad attained perfection and the ability to perfect others as claimed.

> That is why, to this day we never see anyone converting to Islam unless in terror, or in quest of power, or to avoid heavy taxation, or to escape humiliation, or if taken prisoner, or because of infatuation with a Muslim woman, or for some similar reason. Nor do we see a respected, wealthy, and pious non-Muslim well versed in both his faith and that of Islam, going over to the Islamic faith without some of the aforementioned or similar motives.[45]

In general, there were more Islamic-Christian polemics then Islamic-Jewish. Converts from Judaism to Islam like Samawal al-Maghribi (ca 1125–1175), the author of *Silencing the Jews*, were responsible for many of the polemics.[46] Ibn Kammuna also addresses these Islamic objections to Judaism, mainly from

Samawal al-Maghribi. Among these are the claims that the transmission of the Torah is faulty since it was written afresh by Ezra; that the Bible and Talmud contain anthropomorphisms and worthless passages, that they contain nothing on reward and punishment, that the recognition of Moses as a prophet is inconsistent with the rejection of Muhammad as a prophet.

Ibn Kammuna defends the Jewish position by stating, following Sa'adiah, that Judaism is based on scripture, tradition, speculation, and analogy as played out on text and tradition; that Jews follow the prophets and the words of the Sages as God's will and do not seek a pristine revelation from Adam or Abraham; that Jews do not claim that all Judaism comes from reliable tradition; and that Torah was never forgotten by Israel.

Rabbinic Typology on the Kaaba: Rabbi Nissim and Maimonides

In the medieval rabbinic typologies we find erroneous descriptions of Muslim practice. The most notable case is the connection made between "cult of Islam" in Mecca to the worship of Mercury in Greco-Roman religion. Many Jewish sources assume that the Kabba in Mecca was a stone similar to those used in worship of Mercury, or that there was a statue of Muhammad in Mecca.

In a medieval commentary erroneously attributed to the famous sage Rabbi Nissim Gerondi (c. 1310–1375), but actually written by an unknown later scholar, one finds the opinion that Muslims bow to Mohammed. Although the comment is not entirely clear, it appears to be saying that even though the Muslims do not turn Muhammad into a God, one must regard their actions of bowing down to him as idolatry, thus putting them in the category of idolaters.[47]

Maimonides, when asked about this opinion of Islam, rejects it as false. The issue arises in connection with Obadiah the Proselyte, who, having previously been a Muslim, certainly knew the particulars of the religion and had declared that Islam was not idolatry. Obadiah's opinion was ridiculed by one of his teachers in his new faith of Judaism, who claimed that the Islamic religious service at Mecca was idolatrous because it involved the ritual of throwing stones, which constituted worship of "Merkulius." In desperation, the recent convert Obadiah turned to Maimonides, who rejected this erroneous equation of Islam and Mercury as non-empirical.

> The Ishmaelites are not at all idolaters; [idolatry] has long been severed from their mouths and hearts; and they attribute to God a proper unity, a unity concerning which there is no doubt. And because they lie about us, and falsely attribute to us the statement that God has a son, is no reason for us to lie about them and say that they are idolaters . . . And should anyone say that the house that they honor [the Kaaba] is a house of idolatry and an idol is hidden within it, which their ancestors used to worship, then what of it? The hearts of those who bow down toward it today are [directed] only toward Heaven . . . [Regarding] the Ishmaelites today—idolatry has been severed from the mouths of all of them [including] women and children. Their error and foolishness is in other things, which cannot be put into writing because of the renegades and wicked among Israel [i.e., apostates]. But as regards the unity of God they have no error at all.

The long and short of it is that even though at their root these things were estab-lished for idolatry, not a man in the world throws these stones or bows down to that place or does any of the rites for the sake of idolatry—neither verbally nor mentally; their heart is rather surrendered to Heaven.[48]

Maimonides's response offers a reminder that we should not let political differ-ences, even persecution, get in the way of empirical observation of both ritual and theology.

In contrast, Yom Tov b. Abraham Ishbilî (known as the Ritba c.1250–1330), rabbi and Talmudic commentator, considers Islam as monotheistic and as not forbidding their wine. Yet, he calls Islam *avodah zarah* in the context of apostasy. "Although the Muslims profess monotheism, their faith is utterly idolatrous. Consequently, a Jew should suffer martyrdom rather than apostasize. Indeed, whosoever admits their creed, denies by the same token the truthfulness of the Law of Moses in its present state and such a denial is tantamount to idolatry." The reason-ing is that if one denies the Torah of Moses then there is no commonality of monotheism since one is rejecting God's will. Sometimes, Ishbilî is misquoted as if he denied Islamic monotheism, but he does not. David ibn Zimri, the sixteenth-century Egyptian legal decider follows Ishbilî's negative appraisal of Islam. In the twentieth century the Hungarian Klausenburger Rebbe in his Divrei Yatziv also thinks that Islam is idolatry because they reject Torah and worship the Kaaba. Due to his piety and good works, his position is quoted by many contemporary rabbinical authorities.[49]

However the majority view, based on medieval tradition and the philosophic understanding of monotheism, is that Islam is monotheistic. The majority opin-ion of those Jews who lived in Islamic lands was that Islam is monotheistic and non-idolatrous. Maimonides, Yosef Karo, and Rabbi Ovadiah Yosef, all consider Islam as serving the same God as Judaism even if there may have once upon a time been remnants of pre-Islamic paganism. In line with this dominant view, many rabbinic authorities permit Jews to pray at currently functioning Mosques, which were viewed either as a shared sacred space, like the Cave of the Patriarchs in Hebron (al-Khalil), or as a dignified place to turn away from the public market for one's personal prayers.[50] Similar views were found in the Ashkenazi world by Rabbi Yitzhak Elchanan and David Zvei Hoffman, both declaring that Muslims are monotheistic enough to allow Jewish use of the Mosque as a place of prayer.[51] In general, rabbinic texts demonstrate little interest in trying to understand the Islamic faith, whether through its texts or its people.[52]

Law

The contemporary scholar Gideon Libson writes that the similarities between the two legal systems were due either to direct borrowing, or a common culture. Yet, at the time, the dominant culture was clearly Islamic, and neither side will admit borrowing. Still, there is clearly Hanafi influence on the Geonim. Maimonides seems to have been close to the Shafi school. The amount of influence differed from place to place. The rabbinic academy in Sura was more influenced by Islamic law than was the rival academy of Pumbedita.[53]

Early Islamic writings display a widespread sharing of legal thought, prescriptions, and jurisprudence between Islam and Judaism. Zeev Meghan, an Israeli professor of Islam, notes that casuistry about halakhah played a role in the formation and evolution of sharia. He shows that "early Muslim authors cited in Tafsir and other genres often demonstrate a level of familiarity with Jewish laws that does not stop short of sophisticated rehearsals of complex Talmudic sugyot." However, the purpose of these "hundreds of direct statements and detailed digressions regarding what the Jews had been commanded" is often to set up Islam as the optimal religion. Judaism provided an example of errors and excesses. Sharia works with the Talmudic sugya as part of its narrative regardless of how the Talmud actually decided the Jewish law. He writes "It was almost as if in this particular instance the Islamic sources were doing exactly what they have always claimed to be doing: preserving an earlier and more correct understanding of the Jewish religion than the Jews themselves had done."[54]

Even though the Islamic science of evaluating traditions ascribed a low credibility to the Jewish material, Meghen notes how Islamic law integrated Jewish religious law. Islamic legal writings portray Jews as limiting revelation to a one-time unchanging event despite changing circumstances and the contradictions within Jewish law. For them, Islamic law is superior because it responds to these needs. Muhammad received a new revelation specifically to answer the Jews.[55]

According to early sources of Islamic law, God did speak to the Jews, but they have over time developed exaggerated claims of authenticity and excessive strictness. In a precious reversal of the well-known rabbinic story, there is an Islamic story that presents God as offering the Torah to the Jews, who decline the Torah because they want things done their way, not God's. God asks them to pray where they can, but the Jews say only in a synagogue; God wants his teachings in the heart, but Jews wanted the teachings in texts. Halakhah is seen a rejection of Abrahamic religion; Jews are portrayed as sticklers for details, who violate the revelation they have been given.[56]

Jewish texts ask: Can Jews use a Muslim court when there is no Jewish court? Yes, it is a mitzah even when the plaintiff is a gentile, and the defendant or theft a Jew. "In Baghdad we don't but elsewhere they do, court witnesses are excellent in their religion, and avoid falsehood or lies. So it is good."[57]

There are three realms where the Jews felt legally close to Muslims: marriage, circumcision, wine. In these respects, Muslims are depicted as non-Jewish, but also not exactly gentile.

> There are some people who think in their minds that the Ishmaelite woman is not a gentile and does not have the ruling of a gentile. For I have heard it said that the Ishmaelite woman is not to be considered a gentile for the Ishmaelites are monotheists and unite his Oneness. Furthermore, they are circumcised which is not the case with gentiles who are uncircumcised and falsify their faith and have no faith nor religion. And the gentiles and many of them refrain from drinking wine.[58]

Rabbi Zemah ruled that Muslim wine was still unfit to be drunk by a Jew. Similar statements were also made by the Geonim, the heads of Babylonian Jewry from the seventh to eleventh century, Kohen Zedek, Sar Shalom, Nahshon, and other important authorities. However, there are many competing sources that distinguish Muslim wine from idolatrous wine. Rav Hai Gaon (939–1038) wrote "these Muslims are the most solicitous for us and the most protective of us . . . Their wine is not idolatrous—they definitely don't use it in services and their banquets and spices are not used for idolatry." In the ninth century, Rabbi Zemah Gaon ruled that a Jew was permitted to obtain benefit from wine with which a Muslim came into contact. Sar Shalom states that one can have an oath with them.[59] Professor Marc Shapiro quotes Rabbi Joseph Messas, one of the great halakhic authorities of the early twentieth-century North Africa, who writes: "there is no unity [of God] like the unity found in Islam, therefore one who forbids their wine which they have handled turns holy into profane by regarding worshippers of god as worshippers of idols, God forbid."[60]

There was also debate among Kabbalists about the acceptability of praying together with Muslims in Mosques. Below follow two examples of how Kabbalists react to this ritual solidarity with dismay. The first is from the thirteenth-century Kabbalaist Moses de Leon, writing from his Reconquest Castille, and the second is from the early fourteenth-century Joseph ben Shalom Ashkenazi. Neither statement received a widespread audience, yet many probably shared their sentiments.

> There are individuals who believe that the Muslims are not included in the category of gentiles, since they are monotheistic by faith, because they are circumcised and furthermore abstain from certain prohibited foods contrary to the practice of the gentiles. Know then that the Ishmaelites are most certainly to be included in the category of gentiles . . .[61]

> Consider closely the stupidity of our coreligionists who praise and exalt the religion of the Muslims, thus transgressing the precept of the law "Find no grace in them" (Deut. 7:2). Not satisfied with that, when the Muslims profess their faith at the hour of their assembly in the mosques, these Jews who are poor in spirit and who do not share in religion, associate themselves with them reciting for their part the "Hear O Israel."[62]

These statements offer mild forms of rebuke to those praying in Mosques. Judaic writings also contain many exhortations of revulsion that do not offer any insight into the theological perspective on the religious practice of the host culture.

Exclusivism

The majority of medieval Jewish texts discussed in this chapter are inclusivists toward Islam and other religions. They assume that Judaism is the most correct of religions but that there is still some truth in the other faiths. However, some texts portray Islam in a negative exclusive manner as the apocalyptic ruler of the world, the final kingdom to be defeated. There is a Judeo-Arabic tale preserved in the *Genizah,* "The Account of Muhammad's Companions," which relates that the Koran was really written by a group of rabbis from Medina who intimated their names in the "mysterious letters" of the Muslim scripture "in order to save the people of Israel from the evil devices of the wicked one," i.e., Muhammad.[63]

Chaim Vital (1543–1620), in his version of the teaching of the Kabbalist Isaac Luria, builds on the early apocalyptic texts that envision Islam as the final exile. The early Arabian conquest of the Near East and the great crusade battles are the moments and images that define Islam, which is strongly identified with Arabs. One can still find inclusivist strains here in the acknowledgement that Islam is a religious son of Abraham and shares circumcision with Judaism, but the circumcision of Muslims is considered incomplete.

> At the end of days, the Jewish people are destined to be in the exile of Ishmael, as mentioned in *Pirkei de Rabbi Eliezer.* In the *Zohar,* Lech Lecha it says that Ishmael, as the son of Abraham, was circumcised. However, he is still called "A wild donkey of a man" (Genesis 16:12), not a full man, because he was circumcised without the [requisite] pulling back of the remaining foreskin . . . There will be an additional fifth and final exile, harder than the others. This is the exile of Ishmael, who is called "A wild donkey of a man."

> The other nations exert continuous dominion on others. In contrast, Ishmael dwelled alone in the deserts, and did not deal with other nations. Afterwards, Ishmael will rise and become king over the entire world, and over Israel. This refers to "when a man rose up over us" (verse 2), similar to what is said in the Zohar on the verse "a new king rose up" (Exodus 1), because at first he was lower than all the nations and now he rose to kingship . . .[64]

They interpreted Daniel's eschatology as referring to the exile of Ishmael, projecting present woes onto past prophecies as a justification of their doom. Such a portrayal is found in the classic work of Jewish mysticism, the *Zohar,* which while mainly compiled in thirteenth-century Spain, purports to portray the events of a much earlier period in the Holy Land. It emphasizes the degradation and persecution under Islam by coining the maxim "In truth the exile under Ishmael is the hardest of all exiles."

> For three things is the world disquieted, for a servant, when he reigneth and a hand-maid that is heir to her mistress, to Egypt and Ishmael (Islam). There is no nation so despised of the Holy One as Egypt and yet He gave her dominion over Israel; while the handmaid, i.e., Hagar, who bore Ishmael, who tormented Israel so cruelly in the past, still rules over her and persecutes her for her faith. In truth the exile under Ishmael is the hardest of all exiles. Once when going up to Jerusalem, Rabbi Joshua saw an Arab and his son meet a Jew. The Arab said to his son "See there is a Jew whom God has rejected. Go and insult him. Spit in his face seven times for he is of the seed of the exalted ones and I know that the seventy nations shall be ruled by them." So the boy went and took hold of the Jew's beard, whereupon Rabbi Joshua said "Mighty one, mighty one, I call upon the supernal one to come down below." And before he had finished, the earth opened her mouth and swallowed up the Arabs.[65]

This sentiment is echoed in a commentary by the great Moroccan Kabbalist Rabbi Hayyim Ibn 'Attâr, who left Morocco for Jerusalem, where he died in 1743:

> Happy is he who has not suffered exile beneath the Muslims who have enslaved us and embittered our existence. Not only do they leave our labors unrewarded, but they order us to pay them. After having stripped us of our belongings, they demand of us that which we no longer possess and they make us drink of the cup of misery until death.[66]

There are many contemporary homilies on contemporary events from Hasidic influenced sources that use this eschatological exclusivism to understand Middle Eastern politics.[67]

Islamic-Jewish Fatwa

A mid fourteenth-century manuscript from Grenada offers a theological dilemma posed by an unknown Jewish author to the renowned Muslim jurist of Granada Abu Said Faraj ibn Lubb al Shatibi (d. 1381). The manuscript was brought to light and translated by Vincent Cornell and Hayat Kara. The Jewish questioner assumes the Muslim is a follower of the Asherite doctrine of predestination. The questioner also assumes that the Muslim position is that we have free will to either choose Islam or make the wrong choice. The Jew asks the logical question of Islamic predestination: If all people are to freely choose Islam in order to allow for human responsibility, then if there is also predestination does that not mean that God ultimately determines his religion? In the questioner's case, God chose him to be Jewish. The questioner asks: Why is God displeased with his Judaism if it was God's will?[68]

> Oh scholars of religion, a *dhimmi* of your religion
> Is perplexed. So guide him with the clearest proof:
>
> If my Lord has decreed, in your opinion, my unbelief
> But then does not accept it of me, what is my recourse?
>
> He decrees my misguidance and says, "Be satisfied with your fate."
> But how am I to be satisfied with that which leads to my damnation?
>
> He curses me and then shuts the door against me. Is there any
> Way out at all for me? Show me the outcome?
>
> Do I even have the choice of going against his ruling?
> By God, cure my malady with clear arguments!

Jewish Sufis

There is a known history of Jewish Sufism, including most notably Bahye ibn Pakuda, Avraham ben ha Rambam, and the other Egyptian descendents of

Maimonides such as David Maimuni or Joshua Maimuni. The most famous of these works, Bahye's *Duties of the Heart*, is broken into gates of spiritual steps in the manner of the Sufi treatises written by Al-Kusajri and Al-Harawi. In the ninth gate of the book, on the theme of abstinence, Bahye quotes sayings of the Sufis whom he calls *Perushim*, or ascetics. He also exalts the ideals of disinterestedness and equanimity, which has its origin in Sufism.

The writings of Abraham Maimuni, Ovadaiah Maimuni, and the others of this school use the Arabic Sufi lexicon of isolation (ḥalwa), fasting and refraining from sleep, solitary contemplation (*hitbodebut* in Hebrew), discretion (*kitman*) about one's spiritual state, reciting God's names (*dhikr*), prostration, stretching out hands, turning toward the Temple during prayers, ablution of the feet. They also maintain a brotherhood and guidance structure, in which a religious guide—like a sufi *shaykh*—leads novices, and keeps a fellowship order.[69]

The influence in Sufi circles goes in both directions. Hasan al-Basri (died 728 AD), a founding Sufi mystic, introduced many of Isr'il'iyat legends into Muslim thought. Ibn Arabi, the thirteenth-century mystic, had Jewish disciples, one of whom wrote a commentary on *Guide for the Perplexed* for Muslim students. Abu Ali Ibn Hud of Damascus, a thirteenth-century Muslim Sufi, spent his time teaching the *Guide for the Perplexed* to students of all religious backgrounds. One of the Jewish students of Ibn Arabi wrote *The Spiritual Conquests of Time* in tribute to Ibn Arabi's *The Mecca Revelations*, a still un-translated Jewish commentary on the great Islamic mystic. This latter work would be a valuable window into Jewish-Muslim commonalities on revelation. In the interim, we have some more recent cases of Jewish Sufis.[70]

The Jewish Sufis considered these innovations not so much a reform as a restoration of practices that had previously been in vogue in Ancient Israel but which had since fallen into abeyance among the Jews as a result of the tribulations of the Exile and had ultimately passed to the Sufis.[71] Maimonides's son Abraham writes:

> Do not regard as unseemly our reference to the practices of the Muslim Sufis, for the latter imitate the Ancient Prophets of Israel and follow their footsteps . . . the ways of the ancient Saints of Israel which have ceased to be practiced by our own coreligionists have now become the practice of the Muslim Sufis as a result of the iniquities of Israel. Observe, then, these wonderful traditions and sigh with regret over how they have been taken from us and bestowed upon other nations.[72]

Menahem di Lonzano, sixteenth-century rabbi and Turkish mystic, is deeply embedded in his Ottoman context advocating poetic and musical styles of his countrymen. "Do not be surprised at our having employed Muslim melodies, for I have found no other tunes which are so heart-rending. Furthermore, I have done so on account of the scale they employ, for that is what will be used in the messianic era."[73] He also respects the Muslim rules of ablution as a model of purity. "Be sure to cleanse yourself of all impurity, so that the Muslim be not more pious than you."[74]

Ariel Bension (1880–1932), born in Jerusalem, was a rabbi who combined his interest in Sufism, and kabbalah. His father belonged to the elite kabbalistic yeshiva Beit-El in the old city of Jerusalem, to which he also joined. Bension's understanding of kabbalah was influenced by Ibn Arabi's works *Mecca Revelations*, and *Interpreter of Desires*. In his 1932 work on Jewish mysticism, he credits Ibn Arabi for his method for intuition for attaining visions and revelations. Further, he praised Ibn Arabi as a "crucible of . . . poetic imagination" able to present "an artistic description of the world to come far superior and far more beautiful than anything that had been conceived up to his time." Bension claims that the Zohar and Ibn Arabi both conceive of God as light, both consider God as a unity of opposites, and both envision that Divine goodness produces the light of existence, without separating from God.[75]

A related phenomenon is the cult of the saints among Moroccan Jewry saints in which the folk veneration of saintly figures in both traditions overlap in custom and saints.[76]

Siman Tov Melammed

Siman Tov Melammed (before 1793–1823 or 1828, nom de plume Tuvyah) was an Iranian Jewish rabbi, poet, and polemicist. He was the *hakham* (spiritual leader) of the community of Mashad and had to deal with a variety of religious tension, including forced disputations with Shii Imams. In 1839, the entire community was forced to convert to Islam. They lived as relatively secret Jews until the twentieth century. Raphael Patai wrote a book on them called *Jadid al-Islam*.

Melammed's writings are the tip of a much larger world of Jewish Sufi thought in Persia and Central Asia. Melammed wrote, in Persian, a philosophic and mystical poetic commentary on Maimonides thirteen principles called *Hayat al Ruh*, a sufi commentary on the *Guide for the Perplexed*. Within the large treatise, he wrote a poem in praise of Sufis.[77] Melammed praises the Sufis for transcending their physical bodies and the habits of ordinary life to become servants of God. They are radiant and contented from their devotion to God and they lead others back to a straight path to God.

Description of the Pious Sufis Roused from the Sleep of Neglect
Godly and radiant like roses
The Sufis are, the Sufis,
Whose carnal soul is dead,
Doused their desires, the Sufis.
Firmly they grasp the straight path,
Leaders benevolent, guides
Of those who strayed are the Sufis.
Drunk with the cup and soul's sweets,
With love of seeing the Unseen;
Without reins in both hands are the Sufis.
Dead to the world of the moment,
Alive to the here after;
Full of merit and kindness are the Sufis.
God's love is their beloved,

God's affection their decoration,
And that which veils Him from the Sufis.
The most contented of beggars,
Avoiding rancor and dispute;
Freed from the Day of Punishment are the Sufis.

The relationship between Judaism and Sufism must have been seriously debated because there is also a poem by an unknown writer called "Jacob" against Jews becoming Sufis. The poem says to follow Moses and his father Imran and to avoid the path of the famous Sufi Majnun. One should not relinquish one's status as the chosen people for a universal faith.

Jacob: Against Sufis
O people of "Imran's son"
Let not Satan deceive you,
Lest you forfeit religion and faiths;
My life for Moses' life;
Whoever abandons his faith
Becomes a sage like Majnun,
Roaming about, confused;
My life for Moses' life.
Bravely he is called a friend.
But he turns common instead of chosen,
[Now] what religion can he call his own?
My life for Moses' life.

Muhammad versus Moses

Binyamin ben Mishaeel (Kasdan 1672–circa 1732), known by his penname Amina (the faithful), was the most important Iranian Jewish poet. Binyamin wrote religious poems for the synagogue to be recited on the Jewish holidays. In the following poem, he praises Moses in the style of poems in praise of Muhammad. Moses is the highest in rank of the prophets. He states that MH, referring to Muhammad, is not as good as MSH, referring to Moshe (Moses).

Amina: In Praise of Moses, Our Master, Peace Be upon Him
Pure soul and lamp of faith
Chieftain and full moon of the worlds,
In lordship you have been chosen
Highest in rank of all the prophets.
Ere you came into the world
You were with God manifest.
O Moses, O God's interlocutor,

O certain knowledge, essence of certainty.
Your station is above the spheres of the sun and moon
At resurrection, on the Judgment Day

You will encounter M[im] and H[a],
Hearts will incline toward you.
Toward your pure scent and temper.
I am your faithful servant, you

Whose copper visage is well veiled
You are better than M[im] and H[a]
Ou are made of M[im] and Sh[in] and h[a]
You are the glory of *face to face*
The power of our Lord this greatness occurred upon Mount Tur,
This *joy* in *Sivan*'s month we found.
This gathering of the Lord's hosts.
When all these fiery words [to us came].[78]

Conclusion

Rabbi David Rosen, one of the leaders of interfaith dialogue today, writes, "Few religions have as much in common as Islam and Judaism." Rosen emphasizes that they share "fundamental religious concepts, such as reward and punishment relating to a Day of Divine Judgment as well as the belief in the afterlife, Heaven and Hell and future resurrection. Moreover, the structure and modus operandi of their religious jurisprudential codes of conduct—Sharia and Halachah—bear striking similarity." In addition, as this chapter has shown, they share an ethical-monotheistic vision and a view of the "unity of God who is envisaged as just and merciful and who has revealed a way of life in accordance with these values for the benefit of human society."

Judaism does not have the same problems with Islam that it has with Christianity, that is, Trinity, Incarnation, and Resurrection. But to envision a Jewish theology of Islam, there are many questions that would need a fresh analysis to move the discussion forward, especially finding a way to read the negative statements about Jews, either conceptually or contextually, in a way that would minimize their effect.

The word Muslim has both a narrow and a broad meaning. The broad meaning includes Jews as partners in an Abrahamic faith from the revelation to Abraham and promotes a universal truth available to all. It also, obviously, has a specific practice and theology particular to Islam limited to those who accept Muhammad and Islamic law.

Given this, the Jewish position has its own set of questions to address.

- Can Judaism find a place for Muhammad in Judaism as not a madman?
- Can Jews appreciate the Koran?
- Can we think together of a just world order?
- Can we find a place not in the realm of an Islamic polity (dar islam) or in an anti-Islamic polity (dar harb) but walking alongside?
- Can we have a sense that we worship one God, have common laws, common revelation, and common resurrection?

7

Islam: Scholarship and Existential Attitude

As I partially demonstrated in the previous chapter, Islam and Judaism are close not only theologically but also structurally. Both religious cultures emphasize a legal system for the regulation of everyday life. They have the commonalities of circumcision, dietary laws, and daily prayer. Yet, we have not had systematic discussion about the similarities and differences in the role of legal regulations, legal systems, scriptural narrative, philosophy, and lived ritual life of the two faiths. If the two faiths of Judaism and Islam are as similar as stated in the last chapter, then can the two faiths be brought closer together through what they share? Jews have not seriously begun to ask the questions that will lead to a Jewish-Muslim rapprochement.

Despite the fact that Jews have often found it easier to relate to Islam than to Christianity, Jews and Muslims do not affirm a common theological covenant—an affirmation that some thinkers have formulated to bring together Jews and Christians. There are no Jewish versions of Louis Massignon or Kenneth Craig who approached Islam in a theological manner, and there was no rapprochement during the twentieth century, excepting Trude Weiss-Rosmarin. The Jewish-Muslim encounter is now beginning more than a half century behind both the Jewish-Christian and the Muslim-Christian encounter, and the way Jews see Muslims remains colored by the history of Jewish scholarship.

This chapter will start with the basic Jewish academic work on Islam that sought the origins of Islam in Judaism. This approach was typified in the nineteenth century by Abraham Geiger and in the twentieth century by Abraham Katsh. From there we move to consider the regnant historical approaches to the Judeo-Islamic synthesis as presented by Steve Wasserstrom and David Nierenberg. I then look at the fundamentally opposite existential positions of Trude Weiss-Rosmarin, Franz Rosenzweig, and Avi Elqayam. I will capstone that discussion with the existential openness and naturalistic pluralism of Reuven Firestone, which seeks Jewish-Muslim dialogue.

I then deal with the diverse political positions of Eliezer Melamed, Bat Yeor, and other exclusivists, which are informed by contemporary politics, contrasting them with the contemporary open positions that look to find a home for Islam within Judaism—Menachem Forman, Eric Yoffie, and Haim Ovadiah. I conclude by discussing advocates of dialogue and the notion of Abrahamic faiths.

- Koranic scholarship—Abraham Geiger, Abraham Katsh
- Historians—Steven Wasserstrom, David Nierenberg
- Theologians—Trude Weiss-Rosmarin, Franz Rosenzweig, Avi Elqayam, Reuven Firestone
- Twentieth Century Politics—Against Islam
- Twentieth Century Politics—Peace with Islam

Identification with Muslims

The academic affinity of Jews for Islam was part of a much broader cultural trend. The nineteenth-century Jewish vision of connectedness with Islam jettisoned Jews from an environment of Christian persecution and into an era when they imagined Jews were treated with respect. They depicted the Golden Age in Spain as a highpoint for both Muslims and Jews, and the study of medieval Islam was a means of presenting a purified image of Judaism at its peak. The myth of the Golden Age in Spain and the vision of an ideal Jewish existence during those years started in the eighteenth century when the winds of the Enlightenment inspired the lay leaders of the Jewish community in Western Europe to envision a more refined Jewish society. They switched to a Sefardic pronunciation of Hebrew and glorified Maimonides and other Golden Age figures.

In 1821, Heinrich Heine wrote his tragedy *Almansor*. It is set in Alhambra and deals with the adjustment of Muslims to the Christianization of Spain in the sixteenth century. The protagonist, displaying a sensitivity still rare in European circles, decries the burning of a Koran in a public fire in reconquered Spain. "Nearly every literary analysis of the play and the poem has read them as allegories to the predicament of nineteenth-century German Jewry. But *Almansor* also displays a profound empathy for the Muslims themselves, about whom Heine troubled to learn a great deal."

This identification between Jews and Muslims is quite pronounced in the work of British Prime Minister, Benjamin Disraeli (1804–81), who himself was a Jewish convert to Anglicanism. He wrote in his *Tancred* (1847), that the Arabs of the desert were "Jews upon horseback," and that Jews were "Mosaic Arabs," bound by ties of race to "Mohammedan Arabs."

In 1831, Abraham Geiger wrote his award-winning work on Islam (see below), showing the similarities between Judaism and Islam and attributing Muhammad's persecution of some Jews to his disappointment at the Jews not following him. Just as he sought a Jewish context for Jesus, he sought a Jewish context for Islam.

Ignatz Goldziher (1850–1921), Hungarian orientalist and Orthodox Jew, is certainly the strongest and most unusual advocate for Jewish-Muslim understanding in the scholarly history; he regarded Judaism and Islam as kindred religions. Despite his status as an orientalist and a Jew, he was allowed to study with Muslim clerics in Al Azhar in Cairo, and though he called Islam a "Judaized Meccan cult," Goldziher did not treat Islam as derivative in any way. He had the utmost admiration for Islam and thought that Islam had evolved into "the only religion which, even in its doctrinal and official formulation, can satisfy philosophical minds." "My ideal," he said, "was to elevate Judaism to a similar rational level."[1] For Goldziher, Islam is not simply a sibling religion of Judaism; he urges the Jewish minority in Christian Europe to view Islam as a model for its own development.

Jews and Muslims were further linked together as Semitic religions by nineteenth-century linguistics and studies in comparative religion. Judaism and Islam were seen as having shared roots separate from the Greco-Roman Aryan roots of Christianity. In this vast literature, the Semitic faiths were treated as desert religions in which believers followed a stern transcendent deity who demanded sole worship, submission, and obedience. These Semitic religions were considered collective, ritualistic, and mantic prophetic. When this anthropological category was discredited, scholars ceased to pursue the connections between Judaism and Islam. It is also worth noting that while the Jewish vision of Islam was notable in its time for its comparatively sympathetic approach to Muhammad and Islam, some of these positions are clearly condescending and orientalizing by our current standards.

When the Israeli government was founded within the British Mandate of Palestine, there was a general consensus that Israel's education and culture was going to recognize and commit to a relationship with Arabs, Arabic and Islam. Josef Horovitz and Gotthold Weil, served as the first two directors of the School of Oriental Studies at the Hebrew University. They expected European Jews to turn their backs on Europeans as they fled from their persecution. Nevertheless, Hebrew University treated Jewish Studies and Arabic Studies as entirely separate. The approach to history developed at Hebrew University, called the Jerusalem school of history, saw Jews as an autonomous community and independent ethnic group that had been in exile from its homeland, presuming an autonomous Jewish community even within Muslim lands.

The Israeli turn away from European culture halted shortly after the Holocaust, and the war that created the state of Israel left Jews viewing Muslims as antagonists. When Muslims responded to the establishment of the state of Israel with anti-Semitism, reflected by outbreaks of violence against Jewish communities in Muslim lands, "it cast into doubt the very premises of a Jewish scholarly tradition that had presented Islam to Europe as a model of tolerance, especially toward Jews." Over time, Jews lost interest in developing affinity with Muslims.

G. E. Von Grunebaum, Fritz Rosenthal, Shlomo Pines, S. D. Goitein, and others continued to produce studies on Islam, and Judeo-Arabic texts were given special treatment within Jewish studies. Yet, gradually the tone shifted. Bernard Lewis (b. 1916) came to personify the post-war shift from a sympathetic to a critical posture. He still depicts a wonderful golden age of Jewish-Muslim sympathy in the Middle Ages, but grew to emphasize the comparison of contemporary Islamic intolerance with the admirable tolerance of contemporary Western Christendom.[2]

Modern studies have attempted to uncover a cultural kinship between Jewish-Islamic synthesis, seeking commonalities in language, poetry, philosophy, and science. However, there has not been much discussion about developing a religious kinship. We have not seen attempts to develop a Jewish appreciation of Muhammad; no Jewish scholar has spoken of "my brother Muhammad" the way that Buber spoke of Jesus. We have not seen scholarly attempts at formulating a dual covenant with Islam. This scholarly neglect cannot result purely from the perception that the Koran is anti-Semitic since Leo Baeck, Martin Buber, and Joseph Klausner, were willing and able to challenge similar perceptions of Jesus and the New Testament in a pre-Vatican II era.

Abraham Geiger

Abraham Geiger (1810–1874) was a German scholar of Jewish history, rabbi, and founder of Reform Judaism. To reinforce Jewish pride, Geiger worked to demonstrate the importance of Judaism as a source of Western monotheism, including Islam and Christianity. In chapter three, I briefly noted that he portrayed Jesus as a pure ethic of Judaism without the rabbinic legalism. In this chapter, we will see how Geiger portrayed Muhammad as derivative from Judaism.

In 1833, Geiger published a book analyzing the Prophet Muhammad's adaptations from Judaism. Geiger's adept handling of the sources and his careful analysis won him widespread praise from academic scholars of Islam. The original Latin thesis was written for a competition at the University of Bonn, where it took the prize.[3] At the time, the predominate European approach to Islam was that of the French scholar Antoine-Isaac Silvestre de Sacy (1758–1838), founder of modern Arabic studies, who felt compelled to insist that Muhammad was a "skilled imposter." In contrast, Geiger offered a more positive approach, accepting the sincerity of Muhammad. He depicted the Islamic world as an advanced civilization that had historically acknowledged its roots in Judaism.[4] His work introduced a tone of respect into the study of Islam—so much so that Geiger came under some criticism from Christian colleagues for assuming the sincerity of the Muslim prophet.

Geiger dedicated himself to showing that Islam was a sincere revelation that borrowed from Jewish sources; for the first time in the modern era, he brought Islam into the orbit of biblical religion. Yet, it is worth noting his limitations. By twenty-first century standards, Geiger can be faulted for not applying critical methods to the Koran; as a traditionalist, he ascribed the entire Koran to Muhammad. Furthermore, subsequent scholarship rightly criticizes Geiger for overstating Islam's borrowing from Judaism. Despite these limitations, the book is still considered the dawn of historical research on Islam.

Geiger was a partisan of Islam, especially in comparing the experience of Jews under Islam and Christianity. In 1865, he compared Islam, which "always left itself favorable to the cultivation of science and philosophy, with a Christian Church that increasingly nourished a repugnance of science and reason." Geiger offered a clear and resounding voice of dissent in a Europe where Islam continued to be regarded as inimical to science and reason.

Moshe Pearlman, the editor of the English edition of Geiger's book, wrote that according to Geiger the Jews who lived at the time of Muhammad "found themselves unable to take the prophetic claims of the newcomer seriously, and they were quick to express their derision for the howlers he expressed with references to Jewish lore." As such, Geiger originated the perception of modern Jews that Muhammad "had absorbed his notions of Jewish lore from oral communication and impressions gleaned by ear, rather than from the study of Scripture or any other authoritative Jewish text."[5] Geiger used philology to uncover the Jewish origins of Muhammad's ideas. In the Koran, he found similarities to the Jewish idea of God, to Jewish angelology, to rabbinic exegesis, and to concepts like the shekhinah. Pearlman states:

> Geiger set out to trace with precision and exactitude those elements that the herald of Islam had appropriated. Among elements borrowed from Jewish sources that could be traced, Geiger pointed to the notions and terms of the Ark, Eden, Hell, Rabbinic scholars, divine presence, and so on—fourteen ideas and terms in all. . . . In Geiger's judgment the tales of the Hebrew Bible pointed to Jewish sources rather than to Christian informants, for Christians of that period placed greater emphasis on materials of the New Testament."[6]

Geiger wanted to show that Muhammad was sincere and possessed a genuine desire to create scripture for his people and that he was not an imposter as Voltaire and Antoinne Isaac de Sacy had claimed. In Geiger's opinion, however, Muhammad possessed no set religious vision, he devised religious principals ad-hoc in order to demonstrate connections between Muslim practice and Abraham.

> "Theory was quickly devised to keep abreast of practice—Abraham was now declared to have been neither Jew nor Christian, and the Ka'ba, the sanctuary of Mecca with its venerated stone, was designated as the place hallowed by Abraham and his son Ismail."

> "He further proceeded to reinterpret native Arabian customs and, after purifying them of blatant pagan overtones, to associate them with the name of Abraham."

Geiger's approach considered the Jewish influence pervasive even after the development of the Muslim scripture, arguing that early post-Koranic Muslim exegesis "resorted constantly to Judaism to explain the text."[7]

At the end of nineteenth century, Christian scholars entered the discussion as orientalists and laid greater stress on Christianity's influence on the Koran as well as on the Greek language as an intermediary. "Geiger . . . was keenly aware of the actual or possible Christian influences on Mohammed, of a Near-Eastern substratum to his faith, and of the indubitable legacy of pagan Arab lore." Yet, Jews continued their research into the Jewish sources of Islam and proudly claimed the Koran as closer to Judaism than to Christianity.[8] For example, Shlomo Dov Goitein, who depicted Jews and Muslims as members of a single medieval Mediterranean society, noted that the earliest Surah discusses Moses but not Jesus, proving for Jewish scholars that the earliest form of Islam was Judaic with Christian groups and Jewish tribes exerting secondary influences.

Katsh

Abraham Katsh (1908–1998) was a professor of Jewish studies at NYU who wrote and trained a generation of American Jewish Arabists. Proud of the role of the Jewish professors of Arabic, Katsh boasts:

> Through the writings of the modern Jewish Orientalists the affinity of these two great Semitic peoples is stressed. In fact, there is hardly an important Jewish scholarly magazine or Festschrift that does not contain some research dealing with Arabic learning. In the colleges and universities, as well as through the written word, Jewish Orientalists in America share in the intellectual heritage of their Arab colleagues. Just as they played a part in the days of yore as intermediaries in the transmission and unfolding of Islamic culture to the Latin world, so Jewish scholars today are contributing in no small measure to the advancement of Arabic learning in the English-speaking world.[9]

Katsh focuses on the most Jewish parts of the Koran—Surahs two and three—and forges all possible Jewish parallels. His vision is of a single religious world, which would allow him to view Islam through the eyes of rabbinic texts. With this in mind, he generated an extensive rabbinic-style commentary on the Koran showing similarities with Judaism in religious ideas and practice.[10] For example, he finds similarity of purpose among the *shema* and the Muslim affirmation of faith, the *shahadah*. He says, "the Moslem in reciting the *shahadah* accepts the yoke of the kingdom of Heaven, and in uttering the famous (there is no God but Allah), he repeats the biblical phrases, 'For who is God, save the Lord,' and 'There is no God but the Lord.'"

Katsh finds another parallel among Koranic and rabbinic statements on repentance. Citing, "Verily, those who misbelieve after believing, and then increase in misbelief, their repentance shall not be accepted; these are those who err," Katsh immediately brings to mind the Mishnah in *Yoma* 8:9, "If a man said, 'I will sin and repent,' and sin again and repent/ he will be given no chance to repent."

Katsh finds Jewish roots in the practice of Islamic prayer, in contrast Goldziher reached the opposite conclusions, avoiding claims that Islam was derivative of Judaism.

> It is incumbent upon every Moslem to pray five times daily (at sunrise, mid-day, mid-afternoon, sunset and before retiring). Goldziher regards the five daily prayers as of Persian influence. Rabbi Simon Duran (1361–1444), who lived in Algiers, maintains that Muhammad borrowed the custom from the Jewish Day of Atonement. Thus, we learn that the Jews in Arabia during the talmudic period really met five times daily for prayer in the synagogue; twice for the recitation of the Shema', and three times for the three regular "prayers." For practical reasons, the two prayers in the morning were combined into one, as were the two prayers in the evening.[11]

Katsh claims that even the basic language of Islamic submission to God is Jewish. "Abraham in the Bible uses the expression *Yirat Elohim* (the fear of God), which connotes submission or unquestioning obedience to God. To Muhammad this expression would have meant a great deal in formulating his new religion." To construct a parallel for the Islamic phrase "peace be unto Him" and the notion of God as peace giver, Katsh notes that the Koran refers to God as the "Peace-Giver" just as the Bible and Talmud refer to God as *Shalom*.

Katsh even takes the Koranic passage comparing the Jewish violators of the Sabbath to apes and finds Jewish roots for the passage without taking any umbrage at the simian insult. (It is worth noting that the Koran was censuring those Jews who violate the Jewish Sabbath, even though Islam itself does not have a Sabbath concept; this contrasts with early Christian texts that denigrated Jewish law).

> VERSE 61 Then did ye turn aside after this, and were it not for God's grace towards you and His mercy, ye would have been of those who lose. Ye know too of those among you who transgressed upon the Sabbath, and we said, "Become ye apes, despised and spurned."

> Torrey [American scholar of Arabic] states that there is no Aggadic source for "the incident of the Breakers of the Sabbath, who changed into apes." However, it is possible that Muhammad derived this bit of legend from the story in the Talmud about the transformation of a class of sinners into apes, wild beasts and other wild animals. "R. Jeremiah b. Eleazar said: They split up into three parties. One said, 'Let us ascend and dwell there;' the second, 'Let us ascend and serve idols;' and the third, 'Let us ascend, and wage war (with God).' The party which proposed, 'Let us ascend, and dwell there' the Lord scattered them: the one that said 'Let us ascend and wage war' were turned to apes, spirits, devils and night-demons . . ."

> Hirschfeld doubts whether Muhammad knew of this legend.

> The word in question, *qiradatan* is recorded in the dictionaries as plural of *qird*, meaning an ape. If we read *qirdd*, vermin . . . the verse would be a mistaken rendition of Exod. 16:20, 24. The mistake was probably caused by the circumstance that the transformation of living human beings into apes seemed much more fitting than into worms. Now the reason of the transformation is, in the Qur'an, disobedience in connection with the Sabbath, which is the same cause as mentioned in the Pentateuch. Instead of the food left over night, Muhammed has the disobedient persons transformed.[12]

Current Jewish Understandings of Islam: Kugel and Firestone

In popular Jewish consciousness, Islam remains derivative, in a vague undefined way, from Judaism. However, contemporary Jewish academics see both the religions as rooted in the several traditions of the Near East—some biblical, some Arab, and some Aramean. In other words, scholars find biblical stories in Islam, but they also find stories of Muslim origin within Jewish texts.

Early Islam acknowledged the Jewish roots of certain Muslim sources, such as the *Israliyyah* or "Jewish material." There are also *Qisas al-ambiya*, "stories of the Jewish province."[13] Old scholarly accounts of this material often charge the Koran (or Muhammad) with a well-intentioned but incompetent "borrowing" or "appropriation" of biblical and/or para-scriptural traditions. Nineteenth-century

Jewish scholars saw this material as taken directly from Judaism and treated the Islamic works as derivative. Whereas Jews saw the Koranic stories as absorbed from Judaism wholesale, Muslims saw their versions as purified and reliable revisions of tainted and unreliable Jewish stories. In later centuries, a movement arose within Islam to remove the *Isra'ilyyat* from the tradition, since Jewish traditions were categorically unreliable.

James Kugel, a scholar of biblical traditions, compares the formation of the Koran to the formation of the Bible itself. He writes that although the Bible has parallels to Gilgamesh epic, it is not seen as untrue or unreliable relative to its earlier source. The Hebrews borrowed heavily from Ugarits and Canaanites, including their language, priestly system, Temple calendar, and stories. Still later, the Jews borrowed from Babylonians and Persians.[14] Beyond this, Kugel argues that stories have a life of their own outside of the biblical narrative. There was a great deal of expanded biblical narrative in the cultures of the Near East—material similar to the Second Temple literature of the Apocrypha, Pseudepigrapha, and the Dead Sea Sect that circulated independently of the Jewish community, and which sometimes only shows up in Jewish material in the later medieval midrashim.[15]

Ultimately, the pejorative language of "appropriation" and "borrowing" was effectively demolished.[16] For more on the current academic approach, I will focus on Reuven Firestone, though interested readers should also consult the writings of Stanley Wheeler and Jane Dammen McAuliffe.

Firestone points out that from a Muslim perspective, Jewish claims about Islam's cultural borrowing "denies the validity of the Islamic revelation". Muslims view the Koran as a accurate revelation; differences between the Koran and other revelatory texts result from "Jewish and Christian distortion of the Bible". In Firestone's view, Koranic stories are "not made up or adapted from Biblical texts." Rather, he says, "[t]he revelation drew heavily upon the corpus of monotheistic oral traditions" that in part grew out of the Bible and other written scriptures and circulated in Arabia. Over time, the oral tradition had evolved away from the written. Muhammad was sure his accounts were the true versions and the Jews were sure that they were not.[17]

Following from this view, Firestone argues that biblical legends were gradually Arabized in the new environment based on Arabic legends. Hence biblical stories appear within the Koran not due to direct influence, but to intertextuality.[18] Firestone notes that in the Islamic view, Abraham was not a Jew or a Christian but rather a Muslim. Therefore, Muslims did not reject the tales of Abraham of the Jews and Christians (14). Instead, they constructed from these tales, creating a Near-Eastern Abraham that has little in common with the biblical Abraham: "The sacrifice was placed in Mecca, Abraham was a resident of Syria. The legends in Islamic sources are not 'borrowed' but are rather unique creations fully intelligible only when a prior body of discourse—stories, ideas, legends, religious doctrines, and so forth—is taken into consideration along with Isra'ilyyat contemporary Islamic worldview"(19). In general Firestone downplays the role of the Isra'ilyyat, and states that many of those stories are not in Jewish or Christian literature. He promotes the view that Islam excluded the Jewish material not as an anti-Jewish or anti-Christian act but as a point of Islamic pride and integrity.

History

Heinrich Greatz in his *History of the Jews* portrayed Muhammad as an implacable enemy of the Jews, but painted a glowing image of the harmony of Jews and Muslims in Spain under the Umayyad Dynasty from the eighth to the twelfth century. The vision of a golden age in Spain, when the three faiths lived together in respect and tolerance, called convivencia, is an image attractive to many. One of the principal reasons for the persistence of this oversimplified view of convivencia has been the topic's popularity among nonacademics.[19] In Jewish historic memory, Muslims fare better than Christians. While Muslims are seen as engaged in individual conflicts with Jewish community, Christians are remembered as crusaders with a policy of violence against Jews. The actual story is more complex. Steven Wasserstrom offers new perspectives on the religious aspects of the Judeo-Islamic world, and David Nierenberg offers suggestions for a more complex analysis. This brief detour in the Jewish-Muslim history will serve a foundation for theological analysis.

Between Muslim and Jew: Wasserstrom

Steve Wasserstrom, a contemporary scholar of religion, brings up a point that has come up at several other points in this chapter. In contrast with the tradition of Christian-Jewish comparison, most of the studies of the relationship between Judaism and Islam was not done by religionists. For example, the famous advocates of the Judeo-Islamic synthesis, S. D. Goitein and Bernard Lewis are social and political historians not religionists. They used words like synthesis, symbiosis, and mutuality to reflect a common cultural language and lament its end in the modern world.

Wasserstrom moves beyond the language of influence and symbiosis in his consideration of Jewish-Islamic history. Instead, he uses religious criteria of comparison, such as the sharing and interpretation of sancta. In these sancta, Wasserstrom points out instances of convergence and coevolution between Islam and Judaism. Wasserstrom, however, remains a historian; he does not address topics like a Jewish-Islamic Ummah, a common tradition of prophecy, or common roots in the faith of Abraham.

Wasserstrom turns our focus to the first 500 years of Islam. He argues that in the early centuries there was a mixture of traditions, the kind of mixture reflected in the concept of early Jewish-Christians. He points out overlaps in *Hadith* and *tafsir* (commentaries on the Koran and *Hadith*), close connections between the rabbinic leadership and the Caliphate, common theological ideas, and even shared magical texts. He wrote of the insight of the historian Norman Stillman, who notes that in later centuries, Jews and Muslims were educated together. Jews were sent to study arithmetic, geometry, astronomy, and medicine with Muslims in predominantly Muslim schools. Through this sharing, Jews were acquainted with the histories and stories of the Muslim world.[20]

Wasserstrom, going beyond the usual view of Judeo-Islamic synthesis, speaks of "[t]he symbiosis of Jew and Shi'ite" in which the interconfessionalism of Ismaeli Shiites fostered "a rapprochement between Jews and Shiites." The Brethren of

Purity (*ikhwan al Safa*) taught a harmony between faiths and tolerance toward faiths. People could speak of the Jewish Ismaeli-Shiia in the way people now speak of the Judeo-Christian. Furthermore, the Brethren (*ikhwan al Safa*) were influential on the universalism of the Jewish thinkers Ibn Gabirol, Yehudah Halevi, Ibn Ezra, and Nathaniel ibn Fayyumi. Each in their own way saw that there were many paths to God ranging from a general universalism, to each nation having their own prophets, to an inclusivism with Israel in the center.[21] In the context of this Shiite symbiosis, "a group of Jews established the transmission from one generation to another of a testament. Jews are now conserved with the reliability of their authoritative tradition and write chains of tradition to match the Muslim chains of tradition (*silsila*). They claim the testament goes down to the descendents of David."

David Nierenberg

David Nierenberg of the University of Chicago researched the interaction between Jews and Muslims in Christian Spain and found that interfaith interactions were neither tolerant coexistence in convivencia nor were they mutually hostile; intergroup relations are not uniformly ideological. The relationship between Jews and Muslims cannot be boiled down to either coexistence or persecution. There is no single text that can be used to explain the relationship of the two faiths. Nor can the relationship be adequately described by listing events or examples. One must create models that can incorporate both extremes.

> Whatever their persuasion, the methods of all the historians interested in Muslim-Jewish relations have always been more or less the same. Some sift through archives, accumulating examples of peaceful coexistence; others look for grim evidence of persecution and enmity.
>
> First, no history as long and complex as that of Muslim and Jewish interaction can be explained by exegesis of a single text, even when that text is as foundational as the Bible or the Qur'an. Such proof texts can sustain any number of interpretations over time, some of them quite contradictory, as anyone familiar with the Talmud (for example) knows.
>
> Second, societies cannot be classified as tolerant or intolerant merely through the accumulation of "negative" or "positive" examples. Our understanding of the history of Muslim (or Christian) relations with Jews has to be rich enough to explain both the periods of relatively stable coexistence and the periodic persecution that marked Jewish life in both civilizations. Any account of Muslim-Jewish relations that does not simultaneously make sense of, for example, the brilliant career of Samuel Ibn Naghrela and the terrible massacre that ended his son's life is obviously inadequate, for both are very real products of the same society. And finally, historians are not accountants, toting up the assets and liabilities of this and that society in order to declare a particular tradition more solvent (or in this case, more tolerant) than another.[22]

As Nierenberg points out, there is no simple formula to decide if life was better under Christendom or Islam. In the broadest generalities, Jewish life was better most of the time under Islam. However, under both crescent and cross there were periods of tranquility and enmity.

> Just after the expulsion from Spain, Abraham Saba imagined a conversation between two exiles, one from Edom and the other from Ishmael: Each tells of . . . his exile. . . . One tells of the evil done to him by the sons of Esau, and the other tells of what the sons of Ishmael have done to him, and each considers his misfortunes to be the worst possible, so that he almost craves the exile of the other.

> Saba went on to describe some of the differences between Christian and Muslim treatment of Jews, without pretending that he could rank the tolerance of these religions.[23]

Officially, the focus of Nierenberg's research was the reconquest of Christian Spain, a unique era in which Jews lived in close proximity to Muslims but were not subject to Muslim, but to Christian rule. He notes that in this situation "the two groups are free to compete under rules of engagement set by a small group of (largely European and Christian) world powers." In this new social structure, Jews were the officials, tax collectors, and scribes of the chancery, as well as those employed in land and sea services. "A Jew acted as magistrate, and as such sentenced [Muslims] to punishment of whipping or lashes." This situation led to tensions between Jews and Muslims. "When Granada, the last Muslim kingdom of the Iberian Peninsula, negotiated its surrender treaty in late 1491, it included the clause that 'their highnesses would not permit the Jews to have power or command over the Moors, or to be collectors of any tax.' And this was just a few months before the expulsion of the Jews from Spain!"[24]

Turning from social history to theology, Nierenberg points out that both sides used the language of their Christian hosts because "Christians were the ultimate arbiters in this competition between Judaism and Islam. Hence any arguments in the contest needed to be made with an eye on the Christian audience."

> The positions Jews and Muslims took vis-à-vis each other in Christian Spain cannot be understood in any simple sense as the products of "Jewish" or "Islamic" cultural attitudes toward one another. They were that, of course, but they were also very much influenced by what Jews and Muslims understood to be Christian interests and ideologies.

> Are the Jews or the Muslims closer to Christ? The debate is worth describing, because it shows how both Muslims and Jews attempted to borrow from Christian polemics against the other minority group. Clearly, they argue, a Muslim, "who has a lying prophet and an inane and ridiculous law, can receive the law of the Jews." The only doubt is whether "the Jew, who has laws and prophets which we revere and honor as saints, can receive the law of the Moors."

> "It follows that the Jew is closer to the Church, who is a branch cut from the olive that is Christ and has a greater part in Him, than the Moor, who has no connection with Him." Satan, on the other hand, authored Muslim law.

> The Moors, to be sure, are "bestial" and "filthy," but they have never received true law. The Jews have and have rejected it. Rejecting their prophets, they have become a

synagogue of Satan, losing all title to Mosaic law and to the name of "Jews." It follows that . . . the Jews are blasphemous, blind, and obstinate. Moreover, rather than blaspheme, as the Jews do, the Muslims accept Christ: Each year during Holy Week, in Spain and elsewhere in the Mediterranean, crowds of Christian clerics and children participated in ritualized stone throwing attacks on Jewish quarters called "killing the Jews." In 1319, a group of Muslims tried to make the practice their own . . . The point I want to stress is that Muslims in the modern era attacked the Jews as agents of colonial powers in language borrowed from, and addressed to, the dominant colonial powers themselves.[25]

Muslims knew of Christian anti-Judaism; Christian ideas about Jews played an important part in forming Muslim ones. We know that during the first, formative century of Islam, Muslim ideas about Jews were influenced by the views of the millions of Christians whose lands they conquered" (22).

Since there are no general trends, now is the time to research the microhistories of Jewish-Muslim polemics, periods of both hatred and harmony with attention to a particular caliph, a region, and an era. Furthermore, such histories must include the Eastern countries—what are now Afghanistan, Iran, Iraq, and the Central Asia region.[26]

Existential

The historical perspectives on Jewish-Muslim relationships tend to exist in triangulation with Christianity; views of Jewish-Muslim relations depend on views of Jewish-Christian relations. I have already discussed the nineteenth-century view of kinship between Jews and imagined Muslims as a possible counter to European anti-semitism. However, in the twentieth century, Franz Rosenzweig, seeing an affinity between Judaism and Christianity, promoted a view of Islam as a pagan faith in order to reinforce Judeo-Christian kinship. Trude Weiss-Rosmarin, who sees no commonality between Judaism and Christianity, argues that Judaism and Islam are closely related historically, socially, religiously, and geographically.

A completely different approach that rejects the European context for Judaism and wants to set Judaism within Islam is the debated category of Arab Jews. This approach understands Jews in Arab lands as part of Arabic culture, despite their different faith. Avi Elqayam represents this view from a theological perspective. Reuven Firestone advocates an understanding and appreciation of Islam as its own faith position. Finally, Jacob Neusner clearly argues for comparison between the two faiths.

Franz Rosenzweig

Franz Rosenzweig (1886–1929) ranks as one of the most original Jewish thinkers of the modern period. But his approach to Islam follows the eighteenth and nineteenth-century ideas of Islam, and he positions Islam outside of the Western dialogue on faith and the moral will.[27]

Rosenzweig condemned Islam as pagan and not monotheistic, because for him Islam does not display his understanding of the biblical God as love; rather Islam's supreme virtue is submission.[28] According to Rosenzweig, since Islam does not stress a vision of love in religion, then Islam must have a different God. After establishing Islam as pagan, Rosenzweig draws the negative implications. For Rosenzweig, holy war is the sine qua non of Islam, precisely because war is the most sacred act of pagan society in general. However, since Christianity is not pagan, its wars are not holy wars. Franz Rosenzweig was quite prepared to believe that Islam was more humane and tolerant than Christianity during some of its history. But that historical fact remains beside Rosenzweig's point, for he sees Islam as the path of obedience to an entirely different god:

> The concept of the Path of Allah is entirely different than God's path. The paths of God are the disposition of divine decrees high above human events. But following the path of Allah means in the narrowest sense propagating Islam through holy war. In the obedient journey upon this path, taking upon one's self the associated dangers, the observance of the laws prescribed for it, Muslim piety finds its way in the world.

> Unlike the God of faith, Allah cannot go before his own [people] and say to their face that he has chosen them above all others in all their sinfulness, and in order to make them accountable for their sins.

> The path of Allah requires the obedience of the will to a commandment that has been given once and for all time. By contrast, in [Judeo-Christian] brotherly love, the spore of human character erupts ever anew, incited by the ever-surprising outbreak of the act of love.

> Traditional peoples fight to the death. The pagan's personality is an extension of race and state.

Rosenzweig is highly problematic on many levels from his misunderstanding of Islam to his hypocrisy in failing to recognize similarities between his caricature of Islam and his preferred faiths, Judaism and Christianity. He takes the Enlightenment critique of Judaism, which simplifies Judaism as mere submission to the law, and transfers the critique to Islam. He also denies Islam a sense of history or future. He even declares that sacred time, the content of the Jewish and Christian liturgical calendars, does not exist in Islam.

Islam presents the Koran as pure revelation, but for Rosenzweig, creation, revelation, and redemption, which are understood in Jewish and Christian thought as part of God's unfolding plan, become in Islam collapsed together into a single concept of revelation. According to Rosenzweig, if there is continuous revelation, as in Judaism and Christianity, then no idea, act, or spiritual experience can stand between God and the believer (9). Past and future are therefore obliterated in the immediate presence of the divine.[29] However, if Muhammad is the seal of the prophets for a time revelation then he stands between man and God.

Rosenzweig is a crucial voice in the European tradition of depicting Islam as fundamentally violent. One can observe the persistence of Rosenzweig's view by comparing it to Pope Benedict XVI's discussion of Muslim theology at Regensburg on September 12, 2006.[30] In both cases, European religious thinkers are precluding rather than opening dialogue with Islam.

Trude Weiss-Rosmarin

Trude Weiss-Rosmarin (1908–1989) was an Orthodox Jewish-German-American writer, scholar, and feminist activist. She cofounded, with her husband, the School of the Jewish Woman in New York in 1933, and in 1939 founded the *Jewish Spectator*, a quarterly magazine, which she edited for fifty years.

She was an influential critic of the Christian-Jewish dialogue and an advocate of Jewish-Muslim dialogue in her work *Towards Jewish-Muslim Dialogue* (Sept 1967). The book, originally an article in her journal, was written right after the Six Day War. Weiss-Rosmarin warned that victory does not occur on the battlefield but in the winning of the peace.[31] She affirmed Israel as a successor to the ancient Jewish states in the Middle East, but bemoaned Israel's role as an outpost of the West. She drew attention to the Western exclusivism prevalent in Israel, observing the superior attitude of the European-born elite in Israel who referred to Jewish immigrants from Arab countries as the "second Israel" and judged them by Western *mores*.

> A product of Europe and its civilization, Zionism was caught up in the notion of the superiority of Western, i.e., European civilization. This notion caused the Zionists— and Jews as a whole—to *look down* upon the Arabs and their ancient culture in the manner the British *looked down* upon "colonials." The Jews came to Palestine with the determination to make the country an outpost of Western civilization and to "civilize the Arab nations." The unequivocal cultural identification of the Yishuv with the West and the failure to support Arab nationalism in its post-war struggles with the Allies disabused the Arabs of the hope, expressed by Feisal, that the "Jewish cousins" were *cousins* by Arab definition.[32]

> If Zionist movement and Jews generally had been more humble in their encounter with Muslim civilization (and the "Second Israel") and if they had not come to Palestine waving the flag of "Western civilization," Israel might well have benefited from Arab tolerance and humaneness.[33]

> If henceforth Jews will assign to Jewish-Muslim dialogue the importance that is its due, the Arabs, in whose nationalism religion is as important as it is in Jewish nationalism, will eventually—and perhaps sooner than cold-headed realists will dare expect—rediscover that the Jews are their cousins, descendants of Abraham's eldest son, Ishmael, who was Isaac's brother.[34]

> If the young State of Israel is to survive and prosper it must become integrated into the Arab world and be accepted by its neighbors. The crucial challenge confronting Israel is how to conclude an alliance of peace with the Arab nations. We believe that with a complete reorientation, especially a muting of the insistent harping on the theme of "Israel is an outpost of Western civilization" the Arab nations would accept Israel on the basis of the kinship which unites Jews and Arabs.[35]

Weiss-Rosmarin advocates the recognition and revival of the Near-Eastern roots of Hebrew and Israel.

> If there is to be "dialogue" between Israel and the Arab countries, Israel will have to project a new image of herself—the image of a Semitic brother-state in the midst of Semitic brother-states. Instead of proclaiming itself "the outpost of Western civilization," Israel should emphasize that Hebrew is a Semitic language and a sister-language of Arabic. The setting of the Hebrew Bible and the Talmud is not Europe but the Near East—its deserts and its fruitful regions. The biblical ideal of feminine beauty is not the Western dream. It is "the dark and comely beloved" of "Song of Songs," who is swarthy as "the tents of Kedar" and as Arab tents are to this day.[36]

> Our prayers for the end of Exile and for the Return plead: "Renew our days as of old." The *renewal* in the State of Israel should be a *renewal* of Jewishness in the traditional pattern of Hebrew civilization which was born, matured and produced its choicest fruit in the Middle East among kindred Semitic neighbors with kindred mores and, after the birth of Islam (622) in cross-fertilization and symbiosis with a kindred religious civilization.[37]

She cites the works of the Jewish Orientalists on Judeo-Islamic similarities and synthesis: we lived together for more than a millennium; we have commonalities in theology and law; Islam is monotheism; we both have oral traditions and diverse schools of legal reasoning. To these she adds her own observations on contemporary similarities between Jews and Muslims: we share conflicts between the religious education received in madrasas and yeshivot, with modern, secular education; Judaism and Islam both had secular nationalisms rise up to create modern states; we share a common suffering.

> The identity of Jewish and Muslim fate and suffering at the hands of Christians, during the Crusades and in Spain, has not received sufficient attention. It was a period of shared agony and confrontation with a common enemy. This deserves to be better known by Jews and Muslims. The shared fate of oppression and persecution under "Christianity triumphant" is a strong bond of Jewish-Muslim brotherhood.[38]

She advises: (1) American Jewish organizations should foster Jewish-Muslim dialogue. (2) Jewish institutes of higher learning, especially the seminaries, should introduce courses on Islam and Arabic culture (e.g., the way Ignatz Goldziher and Jacob Barth, both observant Jews, taught respectively at the Budapest and Hildesheimer Rabbinical Seminaries). (3) Jewish institutions should assign priority to hosting Muslim lecturers, the way they host Christian lecturers. (4) There should be adult education courses fostering Jewish-Muslim dialogue.[39]

Avi Elkayam

Avraham Elqayam is professor of Kabbalah at Bar Ilan University and active participant in Jewish-Muslim encounter. Elqayam was born in an Arabic-speaking

Jewish family and sees himself as part of the Arabic world. Elqayam rejects the clash of civilizations approach that has placed Jews on the side of the West. He, himself, views Judaism within Arabic Muslim civilization. His own family embodied Arabic Muslim culture, and he argues that we need to develop greater appreciation for the Arabic heritage of the Jews. He presents as his typology of Jews and Muslims the sibling rivalry of Isaac and Ishmael who both come to bury their father Abraham. He is also rejects Western philosophy's contribution to this topic as of no help for the future, specifically pointing out Franz Rosenzweig's anti-Islamic position.[40]

> But are Jews part of the flesh of Western Civilization? I am astonished! My family lived under the Muslim world in Spain and afterward in a small community in Gaza City. They lived submersed in the midst of the Arabic Muslim civilization.
>
> The Torah recounts how Isaac and Ishmael went together to bury Abraham. Therefore, one can legitimately ask about the role of Ishmael in the Jewish spiritual tradition. Our modern philosophers, especially [Franz] Rosenzweig betrayed us. I will turn, therefore, from the world of philosophy to the world of mysticism and Kabbalah.
>
> We need to reconnect the fine threads and the gleanings—that bring us to our brothers Ishmael, that are almost lost to us. It is possible that the time has already passed but we are required at least to try. It is incumbent upon us to begin afresh to build a spiritual bridge between Judaism and Islam, to this I desire.

Elqayam finds three approaches in Jewish mysticism that offer useful approaches to Islam: Kabbalah, Jewish Sufism, and Sabbatianism. Medieval Kabbalah allows us to create a typology of Islam as merciful (*hesed*). In Kabbalah, the world is entirely symbolic of the divine realm; therefore Muslims can fit into Jewish thought as exemplars of mercy. Sufism created a universal meta-religion of prophecy and piety; Sabbatianism created the possibility of syncreticism.

> When you contemplate about Islam, think about Ishmael in the parashah [Hayai Sarah]. Ask what is being symbolized, what is the allusion in the world of divinity. It is surprising to reveal that the Spanish kabbalists saw the essence of Islam as connected to the power of the sefirah hesed. Abraham our patriarch represented hesed and Ishmael comes from Abraham, therefore Islam represents hesed.
>
> In its inwardness, Islam is a religion of hesed. This is the self-consciousness of the Muslims themselves. Muslims are called in Arabic a religion of tolerance. This opinion appears in the writings of Yosef Gikitilla. . . . "The destiny of the Islamic nation amidst the humanity is to represent Divine hesed."
>
> Rabbi Abraham Maimoni was influenced by the Sufi mystical schools. He quoted the learning of Sufis, and praised their use of music, body posture, and prostrations.
>
> Rabbi Abraham Maimoni saw Sufism as a form of meta-religion that bridged between Islamic spirituality and prophetic spirituality. His intention was understandably to imitate the prophets and not the Muslims, except according to his

opinion, only the Muslims preserved the path of prophecy. We have seen in him the spiritual possibility within Judaism that preserves the Jewish identity but which expresses the spiritual world of Islam—the Jew lived in the culture of Islam, drawing leaven from the Muslim world yet making a synthesis between the worlds as a Jew.

Shabbatai Zevi converted to Islam and his followers created a synthesis that mixed both religions, they were Muslims who also kept Jewish practices including the Jewish holidays.

Reuven Firestone

Reuven Firestone, rabbi and professor of Medieval Jewish and Islamic Studies, HUC-JIR/Los Angeles is co-director of the Center for Muslim-Jewish Engagement. Firestone offers well-rounded dedication to Jewish-Muslim encounter. He is an academic historian of early Islam; he is existentially committed to friendship and building bridges with Islam; and he engages in dialogue with Muslims.

Firestone's starting point is not a vision of the history of Islam, but actual exchange and friendship with contemporary Muslims. He has studied Islam in Jerusalem and Cairo and respects the differences between Judaism and Islam. He discusses his initial encounter in college:

> I ended up befriending by chance two young Muslim cousins in Jerusalem and I found myself spending a lot of time with them and their families . . . I eventually found a room in the Muslim Quarter and lived there for two months. It was almost like I had been joined as a family friend to their large family and social network . . . I ate with them, picked up a surprising amount of Arabic, and had discussions about everything from philosophy to food, religion, and of course, politics. This experience shattered my preconceived notions and stereotypes.[41]

He wrote his dissertation on the topic of whom did Abraham sacrifice in Islamic literature, Isaac or Ishmael? His conclusion was that "When all the [Islamic] traditions are collected . . . One hundred thirty authoritative statements consider Isaac to be the intended victim; one hundred thirty three consider it to have been Ishmael."[42] So as an academic he is comfortable declaring this stunning conclusion to a Muslim audience. He does not treat Islam as having already decided for a millennium that the sacrificed son is Ishmael. He is equally historicist in his approach to Koranic claims of its justice or chosenness. His conclusions are that the Arabic texts are not derivative of Judaism but are products of intertextualism among biblical, Arabic, and Aramean narratives.

Firestone wrote an introduction to Islam for Jews. In the book aimed at a popular audience, he presents an academic history of Islam and an overview of Islamic practice. What he does not do is attempt to justify Islamic doctrine in Jewish terms (see Chapter six on a Jewish theory of Islam). He does point out the similarities and parallels, viewing Judaism and Islam as separate religious civilizations from different places, people, histories, and conditions.[43] His is a scholarly perspective: objective, cultural history, with no consideration of theology or revelation. According to his view, the two faiths tell different stories of Abraham, with different values, and many different details; therefore, interfaith narratives that refer to our common Abrahamic stories or our Abrahamic faiths should be used with caution.

Furthermore, Firestone takes a cultural-historical approach to the relationship of the two faiths. Jews and Arabs are both fertile crescent religions growing out of bronze age ideas of chosenness. He tells of the relationship between the two faiths by noting that Arabs had moved to Israel and Iraq; hence there are Arab Nabateans in the Apocrypha, and Arabs are mentioned in the Talmud. Jews in Arabia spoke Arabic and were ethnically Arab. Firestone writes that "the ancient Israelites were keenly aware of their geographical, linguistic, and cultural kinship with Arab peoples. . . . Yet this affinity is tempered by attempts on both sides to maintain a separation."[44]

Firestone notes that scholars sometimes compare the Talmud to the Islamic Hadith, in that both are oral, both reveal God's will, and both record names. But the difference is the source of tradition—in Hadith all goes back to the prophet, while in Talmud the Sages derive the law, which goes back to Sinai (42–43). Firestone wants his readers to understand that Islam, like Judaism, is a complex religion, and that it can't be reduced to simplistic slogans and notions. He wants readers also not to fear Islam or think that all Muslims are extremists. He does note parallels in practice, including a parallel between Torah reading and public Koran reading (*tajwid*), a parallel between the sermon on the Sabbath and *khutba*, and a parallel between Jewish and Islamic purity laws.[45]

Firestone is convinced that Judaism is a dialogic religion, and therefore open to Islam. "Traditional Jewish learning takes place through machloqet or taking opposing positions on principle and working through them, and is dialogical at its core" (84). We have three types of dialogue—argument in the community, discussion between religions, and formal religious polemic—and none of these are good models. "Dialogue today is listening and learning" (86). We need to personally reach out to learn about the other. The most effective dialogue is to read each other's scripture together, since scripture includes formal meanings and informal meanings familiar from growing up as a member of the group. Instead of developing a theology of Islam, he is in favor of pluralism, encounter, and the process of textual reasoning (discussed above).

Jacob Neusner

Jacob Neusner, the scholar of rabbinic literature, writes that to compare the conceptions of Muslim and Jewish faith communities is not difficult, because Islam and Judaism concur that to love God means to participate in a community of those that love God, affirm his unity, perpetually give thanks to Him, and therefore submit to his rule (Islam) or live and rejoice in his kingdom (Judaism). "The contrasts prove subtle . . . Judaism invokes the metaphor of kingdom." Islam "frames things as theological—the sincere, the hypocrite, nuances that God alone can perceive." Neusner points out that both religions both have fasting, absolution, and prayer. They differ in that Judaism orients itself historically and territorially around Jerusalem, and in regards to the eras of the judges, kings, exile, and messianic redemption. Islam orients itself around Divine guidance, compassion, and the creation of an ideal society. There are blessings over food as prayer in Judaism, in contrast there is the mentioning of God's name in Islam—Islam does not have an avoidance of mentioning God's name. Neusner sees the two communities as having similar marriage and divorce laws. However, they differ in almsgiving: Islam offers to help people directly and proximally while Judaism stresses helping others gain self-sufficiency. Neusner would argue that the cords of commonality allow us to begin discussion and to get to know one another, understanding the other both in our own terms and the terms of the other.[46]

The Israeli-Palestinian Conflict

The settlement of Jews in Mandate Palestine followed by the establishment of the State of Israel with the displacement of the native residents from their homes created severe tensions between Judaism and the Arab world. There was a rise of Muslim anti-Semitism that spread from the Arab lands to the rest of the Muslim world. Especially virulent was the new anti-Semitism of the Muslim Brotherhood teacher Sayd Qutb (Egypt, 1906–1966) who rejected the traditional *dhimi* role for Jews and portrayed Jews as a cancer in the realm of Islam.[47]

Followers of Qutb who created the Islamic hard-line position are against the State of Israel, but they also create principles that transcend the narrow political tensions and preclude harmony between the faiths. These statements include, but should not be limited to, stating that the Jews are not a nation, Jews robbed land against God's will, the land of Israel is part of the territory of Islam (*dar Islam*), and that Jerusalem, as Islam's third holiest site, cannot tolerate infidels living in the city.

Jews, in turn, portrayed the Muslim Arabs as their mortal enemies. Within both groups, politics gained ascent over traditional theology. Both sides delegitimize the other faith. Many religious Jews in Israel and the United States currently ignore 2,000 years of Diaspora Jewish law in favor of a return to biblical literalism, viewing the Arab nations as *molekh* and *amalek*—as in a biblical war in which they do not worry about the death of non-combatants. Laws concerning the land of Israel intended for the messianic age are now applied to contemporary events—because of the perception by many in the Settler movement that we are witnessing the start of the messianic age. We will look at two variants of this approach: the legal approach of Rabbi Melamed, and the journalistic approach of Bat Yeor.

Against Islam

Rabbi Eliezer Melamed, rosh yeshiva of Har Bracha and chief rabbi of the community, is a prime example of the religious Zionist thinking prevalent after the Six Day War, which led to the rise of the messianic settlers' movement. He treats all

Muslims as the enemy and characterizes them as liars and killers who constantly wage war.

Islam Lives by the Sword [48]

We are in a state of war with the vast majority of Arab countries, with Islamic believers throughout the world supporting them. We are talking about tens of millions of enemies who are ready to go to war against us at any moment, and hundreds of millions more who voice support for it.

The genetic code of Islam is directed towards a steadfast war to impose the religion of Mohammad on the entire world by means of the sword. And to achieve this goal, everything is legitimate. If they need to lie, they will lie. If they need to kill, they will kill—hundreds of thousands or even millions.

According to the Muslim way of thinking, the world is divided into two areas: *Dar al-Islam* is the area already conquered by Islam. *Dar al-Harb* is the area of war, which the Arabs are commanded to conquer until it is turned into Muslim territory. After a certain territory has been conquered by Islam, it is declared as holy Muslim territory, which is forbidden to be relinquished under any circumstances.

The State of Israel constitutes a double problem from their perspective, for it was established on territory that was conquered by Islam since its foundation (except for a period of approximately 100 years when it was ruled by the Crusaders); and not only this, but the land of Israel is located in the heart of Muslim territory. Therefore, as far as they are concerned, this is the first place they must conquer—either by sword or by guile.

There are similar statements from many religious figures, who, when interviewed, give snippets of a negative and totalizing approach to the Muslim world. For example, former chief rabbi Rabbi Ovadia Yosef, who initially supported the 1993 Oslo accords for pragmatic reasons, has provoked outrage with a sermon calling for the annihilation of Arabs. "The Lord shall return the Arabs' deeds on their own heads, waste their seed and exterminate them, devastate them and banish them from this world. . . . It is forbidden to be merciful to them. . . . They are evil and damnable." Even though these speeches are common from Israeli religious leaders, they usually have a disclaimer issued afterward. In this case, an official spokesman defended the rabbi, saying his remarks referred only to "Arab murderers and terrorists" and not the Arab people as a whole.[49]

A journalistic approach of anti-Muslim discourse is exemplified by the well-known journalist Bat Ye'or, which is the pen name of Gisèle Littman (b. 1933), an Egyptian-born British author, who writes about the history of Christian and Jewish *dhimis*, living under Islamic governments in degradation. She is from a middle-class Jewish family, but she and her parents were forced to leave Egypt in 1957 after the Israeli invasion of Egypt during the Suez War of 1956. Littman's perception is not that of a trained historian; rather she focuses on what she perceives as the entirely negative concept of *Dhimmitude*, which is imposed as a direct consequence of Islamic-mandated jihad. In her opinion, "Muslim theologians and jurists attached so many conditions and humiliations to this real protection that the status of the protected Jews and Christians—the *dhimis*—soon became a status of oppression, deprivation and insecurity," which she calls dhimmitude. Craig R. Smith in a *New York Times* article referred to her as one of the "most extreme voices on the new Jewish right." Her theories of Arabic plans for domination bear similarity "to anti-Semitic conspiracy theories." She is widely cited as an authority on web publications.

Three Approaches to Encounter

I will offer three approaches to encounter, one from an Israeli settler, one from an American from an Arab land, and a third from the head of the American Reform movement.

Rabbi Menachem Froman of Tekoa responds to the tension around him by advocating a universal vision of peace. He lives on the frontlines of hospitality with Islam through his friendship with local Islamic leaders including Hamas Sheikh Yassin (d. 2004) of Gaza City.[50] Froman views the two religious communities as close in their faiths and accepts that Islam portrays itself a religion of peace, and therefore Jews and Muslims must learn to live together. Strikingly, he views an internationalized Jerusalem as a means of creating an interreligious bridge.

> Amidst the difficult bloody battles that we have had since the beginning of Zionism with the Muslims . . . We know . . . that the war between the Jews and the Muslims is the work of the cursed devil. We know that Islam is named after peace.[51]

> Is peace possible with Islam? The question that I wish to pose is the opposite: Is peace possible without Islam? . . . Is it possible to live in peace with the Arab reality without trying to get to know the life of the Arabs? Can anyone who opens up to Arab society deny that religious life is central to it?

> The Israelis as representatives of Western culture and the Palestinians as representatives of the Muslim world can build the bridge between the two worlds. Indeed here in the Holy Land it is possible to build the inter-religious bridge that is so needed for peace in the entire world.

> From the difficult experience of the shared history of the two nations—the Israeli nation and the Palestinian nation—we can learn one important thing—between two brothers—when one's fate is bad, the fate is also bad of the second. Only when it is good for one, it will be, with God's help, good for its double.

> Wouldn't it be wise to launch an offensive aimed at transforming Jerusalem into the capital of the world? . . . Jewish tradition contains many expressions of the idea that Jerusalem is not confined by the bounds of common territoriality. The Midrash, for example, cites it as the place from which Jacob's Ladder connected earth with heaven.

> If the purpose of Zionism is to transform the sublime visions of our heritage into reality here on earth, wouldn't its true fulfillment be the realization of Isaiah's vision here in this temporal city? This is not a utopian vision appropriate only to the End of Days.[52]

Rabbi Haim Ovadia, rabbi of a Sephardic congregation in West Los Angeles writes about the need for dialogue with Muslims as a "Jew of Islam," a relationship only rent asunder by the rise of modern nationalism.

> I am a Jew of Islam . . . It is true that my iPod is packed with Abdul Wahab, Sabah Fakhri and Farid Al Atrache and the Shabbat songs, and liturgy borrows freely from generations of Islamic, Sufi and secular Arabic music, but the connection runs much deeper.
>
> Looking back, we should ask ourselves, what happened to moderate and enlightened Islam? Part of the answer is that when West met East in modern times, it was an encounter infused with arrogance, religious zeal and greed. . . . Is there any wonder that nationalist and religious forces eventually sprang to action in order to counter-act that hostile takeover?[53]

Rabbi Eric H. Yoffie, former president of the Union for Reform Judaism, spoke to the Islamic Society of North America at their 44th Annual Convention in 2007. He sought to overcome ignorance and stereotyping.[54] "There exists in this country among all Americans—whether Jews, Christians, or non-believers—a huge and profound ignorance about Islam. . . . There is no lack of so-called experts who are eager to seize on any troubling statement by any Muslim thinker and pin it on Islam as a whole." The goal, he says, is to work together. "We will help you to over-come stereotyping of Muslims, and you will help us to overcome stereotyping of Jews . . . Anti-Semitism is not native to Islamic tradition, but a virulent form of it is found today in a number of Islamic societies, and we urgently require your assis-tance in mobilizing Muslims here and abroad to delegitimize and combat it."

What of the Concept of "Abrahamic Faiths"?

In recent years, the phrase "Abrahamic faiths" has been the banner under which encounter with Muslims has taken place. The goal of the phrase is to include Muslims within the American Judeo-Christian tradition by referring to Abraham, the patriarch held in common by the three monotheistic religions.

The expression "Abrahamic religion" in the singular, originates from the Koran's repeated references to the religion of Abraham (Surah's 2:130, 135; 3:95; 6:123, 161; 12:38; 16:123; 22:78). This expression refers specifically to Islam, and is sometimes used to contrast Islam with Judaism and Christianity, as when, for example, Abraham is declared to have been a Muslim, "not a Jew nor a Christian"(Surah 3:67 see also Surah 2:135).

The modern source of the term is Louis Massignon (d. 1962), French Islamicist and Christian scholar, who saw the faith of Abraham as a bridge between Christianity and Islam. Since then, Abraham has served interfaith theorists as common ground for the three faiths, now labeled "Abrahamic." Christians view Abraham as the revelation of God's covenant and Muslims view Abraham as the first Muslim. This bridge played a role in Second Vatican Council, where in *Lumens Gentium* #16 Muslims are praised because "they profess to hold the faith of Abraham" and in *Nosta Aetate* #3 Muslims are praised for accepting one God creator of heaven and earth, and for their seeking "to submit to God's will as Abraham did, they link their faith to Abraham." However, Abrahamism is a term from Christian theology, since the revelation and covenant for all people are ascribed to Abraham. For Muslims, Abraham is Muslim; the Muslims themselves see Jews and Christians not as Abrahamic, but as people of the book.

For Jews, Abraham is the start of the Jewish people. Jews in the midrashic literature do see Abraham in many ways similar to Muslims, as the beloved of God, as merciful, and as having found God though rational means. But it is not a Jewish theological term. Furthermore, Jews do not stress the faith of Abraham, but rather stress the action proscribed by Moses and Mosaic prophecy. And Jews understand Islam as related to Yishmael not Abraham.

Even then Abraham is still useful for a starting point for interfaith dialogue and less as a theological similarity among the faiths. In the field, the concept does work: All three faiths view Abraham as the discontinuity with paganism, all three view Abraham as a beacon of obedience to God, and all three faiths have greater commonalities in their views of Abraham than of other biblical figures. Prophet Abraham's willingness to sacrifice all for God is admired by Judaism, Christianity, and Islam. On the other hand, while the Abraham figure in interfaith was to be inclusive and intercommunal and ecumenical, the figure, in fact, radically differs among the faiths. This can be turned into a strength; for it is good for displaying parallel stories among them and a good example for teaching similarities and differences. Even the differences, conflicts of interpretation, and rejections of other views, serve didactic purposes.

There are many other biblical figures that we can compare to show our similarities and differences, including Jacob, Joseph, David, and Jonah. Such comparisons would weave together for teaching purposes Bible and Midrash with Koran and Hadith. The comparisons will show some of our similarities and differences. But how can we respect the alternate versions without claiming the sole truth of our version.[55]

Conclusions

Why did Jews not generate a modern theology of Jewish-Muslim dialogue? First, there are no longer Jews living in many of these lands. Second, the Arab-Israeli conflict blocked any attempts. Finally, the integration of Jews into European culture and the emphasis on the "Jewish-Christian" heritage within it made many Jews forget the prior ages of Judeo-Islamic integration.

At this point, much of contemporary dialogue is still about getting to know the other side, very like the activities between Jews and Catholics in the early 1960s. There are many kum-ba-ya events, synagogue and mosque twinnings, and trilateral dialogue to allow people to ask questions. These activities are useful for helping people to overcome fear and distrust, to create understanding, and to help to reduce tension. People need a basic knowledge of the other side and the ability to work together. Many of the current activities are done at the grassroots level, at college campuses aimed at the younger generation. Teaching the importance of Islamic sources in the works of great Jewish thinkers can create an awareness of the possibilities of encounter. This educational process would be an internal Jewish endeavor and could carry important implications. First and foremost, if Jews are taught about the prior integration of the two faiths then there would be greater clarity that the political war between Arabs and Jews is not a faith war. It could promote an understanding that Islam and Judaism can coexist. Recently, Princeton historian Mark Cohen won the Goldziher prize for his work on Jewish-Muslim understanding.[56]

We lack, however, a tradition of pioneer Jewish thinkers who turned to Islam in a theological way. There are no Jewish versions of Louis Massignon or Kenneth Craig. Trude Weiss-Rosmarin may have been the only one to try. We are starting a half century behind our Jewish-Christian dialogue and a half century behind the Muslim-Christian dialogue.

The majority of Jews can acknowledge that we share the same God. But:

- Can Jews accept the concept of ongoing prophecy?
- Do we think of love of God and fear of God in the same terms?
- Do we share a common vision for society?
- Are our forms of ritual and law the same?
- Can Jews overcome their view of Islam as derivate and learn to see Islam as Muslims see Islam?

Jews and Muslims are similar in their concepts of God and man, and they have similar textual, legalistic, practices. Both faiths reject the Christian ideas of original sin and treating the divine as man. Yet, Islam places more emphasis than Judaism on the concepts of immortality, hypocrisy, and angelic visitors such as Gabriel.[57] Heschel's theory of prophecy exerted a deep influence on the great scholar of Islam Henry Corbin. Heschel noted the language of Islamic religious experience in Maimonides and in turn Corbin noted the similar role in Islam. Would this be the starting point for a dialogue?

We should also not avoid teaching the differences between the faiths. In the recent sessions between Muslim leaders and Catholic leaders recorded in the documents that replied to *A Common Word,* they stated both commonality and difference. They both affirmed the common love of God and love of neighbor, but S. H. Nasr noted that Muslims reject the Trinity, that Catholics lack a legal system for ritual compared to Islam, and that Catholics have different reactions to secularism than do Muslims. What are the basic theological points by which Jews differ from Islam? Clearly, they are the content of prophecy, the reception of prophecy, and the transmission of prophecy.

The Catholic Church moved from teaching contempt to recognizing Judaism as a living faith. We cannot preclude giving any group in Islam that wants dialogue the chance to change and slowly learn tolerance and respect, especially since it serves their own needs for entering a global economy. We recognize that certain Islamic countries currently have a lack of religious freedom, fund hateful literature, have negative views of Judaism, and fail to recognize the State of Israel.

But we cannot compare their worst comments to our best. Both sides have saints and both sides have advocates of hatred. We must, however, remember heroic figures, such as Sister Rose Thering, who confronted her own church with the anti-Semitism that was being taught in its textbooks and helped bring about an interfaith revolution.

In the interim, we need to give those that seek encounter our support. We must not look to the past and use that to dissuade us from working with our counterparts now and in the future. One must first transcend the past and look to the future, then one must transcend polemical arguments on both sides, and then give precedence to common points. But we can look to the past to see how long it took most Western countries to achieve the liberties of the modern world, and know that it will also take many Muslim countries time to achieve this openness. Such starting points will allow for a positive future Jewish theology of Islam.

8

Hinduism and Indian Religions

Most medieval Jews who did not travel knew of the practices of Eastern religions primarily as a form of hearsay, whispers of far-off lands with unfamiliar customs. Because of this perspective, they tended to form very westernized understandings of the East. This approach is typified in a sixteenth century, non-Jewish account of the discovery of the New World, *De Molucco* (1523). Maximilian of Transylvania writes, "The natives of all unknown countries are commonly called Indians."[1] From many traditional Jewish works, one gets a similar sense that all distant people are Indians, Africans, or Tartars. For example, in the *Guide for the Perplexed*, Maimonides (1135–1204) casually states that the Indians and Tartars are the only people who have not joined Abraham's monotheistic mission.

Hinduism

Hinduism is a modern word that refers to the variety of interrelated religions native to the Indian subcontinent. Prior to the nineteenth century, there was for the most part, no concept of a single Indian religion among inhabitants of the Indian subcontinent that would correspond to the modern concept of Hinduism Today, we use the term Hinduism to refer to those Indian religions that share overlapping concepts and practices (*dharma, samsara, karma, moksha*), some of these groups may also share some of their sacred texts (*shastras*) or ideas from one of the six philosophic schools (*astika*). Depending on the context, Jainism, Sikhism, and Buddhism may be considered as part of Hinduism. The correct term used in contemporary interfaith encounter is teachers of the Dharma, or Sanatana Dharma, teachers of the eternal truth. Contemporary approaches to Hinduism make distinctions between the philosophic writings such as Vedanta, the religion of the Temples, and the teachings of a living guru.

- Medieval texts—Saadia, Halevi, Meiri
- Menashe ben Israel, *Zohar*, and gifts to the East
- Wandering Litvaks: David de Bet Hillel, Yaakov Saphir
- Modern Appreciations—Maurice Fleugel, Ezriel Guenzig
- Modern Journeys East, Tagore, Miriam Bokser, David Zeller, and Meditation,

- Halakhah and India—The View From Afar—Meditation, Yoga, and Hair
- The Insider View—Nathan Katz, Barbara Holdrege
- Hindu-Jewish Summit
- A Theology of Hinduism—Alon Goshen-Gottstein

Medieval Jewish Texts

Jewish texts tended to distinguish simply between the Brahmins, who were the Indian priestly class, and between the rest of Indian believers. The Brahmins were seen as having religion and laws similar in form to Western religions.

Jews knew about various aspects of Indian religions through the Arabic (and Persian) mediators.[2] The earliest Muslim scholar to show sustained interest in Indian religious and philosophical texts was al-Bīrūnī (c. 973–1048). A scientist and philosopher, he translated a number of Sanskrit works into Arabic (including selections from Patañjali's *Yogasūtras* and the *Bhagavad Gita*) in connection with his encyclopedic treatise on India. Al-Bīrūnī did not translate the names of foreign deities, nor did he incorporate them into his own theology. Like those who translated polytheistic Greek texts into Arabic, al-Bīrūnī renders the Sanskrit gods (*deva*) with the Arabic terms for angels (*malā'ikah*) or spiritual beings (*rūhāniyyāt*), a theological shift aiding in their acceptance.[3] In addition, most Muslim theologians expanded People of the Book to include Hinduism, allowing for a comparison in scripture. Well-versed Jewish readers would have been acquainted with these translations and would have been thereby shielded from the polytheistic implications of the original texts. These texts create a universal commonality between West and East and were willing to understand Indian religions as monotheistic.[4]

Saadia

Saadia Gaon (d. 942) was the leader of Babylonian Jewry, a halakhic decider, grammarian, biblical commentator, and liturgical poet whose influence on the medieval period was seminal. His theological work, *Emunot veDeot*, set the contours of Jewish belief until today.

Saadia's works reflect the theologically complex interfaith meetings from cosmopolitan humanistic Baghdad. In accounts from the world of medieval Abbasid Islam, we have a well-known report from the end of the tenth century on "the friendly discussions concerning religion held in Baghdad between members of various religions where equal numbers of Muslims, Christians, Jews, Zoroastrians, Manicheans, atheists, and possibly also Buddhists and Brahmins met to debate theological issues. The participants agreed upon absolute tolerance toward one another; when their various faiths were discussed, any dogmatic appeal to authority was ruled out."[5]

Many scholars question whether representatives of the Eastern religions actually participated in these discussions, called Majlis. Instead, they assume that rather than an actual presence, the representatives were literary devices used by Islamic skeptics in order to score theological points. In his presentation of these multi-faith discussions, Julius Guttmann, the historian of Jewish thought, wrote, "Saadyah attacks the view of the sect of the 'Brahima' (Brahmins) to the effect

that man needs no prophets, (but these Brahima may have been an Islamic sect)."
Current trends, more aware of the immense role of Indian religions in Central
Asia and Persia do not reject the possibility of actual meetings (see the discussion
of the Silk Road in the next chapter).[6]

Whether actual contact with Indian religions is historically true or not, Saadia
correctly presents many Buddhist and Hindu theological positions in his work.
Notably, he seems to have an understanding of actual practices of the Indian
subcontinent. For example, he observes, "There are certain Hindus who have
hardened themselves against fire, although it burns them whenever they come
into contact with it."[7] Many of his examples paint Brahmins and Indian culture as
the religious exotic "other," outside of Saadia's own Baghdad culture.

Saadia believed in a single universal truth and a single revelation, thus all truth
in all religion has to coincide with the revelation of Torah. Acknowledging universal
reason, he accepts reason unaided by revelation as capable of reaching the same
truths. Even other religious practices can reach the same universal truth. In his eager-
ness to reject other religious positions in order to prove Judaism as the most logical
religion, Saadia provides disproof of every known alternative religious position and
is as comfortable refuting the lack of a providential creator in Indian thought as he
is rejecting Trinitarian thought. Similarly, in his rather open discussion of Brahmin
ritual, Saadia defends Jewish ritual practices against Brahmanism, acknowledging
its conventional nature, but concluding that Judaism is more logical:

> What if the Brahmins told you, "We have a tradition from Adam ordering us to wear
> garments made of a mixture of wool and linen, and to eat meat soup with milk, and
> to team up an ox and a donkey . . . It is really we who put these allegations into the
> mouth of the Brahmins. As for the Brahmins themselves, they merely maintain that
> these things are permissible, and we, too, admit that they were permissible at the
> time when they were thus held to be, but that it was also fully in consonance with
> reason to forbid them, when man was capable of voluntarily refraining from them,
> on account of some advantage that he might attain thereby.[8]

The other religions, even Brahmanism, do not and cannot contradict the Torah;
their customs merely reflect pre-Sinai practice.

Yehudah Halevi

India had a status of one of the ancient civilizations since Hellenistic times, which
was carried over into the Judeo-Arabic world. Yehudah Halevi casually mentions
that Indian culture is "hundreds of thousands of years old." Halevi chooses Indian
culture and the existence of a King of India as an example of something that we
only know by reliable witnesses due to India's remoteness, but also because of the
great mysterious wisdom that was traditionally attributed to the Indian sages.
Yet, elsewhere Halevi views the Indians as idolatrous pagans and a "dissolute,
unreliable people," lacking any credibility:

> Al Khazari: Does it not weaken thy belief if thou art told that the Indians have antiq-
> uities and buildings which they consider to be millions of years old?

The Rabbi: It would, indeed, weaken my belief had they a fixed form of religion, or a book concerning which a multitude of people held the same opinion, and in which no historical discrepancy could be found. Such a book, however, does not exist. Apart from this, they are a dissolute, unreliable people, and arouse the indignation of the followers of religions through their talk, whilst they anger them with their idols, talismans, and witchcraft. To such things they pin their faith, and deride those who boast of the possession of a divine book. Yet they only possess a few books, and these were written to mislead the weak-minded.[9]

Islamic thought tended to treat Indian culture as possessing wisdom, even if it does not have revelation. Treating India as the land of ancient wisdom, Shem Tov Ibn Falaquera, in his work, *Ethical Epistle*, writes in the thirteenth century and brings a story about an old man who suddenly appears out of nowhere. When asked about his origins, he answers: "I am from the land of India, from the seed of ancient sages. All my ancestors had ancient beliefs, but only I am left, a prophet of wisdom, an old man of cunning."[10]

Meiri and Cultural Influence

Though direct interfaith exchange did not occur until recent centuries, knowledge of Eastern religions circulated as part of the literary world of medieval Jews. In late antiquity, for example, stories such as *Baarlam and Josephat* contain tales that present Buddhism in monotheistic form; similarly, *Aesop's Fables* shows the influence of Indian *Jatakas* tales.

The most influential medieval work of this genre was *Kalilah wa-Dimnah*, which was based on Indian fables contained in the Panchatantra, which was composed in India around 300 C.E. These fables were seen as a Brahmin rival to the Buddhist fable-books and include variants of several of the *Jatakas*, or Buddha birth-stories. The book was translated into Pahlavi around 570 C.E. and thence traveled westward through Arabic sources. According to Abraham ibn Ezra, a Jew had translated it directly from Sanskrit into Arabic. Whether this is factual or not, the passage of Indian wisdom from Arabic into the European languages was conducted by Jewish scholars, even the *Yoga sutras* of Patanjali and the *Bhagavad Gita* circulated in the Judeo-Arabic literary climate.[11] Also, some of the material from *Baarlam and Josephat* and *Kalilah wa-Dimnah* circulated in a Hebrew translation called *The Prince and the Ascetic* of Abraham ibn Hasdai.

Rabbi Menachem Meiri, a thirteenth-century rationalist and Talmudic commentator, who, as a cultured Provencal was aware of these perennial classics, freely quotes them to construct his own pietistic edifice:

The pietistic tales tell about an ascetic who went on a journey and was lost in a field.

A man found him, greeted him and brought him home for food and drink. They talked. The ascetic asked, "What are you doing here and what is your work?" He answered, "I am plowing in order to seed."

Why do you plow?
In order to seed.
And why do you seed?
In order to harvest.
What is you intended purpose in harvesting?
In order to winnow, and to gather to the house and storeroom.
What is your intended purpose in these?
For wealth and prosperity.
What is your intended purpose in collecting money?
To fulfill my desires with pleasures, to have honor among people, to rule my neighbors, and to vanquish my enemies.
Then the ascetic admonished him and said. Thus the prophet forecast the wicked harvest-crushed fruit (*Hosea* 10:13). He sins in all his actions and all details of his labors. Your intentions are not fitting but hated and despised.
The intended purpose in gathering wealth is to provide for you and your family to serve God in righteousness and generosity.[12]

Meiri uses the tales to make his own points about the need to serve God in everything that we do. He removes the foreign elements and adds biblical verses in order to give the tales a Jewish feel. The telling of these tales shows the commonality between faiths of many spiritual virtues; whether Meiri thought these tales originally came from Sufi circles or from Hinduism is irrelevant in his usage. A similar phenomenon is found in the translations of Christian romances into Hebrew and Judeo-German. This occurrence of using a story line from another religious tradition in one's own stories was essential in the creation of the later corpus of tales known as Hasidic tales, which freely used tales of saints from around the globe.

The fifteenth-century Yemeni Jewish scholar Alu'el provides another case of the citation of Eastern material for Jewish purposes. Alu'el cites the yogic teachings on the positive and negative qualities of right and left-hand breaths from the yogic text, *The Pool of Nectar*, in his exegesis of a biblical text (Genesis 13:9). In such a case, the Indian material was only of significance insofar as it contributed to the main point the author was making.[13]

Moshe Idel, the scholar of Jewish mysticism, testifies that he found in a manuscript of Moshe de Leon (late thirteenth century) a discussion and rejection of the Brahmin concept of *maya*, the illusory nature of reality. The discussion focuses on the Indian story of the endlessness of time as vividly portrayed by a never-ending procession of ants. According to Idel, De Leon's purpose was to contrast endless time in the Indian story with the Castilian Kabbalistic ideas on time and creation; once again, the Indian thought served solely as a means of explaining Jewish thought.

Magical Theory of Religion

There is an entire range of early fourteenth-century Spanish thinkers that followed the thought of Abraham ibn Ezra, who explains the religions of India as a form of magic. None of these authors are famous and influential; however, the approach has echoed in many citations and paraphrases in later literature. For example, Rabbi Yosef Tov Elam (fourteenth-century Spain) comments that:

> This is the way of the wise men of India that make mental forms at specific times to bring down the power of the stars, a great wisdom with many books . . . I know a Muslim wise man in this, I know a little to teach and not to do, because it is truly idolatry.[14]

A similar statement is found in the writings of his contemporary, Menachem Tamar, who claims "I met a Jew from India who told me that these things exist there. They make images at specific times and the form speaks."[15]

Menashe ben Israel

Menashe ben Israel (1604–1657) was a Portuguese rabbi, kabbalist, and widely read scholar who lived in the Netherlands. Rabbi Menashe ben Israel was a universalist concerning religions, finding a common core behind them.

Pedro Teixeira, a Portuguese Christian, visited India and wrote a book in 1610 to describe his experiences. Richard G. Marks notes that, "Teixeira expresses only disdain for the religious practices he observed, calling them 'absurdities,' 'follies and superstitions,' and 'diabolical ceremonies.'" Menashe reads Teixeira and records the same practices with approval because they attest to an underlying universal doctrine:

> Even today Indians living between the Gihon River and the Indus, believing in transmigration, act according to [Pythagoras's] custom. And they show great compassion for animals. They walk to the streets of the city and purchase birds from their captors and send them away free. And among them when a bull mates with a cow, it is their custom to spend a great expenditure, as Pedro Teixeira testifies. And in their hour of death, they take in their hands the tail of a cow which they have fed in the thought that they would immediately enter inside it . . . In the kingdom of Gujarat, the men called among them pious ones and men of deeds who put a mask on their faces because they fear to kill with their breath the small flying creatures, which for their smallness cannot be seen by the eye. And thus almost all the people of India believe in the transmigration of animals.[16]

Menashe finds common doctrines in Eastern religions and considers their views of transmigration to have common meaning with Judaism; he also finds Hindu views compassionate at their core.

Developing the ideas of the *Zohar* with some other early modern traditions, Menashe writes that the Brahmins are the descendants of Abraham, and Pythagoreans and other ancients share the religion:

> Similarly, when he [Abraham] went down to Egypt and lived there, he taught this philosophy, after which he sent the sons of his concubines away from Isaac while he was yet alive towards the East to their holy land, India. They also disseminated this

faith. Behold, you may see there the Abrahamites, who are today called Brahmans; they are the sons of Abraham our patriarch and they were the first in India to spread this faith, as Appolonius Tionius, who spoke with them and King Yercha face to face, testified . . . And they spoke the truth, for from the seed of Abraham this ideology was created anew. From there, the new belief spread all over India, as is evident from the writings of that period. Their faith is, however, often thought of as Pythagoras' innovation, since it had disappeared for a few years, but he was not the originator. Also, this was the code followed by Alexander Polister who heard and studied it from the prophet Ezekiel who was his mentor . . .[17]

Foreign Powers

The *Zohar*, the classic of Jewish mysticism, offers a view of Eastern religions as having their own spiritual force. For the *Zohar*, Jewish rites, in contrast to those of the East, work better for bringing down magical influx. In fact, it warns not to be led astray by using the foreign techniques rather than the Jewish practices:

Once I happened to be in a town of the descendents of the easterners, and they told me some of their ancient wisdom. They also possessed books of their wisdom, and they brought me one such book. In this book it was written that, according to the goal that a human being intends in this world, so there is drawn to him a spirit from on high. If he intends a high and holy object, he draws that thing to himself from above, and if he cleaves to the other side (*sitra ahra*), he brings down the thing upon himself.

They said that it essentially depends on the words, deeds, and intention to which one attaches oneself, for the side to which one attaches oneself is drawn down from above.

In that book I found all the rites and practices involved in the worship of the stars and constellations. It included the directions for the rites, as well as instructions about intention in order to draw influence on oneself.

(It is the same for one who wants to attach himself to the Holy Spirit on high through words, deeds, and thought of the intentions of the heart.)

My children, the teachings of that book are close to the words of Torah, but you should keep far away from these books lest your hearts stray after their rites and all those matters, lest, God forbid, you turn aside from the rites of the holy and Blessed One, for all these books lead human beings astray. This is because the people of the East were great sages, who inherited this wisdom from Abraham. He had given it to his sons of his concubines, as it is written, "To the sons of the concubines that Abraham had taken, Abraham gave gifts" (Genesis 25: 6), but later [these gifts] were drawn to the other side.[18]

This passage presents the religious techniques of the East, which in this passage probably refer to Arabia, as originally profound offshoots of Judaism that were misused. This legend has origins in the Book of Jubilees and was developed in various midrashim, however most Jewish versions saw the gifts as knowledge of sorcery rather than the Eastern religions. For example, Rashi, based on *Sanhedrin* 91a, explains that Abraham imparted to them the secrets of the unclean names. Maharal (*ad locum*) explains it as knowledge to counteract sorcery and as a way to exorcise demons that enter into men.

Aryeh Kaplan (d. 1983), a translator of meditation and kabbalistic texts, popularized Menashe ben Israel's understanding of the *Zohar* as applying, not to Arabia, but to Eastern religions in general. He also specifically explains the verse in positive terms and referring to meditation techniques. Kaplan's reading of the *Zohar* as legitimating Eastern religions and meditation was eagerly accepted among those in the late twentieth century with an interest in meditation and spirituality. This opinion has gained currency in circles of returnees to Judaism, who need to find a textual source to maintain a respect for their experiences with Eastern religions. Kaplan's writings are filled with winks and nods that the Eastern religions, especially the practice of mediation, are already in Judaism, leaving the Eastern faiths derivative.

David d'Beth Hillel—Henotheism

The famous Jewish traveler of the second half of the twelfth century, Benjamin of Tudela, gives the most detailed description of the Indians in medieval Jewish literature. He describes the group situated on the western coast of India, as "the children of Cush," pagan, sun-worshipping, and practicing astrology. They are described as practicing black magic, believing in Satan, and following such idolatrous customs as burning people alive. Yet the rule of law is said to prevail in India and the king is even described as a righteous ruler.[19]

David d'Beth Hillel (mid-nineteenth century), a member of the group of Lithuanian expatriates who came to live in the land of Israel under the inspiration of the Gaon of Vilna, undertook a journey eastward through Afghanistan to India. Once in India, he stayed long enough to learn about the local religions, Hinduism, Zoroastrianism, Christianity, and Islam. In his account of the other religions, he consistently views them as devolutionary henotheists, meaning that they had one God at the time of Adam and from there digressed into having lower deities under a supreme God. Their rituals are similar to Jewish practices, and they originally worshipped one God; now they use statues for their deities and mix idolatry into their worship:

> Many of the Hindu purification and mourning ceremonies and other customs bear a strong resemblance to those of the Israelites; since they practice circumcision and sanctify Saturday I should judge them to be descendents of long lost Ten tribes.

> The worship of images, of all kinds of animals and creeping things is very prevalent at Cochin. Very many persons pay divine honor to serpents, which I conceive to have originated in the idolatry spoken of in II Kings, ch. XVIII, v. 4.

> The Parsees . . . pay respect to fire, the sea, rivers, the sun, and the moon. I have enquired of them for this conduct. They answered me that they believe in one God,

but those above mentioned, being the great and primary creations of the almighty, therefore ought to be venerated.

I have been told by many learned Hindus that the ancient Hindus did not worship any idols, and so it is found written in all ancient Hindu books; but I conceive that they had drawn the idolatry from the Samaritans who came to India in the time of Alexander the Great, as it is specified in ancient histories. When he conquered Judea the Samaritans brought to him evil reports against the Jews, and Simeon the Righteous being the High Priest at the time, encountered Alexander and explained to him the cause and that he understood that these were falsities framed through enmity. He then allowed the Israelites to deal with them hardly and it was likely that they came with his army to India and used their customs with their idols (as it is mentioned in II Kings, ch. XVII, v. 29–35). I indeed very much wonder what has befallen the great number of Samaritans as I have never met with one of them excepting those that I have mentioned, or those wicked Jews who came to India after the destruction of Jerusalem by Nebuchadnezzar.

To give all the differences of the Hindus and their customs would occupy many books, for which I have no time, but I shall only in a concise manner give my general opinion of them. All the Hindus believe in Brahmah, Vishnu, and Shiva—Brahmah a creator, Vishnu a preserver, and Shiva a destroyer; but they believe also that there is one self existing or everlasting Being.[20]

While locked into the biblical and rabbinic worldview of his upbringing, Hillel nevertheless showed great openness by trying to find a place in his worldview for his encounters. His approach was to see the practices as mixtures of true and false beliefs.

Saphir-Idolatry

Another wandering Lithuanian Jew whose family also moved to Israel under the influence of the Vilna Gaon, Yaakov Saphir (1822–1885), was given a Middle Eastern education including fluency in Arabic and had undertaken a journey eastward. In his volume, *Even Saphir,* he records his journeys through Yemen first, followed by his travels in India. His friendship with and reports of Yemenite Jewry, previously unknown to European Jewry, are his major claim to fame.

In India, Saphir treated the customs he saw as idolatrous. He shared many views of the Christian missionaries' understanding of Indian religion

There is idolatry in every house; an image of a woman and two children, or male and female, the idol (*me'or*) and his consort carved from stone, or wood, or metal standing on the wall or on the table and a lamp burning continuously before them. Every morning before any activity or eating they place a food offering—this is an idolatrous offering, then they eat and go to work . . . On their holidays they make great images and dress them in fine clothes and precious jewels . . . and the people publicly bear them through the streets and the voice of the people singing with instruments and song until they come to the shore, where they remove the garments and jewels and throw them naked into the sea.[21]

There are many Protestant missionaries in India encouraged because of their great salary, whose whole goal is to bring to their faith whoever comes to their hand ... by creating schools to teach English and all the subjects taught in European schools ... they also have many churches where many of the masses are gathered and they preach to them in the language of the province and many of the people become Christian ... But they are not successful with the Muslims ... because they are strong in their religion, as are the Jews.[22]

Saphir retains his outsider's perspective because of the separation of the Jewish community from the local Indian community. By doing this, he did not wish to acculturate more than his hosts. Saphir considers that "the Jews, even though born in these lands, act completely like Europeans."[23] In contrast to David of Beth Hillel, who actively sought out knowledge of the various ethnic and religious groups of India, Saphir associated solely with those Jews still connected culturally to Baghdad.

Perennialism

Maurice Fleugel (1831–1911) was an Orthodox rabbi in Baltimore who gave up the rabbinate in order to pursue scholarly interests. Among these interests was the study of Kabbalah as a form of Perennialism, where all religions trace their origins to common, ancient roots. Fleugel's Perennialism has similarities to Benamozegh's pluralism and Adolphe Frank's perennialism (discussed in my prior book.)

Fluegel's own specialty involved tracing the influence of Hindu mysticism and Vedanta thought on Judaism. His accepts the nineteenth century idea of Indian influence on Middle-Platonism, including the thought of Philo of Alexandria. Unlike Menashe ben Israel, who assumes that all faith came from Abraham, Fluegel follows certain nineteenth-century trends and believes that common phenomena had common essences. Sufism, Ismaili Islamic thought, Zoroastrianism, Neoplatonism, and Kabbalah are all forms of Vedanta philosophy.

His major contribution to the study of Kabbalah was to show that the *Zohar* preserved the pre-Ptolemaic Babylonian heliocentric astronomy. However, his views on the common essence of Vedanta and Kabbalah have not found wide reception and remain a late nineteenth-century curiosity:

It is necessary to ascertain where and when the Jews became intimately acquainted with the Hindu philosophy, which more than any other exercised an influence on the Zohar. . . .

Concerning the Qabbala and its preceding Hindu philosophy, our immortal F. Man Mueller wrote me on last June (1900) the following: "If you could trace Indian influences in the Qabbala and the other Hebrew philosophical works, that would be very important. Indians certainly came to Alexandria and taught their philosophy. Why should they not have come into contact with Alexandrian Jews, even with Philo and his friends?"[24]

According to that system is the Deity forever hidden from and unknowable to human understanding. God is the Infinite, Unknowable, Substance and Source of all existence. God, Ain-Soph corresponds to Zrvana-Akarana of Persia; to Brahman, All, of the Vedas; to the Biblical Ihvn Elohim; to the Supreme Cause of philosophers . . .[25]

We shall see that this stupendous figure, Adam Qadmon, pervading the Qabbalistic theory, find its parallel in the Hindu *Brahman,* the first manifestation of the Supreme, and in *Manu,* one of the first creation of the *Self-Existent* . . . That Vedic *Self-Existent* corresponds to the Zohar's *Infinite, Unknowable.*[26]

"Brahman is the Supreme Being. The soul of man is called Atman. Self (Athem. Breath. Anima. Atman is the very soul, the essence of man . . . The Brahman is the personified God, the Creator, God manifested . . . In some sense they correspond to the Hebraic abstract, Being and the concrete, Divine Powers.—While the polytheistic gods of the Veda are the angels, the divine messengers and agents of Scriptures.[27]

Ezriel Guenzig

Ezriel Guenzig (c.1868–1931) was a rabbi in Moravia and later, he became the head of the Mizrahi Tahkemoni School in Antwerp. In his time, as editor of the journal *Ha-Eshkol,* he was a conduit of Western and academic knowledge to his Hebrew-reading Orthodox rabbinic audience; unfortunately, he is remembered little today. In 1900, he wrote an appreciation of the recently published works belonging to the series *Sacred Books of the East* edited under the direction of Max Muller. He compares the Hindu positively to Judaism, noting the similarities of the two religious worldviews Kabbalah and Hinduism, especially emanation, *nirvana, eynsof, sefirot,* and theories of the soul. Guenzig's approach consists of focusing on the philosophic works and the ancient scripture to formulate a Hindu monotheism as part of a larger perennialist vision. Rabbinic mentions of Indian thought in the first part of the twentieth-century work in a similar manner.

In perusing these works we find many concepts and images, mores and customs, principles and many doctrines that also stand as the peaks of our religion. We see astounding similarities in many ways between the faith of the Hindus and the faith of Israel, not just in details but even in the principles of purpose, their studies, and their opinions . . . Just as the Therapeutae in Egypt brought Neo-Platonism into Judaism, the Essenes in Judea brought the secrets of Buddhism—the masters of secrets in India—to the masters of secrets in Alexandria and other Jewish works who, in turn, brought these allusions in the secret of our holy writings.

The belief in the Oneness of the creator and the unity of existence is a sublime step in the cultural evolution of humanity, the moral foundation for all religions of Enlightened peoples.

Also the [Hindu] doctrine of the relationship of the individual soul to the universal soul and the spiritual perfection by cleaving to divinity, freed from all desire and physical lusts . . . is found in many Jewish believers and also is found by our ancient wise and the early kabbalists who followed them.

If a scholar delves into the Vedas he will see that the early kabbalists, most of the fathers of the philosophic Kabbalah followed the Hindus . . .[28]

Twentieth-Century Jewish Culture

The Hindu delegation lead by Swami Vivekananda (1863–1902) came to the 1893 World Parliament of Religions in Chicago and presented Indian religion in a way that gained the delegation and the entire religion of Hinduism respect, and English gained the words that became associated with Hinduism. Vivekananda gave hundreds of lectures showing the rational, humanistic, and universal sides of Hinduism. They shifted the perception of Hinduism from ritualistic and heathen to a healthy positive form of religion consisting of monistic philosophy, meditation, and pluralism. Indian culture became associated with a universal spiritual wisdom and discipline.

For example, in 1922, the works of the famed Noble prize–winner poet, Rabindranath Tagore, known as an Indian philosopher and spiritual guide, were translated into Hebrew. Tagore taught a monotheistic approach to Indian religion combined with psychological awareness, oneness with nature, and his fighting of bigotry. In a 1930 interview with the Toronto journal *Jewish Standard*, he recognized the historical logic of Jewish nationalism. He remarked that, "I regard Jewish nationalism as an effort to preserve and enrich Jewish culture and tradition. In today's world this programme requires a national home. It also implies appropriate physical surroundings as well as favorable political and economic conditions."[29]

Tagore's views were widely disseminated by Hebrew essayists and even the fervently Orthodox Agudah magazine, *Ha Neeman*, included poetry by Tagore. Rabbi Irving Bunim, in his commentary to this Mishnah, quotes Tagore's analogy for human freedom. "I have on my table a violin string. It is free . . . But it is not free to do what a violin string is supposed to do, to produce music. So I take it, fix it in my violin, and tighten it until it is taut. Only then is it free to be a violin string."[30] As Bunim puts it, an uncommitted life, free of any higher goals and responsibilities, brings bondage worse than slavery. The Torah, then, is more than just a set of rules and ethics. It is a conduit for human aspiration, allowing us to be, truly, all that we can be. There was even a well-known Yiddish song based on this poem called in Yiddish Far Vos (Why?).

Azriel Carlebach (d. 1955) was the founder and editor of *Ma 'ariv*, one of Israel's leading daily newspapers and had also spent four weeks in India followed by his work, *India: Account of a Voyage*. Carlebach's description of India was, for decades, the only Israeli account and shaped their image of India. Carlebach had been ordained as a rabbi in his youth by Rabbi Abraham Isaac Kook, hence his contribution is that he applied his rabbinical knowledge and "used Biblical and Rabbinic terms to refer to parallel institutions and rituals in the Hindu religious tradition." He avoided calling Indian religious forms as idolatry; rather, he translated Hindu temples and priests using the biblical words temples (*mikdaskim*) and its priests (*kohanim*).[31]

Israelis also knew of the religious thought of India through yet another wandering Lithuanian Jew. Hayyim Spielberg of Vilna survived WWII by escaping to Japan; this experience led him to spend the years between 1941 and 1948 wandering around India as a long route to Israel. In 1948, he wrote an introduction in Yiddish to Indian religions, including Hindus, Jains, Sikhs, and Buddhists. This was translated into Hebrew and served as a basic Israeli guide to Indian religions. For Spielberg, the Indian culture is alive with souls, gods, and sources of blessing:

> What does Judaism say? Each person has a soul. Hinduism reverses the order of things and claims that each soul has a person (or another created body), and it is only a temporary body . . . an animal or insect body can be the dwelling for a wandering soul.
>
> In Judaism, as in Christianity and Islam, man is principle, the soul is an integral part of one's identity. Hinduism does not emphasize the person but the soul.
>
> The Hindu worships the gods with the simplicity of a child, he washes and adorns them and has no doubt at all that they hear his prayers and bless him each day.[32]

Journeying East

American Jews encountered Hinduism beginning in the late 1960s and early 1970s, with the wave of Indian Gurus and spiritual teachers coming to the West. In the 1960s, some American Jews practiced the Hinduism of Transcendental Meditation while others converted to Hindu piety like Baba Ram Das, Krishna Das, or the many that joined ISKON (International Society for Krishna Consciousness).

Israelis in the 1990s and onward have been making post-army visits to India to expand their horizons. Daria Maoz states that most of the Israelis do not seek a true experience of the culture and religion of India and prefer an exposure geared for the enclave of their expatriate fellows. However, she notes that 20 percent of Israeli travelers to India are religious, that is they come from the *dati* sector within Israeli society, having imbibed the knowledge of Torah and practical Judaism and continuing to observe the *mitzvot* as part of their ongoing practice.[33]

This approach continues among Israelis seeking religion in India. Melilah Hellner-Eshed, a contemporary professor of Kabbalah with extensive travels in India, portrays the land as God filled, with no place devoid of Him. God is in each rock and tree and available for an unmediated encounter through colors, scents, sounds. All that one learned about in the classic Jewish sources is still in Indian religion. "Temples, priests, fire, utensils, ritual purifications, all that one learned in Bible and Rabbinics."[34]

The poet, Rivka Miriam, who is observant, and active in Torah study discusses how her Torah knowledge allows her to relate to her experience in India in terms taken from classical Jewish texts. She suggests that divinity is the secret draw of India and Hinduism upon Israelis, and Jews in general:

> And now to Divinity. Meeting its expressions in India brought about a transformation in me. We Jews employ the common expression "there is no place that is devoid

of Him." In India I discovered a world where indeed so it is. I discovered a world in which there is no one who does not believe. I discovered a world where one sees Divinity in every tree and in every stone. But also in every deed and in every matter. The entire world is full of His glory.[35]

David Zeller

David Zeller (1946–2007) is another example of an American who explored the East and then ended his journey as an Orthodox rabbi in Jerusalem, teaching healing mediations. His full story is set out in an autobiography and a memorial biography volume.[36] Zeller's spiritual expedition encompasses the meeting of gurus and yogis first in California and then in India. The intellectual background to understand his experiences includes strong ties to Carl Jung and Carlos Castaneda. Eventually, Zeller became a transpersonal psychologist and head of its professional association.

Additionally, Zeller became friendly with the rabbis who were involved with outreach to the counterculture, including Rabbis Shlomo Carelbach and Zalman Schacter-Shlomi whom he had brought to a Transpersonal Psychology conference dedicated to Yoga in India. Zeller felt that they if they were able to open people's, including outsiders', hearts to Judaism, these rabbis were teaching the same things as the gurus. Zeller felt that "becoming an Orthodox rabbi had not cut [him] off from the other traditions." During his life, he began the Network of Conscious Judaism and Center for Jewish Spirituality and Meditation.

One can see a strong influence in Zelelr's work of Sathya Sai Baba, who taught that there is one God and unity of all religions. Sai Baba's followers do not need to give up their original religion in order to recognize harmony with all. The main objective of the Sathya Sai Organization, as Sathya Sai Baba himself states, "is to help you recognize the divinity inherent in you. So, your duty is to emphasize the One, to experience the One in all you do or speak. Do not give importance to differences of religion, sect, status, or color." Zeller neither accepts nor mentions the problem of those who consider Sathya Sai Baba a full divine incarnation, comparable to a God or in terms of the spiritual benefit of *darshan*. Rather, Zeller wants to show that Judaism is in itself spiritual. He allows a Shinto priest to explain the Tetragrammaton but cautions the priest against pronouncing the name. Zeller's synthesis of his journey is that each religion has a role to play:

> Shinto priest went on to explain, very excitedly, that if you bring energy down from the highest center to the lowest and back up again to the highest, going through the sounds of each center, you get the sound of the Four-Lettered Name of God, the Tetragrammaton. A little nervous, I tried to explain that, in our Jewish tradition, we do not pronounce that name.

> I understood that each people and tradition had been chosen to do a particular task for all of humanity. Just as each organ in our body must fulfill its "destiny" and function for the overall health of the whole body, so each religious tradition has its function in the body of humankind.

While I was on stage singing and teaching about Jewish mysticism and meditation, Swami Vishnu chimed in. "Oh Rabbi, this is just like we teach in yoga philosophy. You see, we really are all one, and all the teachings are here in yoga!"[37]

Zeller could have been included in the chapter on Buddhism since he spent time in India, but he also spent time with Buddhists, Sikhs, and Shinto teachers. More importantly, he was one of a new breed that experienced Eastern religions as a Jew and selected various practices and then returned as Jew. He is the start of the trend of encountering the Eastern religion and then representing it and integrating it as a Jew.

Sant Mat and Sikh Meditation

Miriam Bokser Caravella was an American seeker who set out from her rabbinic family to find true mysticism in India. She studied with Maharaj Charan Singh Ji (c. 1916–1990), the true fifth guru of the Radha Soami Satsang Beas. She worked as a public affair officer for the United States Embassy and at an Indian University. She wrote *The Holy Name*, which is her original synthesis of Sant Mat, specifically in a Sikh variety with Judaism. Caravella found a path of control of mind, a teacher, meditation techniques, and vows of a simple life. She does not point out the differences of her practice from Judaism, but rather emphasizes its similarities. The Holy Name of God in Judaism corresponds to the true reality taught by the guru. Additionally, she conceptualizes the role of *rebbes* (rabbis) and *zaddikim* (spiritual leader) to the Indian Gurus. Sant Mat was a loosely associated group of teachers that started in northern India around the thirteenth century. The group taught an inward, loving devotion to a divine principle. A Sikh version of the group, Radha Soami Satsang Beas, teaches the union of the soul with the Audible Life Stream, the esoteric Holy name of God.

Miriam Bokser Caravella's goal was to reconcile Sant Mat and Judaism by looking for common universal elements. In both Kabbalah and Sant Mat, she points out how the purpose of life is the soul, that man is a microcosm, and that both assume a role for karma.

> Maharaj Charan Singh has bestowed on me the key to mystic understanding, deepening my appreciation of Judaism and increasing my awareness of the universal relevance of Jewish mysticism . . . My purpose is not to compare Judaism with Sant Mat . . . nor am I implying that there is a coherent system of Jewish mysticism which is analougous to Sant Mat.[38]

She adds that the "Mystics of the Kabbalah [. . .] taught that the soul is a spiritual essence distinct from the body, which continues to live when the body dies." She then compares Kabbalah to Kabir, an Indian saint of the fourteenth century, who sang, "The soul is a particle of God; though it is the body, it is never destroyed."[39]

Caravella finds that the Indian notion of Karma, the cycle of action and reaction, is present in the story about the rabbinic sage who "saw a skull floating on the surface of the water. He said to it: because you drowned others, they drowned you. And those who drowned you will, in the end, be drowned."[40]

God's universal oneness is proclaimed in both the Jewish doxology, the *Shema*, and Sikh hymns:

> There are outer names of God that we encounter in prayer and scripture, and which can be read, written, and spoken. . . . But there is also the inner Name, the divine reality which the prophets of the Bible and mystics throughout history actually experienced . . . This name or power is inexpressible.

> According to Singh, "there is conflict only when we dwell on the names expressed in words . . . and forget the music of the true name."[41]

God is interested in our salvation of the soul and this is done by victory over the enemies hidden within us and our worldly tendencies that keep us bound to karma. Sant Mat "teaches that the path home is through overcoming the barrier of mind, proclaiming that to conquer the mind is the true warrior" to which Caravella compares the rabbinic statement: "Who is might? He who subdues his passions." (Avot 4:1) She treats Jewish Law (halakhah) as eternal truth, cosmic law, and eternal revelation.[42]

On the question of idolatry, Caravella states that the guru is an embodiment of the Divine name and not divine:

> The Master is not a pretender to divinity. Love for the Master is not avodazara, "idolatrous worship" of a being other than God. Since the Master has merged in the divine Name, he embodies that Name.

> The Master is the one place on earth, open to human experience, where the divine essence can be perceived. He is the intersection of the Divine with the physical realms. The divine energy has become concentrated and crystallized in this one point so that we can know it. The Master is the doorway through which we can experience the Divine.

> God is the Shabd, the ineffable divine essence. The Master has realized this essence within himself and has merged into it. Thus, for all intents and purposes, he has become identical with God. Though his body is finite and of the material plane, his spiritual radiance is so great that he appears as a divine being walking among men—like the prophet Moses, whose face shone with beams of light.[43]

Many religions have the same symbols of light and sound "to teach that the human body is the only true temple or tabernacle, and that within the temple of our bodies burns the divine eternal flame; there echoes the divine inner melody, God's holy name."[44]

On Being Hindu and Jewish

This path of being Jewish and a follower of a Hindu guru was common in the 1960s and 1970s. The path of meditation and the Hindu teaching on the soul were treated as universal wisdom. We also have specific cases of famous Vedanta gurus of Jewish background such as Swami Vijayananda, who claim to be Vedanta without becoming Hindu. This works because conservative Hindu leaders such as Anandamai Ma do not accept non-Hindus into Hinduism. Rather, they themselves teach Vedanta as a universal path outside of the rituals of Hindu practice of diet, marriage laws, and holidays.

Mirra Alfassa (1878–1973), known her followers as "The Mother," was born Jewish and became the muse and voice of Sri Aurobindo, the guru, poet, and theologian of spiritual evolution. When Sri Aurobindo retired into seclusion in 1926, she founded his ashram with a handful of disciples and became the leader of the community, a position she held until her death. Sri Aurobindo considered her an incarnation of the Mother Divine and called her by that name: the Mother. 'The One whom we adore as the Mother is the divine Conscious Force that dominates all existence, one and yet many-sided that to follow her movement is impossible even for the quickest mind and for the freest and most vast intelligence." She founded a utopian community, Auroville, about eight kilometers outside of Pondicherry.

The famous case of a universal Vedanta teaching in the West is the Maharishi Mahesh Yogi, who taught a simplified path of meditation called Transcendental Meditation (TM) and gained many Christian and Jewish followers who did not see any contradiction between their TM practice and their birth religion.

Swami Vijayananda, already mentioned, stayed in India, following his meeting Anandamai Ma. Even though he came under her spiritual direction, he never converted to Hinduism. In part, this was due to the fact that there is no classical conversion ceremony, but more pointedly, this goes back to Ma's own reticence, apparently influenced by her own conservative Bengali background, to accept non-Hindus as converts. For the Jewish Vijayananda this was most convenient.

He never sought to forego his Jewish identity. Indeed, in his own self-understanding, he had never become a Hindu. He had only taken up Vedanta as his preferred spiritual path. Here Vedanta is seen as above a particular religion, rather than as identical with Hinduism. Thus, he remains a Jew, due to the impossibility of conversion to Hinduism.

The Maharishi Mahesh Yogi is the prime example, teaching meditation as a technique, while divesting it of its religious meaning. While Maharishi did not make God the focus or goal of the system, the Divine, as understood in classical vedanta, maintains its place of importance in his various writings.[45]

Halakhah: The View From Afar

The stream of Jews who headed East also included those who eventually returned to the west. They came with a variety of new questions, which were generally answered based on the limited availability of Western knowledge. Over time, the questions begin to turn from commerce to religious topics such as meditation and yoga. At the start of the twenty-first-century, a debate over the use of tonsured Temple hair becomes a locus for evaluating the questions asked from afar.

Over the last 250 years, knowledge of Indian religions has slowly entered into the discourse of halakhic legal decisions. A ruling by Rabbi Ezekiel Landau (Prague,

1713–1793) provides us with an early eighteenth-century example of such discourse. Rabbi Landau responded to a man who had visited colonial India and married a Hindu woman and who now wanted to be returned to his status as a *kohen* (priest) in the London Jewish community. Rabbi Landau ruled that the person asking the question had engaged in Hindu rites solely to marry his wife, including entering a Hindu temple and bowing, then later divorcing her and doing penance, could still recite the priestly blessings. In his ruling, Landau relies on the minority opinion among medieval Jewish legal authorities in which a priest who engaged in idolatry may still recite the priestly blessings. Landau notes that even according to the majority opinion that an idolatrous *kohen* cannot recite the priestly blessings, he should be allowed to perform these duties, because he did not genuinely believe in the Hindu gods, but simply went through the motions to please his wife.[46]

As the nature of relations between East and West changed, with it changed the subject matter of halakhic decisions. By the early twentieth century, products were regularly imported from India to the West; hence, Rabbi Pesah Zevi Frank dealt with the problems related to the importation of powdered milk from India. Rabbi Frank permitted the milk despite the Hindu concept of sacred cows and milk offerings.[47]

Meditation

Jewish returnees from Indian Ashrams, who brought with them the influence of Eastern forms of Yoga and meditation, generated a new series of halakhic questions. A practical question came before Rabbi Yitzhak Yaakov Weiss (d. 1989) of the London rabbinical court: Can a Jew practice Eastern forms of meditation? His answer was, "No!"

A full and permissive answer came from Rabbi Hayyim David Halevi (b. 1924), former Sefardi Chief Rabbi of Tel Aviv, who was a major force in deciding practical matters, many of sociological import, in contemporary Israeli halakhah:

> How real is the distinction between worship (Jewish meditation) and the technique of Transcendental Meditation? The latter encourages a person to empty his mind from continuous daily thoughts, which create the psychological tension through focus on a specific mantra, a word without meaning to the meditator, which is emptiness in order to attain emptiness. But Judaism attains the same goal of emptying a person of all worrisome thoughts, but by filling him with holy feelings of the Divine existence, by turning to God. Not concentrating on emptiness but concentrating on the full content of holiness.[48]

> The initiation ceremony of Transcendental Meditation, and similarly the mantra given to the meditator, has absolute colorings of idolatry, forbidden when used for a forbidden purpose. The technique of Transcendental Meditation, however, by itself is not forbidden, if a person does it without the initiation ceremony, and without the guidance of those teachers [gurus].[49]

The most significant aspect of the response is that Rabbi Halevi is willing to discuss the topic of meditation, and that in his response he mentions that he took the effort to read books about Hinduism and Transcendental Meditation. His answer distinguishes the techniques of meditation from the religious aspects; only the latter he declared as forbidden. In general, TM required food offerings. It is interesting to note that Rabbi Halevi's practical response produced a theoretical statement on the difference between the two faiths as being the difference between fullness versus emptiness. In his response, he defined the line between meditation and Hinduism as crossed when one enters into the realm of ritual or allegiance to a guru.

Yoga

Modern yoga, especially the posture-driven variety that is popular in North America, is the product of a particular historical moment in which premodern forms of yoga (such as *hatha yoga*) were merged with European physical culturalist thought and callisthenic practices, Hindu universalism, and emerging ideas of a modern body. The American yoga of the 1970s was entirely physical education. In the 1990s, Yoga in America was combined with Buddhist insight meditation and new age spirituality. Now, some of the original Hinduism is returning for some Yoga classes including the invoking of Hindu deities. There has been a strong push by American Hindus to reclaim Yoga as part of Hinduism. The Hinduism has also returned back from those visiting modern Ashrams in India. There are *responsa* permitting yoga and meditation as a physical activity with caveats not to bow, invoke deities, offer flowers, or worship. But what of asanas that have a reference back to a Vedic deity? What of the Sun salutation, where the sun in our culture has none of the original Helios worship references? Or what about the original origins of breathing techniques? As a rule, Jews do not determine permissibility by finding obscure occult origins on Wikipedia. The Jewish criterion in halakhah is the current or at most its recent meaning. If the original meaning is forgotten, then it is forgotten.

Exclusivist Parallelism

A contemporary example of the Jewish encounter with Hinduism can be seen in those who teach returnees to Judaism in yeshivas. These teachers receive students who have formerly practiced Eastern religions. While entirely exclusivist in reserving a Jewish relationship with God, these teachers have a serious ability to listen to their students and not to work from preexisting rejectionist categories. They have no choice but to acknowledge the great gifts of contemplation given to someone who spends time in an ashram. The fundamental phenomenological maturity of their approach offers a model for accepting an empirical approach to eastern religions, in line with the empirical approach described in earlier chapters. Yet his trying to connect Hebrew and Sanskrit through anagrams appears almost juvenile, as is evident in the excerpts below from Matityahu Glazerson's *From Hinduism to Judaism*:

This book was written after many conversations with Jews who decided to return to a staunch observance of the Jewish faith after encounters with such Eastern schools of spiritual practice as Yoga, Transcendental Meditation and even levitation. Some of these people had spent long periods of time in India and Tibet. Despite some lightening inner experiences during their involvement with Eastern sects, these spiritual seekers felt that they were still far from attaining the total bliss promised to them by their mystic teachers. Not only did their dreams of happiness remain unrealized; the arid spiritual emptiness in their souls grew more and more with each experience. This is because, according to our teachings, the nature of the Jewish soul is different than that of a gentile soul. We believe that the source of a Jewish soul lies in the upper worlds, and that it is possible to reach that source only through strict adherence to the commandments of the Torah (the Five Books of Moses).

It is my belief that the wisdom of *Hodu* (India) only contains the *Hod* (glory of) the world of Judaism, while the source and the root of the light of God is to be found only in the Torah of Israel.

The teachings of Hinduism explain that through proper breathing a man can acquire certain life-giving energies which are drawn from an intangible cosmic "center" of the universe and that these energies can create in him an optimal physical condition and can intensify the personal reality of his life. This same philosophy is expressed by studying the letters of the Hebrew alphabet, with which God created the worlds and through which these worlds reveal themselves. Let us examine the relationship between the words *avir* (air) and *bari* (healthy).

The name Brahman, through which Hinduism attempts to achieve the divine essence that resides beyond the forces of nature and time, contains the same elements as the name Abraham.

Another pivotal term in Hinduism is (*Prana*), the force through which the unseen existence is revealed to man. In Kabbalistic thought, this force, which enables man to harness the hidden upper powers, is the attribute of God called *tiferet* (glory), the root of which is the *pa'ar* (also glory).

Like Judaism, Hinduism emphasizes the importance of saying a blessing before eating. Both also preach that the mood and attitude of a man at the time of his meals influence the organs and the digestion process.[50]

The question today is: How do we approach the many Jews heading to the East to seek spirituality? It is both an educational and an interfaith question. With that in mind, one must ask: what can be learned, practically, in an ashram or monastery and be brought back to the community? What can exposure to the East do to help strengthen Judaism?

Halakhah and Hair

The age of globalization has paradoxically led to more categorical opinions. For example, Haredi Jews discovered in 2004 that the hair used in the wigs used for the Jewish religious requirement of hair covering originated from the Temple in Tirupati, India. Most of the discussions of the permissibility of the hair assume that Hinduism is idolatry, and the only question to the rabbis concerns whether there was a Temple offering of the hair, in the technical sense, or not. The sending of rabbinical investigative teams to India in 2004, without any ethnographic or cultural interest, has paradoxically led to an even greater sense of the otherness of Indian religions.[51]

In the recent Orthodox Jewish controversy over the permissibility of using the tonsured Temple hair to make women's wigs, I served as a minor border crossing of knowledge. On the day before the ban on the wigs was going to take effect, one of the Israeli rabbinic figures involved frantically called me as an outside expert. As I started to approach my answer by setting up an explanation of Hinduism and the role of temples, I was cut off with the question, "Hindu, Buddhist, what difference does it make?" The question clearly indicated that there was no basic conceptual category of Hinduism, religion, or other religions. Nor was there any rubric, outside of the Talmud's presentation of Greco-Roman offerings to the gods, to frame unfamiliar activities. The only question was whether this presumed idol was worshiped through a hair offering or not. Afterward, when consulting with another colleague who had received the same phone call, I was told that he too, had received the same reaction.

In a recent pair of scholarly articles by Benjamin Fleming and Annette Yoshiko Reed, they address this problem that the hair created directly. The question that they pose is: Modern western views on Hinduism focused on the image-worship and the polytheism, but what happens when Hinduism is confronted by someone who never heard these categories?[52]

> [A]ccording to the halakhic interpretations, it was not the association of the act with a Hindu god or image that made the wigs problematic for Jewish women; rather, it was the possibility that the hair is given as a sacrificial offering to the god. In order to make an assessment, observers were sent to Tirupati to witness the Hindu practices first-hand, to determine whether or not the devotees were "offering" the hair. They did so with great attention to the details of the Hindu practices, but they interpreted them in conjunction with laws about Greco-Roman religion in the Mishnah and Talmud. The conclusion of most was that the hair was, in fact, cut as an offering to the god.

Fleming explains how the twentieth-century rabbis arrived at the conclusion that the hair was a sacrificial offering. They did not understand that tonsuring is not the same as *darshan* (vision of a deity) or an offering to a god, and that the cutting of hair can be likened to the washing of dirt from the body. They did not understand that barbering is not a temple ritual since it is done by outcaste barbers—not Brahmins. They did not ask questions about the entire pilgrimage process to the Tirupati Temple complex. In all of it, there was an assumption that this is idolatry, the only question is whether there was an offering. "The pilgrims were asked: If your intention is to give a present why do you cut it here and therefore have to wait for hours in a queue? Why don't you cut it at home and send it to the God?" They received answers that it is more virtuous not to cut it at home therefore "we want to cut it here because here we are in a holy place . . . and the idol loves our hair." So they concluded it was forbidden. Eventually, this first thought was overruled with more information."

One of the issues debated in the halakhic literature was if Hinduism should be understood by its educated teachers or by its uneducated practitioners. Those who saw the process as idolatry tended to think we should follow the latter and those who did not consider it idolatry followed the former. A similar phenomenon occurs in Western scholarship, which bases its conclusion on the common people visiting the Temple and concludes that there is real presence in the visions of the statue. In contrast the majority of educated Hindus and the trained teachers would explain Hinduism as affirming a Supreme Being greater than the manifestation as Temple deities.

Pointing to future decades when there will be greater Jewish-Hindu understanding, Fleming and Reed wrote:

> Perhaps most striking, in this regard, may be the manner in which the halakhic discourse about avodah zarah has served to efface the structural and ritual similarities between Jewish and Hindu practices surrounding the cutting of hair, precisely by virtue of the selective appeal to the cultic practice of the Jewish past (i.e., sacrifice in the Jerusalem Temple) as the model for the interpretation of non-Jewish ritual practice in the present. Tacit—perhaps already in the Mishnah—is the effacement of the very possibility of any parallels between avodah zarah and contemporary Jewish practice.

The actual legal reasoning for the eventual leniencies does not concern us here since that is entirely within their the halakhah canon of knowledge. Leniencies to wear the hair were found by a variety of rabbis; some of their reasoning was based on the barber's lack of intention for worship, on the tonsuring as a non-ritual act, and on the lack of probability that one has the Temple hair.

Much work needs to be done for Jewish law to create an understanding of the myriad issues around Indian religions. Daniel Sperber (b. 1940) a noted rabbi, professor and author of halakhic works is attempting to produce a halakhic introduction to Hinduism that is informed by knowledge of Hindu thought and practice. Sperber follows the legal approach of trusting the leadership over the laity and therefore relies on the Westernized presentations that he receives. His goals are to explain Hinduism as non-idolatrous and to explain the manifestations of Hindu worship. Sperber's work is still in progress, but it will certainly generate discussion when it is done. In the meantime he has already noted:

> [T]he respect and devotion they accord to them is not necessarily worship. Thus, for example, the cow is viewed as a source of life, for it gives milk, dung which is used for fuel . . . and as such it is a life-giving gift of God, and has a sacred character much as we Jews accord kedushah, holiness to certain life-giving gifts, such as Torah—albeit a spiritual, rather than a physical gift.

> [I]t should also be noted that Hindu monotheism is by no means identical to Jewish monotheism.

> However, while a Jew may not accept the Hindu Advaita Vedanta philosophic stance, and may regard it, from his own viewpoint as heterodox, it can hardly be seen as idolatrous.[53]

View from Near

The view from near has been slow in arriving and diverse in its directions. There are academics who specialize in Indian religions who have Jewish backgrounds by which to evaluate their studies. There are ethnographers of the Jews of India and there are the accounts of those Indian Jews who have moved to Israel. Recently, there have been a momentous series of dialouges between Israeli rabbis and Indian teachers of the Dharma. Finally, Alon Goshen-Gottstein, a rabbi and scholar, has made it his own personal quest to reach a Jewish understanding of Indian religions.

Nathan Katz

Nathan Katz , a professor of Indian religions who returned to Jewish observance offers a cultural bridge between Judaism and Indian faiths. He was trained in language by the US government during the Vietnam War era and has written on Hinduism, Jainism, and Buddhism. He returns to India regularly and was one of the Jewish leaders who met with the Dali Lama. He has made himself the hub of Indo-Judaic Studies. Katz's approach is mainly ethnographic and he is reticent to offer full theological discussion. In one of his autobiographic moments he does offer the following reflections.

> The question of one G-d versus many gods confounds every Westerner who approaches Hinduism. On the apparent level, Hinduism has many gods who are depicted by murtis, statues or idols. Idolatry, of course, is not only condemned in the Torah's second commandment, it even contradicts the much less doctrinaire seven Noachide commandments that are said to be obligatory for all descendants of Noah, which is to say for everyone (according to Judaism).
>
> Yet when the swami speaks of G-d as the Light, beyond all form and distinctions, the initial understanding is put into question. And the more one delves into the philosophies underlying Hindu practice, the more the initial level is reduced to a comic book version of a profound and serious theology.
>
> I knew beyond any doubt that Hinduism teaches a way of being in the word that is consonant with the Biblical principle that we humans are all created b'tselem Elokim, in the image of G-d. Whatever we may think of her more mundane religious practices, it cannot be denied that Hinduism creates a cultured human whose actions honor both humans and our Creator.[54]

Katz calls us to begin the discussion in earnest and to realize that our first perceptions are not necessary accurate.

Katz, as an ethnographer, offers a contemporary look at the Cochin Jews that yields a different picture of the relationship of Jewish life to Hindu life than that shown by outsiders. Cochin Jews were embedded in Indian culture and performed their own Jewish rites in a Hindu manner. Such observation opens the question again: What would Rabbi Yaakov Emden or Rabbi Shmuel David Luzzatto have said had they lived in India?

> The three elements characteristic of Hindu Temple festivals, display, procession, and disposal, are also characteristic of Simchat Torah in Cochin. Like a Hindu deity the Torah scrolls are removed from their usual holy abode, the Jewish *aronhakodesh*, paralleling the Hindu *sanctum sanctorum*, and displayed on a temporary structure, the Jewish temporary ark, paralleling the Hindu cart. Like the deity they are carried through a public area, in this case the synagogue courtyard. As the deity's image is disposed of at the end of the festival, so the temporary ark—not of course the Torah scrolls—is demolished ritually.... In Hindu India, however, it is the Jewish priestly-ascetic and noble-kingly threads that have been emphasized, and the fiery ethical imperatives of the prophets have been less central.[55]

As such experience shows, Jews *do* acculturate into their surroundings and the age of globalization may yield new juxtapositions.

There are many signs of acculturation to Hindu religious thought patterns to be found in the works of Indian Jews. For example, in a basic primer on Jewish belief written by a twentieth-century Jew from India for Indian Jews, the author describes the synagogue first as a place of the dwelling of the *shekhinah* (dwelling) and the purpose of prayer as blessing and mental tranquility. While not explicitly an engagement with Indian religion, it does however present Judaism in terms similar to the other Indian beliefs, thereby creating a commonality. There are several other scholars working on the ethnography of Jews in India that specialize Bene Israel, Cochin Jews, Baghdadi Jews, their studies will may yield new insights for the theological issues.[56]

Regarding the integration of the Cochin community, it is worth noting that Ezekiel Rahabi (c. 1694–1772), the Dutch East India Company's principal merchant and diplomat in Malabar, organized inter-confessional activities between the Jewish community and other religions in India; alas, we do not have these transcripts.[57]

Veda and Torah

Barbara A. Holdrege, professor and comparative historian of religion at the University of California, Santa Barbara, wrote a major work offering theme and variations on comparing the text of Torah with that of the Veda. She shows that there are strong theological reasons for the parallels in cosmology and power of the word. For example, both religions use the image of the body to represent scripture and both scriptures are considered the blueprints of creation. But, she also points out the differences between the two. Judaism emphasizes the role of a personal God giving revelation to His chosen people in the phenomena of prophecy and the event of Sinai, where in contrast, the Veda emphasizes its eternal source available to everyone as the universal enlightened wisdom:

> Veda and Torah are each at times depicted as the subtle plan or blueprint of creation, its constituent sounds or letters constituting the primordial elements of the divine language from which the realm of forms is structured.

The transcendent reality of Brahman that is represented as the ultimate source of the Veda is impersonal; it is not a personal God with whom one enters into a personal relationship. Thus, the Veda is at times designated as apauruseya: not derived from any personal agent.

The revelation at Mount Sinai, in contrast, is described in personal terms as a covenant between a personal God and his chosen people, involving gifts on the part of the divine and obligations on the part of the Israelites. The Israelites are not described as utilizing a technique to attain knowledge of Torah. Moses' role is more parallel to that of the rsis [seer, one who see the higher truths] in that although he is not depicted as practicing a specific technique, he is represented as acquiring the Torah at least partially through his own efforts.

The distinction between acquisition of Veda through a technique and reception of the Torah as a gift is founded on a more fundamental distinction concerning the divine source of the knowledge—whether impersonal, the case of Veda, or personal, in the case of Torah. Rabbinic and zoharic discussions of the revelation of the Torah, on the other hand, are concerned to explicate every detail of the Sinai event: when and where the Torah was given, to whom it was given, how it was given, and so on. The Veda is at times identified with the creator Prajapati or Brahma, the demiurge principle, who is extolled as the embodiment of knowledge and Veda incarnate.[58]

Holdrege's distinction between the prophetic element of Torah and the universal wisdom of Veda is the commonplace Muslim observation on the difference between Islam and Hinduism. If prophecy is used as the most important yardstick for measuring a religious tradition, then Hinduism which is without prophecy gets thrown in sharp relief from Judaism. Abraham ibn Ezra stressed that God spoke directly to Moses to exclude the Hindu position that it is impossible for God to talk to humans. (Exodus 19:9, long version.) On the other hand, using the criteria of prophecy allows Jews to say that their involvement with Hinduism, is only the study of a universal wisdom, which does not contradict Jewish revelation with an alternative revelation.

In 1976, Hannaiah Goodman, a student at the time, wrote to Gershom Scholem asking about the ability to make academic parallels between the two faiths. Scholem answered in the negative based on his own mastery of what had been already written. He did however cite as an example of the minimal results available his own observation about the two Shekhinas and Shakti. Scholem writes: "One might almost say, to use the terms of Indian religion, that the upper Shekhinah is the Shakti of the latent God; it is entirely active energy, in which what is concealed within God is externalized." Goodman nevertheless wrote an important bibliographer on prior attempts and helped organize scholars such as Katz and Holdrege to hold academic meetings on the topic.[59]

Hindu-Jewish Summit

On February 5–6, 2007, the first Hindu-Jewish leadership summit took place in Delhi consisting of a delegation of the Chief Rabbinate of Israel with major religious leaders of Hindu dharma. Rabbi Yona Metzger said although interreligious dialogue has increased recently, the Hindu-Jewish declaration is a significant move, which highlights the necessity of expanding interfaith community to eastern traditions. "For thousands of years we have marched on parallel causes and now built bridges of cooperation between the two religions. Jews have lived in India for 2,000 years and have never been discriminated against. This is something unparalleled in human history," added Rabbi Metzger.[60]

This meeting led to a "Declaration of Mutual Understanding and Cooperation from the First Jewish-Hindu Leadership Summit." The document was remarkable as an Orthodox Jewish acknowledgement that Hinduism accepts One Supreme Being, monotheism, and that there exists commonality between Jewish and Hindu revelation and ethics. The participants affirmed that:

> Their respective Traditions teach that there is One Supreme Being who is the Ultimate Reality, who has created this world in its blessed diversity and who has communicated Divine ways of action for humanity, for different peoples in different times and places.

> The representatives of the two faith communities recognize the need for understanding one another in terms of lifestyles, philosophy, religious symbols, culture, etc. They also recognize that they have to make themselves understood by other faith communities. They hope that through their bilateral initiatives, these needs would be met.[61]

In fact, during the first Hindu-Jewish summit meeting, Israeli Chief Rabbi, Yonah Metzger, visited the Delhi Akshardham Temple complex.

A second Hindu-Jewish Leadership Summit took place in Jerusalem on February 17–20, 2008. In this meeting, the leaders went further in their declarations and considered Hinduism as a shared "Creator and Guide of the Cosmos."[62] The Jewish delegation also accepted that true Hindus accept One Supreme Being and do not think that the representations are idols:

> 1. In keeping with the Delhi declaration, the participants reaffirmed their commitment to deepening this bilateral relationship predicated on the recognition of One Supreme Being, Creator and Guide of the Cosmos; shared values; and similar historical experiences. The parties are committed to learning about one another on the basis of respect for the particular identities of their respective communities and seeking, through their bilateral relationship, to be a blessing to all.

> 2. It is recognized that the One Supreme Being, both in its formless and manifest aspects, has been worshipped by Hindus over the millennia. This does not mean that Hindus worship "gods" and "idols." The Hindu relates to only the One Supreme Being when he/she prays to a particular manifestation.[63]

The Hindu Dharma teachers' entrance into interfaith with the West has the possibility of placing a renewed emphasis on Neo-Hinduism, the nineteenth and twentieth-century position that Indian religions worship of a single Absolute Being; all other deities are only manifestations.

Nathan Katz notes that, "While interreligious dialogue has been a 'tool for evan-gelization' in the hands of Christian missionaries, when Jews and Hindus converse, there are no ulterior motives [. . .] The Hindu-Jewish dialogue is also about our experiences of oppression and intolerance" from other faiths.[64] In a comparative religion class, Judaism and Hinduism can be easily compared as ritualistic religions that ward off their more spiritualized daughters—Christianity and Buddhism. One finds similarity in ritual laws, sacred space, sacred time—but now what? What do these comparisons mean? How does the study of Hinduism help in my own faith? Can we ask: how does this fact about Hinduism affect my Judaism?

On Hinduism

Although we still do not have any Jewish religious texts that are truly familiar with the theologies of the Indian subcontinent in order for a real discussion, it is still important to ask the basic question about how Judaism would conceptualize what is now called Hinduism. There are three points about Hindu deities to consider: absolute divinity, manifestations as gods, and representations. Indian religions present a dichotomy between one incorporeal essence and millions of manifes-tations as specific gods, between meditations beyond any image and incredible varieties of representations, icons, statues, and deities.

As early as the *Rig Veda*, we have a statement: "Truth is One; the wise call it by many names." The Upanishads further clarify the nature of the Godhead as being without attributes. If we start our discussion with a Hindu theologian, we have a form of monotheism as presented in Shankara (c. 788–820 C.E.) and other monists; this monotheism can easily be compared to Western varieties. But we also have a multiplicity in Brahman, Vishnu, and Shiva, which for gentiles would count as a multiplicity in god, the category of association (*shituf*). Whatever Jewish texts would say about Christians might be extended to Hinduism, but a further encounter is needed.

We can learn from the translation process into Arabic of these Hindu works that translated diva as angels thereby the reader would consider the many deities as mere angels. It lets us note that the millions of Indian deities may not function as the Western concept of God, and that only the absolute may correspond to our concept of God. Part of this activity of translating Indian religions into Jewish terms may require us to separate popular (idolatrous) religion from the abstract philosophic ideal of the religion. When Hindus are universalistic about one absolute principle, then Jews can discuss Indian religions with greater ease than when they discuss 330 million gods or the exclusivist worship of local deities and their statues.

Rabbi Adin Steinsaltz, contemporary author and translator of the Talmud into Modern Hebrew, came to the same conclusions a few years prior. Indian religions are sufficiently monotheistic for gentiles. He expands the laws of association (*shituf*) (discussed in my prior book) to include Buddhism and Islam:

> In the ancient religions grouped under the name of Hinduism, there are many gods and local shrines, but the theological principles that guide belief and provide

a uniformity of moral standards assume that all the deities revered in India or else-where are forms of, expressions of, or names for, one ultimate reality or God.

Under the Noahide laws, it is possible to assume that Hinduism and Buddhism are sufficiently monotheistic in principle for moral Hindus and Buddhists to enter the gentiles' gate into heaven. Jewish law regards the compromises made or tolerated by the world's major religions as ways of rendering essentially monotheistic theologies easier in practice for large populations of adherents.[65]

In one of his books on Judaism, Rabbi Eliezer Berkovits asks about the inherent chasm between man and the Divine in the encounter with God: how can we stand in the presence of the Divine source of all energy and power of the universe? To emphasize his point, he surprisingly quotes the *Bhagavad Gita* on human smallness before the divine, "suppose a thousand suns were to arise tomorrow in the sky?" God's infinite greatness remains beyond human understanding.[66] The *Bhagavad Gita* has both monistic and theistic readings; the theistic readings can easily find resonance with many Jewish positions.

As recently as 2009 Rabbi Aharon Lichtenstein, rosh yeshiva at Yeshivat Har Etzion gave a discourse for over an hour on the *Bhagavad Gita* as an illustration of the Torah's concept of duty. For him, the Torah teaches the need to do the right action without worry for the results similar to *Nishkam Karma*. "To action alone hast thou a right and never at all to its fruits; let not the fruits of action be thy motive; neither let there be in thee any attachment to inaction" (Bhagavad Gita 2.47). He also used it to teach the need for the Torah scholar to have self-control, discipline, and freedom from attachment. "With the body, with the mind, with the intellect, even merely with the senses, perform action toward self-purification, having abandoned attachment. He who is disciplined in Yoga, having abandoned the fruit of action, attains steady peace (2.48).

Alon Goshen-Gottstein

One of the few who has devoted themselves to Hindu-Jewish encounter is Alon Goshen-Gottstein, a contemporary rabbi trained at Yeshivat Har Etzion and a professor of rabbinic literature, who for the last decade has been working full time on interfaith activities, especially developing a Jewish theology of other religions. Goshen-Gottstein has spent time in India and is personally enmeshed in currently working to place on the table all the issues in a Jewish-Indian religion encounter. He writes: "The issues at hand are complex to such a degree that, at least in my own view, we cannot simply move from a description of a reality to passing 'judg-ment' or issuing halachic *pesak* in relation to it." "These challenges are new and can draw only minimal guidance or inspiration from the meager contact that has taken place over the centuries." My own work in this book on these issues has been deeply influenced by Goshen-Gottstein's work and his work was indebted to earlier versions of this chapter:

I have spent months in some of the leading Ashrams. I should mention in particular the Sivananda Ashram in Rishikesh, and the Sadhana Kendra Ashram near Dehradun.

Both ashrams have become home, in different ways. In both I received immensely from the wisdom and spiritual perspective of resident sages. Swami Yogaswaroopananda has spent dozens, well over a hundred I imagine, of hours with me, discussing issues that are seminal to a Jewish understanding of Hinduism, particularly issues related to the worship of idols and how these are viewed in Hinduism. Chandra Swami has shared his wisdom on a large range of issues, relevant to this project.[67]

But also India's great thinkers seem to have never had the opportunity to consider Judaism on its own terms. Swami Vivekananda is paradigmatic. An examination of his references to Judaism reveals that he only knows Judaism as the forerunner of Christianity. The only Judaism known to Vivekananda is that of the Old Testament.

[I]n Diaspora, Hindus are challenged to explain what the idols they worship are and how they are to be understood. She notes that Temple literature in the United States presents Hindu deities in ways that conflict with traditional practice, but that do make Hinduism more palatable to the Western audience. Idols are, accordingly, merely symbolic.[68] The issue is not whether Temple pamphlets in North American Temples are getting it theologically or ritually right or not.

It is not enough to dismiss certain voices as apologetic. Today's apologetics are tomorrow's faith, especially when it comes to a religious tradition that is as pliable and morphs as easily as Hinduism does.[69]

David Shulman, professor of Hinduism at Hebrew University, points out that Hinduism does not has a sharp dividing line of human and divine. Goshen-Gottstein who has been in contact with many gurus and has spent several seasons in India points out how within the Indian culture "The Guru is approached *as if* he were God." On one hand, this is a problem for Jewish monotheism, in which "there is a fundamental disdain from the divinization of the human person in classical Judaism. Yet the 'as if' approach is, of course, reminiscent of various midrashic statements that inculcate a religious attitude by means of 'as if' statements, that narrow down and break down the divide between the human and the divine." From the Hindu perspective, "Who but god, argued the Swami, would have such power. The leap from the powerful and miraculous to the divine is made with an ease that leaves the Jewish observer ill at ease." Goshen-Gottstein notes that some Jewish figures, such as R. Isaac Luria were called the divine (*ha-elokhi*), but without the same connotations as in India.[70]

Goshen-Gottstein quotes the opening of Maimondies, Mishneh Torah: "The foundation of foundations and the pillar of wisdom is to know there is a primordial Being, and that He brought about all that is. And all that is (exists), of heaven and earth and what is between, exist only on the account of the Truth of His Being."[71] Goshen-Gottstein ponders how the Hindu emphasis on the divine nature of reality of the Vedanta is only one prefatory note in Maimonides. Jews do not contemplate God as much as Hindus do. To imitate this, Jews would have to have a study program of discussions of God in medieval philosophy, kabbalah, and Habad Hasidut.

The first, and most obvious, was how easily this text could have been composed by a vedantin. God alone is. All else is secondary and derivative of His existence. In truth,

> God alone exists. Nothing is real as God is real. God alone is Truth. God alone is Being. These are the most fundamental teachings that the student of this Hindu philosophy encounters regularly.
>
> Many well educated and pious Jews may never read this text, and if they do it may not play a formative role in their thinking of God. By contrast, reflection on these ideas is the spiritual bread and butter of vedanta . . .
>
> For the vedantin, these issues are what spiritual teaching are all about, and their elaboration, exploration, meditation and realization are the goal and the path of the spiritual life.
>
> The vedantin would well agree with this, with one major difference. All that exists exists because it shares in God's existence . . . We return to the notion of the all pervading God, whose life fills all of creation, and for whom creation serves as its outer expression.[72]

Hinduism and Indian thought distinguishes between relative and absolute, or in other formulations, between form and formless. The Hindu terms are *nirguna* and *saguna*, with and without attributes. God can be approached in His aspect as absolute, without attributes, qualities or through qualities, form, and manifestation. Judaism may not worship in form, but in some higher sense its approach to God is still *saguna*, with attributes hence implicated in form. This places Jewish opposition to worship in form, what Judaism considers idolatry, in a broader theoretical matrix. There is a greater need for philosophic and Kabbalistic matrix for understanding Indian thought. David Shulman puts forward the hypothesis that Jews worship a *saguna* God with no visible form, while Hindus worship a formless *nirguna* God, who can take on form. If things are seen in this light, then the two faiths no longer can be placed in simple dichotomies.

A significant part of the challenge that Hinduism poses is the encounter with religious virtuosi, the gurus, some of whom are indeed of extraordinary value. Judaism tends to praise other faiths by their morality not their saintliness. What do we do now?

> When a Jewish person looks at the lives of holy people in India, he is thus confronted and challenged on two levels. The first is the ability to recognize and to accept that extraordinary holiness and spirituality can be found in practitioners of Hinduism . . . Recognizing holiness in another tradition implies a certain degree of recognition and acceptance.[73]

Goshen-Gottstein admonishes us that he is not aware of a single attempt to state what Judaism has to offer, as an inspiration or as a corrective, to a Hindu worldview. Hindus are much more self-confident in the universality of their message as the fundamental spiritual truth that all religions should be teaching. If Judaism belittles the spiritual value of the Hindu religion by identifying it with simplistic idol worship, then Judaism comes off as simplistic in its conceptualization. Jews narrowly tell Hindus to outgrow your idol worship, but empirical observers see the Hindu tradition as one that worships one Supreme Being and has the potential to cultivate spiritual teachers of immediate empirical and spiritual worth.

On the other hand, many Neo-Hindu theological positions of a Supreme Being that transcends categories and denies reality to the images create an unbound god above any religion or human category. Then, one is not comparing two religions but is rather creating a new universal mysticism. Whereas Jewish-Christian encounters in the 1950s created a language of covenant, Hindu-Western encounter in the mid-twentieth century created a form of Supreme Being above religion. Despite all these hurdles: How can we find a place for Hinduism within our own theology?

Buddhist Encounters

Nineteenth-century European and Americans did not meet living teachers, visit Buddhist institutions, nor did they engage in true Buddhist practice. Rather, Buddhism known through books served an intellectual landscape to serve as a foil to Western Christendom. Buddhism was portrayed either as life affirming Transcendentalism, or in other eras it was portrayed by the opposite as nihilism in terms of negativity, seeking death, and denying individuality. From the eighteenth-century until the 1970s, many Westerners presented Theraveda Buddhism, the meditative monastic Buddhism of Southeast Asia, as teaching pessimism and the transitory nature of the world. One seeks to escape this vanity by attaining nirvana, the cessation of mental activity.[1] The positive appreciation of meditation is a recent association.[2]

Judaism does not have any extensive early records of encounter with Buddhism Currently, most of the modern encounters of Judaism and Buddhism are within Judaism itself, between ethnic Jews who have been exposed to Westernized Buddhism or adapted meditation as part their Judaism. I have included Confucianism and Taoism in this chapter because when discussing Chinese religion, the three are interconnected.

- Silk Road and Ibn Rashid
- Enlightenment Translations: *Meoreot Zvi, Shevilei Olam*
- Moderns: Kook, Koehler, Buber, Teshima, and Matt
- Seekers: Lew and Gellman
- China and Confucianism

On the Silk Road

Contrary to current perceptions, medieval Buddhists fostered a world of internationalism—serving as bankers that urged monetization, urbanization, and political consolidation. Before the Islamic conquests, Tukharistan (northern Afghanistan) and Sogdiana (southern Uzbekistan) were strongholds of Buddhism and encompassed the most important way stations on the routes that moved Buddhism from India to China. In Afghanistan, the gigantic Buddhas, that graced the Bamiyan valley until a few years ago, are a testament to the long legacy of Buddhism on the silk and spice routes, as well as a testimony to the relative openness of Islam to Buddhism for 1,300 years. Jews are reported in and on the silk route in Tibet and China.[3]

Muslims, and their Jewish co-travelers, traversed the Indian and Chinese lands looking for knowledge of pharmacology, medicine, mathematics, and well as spices and musk. In the ninth century, the circle of followers of the Muslim philosopher al-Kindi (d. ~873) possessed accounts of these journeys.

The Mongolians who conquered much of Central and Middle East were Tibetan Buddhists; the famous Kublai Khan (d. 1295) followed the Kagyu form of Buddhism. Much of the Mongolian leadership converted to Islam over time, but Buddhism held its own within Muslim lands. In the seventeenth century, the Fourth and Fifth Dalai Lamas were violent warriors maintaining and consolidating Tibetan power. The roles of the small minority of Jews in these events have yet to be fully explored; however we do have information about one important figure, Rashid al-Din.

Rashid al-Din

Rashid al-Din (1247–1318) (also called Fazlallah Tabib al-Hamdani, "the physician from Hamadan"), entered the service of the Ilkhan Abaqa (r. 1265–1282), the second Mongol Emperor, as a physician. Then he became a deputy to Sadr al-Din Zanjāni, the vizier of Arghun's son, Ghazan Khan (1295–1304). A few months later, Sadr al-Din was put to death and his place was taken by Sad al-Din Sāvaji who made Rashid al-Din his associate. In this capacity Rashid al-Din introduced substantial administrative reforms during Ghazan's reign. He amassed tremendous power and wealth and owned property in almost every corner of the Mongol Empire. Eight of his fourteen sons were appointed governors of provinces. In the suburb of Tabriz he constructed a little town, called by his name Rab-i Rashidi, to which he brought intellectuals and artists from different Islamic lands. We are informed from some early sources that he had embraced Islam around the year 1278. When they tried to introduce paper money, economic crisis ensued and he was accused of poisoning Ghazan Khan, by prescribing the wrong medicine. During his trial, his Jewish background was mentioned very often. Rashid al-Din and his 16-year-old son, Ibrahim, were put to death in 1318 by the new emperor. He and his son were buried in the Jewish cemetery.

Rashid al-Din is considered one of the greatest scholars in Persia. Besides Persian, he knew Arabic, Hebrew, Turkish, and Mongolian languages. He produced several monumental books, the most important of which was *Jāmi-al-Tavārīkh World History*, known to be the first world history; he used a whole team of experts. The book contains, within the context of the history of India, a separate section dedicated to the life of the Buddha as well as separate sections on Southeast Asian Theravada, Tibetan, and Chinese Chan Buddhism. Rashid al-Din knew Buddhists and had visited Buddhist Temples and explains the various philosophies of Buddhism. An analysis of this widely read text can provide us with some clues regarding how Persian and Central Asian Jews viewed Buddhism.[4]

Important presentations for our purposes include his explaining Buddhism in Koranic terms through describing Buddha as a prophet who received revelation of a book. He compared Sufism to Indian asceticism, as well as Muslim paradise to Buddhist heavens and hells. Ronit Yoeli-Tlalim, a scholar of Central Asia, has analyzed Rashid al-Din's *Life of the Buddha* and noted the influence of Mahayana and Vajrayana perspectives. On the process of translation, she notes that the Buddhist term "higher rebirth" is translated as paradise and the concept of "transcending transmigration (*samsara*)" is translated as "to reach the Real (Haqq)." The word *karma,* which refers to actions, is translated as action by nature or the prime mover. And just as we found in the discussion of Hinduism, al-Din translates Buddhist deities as angels. On the question of God, many of the contemporary Muslim thinkers considered Buddhists as worshiping the great Abrahamic God, an inclusivism of placing Buddhism in Biblical categories. Rashid al-Din reports on Chinese Amitabha Buddhism, where the worshipers treat Buddha in a theist way and recite daily ablutions in order for the Bodhisattva of compassion to take people out of hell. Al-Din also knows of the Buddhist-Daoist worship of the big dipper and body meridians, on which he comments that they follow their own personal opinions and not the guidance of a prophet.

Meoreot Zvi

Meoreot Zvi (Lvov, 1804) is a narrative of the events surrounding the life of Shabbatai Zvi along with a description of his prophecies, visions, magic, and charismatic gifts used in generating a following. The work is dependent upon Enlightenment travelogues to the East with their vivid reports of distant lands combined with condescending evaluations of the foreign cultures. The passage is remarkably positive for a rabbinic text without exclusivist condemnation as idolatry; rather it is of a more subtle Western European style of derogatory ethnography. The author tended to mix passages from more than one author so that authors as diverse in time and place as Athanasius Kircher (d. 1667) and Thomas Astley (d. 1745) are mixed. The idea that ecstasies are either divine or demonic is an early modern Catholic language, depicting a world of exorcisms and possession. The mention of their impure spirit rather than the traditional Jewish discussion of idols, reflects a source in a Christian missionary travelogue. On the other hand, Protestants circulated these works to show the similar paganism of the Catholic Church. The author shows that he read such works and provides many parallels between Shabbatai Zvi's actions and Eastern practices. His goal is to present a captivating account of Shabbatai Zvi with conflicting valences in Enlightenment style, this religious imaginary is important because later the same author will be involved in editing stories of the Baal Shem Tov.[5]

> In the province in the sky, which is the great [Lhasa] valley in the land of Tibet next to East India is their great city Potala. There resides the great monk of all their idolatrous monks, called the [Dalai] Lama, who is father of impurity from which all the monks derive their way of crookedness from one of the spirits of impurity.

The matter is like this: The monks called Brahmins make a golem from clay in the image of a man with their magic until skin, flesh, bones, and veins appear. Afterward, they adjure it with (demonic) spirits of the impure spirit because of their crookedness. Then an actual living man literally appears and its appearance is like the golem made from clay by our [Jewish] masters of the names. [The Jewish masters of the name] do everything with the predetermined received skills; in contrast they [the monks] adjure spirits of the false seven heavens. They are all experts in adjuring spirits of impurity, especially the face-spirit of impurity. By their oaths a face-spirit continuously appears illuminated, sometimes it changes and there will appear a continuous image of the previous (demonic) [Dalai] Lama, who had died.

At the time of a particular festival of theirs, the monks bear [the Dalai Lama] through the streets of the city in a throne sheathed in linens, with his face covered. His face does not appear to the masses, because he is holy in their opinion. When he dies they treat the incoming ruling Lama with the same authority as they did for the preceding Lama. The monks deceive the masses with the image saying that their Lama is the living and eternal God, holy and awe-inspiring.

Any one of the masses that is, at least worthy to drink from the urine of the Lama (which the monks themselves urinate) is sanctified with a special holiness. Those sanctified with the drinking of this urine are called holy and pure due to all types of holiness.

Thousands and tens of thousands go on pilgrimage to him from far and he prophesizes the future for them, and the monks write healing amulets with his name inside. Even the emperors who rule over them, and every prince of the kingdom, must receive authorization for his rule from him or he will not be received as king over them.

As a historic point, the eighteenth-century Enlightenment actually entertained using the urine-cure as one of the wondrous cures available from the East. The description of the creation of golem-like figures in Tibet reappears for the general English reader in Alexandra David-Neel's, *Magic and Mystery in Tibet.*

Another passage from the book compares the extreme penances of the followers of Shabbatai Zvi with Eastern practices.[6] The book describes the annual "*Rathayatra*" (Car Festival), which attracts devotees and pilgrims. *Rath* means chariot, *Yatra*—a pilgrimage or procession. It originated in Jagannath Puri on the eastern coast of India. *Jagannath* is a Hindu god worshipped primarily by the people of Indian states of Odisha and Bengal, and is generally considered an aspect of the god Vishnu or his avatar Krishna—and was connected to Buddhism by westerners. Throwing under the wheels has been mentioned in accounts of the Sri *Jagannath* festival in Puri. Piercing is an exaggeration of a penance called *kavadi*; in which people pull carts attached to body piercings, or suspend themselves by tying cords from the piercings to trees, etc., widespread in Tamil Nadu, Sri Lanka, Malaysia—anywhere Tamil culture pervades.

The people of ancient Martaban, near the city Pegu [currently Bago] in East India [currently Burma] on the day of their idolatrous holiday, have all the monks take out an enormous and long wagon of seventy wheels from their house of idolatry to the streets. Their idolatry is at the head of the drawn wagon, while behind and next to it they draw many renowned monks. [These monks] went up all seven false heavens and they brought down prophecies and apparitions of impurity. Many hundreds of people from the city, as a great honor, vie to pull the wagon.

The sinners in that nation in order to atone for their souls engage in sanctification and surrender for several months before the idolatrous holiday with fasts and unbearable great mortifications. When they draw the wagon through the street with their idolatry, the penitents throw themselves under the wheels, one here and one there. In an instant the wheels cut them into many pieces like the scapegoat. This penance is their greatest form of penance. One of their lesser penances is where the penitent cuts into his left thigh two great holes and tie into them a fine cord. He attaches the other end to the wagons of idolatry in order to be drawn after the [cart of the] idols.

Shevilei Olam

Samson ha Levi Bloch (1782–1845) was a Galician rabbi and author with a wide interest in all aspects of the Jewish Enlightenment. He wrote a three-volume work surveying the geography and history of the world based on similar recent works in German. There are several other early nineteenth-century works of a similar nature, but Bloch's work won acceptance through his unique style and his having personally traveled to sell his books. Ultra-Orthodox Rabbinic figures, such as Rabbis Moses Sofer and Mordechai Banet, considered the book worthy to read. The work was reprinted and for three generations served as a basic conduit of knowledge. The first volume of the work, *Shevilei Olam* (1822), surveys the entire breath of Asia, including countries and regions such as India, Central Asia, China, Japan, Burma, Vietnam, and Indonesia. The perspective of the accounts is that of European interest and the rise of the British Empire. Therefore, the accounts stress empire, free trade, maritime connection, and the role of liberty.

In Bloch's account of Tibet, he presents descriptions of the court and Temples of Tibet as well as their vassalage to China. He explains Lamaism as the elevation of the lowly human body, which does not actually reflect the Tibetan doctrine of a spiritual body. It is ironic, however, since this is the correct explanation of Hasidism, and Bloch wrote an anti-Hasidic tract. The book is rich in detail that could have been used in this book to describe numerous countries and religions.

The religion of the land is Buddhism (Phowa, which in the Hindi language is Bodhi) or the religion of the Dalai Lama, their teacher and high priest. This faith has attracted over 100 million believers and is found all over Eastern Asia with countless temples. Buddhism reaches as far as the island of Ceylon (Sri Lanka). There are countless temples in the region. The foundation of this faith is the desire to achieve a state of sublimity in a mundane form. Followers of the faith attempt to reach a lofty spiritual state while in a human body. According to doctrines, the holy presence (*shekhinah*) contracts into the body of the high priest, who lives eternally. When his time in this world has expired, knowledge of what is to come is immediate. The holy spirit reveals who the high priest's soul will be reborn into in the next realm of being. Sometimes it occurs to a nursing baby, and the spirit rests upon him. In this way he lives eternally

The stories from the work of Creation and the sin of the Tree of Knowledge are taken from our Holy Torah, and the ideas of reincarnation, the pleasures of the world to come, and the hells are from the Hindu faith.

Bloch also deals with the religions of India and the more complex mixtures of China and the East Indies. He accepts the moral foundations of the original sources, such as the colonialists condemning and banning widow burning (*sati*).

To expiate any sin, the Hindus bring offerings, undergo baptisms, pray, fast, and make pilgrimages to holy people and holy sites, and give alms. In every city, there are places of prayer to the aforementioned Vishnu and Shiva, but not (necessarily) to Brahma. On the walls various sorts of painted images and idols are depicted inside the temples.

Originally, in India, widows were sent to their death with their husband on pyres. Both were cremated together and so they will die together . . . Hindu scripture says that, "A man and his wife that die together, will be entwined in a sweet, eternal, loving embrace." This is truly the source of this abominable custom. The widows who go to their burning upon the pyre do not cry; they go joyfully.[7]

Alexandrov and Rav Kook

Rabbi Shmuel Alexandrov (d. 1941) had been a close friend of Rabbi Abraham Isaac Kook in Volozhin, where they both studied. Unlike Kook, however, Alexandrov never left Russia and instead became a rabbi in Bobruisk. Until his death at the hands of the Germans in 1941, Alexandrov was a spiritual leader to many rabbis, particularly during the severe religious persecutions of the 1920s and 1930s in the Soviet Union. He was also a Kabbalistic mystic and a devotee of the Maharal of Prague, of whom he was a twelfth generation descendant.

Alexandrov propounded a mystical theory of the relationship between Jews and gentiles, containing deep roots in the Kabbalah and Maharal. According to him, of the two trees in the Garden of Eden, the Tree of Life and the Tree of Knowledge, the former is an exclusively Jewish possession (i.e., the Torah), while the latter belongs to the gentiles. Among the Tree of Knowledge's fruits are scientific-technical progress, philosophy, and art; nevertheless, there exists a historical mystical exchange of the fruits of both trees. By giving to the world the fruits of the Tree of Life Jews consecrate the gentile world, while simultaneously Jews receive from the gentiles the fruits of vital knowledge and ideas.

Alexandrov seeks to find a place for the wisdom learned from other religions, especially the idea of Buddhist nothingness. Alexandrov boldly claimed that one universal truth forms the basis of all religions; hence, the Buddhist concept of nirvana and Hasidic concept of ayin point to the same concept in different words. He made this assertion based not on the study of texts nor from encountering Buddhists, but rather from the conceptualizations of religion found in the writings of Schelling and Schopenhauer, German Idealists of the nineteenth century. Alexandrov postulates a universal religion given by Moses and reiterated by Plato, which overcomes abstract intellect and seeks the emotional and psychological, offering individual salvation.[8]

Since Alexandrov weaves his ideas from comments on Kabbalistic texts, his statements are hard to translate, and many consist of fragmentary comments on earlier texts. It is important to note that he reinterprets the thought of his forefather, the Maharal, to suggest that the dialectic of Israel and the nations, presented by the Maharal, will be overcome at the end of days when all national differences will be abolished by the coming of the Messiah.

Rabbi Abraham Isaac Kook found this approach to concede too much to universalism. He responds to Alexandrov's pluralistic claims with an inclusive claim that all truth is from Judaism using the spectrum of colors metaphor of the *Zohar*:

> The name of the God of Israel is the infinite, incomprehensible root of all existence, because He is the existence of the world who can be comprehended and spoken of only through the nuances of colors through many deeds and abundant peace, his profusion of love and courage. Israel proclaims, "This is my God and I will adore Him," and can see these [colors], not the barren wilderness of Islamic monotheism, nor Buddhism's negation.

> The approach of the East in general and with Buddhism in particular consists of the recognition of the [absolute] evil of [this world's] evil and from this an absolute despair is proclaimed on existence, in which the success of existence only comes from its destruction.

> As for the reality of nothingness in the statements of those of Buddhist leanings, it seems that they mean the reality of the force which aspires to negate and nullify absolutely . . . Jewish consciousness, however, in the goodness of God's knowledge, brings about a recognition of the absolute reality. . . . Thus we find that even this contradiction between Buddhism and Judaism is not absolute opposites, because reality as viewed without God is everywhere evil and bitter, and in its midst lies the longing for absolute negation, which will in the end be fulfilled.[9]

Like Benamozegh, Alexandrov had observed that Jews throughout history acquired knowledge from the wisdom of all nations during the exile, and claimed that contemporary Jews can continue this process through study of Buddhism and other religions. Rabbi Kook, on the other hand, found all of religion in Judaism, minimizing any need to study other religions.[10]

This debate played itself out in their differing concepts of religion. For Alexandrov, an infinite inner core resides behind the particular Jewish commandments; the current versions express the infinite by limiting it to concrete forms, while for Rav Kook, the commandments in their concrete, particular forms contain an infinite essence that needs to be brought into daily life. For Alexandrov, Judaism and its commandments are themselves limits on the infinite Divine, while for Kook, the commandments are the very conduits of the infinite.

Leo Baeck

Leo Baeck (1873–1956) was one of the most important liberal Jewish theologians of the twentieth century. Baeck's description of Buddhism, as well as other religions, tends toward caricature, being largely inattentive to the subtleties monolithic. For Baeck, Buddhism denotes passivity and inactivity as well as denying the value in the world. In contrast, only Judaism offers moral duty:

> [Judaism] declares the world to be the field of life's tasks and offers a moral affirmation of the value of man's relationship to the world by deed and will; the latter [Buddhist] declares that man's task is to devote himself to self-meditation without the exercise of his volition . . . Judaism leads to the desire to work for the kingdom of God in which all men may unite, while Buddhism leads to the desire to sink into the One, into nothingness, there to find deliverance and salvation for the ego.

> Buddhism seeks "extinction," departure from humanity and from the world. Thus Judaism is a religion of altruism, since it declares that man to be striving toward perfection who has found his way to God by seeking his brethren and who serves God by loving and being just to them. Buddhism on the other hand, is the religion of egotism, since it attributes perfection to the man who retreats from mankind in order to discover the only true approach to himself.

> While Buddhism is a world-negating tradition, working for release from responsibility and involvement, Judaism is a world-affirming religion; its optimism takes the form of ethical action within the community.[11]

> Buddhism's doctrine of love fondly preaches mercy and benevolence toward every living thing, but in its inner core this feeling is one of sentimentality and melancholy. It lacks the reverence for the fellow man which distinguishes Jewish teaching; it lacks the great "Thou shalt", the imperative force and urgency, the social and messianic elements which are emphasized by Judaism. Beyond mere feeling Buddhist morality does not go. That is what gives its characteristically passive and negative stamp.[12]

In the last passage, Baeck firmly questions any Buddhist sense of love and mercy before its world-denying melancholia. There are negative statements toward other religions similar to Baeck found in the writings of his older contemporary, Kaufman Kohler (c.1843–1926) who, besides being a major Reform rabbi, was also the principle theologian of the widely read *Jewish Encyclopedia* (1901). He encapsulated for his wide Jewish readership his position that "Buddhism and Confucianism never engendered love of mankind."[13]

Martin Buber: Zen and Tao

Martin Buber (1878–1965) is an important twentieth-century Jewish philosopher and biblical commentator, best known for his philosophy of dialogue. Buber translated tales of the Chinese Taoists and was one of the first to compare

Hasidism to Zen Buddhism.[14] In all of his comparisons, Buber looks to praise the adept who lives in the moment; and he condemns metaphysical speculation.

Both Zen and Hasidism share teaching through tales, but "In the Hasidic tale the symbolic character of the occurrence is stressed, whereas in the Zen tale it remains concealed," and only in the literature is the meaning of the utterance discussed.[15] In addition, "both in Zen and in Hasidism the relation between the teacher and disciple is central."[16] They train one to live in the concrete world, however Zen seeks to transcend the world, while in Hasidism correct action raises a spark and thereby puts one directly in contact with the Divine and the redemption of the world. For Buber, Buddhism identifies the world and the self while Hasidism identifies God and the world but leaves the self intact:

> We must consider afresh what seemed most clearly to us to be common to Zen and Hasidism, the positive relationship to the concrete. We have seen that in both the learning and developing man is directed to the things, to the sensible being, to activity in the world.
>
> But the moving force thereto is fundamentally different in each. In Zen the intensive pointing to the concrete serves to divert the spirit directed to knowledge of the transcendent from the discursive thought . . . it is not the things themselves that matter here, but their non-conceptual nature as symbol of the Absolute which is superior to all concepts. Not so in Hasidism. Here the things themselves are the object of religious concern, for they are the abode of the holy sparks that man shall raise up [. . .] By concerning himself with them in the right way man comes into contact with the destiny of divine being in the world and helps in the redemption . . . The realism of Zen is dialectical, it means annulment; Hasidic realism is Messianic, it means fulfillment.[17]
>
> Buddhism, originally as an historically-defined religion which was even transformed into Mahayana into a religion of revelation, becomes here a mysticism of the human person, a mysticism outside of history, no longer bound to any unique event . . . It is entirely different with Hasidism. However much the Kabbalistic doctrine of emanations altered the view of the relation between God and the *world*, the view of the relation between God and the *human soul* remains essentially what it was. We do, indeed, hear in Hasidism ever again that God is the substance of our prayers, but we do not hear that He is our substance.[18]

In Buber's model of world religions, there are different paths to salvation that Buber limits to three major paths. "These three manifestations are the Chinese Tao-teaching, the Indian teaching of release, and the Jewish/original–Christian teaching of the kingdom of God."[19] In each of these, one has a direct connection to the concrete without doctrinal and legal interference. As is known from his other writings, the prophets, Jesus, kabbalah, and Hasidut overcome western dogmatism and legalism:

> Buddha overcomes the Vedic science with the abolition of the "view" that does not belong to the accomplished man on the "path," and the Brahmin law with the abolition of castes in the order. Thus, Lao Tzu overcomes the official wisdom through the teaching of "non-being," the official virtue through the teaching of "non-doing."[20]

Jacob Teshima

Jacob Yuroh Teshima (b. 1942) was a student of Heschel and studied at both the Hebrew University and at the Jewish Theological Seminary of America. His father, Abraham Ikurō Teshima, was the original convert and founder of the Makuya sect, a biblical faith with many followers in Japan. Even though technically not a Jewish author, the sect believes in a return to the Bible as a Protestant group combined with a Jewish understanding of those texts. In addition, they are active advocates for Israel and Jacob's father Abraham was close to Martin Buber, who was the first person to point out the similarity between Zen and Hasidism.

Jacob Teshima has spent many decades writing popularizations of the Talmud and rabbinic ethics for Japanese and Korean readers. Teshima is the only non-Jewish author that I include in this chapter because his important work on Zen and Hasidism was done under Jewish auspices and is widely cited in Jewish circles as if it was from Heschel himself. In addition, his movement remains connected to mainstream Jewish causes and stays connected to the Jewish community. The basic difference, for Teshima, between the faiths is that Zen is about no-thinking and everyday mindfulness while Hasidism is about God:

> A survey of the basic practices: zazen in Zen Buddhism and devequth in Hasidism. Although in essence both zazen and devequth are contemplation, zazen is the practice of no-thinking and looking into one's own nature whereas devequth is meditation on God . . . The essential difference between the Hasidic and the Zen versions of the annihilation of selfhood is that in Hasidism the individual accomplishes bittul ha-yesh through encounter with God, while in Zen Buddhism the individual maintains wu-nien through realization of his own universal nature . . . It is the maintenance of the unconscious "everyday-mindedness."

> There is substantial difference between Hasidism's devequth and Zen's *chien-hsing*. In devequth, a person cleaves to God, who is an external and independent entity from him and who is the Infinite One embracing all creation. In chien-hsing, a person looks at his own nature, which is, however, identical with the vessel of Dharma (Reality).

> Zen requires of a person wu-nien (non-activation of thought) in order to contemplate his own nature. If he activates the process of thinking in the mind, he will be disturbed immediately by his own act and unable to look into his own nature. Therefore in the practice of Zen, especially in zazen, he is required to remain as he is. It could be compared with a ship floating on the ocean without an anchor . . . On the other hand, devequth is to cast anchor into God. The anchor of a Hasid is kavvanah, which is active awareness of the Divine Presence. In comparison to the complexity of Kabbalistic kavvanoth, Hasidic kavvanah greatly reduced the need to activate the thinking process. Once a Hasid has engraved the impression of the Divine Presence or the Tetragrammaton upon his subconsciousness, there is no need for him to reactivate thinking of God in the mind. The notion of God, then, automatically appears in the mind whenever the mind is free from other thoughts. In this point, Hasidism's *kavvanah* is close to Zen's wu-nien.

. . . Buddhism denies the somethingness of the universe and tries to reduce all being into non-somethingness. . . . Hasidism attempts to reduce all being into super-somethingness. Perhaps the quality is identical, but the process is entirely different.[21]

Daniel Matt

Daniel Matt, academic scholar of the Kabbalah and translator of *The Zohar: Pritzker Edition*, developed the symbol of *Ayin*, God's nothingness, in a way that has found resonance among many looking to connect Kabbalah to the Buddhist nothingness. Matt is a careful scholar and explains the texts within their original historical context of Judeo-Arabic Neo-Platonic ideas of the One and the many. Yet he tantalizes his reader by offering Kabbalah as "beyond the Personal God" to descriptions that sound like a generic version of the Buddhist concept of emptiness *Sunyata*, and no-thingness. Many popular writers have expanded Matt's implicit equivalence to be an explicit equation, in which all references to the Hebrew term *ayin* or *eyn* meaning nothingness, contained within Jewish thought, such as "Eyn Od Milvado," are understood in Buddhist terms and with Buddhist parallels:

> Among their new names for God, Eyn Sof is the most famous but not the most radical. Having carved away all that is false, they discover a paradox of a name: ayin, Nothingness . . . What does it mean to call God Nothingness? It does not mean that God does not exist. In the words of a fourteenth-century kabbalist, David ben Abraham Halavan,
>
> > Nothingness (ayin) is more existent than all the being of the world. But since it is simple, and all simple things are complex compared with its simplicity, in comparison it is called ayin.
>
> Ayin is a name for the nameless. It conveys the idea that God is no thing, neither this nor that. Rather, as ayin, God animates all things and cannot be contained by them. The paradox is that ayin embraces "everything" and "nothing." This nothing-ness is oneness, undifferentiated oneness, overwhelming the distinctions between things. God is the oneness that is no particular thing, no thingness, Nothingness with a capital N.[22]

Encounters

The first Prime Minister of Israel, David Ben-Gurion, was attracted to Theraveda Buddhism as part of his general interest in stoic heroic values, reading the *Dhammapada* together with Spinoza, and the Bible. Ben-Gurion offers his thoughts on Buddhism and what he learned from the Buddhist scholar and Prime Minister of Burma, Thray Sithu U Ba Khin, whose country achieved independence alongside the new state of Israel:[23]

> "He abused me, he defeated me, he robbed me"—in those who harbor such thoughts hatred will never cease. For never does hatred cease by hatred here below. Hatred ceases by love; this is an eternal law.

This saying in the *Dhammapada,* one of the collections of the Buddha's sayings, is a major principle in his teachings. Another is the conquest of the instincts: If one man conquers in battle a thousand times a thousand men, and if another conquers himself, he is the greatest of conquerors.

And just as Buddha enjoined love to all men and all living things, and the conquest of the instincts, so he enjoined men to pursue truth: Like a beautiful flower, full of color, but without scent, are the fair but fruitless words of him who does not act accordingly.[24]

In 1961, a delegation of politicians and journalists visited Burma. The Buddhists found the Israeli delegation as "materialistic in outlook and more interested in the present values of Buddhist Meditation than in what one would gain in the after-life." Their Buddhist host wanted them to understand that the goal of Buddhist meditation is the realization of nirvana, a cessation of mental activity.

During the Korean War, Jews were exposed to various religions in Japan, Korea, and Indochina, they met Buddhists, Shintoists, and other eastern religions. The effect was that when they arrived home they engaged in interfaith activities in suburbia, working together with Protestants and Catholics as religions of democracy. In contrast to the majority, Philip Kapleau (1912–2004), who was serving as an Allied military court reporter for the Tokyo War Crimes Trials, discovered Zen Buddhism in Japan and returned to become an influential Zen Roshi as well as author of the influential *The Three Pillars of Zen.*

Even though some American Jews were first attracted to Hinduism, others became attracted to Zen Buddhism, or at least to Beat Zen Buddhism. American Jews first became acquainted with Vipassana Buddhist meditation during the 1960s while traveling or while serving in the Peace Corps. When they returned to the United Stiles, they taught Buddhist meditation in retreat centers to a broad audience without the doctrines of the religion, without concern of karma or liberation, and without practicing the many Buddhist rituals and feast days. Some of these Jews such as Joseph Goldstein, Jack Kornfeld, and Sharon Saltzberg were the first to bring insight meditation to the United States and founded the Insight Meditation Society (IMS).

Rodger Kamenetz's best-selling book *The Jew in the Lotus: A Poet's Rediscovery of Jewish Identity in Buddhist India* is about the 1990 visit of a delegation of Jewish rabbis and other notables to Dharamsala, India, the Dalai Lama's home in exile. In some ways though, the book is about Rodger's journey from religious non-participation to his adopting Jewish Renewal's version of Judaism. After this much publicized meeting with the Dali Lama, the attraction was galvanized into the Buddhist-Judaism (Ju Bu or *Bu-Ju*) trend. This trend embraced a popular Buddhism of meditation without any doctrine, divinity, or scripture that could possibly contradict Judaism. A well-known book to discuss this trend is *That's Funny, You Don't Look Buddhist: On Being a Faithful Jew and a Passionate Buddhist* by Sylvia Boorstein. The author explains that her Buddhist practice has made her a better Jew, and that by allowing her *Yiddishkeit* (Jewishness) to show, she has become a better Buddhist. Jewish meditation has become widespread, which is not meditation based in Jewish tradition or practice. Rather, it is Buddhist meditation that lives within the Buddhist world of *Dharma*, but now has a Jewish cultural veneer. We even have contemporary Jews writing Hasidic tales in which Buddhist teachings are placed in the mouths of fictitious nineteenth-century Chassidic Rebbes, offering a Jewish patina of authenticity to Buddhist teachings.[25]

Alan Lew

Rabbi Alan Lew (1944–2009) was the spiritual leader of San Francisco's Congregation Beth Sholom. He was also at the forefront of attempting to cultivate a spirituality bridging Judaism and Buddhism. Lew's coming of age as a Jew actually occurred while he sought to deepen his Zen Buddhist practice. Disillusioned by the Judaism that he had experienced as a child, Lew considered becoming ordained as a lay Buddhist priest. However, he found himself unable to sew a priestly garment while on a retreat in the 1970s at Tassajara, a Zen center in Carmel Valley. As he meditated on that resistance, Lew said that "there was some sense of conflict between my being ordained as a Buddhist with my being Jewish." It became a turning point, which lead Lew toward Judaism and, ultimately, to rabbinical school.

Lew seems to have a Buddhist view toward reality in terms of its root metaphors, not in terms of the religion itself. Life is a great sea of Being, an endless flow; we are all interconnected, and we all feel other people's suffering. He formulates Judaism as mindfulness using the metaphor of "layered grid of awareness" as a bridge idea, noting that both Buddhism and Judaism have a layered grid of awareness. Jewish prayer is about energy exchange and mindfulness:

> That we are afloat in a great sea of being, an endless flow of becoming in which we are connected to all beings . . . We die to the world every time we breathe out, and every time we breathe in, every time our breath returns to us of its own accord, we are reborn, and the world rises up into being again.[26]

> Every spiritual tradition I am aware of speaks of a kind of layered mindfulness, a sensibility that works up and out of the body, to the heart and then to the mind and then finally to the soul. The Buddhist sutra On Mindfulness describes this kind of layered grid of awareness, and the Kabala, the Jewish mystical tradition, speaks of it too. According to the Kabala, we start out with our awareness in Asiyah—the world of physicality, the world of the body, our most immediately accessible reality. Then we become aware of the heart, yetzirah—the world of formation or emotion, that shadowy world between conception and its realization in material form. From there we move on to the world of pure intellect, Briyah, or creation, and then to Atzilut, the realm of pure spiritual emanation.[27]

> I would visualize the words as an energy exchange—the words going up to God and God's attention coming down. Prayer began bringing me to the same place my Zen practice had taken me . . . Before I prayed, I would study, in a prayer shawl and teffilin, sitting in half-lotus.[28]

> So yoga and directed meditation became part of the practice I offered at my synagogue. The meditation group changed the whole tenor of the Friday night minyan.

Suddenly the service had great density and feeling [. . .] My goal was to help Jews deepen their Jewish practice with Buddhist-style meditation techniques.[29]

Meditation and Jewish practice lead us to experience the oneness of all beings. We are all connected; each of us is created in the divine image, and other people's suffering is our own . . . But the first noble truth is that everything is suffering, and both Judaism and Buddhism insist that the only appropriate response to this suffering is to turn toward it, to attend to it. Avalokiteshvara, the Bodhisattva of Compassion, is "The Hearer of the Cries of the World," and the Torah God is repeatedly described as hearing the cries of the oppressed.[30]

Alan Lew believed "There was nothing in my experience of beginning to study Buddhism or to practice mindfulness meditation and loving-kindness meditation, which are the principal practices that the Buddhists taught, that ever seemed to challenge my being a Jew at all." Buddhist meditation and the minimalism of Zen are considered the definition of Buddhism, without recourse to Buddhist scripture, philosophy, or ritual life. It seems strange to some that Bu-Jews completely remove the religion from Buddhism and teach the meditation outside of the rest of the very religion it is founded upon. Apparently, today many people in the West feel one can honor their birth religion while concurrently being a Zen Buddhist. Can we combine both traditions?

It would be instructive to compare Lew with Paul Williams' work, *The Unexpected Way,* who advocates theism over Buddhist theology. As a trained professor of Buddhism at the University of Bristol, Williams is familiar with the languages and the religion of Buddhism. Williams's study of Buddhism leads him to reject a religion without a theistic God, revelation, redemption, reward, and providence. He writes a coherent, rational, and theological critique of Buddhism and a defense of theism from a Catholic point of view. Reading Lew in light of Williams, one is struck by the lack of any engagement with the theology of Judaism or where Judaism differs from Buddhism, or any Buddhism beyond the metaphors. One would not know from Lew that Jewish theology does not view reality as "afloat in a sea of Being."[31]

Some might argue that Lew serves as a good paradigm for those who do not mix their Buddhism and their Judaism, keeping the Buddhist meditation separate from Jewish theology. Lew was able to make those Jews who had found spirituality in the Zen and Vipassana Buddhist worlds feel comfortable in an authentically Jewish context. The foundation of his meditation practice was to find and inhabit the silence, and then to develop a practical meditation practice that proceeded from that point. The virtue of silence serves as a bridge to say that sitting in impermanence compares to the silence in Jewish texts. It is just taking the best practices that they see reflected elsewhere.

Unfortunately, this taking of the wisdom of the best practices has Jews conflating kabbalistic and Hasidic texts with Buddhism with an implicit implication that if a Kabbalist practiced silence for a few minutes and Buddhism practices meditation for days and weeks of silence then the two faiths have the same practice. One religion's essence of meditation is equated with a mere preparation for prayer in another faith. In addition, this apologetic approach does not have a problem of ignoring the differences between the Heart Sutra and Kabbalah, or with saying that the two faiths share the interconnection of being as "there is nothing but him" (*eyn od milvado*) and "afloat in a great sea of being" without accepting all the Buddhist cultural values and emotional connections inherent in the latter.

It might be more fruitful to accept convergence of religions (Pannikar), or how the other faith allows one to gain wisdom to see one's own religion in a new light (Clooney), or even more productively to be able to state clearly that the two religions have different goals, and aspirations (Mark Heim) (see Chapter 1). But when Lew combines the faiths and writes, "Personally, when I prepare for Pesach, it's Passover Mind. Like Sesshin Mind, I am focused and it becomes 'whole body and mind.'" He might be better served to admit that the message of Zen and Passover are different.

Can one write a book on non-dualist Judaism from the sources of Judaism? One definitely could, but this would directly present Jewish thought in conversation with Buddhism in a way that Lew does not. Alon Goshen-Gottstein posed similar questions, discussed in chapter eight, about speculations about God and reality in both Judaism and Hinduism. The Jewish concepts of Nondualism, as "'there is nothing but Him' (*ein ode milvado*), has no need to use Buddhist language and reference the Heart Sutras' 'form is emptiness; emptiness is form,'" unless one were trying to specifically address Jews who were more comfortable with the language of Buddhism. However, I am far from convinced that "ein od milvado" is the same as the Heart Sutra. It would take comparative studies to discuss the similarities and differences. When do the Heart Sutra metaphors and cosmology come into conflict with the Jewish vision? Or, when do we move from "seeing the best in others" into syncreticism? Buddhism does not offer the experience of the revelation at Sinai and much of Buddhism is not theist. There is a huge gulf between the two religions. Professor Nathan Katz of the Florida International University, who was part of the Jewish journey to meet the Dalai Lama, states:

> According to Judaic belief, we entered into a covenant with God at Mt. Sinai. To seek refuge in the Buddha rather than in God is to violate the very principles upon which our relationship with God is based.

Katz practiced Buddhism for fifteen years and thinks there are irreconcilable differences between the two religions. "I would say the fundamental difference between the two traditions is one is theistic and one is not. And even if you take the most esoteric, Judaic concepts of God, they still don't reconcile with the Buddhist criticism of all concepts of God."

On the other hand, the recent work by Christian theologian Paul Knitter, *Without Buddha I Could Not Be A Christian.*, boldly proclaims himself a syncreticist who follows two religions simultaneously. Knitter describes how his seminary students see it as adultery. But Knitter argues that Buddhism allows him give up the traditional categories of God, religious language, and revelation. Alan Lew avoided the Buddha, Buddhist ritual, and Buddhist holidays creating what he called "Buddhist style" practices for import into Judaism. Knitter, however, is not satisfied with Buddhist style and feels that even accepting refuge in the Dharma does not conflict with being a Catholic.[32] However, Norman Fischer, the Senior Teacher at the San Francisco Zen Center, and co-founder with Alan Lew of Makor

Or Jewish Meditation Center in San Francisco, is similar to Knitter, in that, he keeps both religions and practices. Fischer is active in Jewish causes and advocates Jewish prayer and ritual, as well as a Jewish home life.

Jerome (Yehuda) Gellman

Jerome (Yehuda) Gellman is a professor of philosophy, at the Ben-Gurion University, who recently attempted to tackle the question of Buddhism afresh. Gellman found that study of Buddhist classics and the practice of Buddhism has enhanced his Orthodox Jewish piety and practice. Most people are worried about the Buddhist statues as a form of idolatry but Gellman knows Buddhism predominately from the reading of the medieval classics and the modern commentaries. His problem is exactly the opposite of the prior discussion: Is Buddhism atheistic?[33]

Gellman deals with the interpretive schools of Buddhism that argue that in the early Pali canon the Buddha did not teach for or against any metaphysical doctrines, but only gave guidance on how to be free from the anguish of one's life, metaphysical questions were 'questions to be set aside' because they were not relevant for liberation. God is not denied, rather counter-productive or irrelevant.

Gellman's problem is that "as Buddhism developed it became more explicitly atheistic in tone and substance." Nagarjuna (second century), argued extensively against the metaphysical coherence of the concepts of God, and of self. "There is no soul, no heaven, or reward, just liberation from the illusions"[34] The Buddhist goal is "the desire to be released from the egocentric predicament" of birth, sickness, old age, and death." God easily becomes a source of egocentric satisfaction, granting well-being for good deeds and answering prayers for help.

Must Jews reject the atheism of Buddhism? Gellman answers by considering that "Buddhist atheism is thus profoundly different from Western atheism," which is grounded in the belief that "humanity, through human 'reason,' replaces God and takes its destiny into its own hands." In contrast, Buddhist atheism shares much with Hasidism in that in both one seeks to nullify the self, to erase the ego-driven mind, and see the world as an illusion.

> My knowledge of Buddhist literature and my familiarity with Buddhist practices have added greatly to my religious sensibilities and understanding . . . I have learned of ways of holiness that I would not have imagined as a Jew.
> This is a crucial point. That positing the existence of God can, if done wisely, serve the same end of internalizing the vulnerability of life and can further the same desire to find release from egocentrism.

> A traditional Jew could look deeper than the early non-theism that comes from the reticence towards metaphysical ontologizing, and a traditional Jew could look deeper than the metaphysical ontologizing of Buddhist atheism, so as to get to the ground of that ontologizing, to the attitude that drives the ontologizing in the first place. When that is done, a traditional Jew could find, as I have, a kinship with Buddhism, without agreeing with its non-theism.

> A traditional Jew such as myself can discover in Buddhism practices for self-decentring that do not exist in Judaism . . . In the end, Buddhism remains godless

and in contrast Judaism commands me to love God with all my heart, with all my soul, and with all my power.

I recognize that Buddhists, given the holy motivations and purposes of their proclaimed atheism, might be touched by God in a way that traditional Jews might not be. To sincerely seek freedom from egocentrism is, to me as a traditional Jew, to be touched by God, since my God is a warning.

For many, the current state of encounter is based on paperback knowledge of Buddhism as atheism as shown in a recent rabbinical newspaper columnist when asked a question about journeying to the East:

Q: I visited an Asian restaurant . . . There seemed to be active idolatry taking place. There was a statue of Buddha, where they had placed a large bowl of oranges and burning incense right in the entrance to the place. . . . Is this place considered a *"Bais Avodah Zorah"* [an idolatrous Temple]?

A: Buddhism is different. There the reference is to a great religious teacher called "the enlightened one." It is hard to imagine why this might be called *Avodah Zarah*.[35]

The rabbinic author uses his college paperback knowledge of Buddhism in order to answer the question and decide Jewish law (without knowledge of the actual devotional and ritual elements of the Buddhism). However, the theological question of what Buddhism means from a Jewish perspective is separate from how Orthodox Jews deal with the halakhic question of the status of statues of the Buddha in kosher vegetarian restaurants.

Dovid Sears, a widely published Breslov author whose life journeys took him to Eastern meditation before he became a Hasid, remains engaged enough to offer his perspective of the differences between Judaism and Buddhism. His list includes the distinction between theism and non-theism; the contention that Hasidic contemplation leading to the dissolution of the ego leads to the greater goal of spiritual work in the world and is not an end in itself; and the perception of impermanence in Hasidic thought focuses on materialism and the ego, without negating the world or worldly engagement. On the other hand, both Hasidism and Buddhism affirm the need for a rebbe or guru, both teach compassion based on an encompassing sense of unity of all creation, the need to transmute negative energies, the virtue of equanimity, and the acute belief life after life. He also draws a parallel between the Jewish belief in the messiah and the Mahayana belief in Matreiya Buddha.[36]

Confucianism and Acculturation

The Jews in China acculturated into the Chinese lands and way of thinking; they also saw the two approaches of Judaism and Confucianism as similar. For the Jews of Kaifeng, China, that equation came naturally, and they proclaimed it on the walls of their synagogue. Michael Polleck, the author of a book on the Jews of China, writes that "as part of the effort to maintain good relations with their neighbors, the Jews of Kaifeng diligently tried to understand Chinese culture,

Confucianism, and seek a common ground." Following the similarities of the religions:

> In their main focus of ideas and established practices both [Judaism and Confucianism] are exclusively concerned with honoring the Way of Heaven, venerating ancestors, valuing the relations of ruler and subject, obedience to parents, harmony within families, correct ordering of social hierarchies, and good fellowship among friends: nothing more than the 'five cardinal relations" of mankind.[37]

On the wall of the synagogue, the Jews of Kaifeng had a huge stele that proclaimed the following similarities of Hebrew scripture and Confucian sacred writings (one should note that they translated Torah as Tao):

> From the time of Noah, when beauteous creation arose, until now, talented men of the West Region have sought the principle that produced Heaven, Earth, and Man;

> From the time of Abraham, when our religion was established, and subsequently, men of China have diffused instruction, and obtained complete knowledge of Confucianism, of Buddhism, and Taoism.

> Before the Great Void, we burn the fragrant incense, entirely forgetting its name or form;

> Tracing back to the Western World, we resist our evil desires, and solely attend to purity and truth.

> The First Ancestor [Abraham] alone received the religion from Heaven and honored Heaven, therefore we remember the Ancestor;

> When living he was able to prevent and abstain from killing [Isaac], therefore we preserve life.[38]

> The Way [Torah] has its source in Heaven, and the fifty-three sections record the facts concerning the creation of Heaven, Earth, and Man. The Religion is based on holiness, and the Twenty-seven Letters are used to transmit the mysteries of the Mind, Way, and Learning—Ai Fu-sheng[39]

In tracing Abraham as our common ancestor, even Confucianism (and Buddhism and Taoism) can be considered an Abrahamic faith. From a Chinese perspective, ancestors honor heaven and preserve life; so too does the ancestor Abraham. For some scholars, these quotations from the stele are not to be taken as serious beliefs; rather, they were done to find favor in the eyes of Confucian authorities with some loyalty to the throne. For others they are a sincere attempt to understand their own faith and the faith of their surrounding culture. But we cannot know for sure the actual intention of the stele. The ethnographic reports seem to imply great religious acculturation of the Jews in China, and we do know that Confucianism was seen as malleable and able to integrate with other beliefs by both Taoists and Buddhists. This stele points to possible discussions and encounters that did occur, even if they were not recorded.[40]

We can compare this stele to the similar writings of Muslims in China in order to contextualize the translation. The Muslims considered it a cultural imperative for Muslims to express themselves in Chinese categories. The monotheistic unity of being *(tawhid)* is translated as the Chinese "all comes from the One." God is translated as the Chinese concept of real Lord. Religion and submission are translated as virtue, in the Confucian sense. The Muslims emphasized the role of the sage and heaven as equivalent to their terms of scholar, prophet, and patriarch. Islam even took sides in the debates between Chan and Soto Zen on whether there is slow or immediate enlightenment, Muslims saw the former as typical.[41] These medieval Islamic translations may prove useful as Judaism comes to have increasing presence in China.

Conclusions

Peter Phan, a Georgetown professor, tells a story of how his Catholic mother changed her attitude toward the Buddha from false god to holy man:

> In 2000, twenty-five members of my family returned to Vietnam, many for the first time since leaving the country as refugees a quarter of a century earlier.
>
> As we entered the courtyard, dominated by a huge statue of the reclining Buddha, the whole place was suffused with a prayerful silence periodically punctuated by the muffled sounds of a gong.
>
> My mother stood reverently in front of the Buddha, her eyes fixed on him, her palms held together at her chest, her lips murmuring a prayer. When she finished, she rummaged in her handbag, took out a handful of American dollars, and dropped them into the coffer. As we left, she turned to me and said: "The Buddha is a holy man."
>
> Just a couple of decades earlier, my mother's gesture would have been condemned as idolatry. In her youth (she is now eighty-two) she had been taught that only Christianity—more precisely, Roman Catholicism—was the true religion, and all other religions the work of the devil.
>
> How, then, could an old woman like my mother, God-loving and church-fearing, a twice-a-day churchgoer raised to believe that no one except Catholics can be saved, do what she did that day in that pagoda?
>
> And what, exactly, happened between the 1960s and 2000 that enabled her to honor the Buddhist nun, pray to the Buddha, and contribute money to the maintenance of the pagoda? The answer lies in the dramatic expansion during our era of interreligious dialogue, particularly as it has been espoused by the church since Vatican II.

What can we learn from the story? What do we see when we witness the other? Do we now see the piety and wisdom in the practice of eastern religions? How do we explain the sea change in Jewish perceptions?

The last two chapters are the start of a bigger process of a renewed Jewish encounter with Eastern religions. A relation of Judaism to the many religions of the world, such as Buddhism, Hinduism, Taoism, Sikhs, Jains, and others, the encounters and the mutual hospitality has barely even started. The question is: how do we relate to these faiths when we gain actual knowledge of the other faith? What would R. Menachem Meiri, R. Eliezer Ashkenazi, or R. Yaakov Emden have written if they had congregations in China, Japan, or Thailand? Does our ability for airline travel and firsthand knowledge of these religions change our self-understanding of Judaism? This chapter is likely to change the most in the upcoming decades.

Notes

Chapter 1

1. Wilfred Cantwell Smith, *The Faith of Other Men* (New York: Harper, 1972), 133, reprinted as *Patterns of Faith Around the World* (Oxford: Oneworld), 138.
2. Max Müller, *Introduction to the Science of Religion* (London: Longmans, Green, 1873).
3. John Hick and Brian Hebblethwaite, *Christianity and Other Religions: Selected Readings* (Philadelphia: Fortress Press, 1980).
4. Tzvetan Todorov, *Morals of History* (Minneapolis: University of Minnesota Press, 1995); Gerardus Van DerLeeuw, *Religion in Essence and Manifestation* (New York: Harper & Row, 1963); Eric Sharpe, *Comparative Religion: A History* (New York: Scribner's, 1975).
5. Eric Sharpe, *Comparative Religion: A History* (New York: Scribner's, 1975).
6. Mircea Eliade, *Mystic Stories: The Sacred and the Profane* (New York: Columbia University Press, 1992).
7. Joseph Campbell with Bill Moyers, *The Power of Myth* (New York: Doubleday, 1988).
8. Paul Tillich, *Christianity and the Encounter of the World Religions* (New York: Columbia University Press, 1963); Wilfred Cantwell Smith, *Towards a World Theology* (London: Macmillan, 1980).
9. John Hick and Brian Hebblethwaite, *Christianity and Other Religions: Selected Readings* (Philadelphia: Fortress Press, 1980); J. B. Webster, *The Cambridge Companion to Karl Barth* (Cambridge: Cambridge University Press, 2000); J. A. DiNoia, "Religion and the Religions," in *The Diversity of Religions: A Christian Perspective* (Washington: Catholic University of America Press, 1992).
10. Eric Sharpe, *The Theology of A. G. Hogg* (Madras: Published for the Christian Institute for the Study of Religion and Society, Bangalore, by the Christian Literature Society, 1971).
11. Ibid, 67, 75, 80.
12. Ibid, 101, 212.
13. Hendrik Kraemer, *Religion and the Christian Faith* (Philadelphia: Westminster Press, 1957); Tom Perry, *Radical Difference: A Defence of Hendrik Kraemer's Theology of Religions* (Waterloo: Published for the Canadian Corp. for Studies in Religion = *Corp. Canadienne des Sciences Religeuses* by Wilfrid Laurier University Press, 2001).
14. Alan Race, *Christians and Religious Pluralism: Patterns in the Christian Theology of Religions* (Maryknoll, NY: Orbis Books, 1983); John Hick, *God Has Many Names* (London: Macmillan, 1980). Current readable summaries are provided by Paul F. Knitter, *Introducing Theologies of Religions* (Maryknoll, NY: Orbis Books, 2002); Veli-Matti Kärkkäinen, *An Introduction to the Theology of Religion: Biblical, Historical, and Contemporary Perspectives* (Downers Grove, IL: InterVarity Press, 2004).

15. Alan Brill, *Judaism and Other Religions: Models of Understanding* (New York: Palgrave Macmillan, 2010), Chapter 7.

16. Francis X. Clooney, *The New Comparative Theology: Interreligious Insights from the Next Generation* (New York: T&T Clark, 2010).

17. S. Mark Heim, *Salvations: Truth and Difference in Religion* (Maryknoll, NY: Orbis, 1995); Idem., "The Depth of the Riches: Trinity and Religious Ends," in *Christianity and the Religions: A Dialogue*, ed. Viggo Mortensen (Grand Rapids: Eerdmans, 2003).

18. Stephen Prothero, *God Is Not One: The Eight Rival Religions That Run the World—and Why Their Differences Matter* (New York: HarperOne, 2010).

19. Paul Ricoeur, "From the Hermeneutics of Texts to the Hermeneutics of Action," in *From Text to Action* (Evanston: Northeastern University Press, 1991), 105–222.

20. Paul Ricoeur, *The Course of Recognition* (Cambridge: Harvard University Press, 2005).

21. Raimundo Panikkar, *The Unknown Christ of Hinduism: Towards an Ecumenical Christophany* (Maryknoll: Orbis Books, 1981).

22. Ewert Cousins, "Judaism-Christianity-Islam: Facing Modernity Together," *Journal of Ecumenical Studies* 30:3–4 (Summer-Fall, 1993): 417–425.

23. Jacques Dupuis, *Toward a Christian Theology of Religious Pluralism* (Maryknoll: Orbis Books, 2001), 260–262.

24. Joseph Ratzinger, "Dominus Iesus," *Congregation for the Doctrine of the Faith*, The Vatican, 06 Aug 2000, http://www.vatican.va/roman_curia/congregations/cfaith/documents/rc_con_cfaith_doc_20000806_dominus-iesus_en.html; Pope Benedict XVI, *Verbum Domini*, The Vatican 10, 10, 2010; http://www.catholicculture.org/culture/library/view.cfm?recnum=9460.

25. http://www.bc.edu/research/cjl/meta-elements/texts/documents/interreligious/alexandria2002.htm.

26. For examples of conflict of religions and tribal views of the gods, see George Weigel, *Faith, Reason, and the War against Jihadism: A Call to Action* (New York: Doubleday, 2007), Chapter 1; Alain Besancon, "What Kind of Religion is Islam?" *Commentary* (May 2004). According to Besancon, Abraham of Genesis is not Ibrahim of the Quran, Moses is not Moussa.

27. Diana L. Eck, *Encountering God: A Spiritual Journey from Bozeman to Banaras* (Boston: Beacon Press, 1993), 50.

28. Miroslav Volf, *Allah: A Christian Response* (New York, HarperOne, 2011), 190.

29. Pontifical Council for Interreligious Dialogue, *Dialogue and Proclamation*, Rome (May 19, 1991), 42, http://www.vatican.va/roman_curia/pontifical_councils/interelg/documents/rc_pc_interelg_doc_19051991_dialogue-and-proclamatio_en.html.

30. Second Vatican Council, *Nostra Aetate* (1965), 1.

31. David Smock, *Interfaith Dialogue and Peacebuilding* (Washington: United States Institute of Peace Press, 2002); Mohammed Abu-Nimer, *Dialogue, Conflict Resolution, and Change: Arab-Jewish Encounters in Israel* (Albany: Albany State University of New York Press, 1999); Idem., *Reconciliation, Coexistence, and Justice: Theory and Practice* (New York: Rowman & Littlefield, 2001); Mohammed Abu-Nimer and Muhammad Shafiq, *Interfaith Dialogue: A Guide for Muslims* (Herendon: International Institute for Islamic Thought, 2007).

32. Shaar Yashuv Cohen, "Israel and the nations: Past, Present, and Future," lecture delivered at Mekhon Meir, *Zahut* (Tevet 18, 2006); Rabbi Shaar Yashuv Cohen has unpublished guidelines to dialogue that should be published and translated. In sum, he only restricts interfaith dialogue to the shortlist of topics in the letter of Rabbi Joseph Soloveitchik in Joseph Dov Soloveitchik and Nathaniel Helfgot, *Community, Covenant, And Commitment: Selected Letters And Communications Of Rabbi Joseph B. Soloveitchik* (Jersey City: KTAV Pub. House, 2005).

33. "Rabbis and MKs Upgrade Israeli-Christian Relations," *Arutz Sheva* (January 2005), http://www.israelnationalnews.com/News/News.aspx/75808.

Chapter 2

1. Yerushalmi Abodah Zarah 1:2, 20–23; Catherine Hezser, "Jews and Gentiles in Yerushalmi Avodah Zarah," in *The Talmud Yerushalmi and Greco-Roman Culture Volume 3* (CITY: J.C.B. Mohr, 2002), 335–354; Friz Graf, "Roman Festivals in Syria Palestina," ibid., 435–452.
2. Yerushalmi Abodah Zarah 1:4, 29.
3. Paul Veyne, *Did the Greeks Believe in Their Myths? An Essay on the Constitutive Imagination* (Chicago: University of Chicago Press.1988); Dan Sperber, *On Anthropological Knowledge: Three Essays* (Cambridge: Cambridge University Press & Editions de la Maison des Sciences de 'Homme, 1985).
4. Acts 13:6–11; 19:13–16; Josephus, *Jewish Antiquities* (Cambridge: Harvard University Press, 1998), 8.44–46; "Lucian, The Lover of Lies," 31.
5. *Pesikta de-Rav Kehana Mandelbaum* edition piska 4; cf Tanhuma B, Hakkut 26; PR 14:14; *Numbers Rabbah* 19:8.
6. Emmanuel Friedheim, "Sol Invictus In The Severus Synagogue At Hammath Tiberias, The Rabbis, And Jewish Society: A Different Approach," *Review of Rabbinic Judaism* 12, 1 (2009): 89–121.
7. *Sifrei* Deuteronomy *shoftim,* para 146, 160.
8. S. R. Hirsch, *Commentary on the Pentauech,* trans Levy Genesis 28: 18; A. Y. Kook Iggerot volume 3: 10, #746 Abraham Isaac Kook, *Igrot ha-Re'iyah* (Yerushalayim, Mosad ha-RavKuk, 722).
9. Rivka Ulmer, *Egyptian Cultural Icons in Midrash* (Berlin: Walter de Gruyter, 2009).
10. Carlos Eire, *War against the Idols: The Reformation of Worship from Erasmus to Calvin* (Cambridge: Cambridge University Press, 1986*).*
11. Guy Stroumsa, "John Spencer and the Roots of Idolatry," *History of Religions* 40 (2001): 1–23; Mark Silk, "Numa Pompilius and the Idea of Civil Religion in the West," *Journal of the American Academy of Religion* 72: 4 (2004): 86–96.
12. Richard Hardin, *Civil Idolatry: Desacralizing and Monarchy in Spenser, Shakespeare, and Milton* (Newark: University of Delaware Press, 1992).
13. Jan Assmann, *The Price of Monotheism* (Stanford: Stanford University Press, 2010).
14. David Pailin, *Attitudes to Other Religions: Comparative Religion in the 17th and 18th Century Britain* (Manchester: Manchester University Press, 1984).
15. Joan Pau Rubiés, "Theology, Ethnography, and the Historicization of Idolatry," *Journal of the History of Ideas* 67:4 (2006): 571–596.
16. On Castro, see Yosef Kaplan, *From Christianity to Judaism: The Story of Isaac Orobio de Castro* (Oxford: Littman, 1989). The book is called *Divine Forewarnings Against the Vain Idolatry of the Gentiles* [latin] 1679. The translation here was done by Adam Sutcliffe at King's College London, http://www.earlymodern.org/workshops/2009/sutcliffe/text01/english.php?tid=141.
17. See Chapter 1.
18. These passages are from Benedictus de Spinoza, *Theological-Political Treatise* (Cambridge: Cambridge University Press, 2007), preface, 13, 14, and 15.
19. http://www.guardian.co.uk/science/2008/may/13/peopleinscience.religion (accessed July 7, 2011).
20. Moses Mendelssohn, *Jerusalem and Other Writings,* 68–9.
21. Samson Raphael Hirsch, Horeb, Section 1 toroth, 10.

22. Ibid., 6.
23. Ibid., 7.
24. For others influenced by Schelling, see Werner Jacob Cahnman, "Schelling and the New Thinking of Judaism," *German Jewry: Its History and Sociology; Selected Essays* (Brunswick: Transaction, 1989).
25. A. I. Kook, *Kevatzim Mi-Ketav YadKodsho* 2, *pinkas ha-dapim* 1, 59: 20.
26. A. I. Kook, *Li-Nevokhei ha-Dor*, 29–30.
27. Ibid., 29.
28. A. I. Kook, *The Lights of Penitence* (New York: Paulist Press, 1978), 295–296.
29. Louis Grossman, *Some Chapters on Judaism and the Science of Religion* (New York: Putnam, 1888).
30. Michael Friedlander, *The Jewish Religion* (New York: Pardes, 1946), 22, 25–29.
31. Bernard Martin, "Scriptural Authority, Scriptural Interpretation & Jewish-Christian Relations," in *Evangelicals and Jews in Conversation On Scripture, Theology and History,* trans., Marc H. Tanenbaum, Marvin R. Wilson, and A. James Rudin (Grand Rapids: Baker Book House, 1978).
32. Gershom Scholem, *Major Trends in Jewish Mysticism* (New York: Schoken Book, 1954), 7–8.
33. Ibid., 35.
34. Gershom Scholem, *On the Mystical Shape of the Godhead: Basic Concepts in the Kabbalah* (New York: Schoken Books, 1991), 15–16.
35. Nathan Söderblom, *The Living God: Basal Forms of Personal Religions* (Gifford lectures, 1933); Eric Sharpe, *Comparative Religion: A History* (New York: Scribner's, 1975); Idem., *Nathan Soderblom and the Study of Religion* (Chapel Hill: University of North Carolina Press, 1990).
36. Abraham Joshua Heschel, interviewed by Harold Fletcher, *Two Conversations with Abraham Joshua Heschel*, The National Broadcasting Company, May 9, 1971, available from "The Eternal Light," program, 3.
37. Abraham Heschel, *The Prophets* (New York: Harper & Row, 1962), 472–3.
38. Fritz A. Rothschild, *Jewish perspectives on Christianity: Leo Baeck, Martin Buber, Franz Rosenzweig, Will Herberg, and Abraham J. Heschel* (New York: Crossroad, 1990), 308.
39. Joseph Dov Soloveitchik, *Halakhic Man* (Philadelphia: J. P. S., 1983), 220.
40. *And From There You Shall Seek*, by Joseph B. *Soloveitchik*, translated by Naomi Goldblum (Jersey City: Ktav, 2008).
41. "Sacred and Profane, Kodesh and Chol in World Perspective," reprinted in Epstein, *Shiurei HaRav: A Conspectus Of The Public Lectures Of Rabbi Joseph B. Soloveitchik* (Hoboken, NJ: Ktav, 1994), 6.
42. Joseph B. Soloveitchik, *And From There You Shall Seek* (Jersey City: Ktav, 2008), 41, 7, 19.
43. Ibid., 10, 40.
44. Ibid., 43.
45. C. S. Lewis, "Christianity and Culture," in C. S. Lewis and Walter Hooper, *Christian Reflections* (Grand Rapids: W. B. Eerdmans, 1967), 33, 24.

Chapter 3

1. James Parkes, *The Conflict of the Church and the Synagogue: A Study in the Origins of Antisemitism* (Cleveland: World, 1961); *Essential Papers on Judaism and Christianity in Conflict: From Late Antiquity to the Reformation,* ed. Jeremy Cohen,

NOTES **259**

(New York: New York University Press, 1991); Edward Flannery, *The Anguish of the Jews* (New York: Paulist Press, 1985).

2. Jules Issac, *Jésus et Israël* (Paris: Michel, 1948); ibid., *The Teaching of Contempt; Christian Roots of Anti-Semitism* (New York: Holt, Rinehart and Winston, 1964).

3. Robert Chazen, *Reassessing Jewish Life in Medieval Europe* (New York: Cambridge University Press, 2010), 191, also see ibid., *Fashioning Jewish Identity in the Medieval Western Christendom* (Cambridge: Cambridge University Press, 2003); David Nierenberg, *Communities of Violence: Persecution of Minorities in the Middle Ages* (Princeton University Press,1996); ibid., "What Can Medieval Spain Teach Us About Muslim-Jewish Relations?" *CCAR Journal* (Summer, 2002): 17–36; ibid, "The Birth of the Pariah: Jews, Christian Dualism, and Social Science," *Social Research* 70.1 (Spring, 2003), 201–236; ibid., "Enmity and Assimilation: Jews, Christians, and Converts in Medieval Spain," *Common Knowledge* 9 (2003): 137–155. Joseph *Shatzmiller, Jews, Medicine, and Medieval Society* (Berkeley: University of California Press, 1994); ibid., *Shylock Reconsidered* (University of California Press, 1990).

4. Wout van Bekkum, "'The Rock on which the Church is Founded': Simon Peter in Jewish Folktale," in *Saints and Role Models in Judaism and Christianity* (Leiden: Brill, 2004), 289–310.

5. Morris Goldstein, *Jesus in the Jewish Tradition* (New York: Macmillan, 1950); J. H. Greenstone, "Jewish Legends about Simon-Peter," *Historia Judaica* 12 (1950): 89–104; Sid Leiman, "The Scroll of Fasts: The Ninth of Tebeth," *Jewish Quarterly Review* 74 (1983), 174–195; http://web.archive.org/web/20040202141247/ccat.sas. upenn.edu/~humm/Topics/JewishJesus/toledoth.html.

6. Daniel J. Lasker, *Jewish Philosophical Polemics Against Christianity in the Middle Ages* (New York: Ktav, 1977); 109.

7. Ibid., 74.

8. Ibid., 133.

9. Daniel J. Lasker, *The Refutation of The Christian Principles by Hasdai Crescas* (SUNY, 1992): text itself: 23–84.

10. Moses Mendelsohn letter to Karl Wilheim Ferdinand, prince of Bunswick, trans. Alfred Jospe, *Jerusalem and Other Jewish Writings* (New York: Bnai Brith, 1969), l23–24.

11. Hirsch, "Die Religions Philosophie der Juden," 728, quoted in Dan-Sherbok Cohen, *Judaism and Other Faiths* (London, Palgrave Macmillan, 1994), 22–23.

12. Judishe Schriften Cohen, vol. 2, 208 quoted in Dan-Sherbok Cohen, *Judaism and Other Faiths,* 25.

13. Leo Baeck, *Judaism and Christianity* (Philadelphia: Jewish Publication Society of America, 1948), 39.

14. Ibid., 35.

15. Leo Baeck, *Essence of Judaism* (New York: Schocken Books, 1961), 182–3, 252, 276.

16. Ibid., 62, 70.

17. Martin Buber, *Two Types of Faith* (New York: Harper, 1961), 26, 35.

18. Martin Buber, "The Question to the Single One," in *Between Man and Man* (Boston: Beacon Press: 1955), 193.

19. Ibid., *Two Types of Faith* (New York: Harper, 1961), 12, 91.

20. Preface by Balthasar in Martin Buber, *Two Types of Faith* (New York: Harper, 1961), 8, 114, 117.

21. Franz Rosenzweig, *The Star of Redemption* (New York: Holt, Rinehart, and Winston, 1971), 193, 200, 232; Leora Batnitzky, "Dialogue as Judgment, Not Mutual Affirmation: A New Look at Franz Rosenzweig's Dialogical Philosophy," *The Journal of Religion* 79, 4 (1999): 523–544. Passage specifically from 524.

22. Fritz Rothschild, *Jewish Perspectives on Christianity: Leo Baeck, Martin Buber, Franz Rosenzweig, Will Herberg, and Abraham J. Heschel* (New York: Crossroad, 1990), 170–177.

23. Franz Rosenzweig, *The Star of Redemption* (New York: Holt, Rinehart, and Winston, 1971), 193, 200, 232; Leora Batnitzky, "Dialogue as Judgment, Not Mutual Affirmation: A New Look at Franz Rosenzweig's Dialogical Philosophy," *The Journal of Religion* 79, 4 (1999): 5.

24. Eugen Rosenstock-Huessy and Franz Rosenzweig, *Judaism Despite Christianity; The Letters on Christianity and Judaism Between Eugen Rosenstock-Huessy and Franz Rosenzweig* (University of Alabama: University of Alabama Press, 1969), Letter 15.

25. Fritz Rothschild, *Jewish perspectives on Christianity: Leo Baeck, Martin Buber, Franz Rosenzweig, Will Herberg, and Abraham J. Heschel* (New York: Crossroad, 1990).

26. Franz Rosenzweig, *The Star of Redemption* (New York: Holt, Rinehart, and Winston, 1971).

27. Hans Joachim Schoeps, *The Jewish-Christian Argument: A History of Theologies in Conflict* (New York: Holt, Rinehart and Winston, 1963), 127, 140.

28. Hans Joachim Schoeps, *The Jewish-Christian Argument*, 164–6.

29. Ibid., 162, 166, 167.

30. Ibid, *Jewish Christianity; Factional Disputes in the Early Church* (Philadelphia: Fortress Press, 1969), 67.

31. Hans Joachim Schoeps, *The Jewish-Christian Argument*: XIV.

32. http://www.jcrelations.net/en/?item=983 (accessed July 2010).

33. Walter Wurzburger, "Justification and Limitations of Interfaith Dialogue," *The Commentator*, 8 Mar, 2005, http://www.yucommentator.com/2.2828/justification-and-limitations-of-interfaith-dialogue-1.299135. Originally in Walter Wurzburger and Eugene Borowitz, *Judaism and the Interfaith Movement* (New York: Synagogue Council of America, 1967).

34. Ibid.

35. Trude Weiss-Rosmarin, *Judaism and Christianity: The Differences* (New York: The Jewish Book Club, 1943), 15, 24, 76, 81.

36. Ibid., 83, 86, 91, 103, 151.

37. Joseph H Hertz, *The Pentateuch And Haftorahs* (London: Soncino Press, 1963), 759.

38. J. H. Hertz, *Affirmations of Judaism* (London, 1927), 307.

39. George L. Berlin, *Defending the Faith: Nineteenth-Century American Jewish Writings on Jesus and Christianity* (New York: SUNY Press, 1989).

40. Abba Hillel Silver, *Where Judaism Differs* (New York: Macmillan, 1956).

41. Frank Talmage, *Disputation and Dialogue: Readings in the Jewish-Christian Encounter* (New York: Ktav, 1975), 291.

42. Eliezer Berkovits, *Faith After the Holocaust* (New York: KTAV, 1973), 49.

43. Ibid., 41, 46–47.

44. Eliezer Berkovits, *Faith After the Holocaust*, 49, 64.

45. Eliezer Berkovits, *Faith After the Holocaust*, 49, 64.

46. Yossef Charvit, "From Monologues to Possible Dialogue: Judaism's Attitude towards Christianity According to the Philosophy of R. Yéhouda Léon Askénazi (Manitou)," in *Interaction Between Judaism and Christianity in History, Religion, Art, and Literature*, eds. Marcel Poorthuis, J. Schwartz, and J. Turner (Leiden: Brill, 2009), 319–336, quotes 325, 332.

47. Yossef Charvit, "From Monologues to Possible Dialogue," 328.

48. Emmanuel Lévinas, *Totality and Infinity: An Essay on Exteriority* (Pittsburgh: Duquesne University Press, 1969), 38.

49. Denis Donoghue and Emmanuel Lévinas, "In the Time of Nations," *The New York Review of Books*. 43, no. 5:37 (1996): 164.

50. Emmanuel Lévinas, "Simone Weil Against the Bible," in Emmanuel Lévinas, *Difficult Freedom: Essays On Judaism* (Baltimore: Johns Hopkins University Press, 1990), 176–177.

51. Emmanuel Lévinas, "Judaism and Kenosis," in *In The Time of the Nations*, ed Michael B. Smith (Bloomington: Indiana University Press, 1994).

52. R. T. Kendall and David Rosen, *The Christian and the Pharisee: Two Outspoken Religious Leaders Debate the Road to Heaven* (New York: Faith Words, 2007), XV.

53. Elie Wiesel, *All Rivers Run to the Sea: Memoirs* (New York: Knopf, 1995), 354–55.

Chapter 4

1. Moshe Weinfled, "Theological Lexicon of the Old Testament," in *Encyclopedia Judaica*, vol. 1, ed. Cecil Roth (New York, Macmillan, 1994), 256–56.

2. Solomon Schechter, *Aspects of Rabbinic Theology* (New York: Schocken Books, 1961).

3. "Westminster Confession of Faith (1647): Chapter 7:3," Center for Reformed Theology and Apologetics, November 2, 2008,_http://www.reformed.org/documents/index. html?mainframe=http://www.reformed.org/documents/westminster_conf_of_faith. html.

4. Reinhold Niebuhr, *The Nature and Destiny of Man: A Christian Interpretation* (New York: C. Scribner's Sons, 1941); Reinhold Niebuhr, *The Self and the Dramas of History* (New York: Scribner, 1955); Mark Silk, *Notes On The Judeo-Christian Tradition In America* (Philadelphia: American Studies Association, 1984), 65–85.

5. See the section on Scripture, *Catechism of the Catholic Church*; "Catechism of the Catholic Church," Part I: "The Profession of Faith," Article 3, nos. 101–141, The Vatican, November 3, 2008, http://www.vatican.va/archive/ENG0015/_INDEX.HTM.

6. "Catechism of the Catholic Church," no. 781, The Vatican, November 3, 2008, http:// www.vatican.va/archive/ENG0015/__P28.HTM#-10O. This section of the Catechism draws on Pope Paul VI, "Lumen Gentium," Chapter II, No. 9, Eternal World Television Network, November 3, 2008, http://www.ewtn.com/library/councils/v2church.htm.

7. Franz Mussner, Tractate On The Jews: The Significance Of Judaism For Christian Faith (London: SPCK, 1984), 164–76; Jakób Jocz, *The Jewish People and Jesus Christ: A Study In The Relationship Between The Jewish People and Jesus Christ* (London: SPCK, 1954); Augustin Bea, *The Church and The Jewish People: A Commentary On The Second Vatican Council's Declaration On The Relation Of The Church To Non-Christian Religions* (New York: Harper & Row, 1966); Jacques Maritain, *The Mystery of Israel and Other Essays* (Paris: Desclée, De Brouwer, 1965).

8. John M. Oesterreicher, *Why Judeo-Christian Studies* (Newark: Institute of Judeo-Christian Studies, 1954).

9. Mary C. Boys, *Has God Only One Blessing? Judaism As A Source Of Christian Self-Understanding* (New York: Paulist Press, 2000); James Parkes, *Prelude To Dialogue: Jewish-Christian Relationships* (New York: Schocken Books, 1969); John Pawlikowski, *Jesus And The Theology Of Israel* (Wilmington: Michael Glazier, 1989).

10. Lily Edelman, *Face To Face: A Primer in Dialogue* (Washington, D.C.: B'nai B'rith, Adult Jewish Education, 1967), 23.

11. Jacob Agus, *Modern Philosophies of Judaism, A Study of Recent Jewish Philosophies of Religion* (New York: Behrman's Jewish Book House, 1941), 153.

12. Ibid., forward.

13. Ibid., 208.

14. Ibid., 191.

15. Jacob Agus, *Dialogue and Tradition; The Challenges of Contemporary Judeo-Christian Thought* (London: Abelard-Schuman, 1971), 67.
16. Ibid., 492–3.
17. Agus, *Modern Philosophies of Judaism*, 193.
18. Agus, *Dialogue and Tradition,* 66.
19. Edelman, *Face To Face: A Primer in Dialogue,* 21.
20. Agus, *Dialogue and Tradition,* 183.
21. Fritz A. Rothschild, *Jewish Perspectives on Christianity* (New York: Continuum, 1996), 251, 253, 255.
22. Robert Gordis, "The Judeo-Christian Tradition-Illusion or Reality," in *Judaism in a Christian World* (New York: McGraw-Hill, 1966), 154–55.
23. Arthur A. Cohen, *The Myth of the Judeo-Christian Tradition* (New York: Harper & Row, 1969).
24. Robert N. Bellah, *The Broken Covenant: American Civil Religion in a Time of Trial* (New York: Seabury Press, 1975).
25. Paul Ramsey, *Basic Christian Ethics* (New York: Scribner, 1950); James M Gustafson, *Can Ethics Be Christian?* (Chicago: University of Chicago Press, 1975).
26. Paul M. Van Buren, *A Theology Of The Jewish Christian Reality* (New York: Seabury Press, 1980). At the end of his life, Van Buren commented on a book by Jon Levenson called *The Death and Resurrection of the Beloved Son* (New Haven: Yale University Press, 1993) where Van Buren came to accept more rivalry between the faiths than dual covenant; Paul M. Van Buren, "Can Jews and Christians share the same Bible stories without abandoning the core truth claims of their respective religions?" http://www.icjs.org/info/vanburenessay.html (December 4, 2008) [No longer accessible.]
27. Martin Marty, *Modern American Religion: Under God, Indivisible, 1941–1960* (Chicago: University of Chicago Press, 1986).
28. Joseph B. Soloveitchik, "Confrontation" & "On Interfaith Relationships," in *A Treasury of Tradition,* ed. Norman Lamm and Walter S. Wurzburger (New York: Hebrew, 1967), 79–80; Lawrence Kaplan, "Revisionism and the Rav; the Struggle for the Soul of Modern Orthodoxy," *Judaism* 48:3 (1999).
29. Judith H. Banki and Eugene J. Fisher, eds., *A Prophet for Our Time* (New York: Fordham University Press, 2002).
30. Harold Kasimow, *No Religion Is an Island: Abraham Joshua Heschel and Interreligious Dialogue* (Maryknoll, NY: Orbis Books, 1991), 5.
31. Heschel cited in ibid., 6, 7, 13,
32. Heschel cited in ibid., 14, 18–19, 21.
33. Samuel H. Dresner, *The Jew in American life* (New York: Crown Publishers, 1963), 243.
34. Fritz A. Rothschild, *Jewish Perspectives on Christianity* (New York: Crossroad, 1990), 331.
35. Abraham Joshua Heschel and Susannah Heschel, *Moral Grandeur and Spiritual Audacity: Essays* (New York: Farrar, Straus & Giroux, 1996), 242 (n114).
36. Heschel cited in Kasimow, *No Religion is an Island,* 22.
37. James A. Sanders, "An Apostle to the Gentiles," *Conservative Judaism,* 28:1 (Fall, 1973): 61–63, quoted in Kasimow, *No Religion Is an Island,* 80.
38. Abraham Joshua Heschel and Susannah Heshel, *Moral Grandeur and Spiritual Audacity: Essays* (New York: Farrar, Straus & Giroux, 1996), 408.
39. Television Interview with Carl Stern 1972—"The Eternal Light" available on http://www.youtube.com/watch?v=2bdFFEiDnmU (accessed June 3, 2011).
40. David Ellenson, "Two Responsa of Rabbi Moshe *Feinstein,*" *Chronicle of Hebrew Union College,* LII: 1 and 2 (Fall, 2000–2001).

41. William Hutchison, *Religious Pluralism in America* (New Haven: Yale University Press, 2003).
42. Alan Brill, "Triumph Without Battle: The Role of Dialectic Theology in Rabbi J. B. Soloveitchik's Theology of Culture," [Hebrew] in *Rabbi in the New World: The Influence of Rabbi J. B. Soloveitchik on Culture, Education and Jewish Thought*, ed. Avinoam Rosenak and Naftali Rothenberg (2011).
43. Joseph B. Soloveitchik, "Confrontation" in *A Treasury of Tradition*, ed. N. Lamm and Walter S. Wurzburger (New York: Hebrew Publishing Company, 1967), 17.
44. Soloveitchik, "Confrontation," 18–20.
45. Ibid.
46. Soloveitchik, "On Interfaith Relationships," 79.
47. Soloveitchik, "Confrontation," 21.
48. Ibid., 24.
49. Ibid., 21–24.
50. Ibid., 28.
51. Among the criticisms of the approach of Soloveitchik, we find several major essays. (1) Israel Moskovitz thinks Soloveitchik is wrong because one can grasp concept of other faiths; no major or special training needed to understand another religion; religion is taught in books and is portrayed on the popular level; and converts know about other faiths without being a member yet. "From Auschwitz to Acceptance" in Lily Edelman, *Face to Face: A Primer in Dialogue* (Washington, D.C.: B'nai B'rith, Adult Jewish Education, 1967); (2) David Novak is troubled by the Barthian premise that of the non-communicatable "metaphysical community" that ignores that our secular work in ethics, public morality, dogma doctrine, values are all metaphysical. David Novak, *Jewish-Christian Dialogue: A Jewish Justification* (New York: Oxford University Press, 1989); (3) David Rosen is bothered by the sense of alienation from the world coupled with the lack of mission for Judaism in the modern world, he is also bothered by the lack of an acknowledgement of the state of Israel, the lack of a future vision, and the viewing of religion as a minority within a sea of secularism. Rosen also assumes that religion is situated in culture. David Rosen, "Christians and Jews in a Radically New Relationship." Human Rights Oration given in Sydney, Australia, May 13, 2001, http://www.jcrelations.net/en/displayItem.php?id=956 (November 11, 2008); David Rosen, "'Dabru Emet': Its Significance for the Jewish-Christian Dialogue," An address given at the twentieth anniversary celebration of the Dutch Council of Christians and Jews (OJEC) at Tilburg, The Netherlands, November 6, 2001, November 11, 2008. http://www.jcrelations.net/en/displayItem.php?id=1477.
    Rosen's position has several arguments against Soloveitchik's position. Rosen accepts natural theology thereby creating commonalities, he works with a Rav Kook framework of no division of sacred and profane, he has a Zionist vision of needing to directly confront the challenges of a modern state, and he tries to integrate R. Yaakov Emden considering Jesus as a moral teacher into a broader perspective on Christianity as a whole. (4) Marc Tannenbaum thinks that one cannot work together as long as the people that one is working with think that you need to be redeemed. See above in this chapter. (5) Eugene Korn, "The Man of Faith and Religious Dialogue: Revisiting 'Confrontation,'" *Modern Judaism* 25, no. 3 (October 2005): 290–315, argues that the historic changes of the last half century require a change in position. (6) Marshall Breger Rabbi Joseph Soloveitchik's "Confrontation: A Reassessment," *CCJR Journal* 1 (2005–6): 151–169, thinks that one can indeed communicate religious ideas both in theory and practice. More importantly, Breger finds difficulty in that Soloveitchik thinks that the status of the Catholic-Jewish relationship is essential and determinist.

Breger finds the Soloveitchik approach to create a "surreal approach to the place of the Jews in the modern world. It is as if we are the center of the universe and make judgments of independent actors without reference to the view of others," (168). And as he concludes, if Christians are adjusting their historically pejorative understanding of Judaism—why should we not assist them with proper accurate understanding of Jewish doctrines? Breger's article gives a full bibliography to the topic.

52. Walter Wurzburger, *Judaism and the Interfaith Movement*, ed. Walter Wurzburger and Eugene Borowitz (New York: Synagogue Council of America, 1967), 7–16.
53. David Holwerda, *Jesus & Israel: One Covenant or Two?* (Grand Rapids: Eerdmans, 1995), 11; Karl Barth, *Church Dogmatics, Vol. 2, The Doctrine of God* Part 2. (Edinburgh: Clark, 1957), 195, 199; John J. Johnson, "A New Testament Understanding of the Jewish Rejection of Jesus: Four Theologians on the Salvation of Israel," *Journal of the Evangelical Theological Society* 43 (June 2000): 237. Johnson writes: "Barth seems far more optimistic than Augustine about the ultimate salvation of the Jews."
54. Michael Wyschogrod, *Abraham's Promise: Judaism and Jewish-Christian Relations* (Grand Rapids: William B. Eerdmans, 2004), 16, 109, 110, 175, 178, 184, 212.
55. Joseph Dov Soloveitchik, *The Lonely Man of Faith* (New York: Doubleday, 1992), 29–30.
56. Greenberg, *For The Sake of Heaven and Earth*, 185.
57. Ibid., 204.
58. Eugene J Fisher, *Twenty Years of Jewish-Catholic Relations* (New York: Paulist Press, 1986); Eugene J Fisher, *Visions of the Other: Jewish and Christian Theologians Assess the Dialogue, Studies in Judaism and Christianity* (New York: Paulist Press, 1994); John T. Pawlikowski, *Christ in the Light of the Christian Jewish Dialogue* (New York: Paulist Press, 1982); John T. Pawlikowski with Judith Banki of *Ethics in the Shadow of the Holocaust. Christian and Jewish Perspectives* (Franklin, WI: Sheed & Ward, 2001).
59. Victoria Clark, *Allies for Armageddon: The Rise of Christian Zionism* (New Haven, Connecticut: Yale University Press, 2007); Stephen Sizer, *Christian Zionism: Road Map to Armageddon?* (Leicester: Inter-Varsity Press, 2004).
60. John W. Kennedy, "The Ultimate Kibitzer," *Christianity Today*, February 24–25, 2009, http://www.christianitytoday.com/ct/2009/february/27.32.htm.
61. Yechiel Eckstein, *The Journey Home: An Orthodox Rabbi and a Christian Journalist See Israel Through Each Other's Eyes and Strengthen Their Faith* (Shavti House, 2001), 7, 106.
62. Ibid., 204.
63. Ibid.
64. Noahite Laws—see Alan Brill, *Judaism and Other Religions: Models of Understanding* (New York: Palgrave Macmillan, 2010).
65. Shlomo Riskin, "Shabbat Shalom: Parshat Shemini Leviticus 9:1–11:47," http://www.ohrtorahstone.org.il/parsha/5763/shemini63.htm (November 11, 2008).
66. Shlomo Riskin, "Covenant and Conversion: The United Mission to Redeem the World," Institute for Theological Inquiry, http://www.yale.edu/ris/theologyconference/documents/Shlomo_Riskin.pdf.
67. http://cjcuc.com/site/2011/05/24/cjcuc-statement-on-a-jewish-understanding-of-christians-and-christianity/ (accessed June 3, 2011).
68. Joseph Ratzinger, *Dominus Iesus*, Congregation for the Doctrine of the Faith (August 6, 2000); Joseph Ratzinger, *Many Religions, One Covenant: Israel, the Church, and the World* (San Francisco: Ignatius Press, 1999).
69. Defending *Dominus Iesus* in an interview with the *Frankfurter Allgemeine Zeitung*, (2000) Cardinal Ratzinger, said that for him, law is really about the spirit, therefore he acknowledges that Jews have the same message of the spirit.

Chapter 5

1. Joseph Kimhi, *The Book of the Covenant of Joseph Kimhi* (Toronto: The Pontifical Institute of Mediaeval Studies, 1972), 28–29.

2. Ibid., 11.

3. R. J. Zwi Werblowsky, *Jewish-Christian relations* (London: Council of Christians and Jews, 1973).

4. The French-Jewish Ad Hoc Committee, "Christianity in Jewish Theology," *Revue des Études Juives* 160 (2001): 495–497, http://www.ccjr.us/dialogika-resources/documents-and-statements/jewish/765-fr-jewish-comm1973.

5. The original had the following comment: In the famous anecdote in *Sanhedrin* 107b and *Sotah* 47a (texts that were censured by the Christian censorship, but which can be found again in *Hesronot Ha-Shas*), a certain regret comes through, when a *barayta* says the following: "May the left hand always push away, but may the right hand bring closer, contrary to what Elisha did when pushing away Gehazi with both hands or Joshua b. Perahya when pushing away Jesus with both hands."

6. The original had the following comment: Juda Hallevi, the most exclusivist among our thinkers, wrote: "We deny to no one, no matter to which faith community that person might belong, a reward from God for his/her good deeds" (*Kuzari* I, § 111,). The term "Israel" in the sentence, "All Israel has a part in the 'olam ha-ba' means the righteous from all the nations," unless they impute iniquity to God (Aqedat Yitshaq, Shemini, gateway 60).

7. The original had the following comment: Bahya Ibn Paquda justified what he took from the non-Jewish philosophers and other ascetics from the Talmudic saying: "You have not acted like the most righteous 'among the non-Jews,' but you have acted like the most depraved" (*Babli, Sanhedrin* 39b): "Whoever says a wise word, even among the nations of the world, is called *Hakham*" (*Megilla* 16a; *Hobot ha-Lebabot*, Preface).

8. Jewish-Christian Relations, "National Jewish Scholars Project: Dabru Emet: A Jewish Statement on Christians and Christianity," Jewish-Christian Relations http://www.jcrelations.net/en/displayItem.php?id=1014.

9. Tikva Frymer-Kensky, et al. *Christianity in Jewish Terms* (Boulder: Westview Press, 2000), 124.

10. David Novak, *Talking with Christians: Musings of a Jewish Theologian* (Grand Rapids: William B. Eerdmans, 2005), 5, 23, 27, 29, 30.

11. Ibid., 160, 33–37.

12. Ibid., 16–17.

13. Marvin A. Sweeney, "Why Jews Are Interested in Biblical Theology: A Retrospective on the Work of Jon D. Levinson," *Jewish Book Annual* 55–56 (1997–99): 135–68.

14. Jon Levenson, *Sinai and Zion* (New York: HarperOne, 1987), 38–40, 77.

15. Jon Levenson, *The Death And Resurrection Of The Beloved Son: The Transformation Of Child Sacrifice In Judaism And Christianity* (New Haven: Yale University Press, 1993), x.

16. Ibid., 232.

17. Ibid.,186.

18. Jon Levenson, "Can Jews and Christians Share the Same Bible Stories Without Abandoning the Core Truth Claims of their Respective Religions?" ICJS' Interactive Discussion, The Institute for Christian & Jewish Studies, 232.

19. Jon D. Levenson, "The Same God? Who Do Christians and Muslims Worship?" *The Christian Century* 121: 8 (2004): 32–33.

20. Jon D. Levenson, "The Agenda of *Dabru Emet*," *Review of Rabbinic Judaism*, 7:1(2004): 1–26; citation specifically from pp. 9, 12.
21. Levenson, "The same God? Who do Christians and Muslims worship?"
22. Sharon Goldman, "The World Repaired, Remade An Interview With Jon D. Levenson," *Harvard Divinity School Bulletin* vol. 35, no. 1 (Winter 2007). Available at http://www. hds.harvard.edu/news/bulletin_mag/articles/35-1_levenson.html (accessed June 13, 2011).
23. Peter W. Ochs, "The God of Jews and Christians," in *Christianity in Jewish Terms*, ed. Tikva Frymer-Kensky (Boulder: Westview Press, 2000), xii.
24. Ibid., 59–61.
25. Peter W. Ochs, "The God of Jews and Christians," in *Christianity in Jewish Terms*, ed. Tikva Frymer-Kensky (Boulder: Westview Press, 2000), 59.
26. Ibid., 61.
27. Ibid., 69.
28. Ibid., 67.
29. Jeffrey W. Baile, "Reading Scripture Across Interfaith Lines," *The Christian Century* (September 2006): 36–42.
30. Meir Sendor, "The Violence of the Neutral In Interfaith Relations," in *Theology of Other Religions*, ed. Alon Goshen-Gottstein and E. Korn (Portland: Littman Library, 2012).
31. Michael Signer, "Searching the Scriptures," in *Christianity in Jewish Terms*, ed. Tikva Frymer-Kensky (Boulder: Westview Press, 2000), 86, 97.
32. *Transforming Relations: Essays on Jews and Christians throughout History in Honor of Michael A. Signer*, ed. Franklin T. Harkins (University of Notre Dame Press, 2010).
33. Idem., *Judaism and Christianity in the Age of Constantine: History, Messiah, Israel, and the Initial Confrontation* (Chicago: University of Chicago Press, 1987).
34. Jacob Neusner, *Telling Tales; Making Sense of Christian and Judaic Nonsense: The Urgency and Basis for Judeo-Christian Dialogue* (Louisville: Westminster/John Knox Press, 1993), 95.
35. Jacob Neusner, *Rabbi Talks with Jesus*: (Montreal: McGill-Queen's University Press; Rev. ed, 2000).
36. Kurt Cardinal Koch, "Theological Questions and Perspectives in Jewish-Catholic Dialogue" available at http://www.ccjr.us/dialogika-resources/documents-and-statements/roman-catholic/kurt-cardinal-koch.
37. Jack Chester Memorial Lecture on the Tenth Anniversary Celebration of the Sue and Leonard Miller Center for Contemporary Judaic Studies at the University of Miami on March 5, 2009.
38. Jacob Neusner, *Telling Tales; Making Sense of Christian and Judaic Nonsense: The Urgency and Basis for Judeo-Christian Dialogue* (Louisville: Westminster/John Knox Press, 1993), 12.
39. Ibid., 22, 116, 163–4.
40. A. Roy Eckardt, "Telling Tales: Making Sense of Christian and Judaic Nonsense: The Urgency and Basis for Judeo-Christian Dialogue," *Theology Today* (October 1993): 502–3.
41. Pinchas Lapide and Jurgen Moltmann, *Jewish Monotheism and Christian Trinitarian Doctrine*, forward by Jacob Agus (Philadelphia: Fortress Press, 1981), 19–22.
42. Pinchas Lapide and Karl Rahner, *Encountering Jesus—Encountering Judaism: A Dialogue* (New York: Crossroad, 1987), 49.
43. Lapide and Moltmann, *Jewish Monotheism and Christian Trinitarian Doctrine: A Dialogue*, 104. He also did an early study on Jesus in Israeli textbooks showing that

Jesus was treated as part of Jewish history, unfortunately the situation has almost reversed itself in recent decades, see Pinchas Lapide, "Jesus in Israeli Textbooks," *Journal of Ecumenical Studies* 10 (Summer, 1973): 515–531.

44. Lapide and Moltmann, *Jewish Monotheism and Christian Trinitarian Doctrine*, 28.
45. Ibid., 34.
46. Ibid., 31, 42, 61, 62.
47. Lapide and Rahner, *Encountering Jesus—Encountering Judaism: A Dialogue* (New York: Crossroad, 1987), 36–40, 67–8.
48. Lapide and Moltmann, *Jewish Monotheism and Christian Trinitarian Doctrine*, 59.
49. Lapide and Rahner, *Encountering Jesus—Encountering Judaism*, 12, 36.
50. Lapide and Moltmann, *Jewish Monotheism and Christian Trinitarian Doctrine*, 69.
51. Lapide and Rahner, *Encountering Jesus—Encountering Judaism*, 1.
52. Ibid., 11.
53. Ibid., 177.
54. Pinchas Lapide, *Paul, Rabbi, and Apostle* (Minneapolis: Augsburg, 1984), 54–55, 69–70, 39, 85.
55. For an example of the criticism he received, see Pnina Nave Levinson, "Christian Preacher," *Evangelische Information* 24 (June 1979): 75.
56. Alon Goshen-Gottstein, "Judaisms and Incarnational Theologies: Mapping Out the Parameters of Dialogue," *Journal of Ecumenical Studies* 39: 3 (2002): 219–247.
57. Alon Goshen-Gottstein, "God the Father in Rabbinic Judaism and Christianity: Transformed Background or Common Ground?" *Journal of Ecumenical Studies* 38 (2001): 85 (n81).
58. Alon Goshen-Gottstein, "Thinking of/With Scripture: Struggling for the Religious Significance of the Song of Songs," *The Journal Of Scriptural Reasoning* 3: 2 (August 2003).
59. Joseph Salvador, *das Leben Jesu Und Sein Lehre* (Dresden: Walther's Buchhandlung, 1841), 348, quoted in Dan Cohn-Sherbok, *Judaism and Other Faiths* (New York: Palgrave Macmillan, 1994), 87.
60. Joseph Salvador, *Paris, Rome, Jérusalem, Ou La Question Religeuse au XIXe Siécle,* (Paris: Michel-Lévy Frères, 1860), quoted in Dan Cohn-Sherbok, *Judaism and Other Faiths* (New York: Palgrave Macmillan, 1994), 89.
61. Martin Buber, *Origins of Hasidism* (New York: Horizon Press, 1960), 110.
62. Fritz A. Rothschild, ed., *Jewish Perspectives on Christianity* (New York: Crossroad, 1990); Jonathan D. Brumberg-Kraus, "A Jewish Ideological Perspective on the Study of Christian Scripture," *Jewish Social Studies* 4:1 (Autumn, 1997).
63. D. F. Sandmel, "Joseph Klausner, Israel, and Jesus," *Currents in Theology and Mission* 31: 6 (2004): 456–464.
64. David Flusser, *Jesus* (New York: Herder and Herder, 1969).
65. Géza Vermès, *Jesus and the World of Judaisim* (Philadelphia: Fortress, 1983); John Dominic Crossan, *The Historical Jesus: The Life of a Mediterranean Jewish Peasant* (San Francisco: HarperSanFrancisco, 1991); M. J. Borg, *Meeting Jesus Again for the First Time* (San Francisco: HarperSanFrancisco, 1994); N. T. Wright, *Jesus and the Victory of God* (Minneapolis: Fortress, 1996); E. P. Sanders, *Paul and Palestinian Judaism* (London: S. C. M, 1977); Géza Vermès, *The Changing Faces of Jesus* (New York: Viking Compass, 2001); Paula Fredriksen, *Jesus Of Nazareth, King of the Jews: A Jewish Life and the Emergence of Christianity* (New York: Vintage Books, 2000).
66. Géza Vermès, *Jesus the Jew* (London: S. C. M, 2001), 17.
67. Amy-Jill Levine, *The Misunderstood Jew: The Church and Scandal of the Jewish Jesus* (San Francisco: HarperSanFrancisco, 2006).

68. Beatrice Bruteau, *Jesus through Jewish Eyes: Rabbis and Scholars Engage an Ancient Brother in A New Conversation* (Maryknoll: Orbis Books, 2001), 59.

69. Krister Stendahl, *Paul Among Jews and Gentiles and Other Essays* (Philadelphia: Fortress Press, 1977); Nicholas Thomas Write, *Paul: Fresh Perspectives* (London: SPCK,2005); E. P. Sanders, *Paul and Palestinian Judaism: A Comparison of Patterns of Religion* (Philadelphia: Fortress Press, 1977); James D. G. Dunn, *Jesus, Paul, And The Law: Studies in Mark and Galatians* (Louisville: Westminster/ John Knox Press, 1990); James D. G. Dunn, *The New Perspective On Paul* (Grand Rapids: W. B. Eerdmans, 2007).

70. Daniel Boyarin, *A Radical Jew: Paul and the Politics of Identity* (Berkeley: University of California Press, 1997); Pamela Eisenbaum, *Paul was Not a Christian: The Original Message of a Misunderstood Paul* (New York: HarperOne, 2009); Paula Fredriksen, *Augustine and the Jews: A Christian Defense of Jews and Judaism* (New Haven: Yale University Press, 2010); Adele Reinhartz, *Befriending the Beloved Disciple: A Jewish Reading of the Gospel of John* (New York: Continuum, 2001).

71. Daniel Boyarin, *Borderlines* (Philadelphia; University of Pennsylvania Press, 2004); Idem, "Gospel of the Memra: Jewish Binitarianism and the Prologue of John," in *The Harvard Theological Review* 94:3 (July 2001): 243–284; idem, *A Radical Jew: Paul and the Politics of Identity* (Berkley: University of California Press, 1994).

72. Daniel Boyarin, *Borderlines,* 229.

73. Ibid., 17–19.

74. See Alan Segal, *Two Powers in Heaven: Early Rabbinic Reports About Christianity and Gnosticism* (Leiden: E. J. Brill, 1977).

75. Daniel Boyarin, *Borderlines* (Philadelphia; University of Pennsylvania Press, 2004), 125.

76. Ibid., 17.

77. Ibid., 33, 35.

78. Ibid., 121.

79. Moshe Idel, *Ben: Sonship and Jewish Mysticism* (New York: Continuum Books, 2007), 146–147.

80. Ibid., 147.

81. Daniel Boyarin, *Borderlines* (Philadelphia; University of Pennsylvania Press, 2004), 138.

82. Daniel Boyarin, *The Jewish Gospels* (New York: The New Press, 2012).

83. Idel, *Ben: Sonship and Jewish Mysticism.*

84. Ibid., 589–592.

85. Ibid., 123, 593.

86. Ibid., 592.

87. Ibid., 587.

88. Peter Schäfer, *Mirror of His Beauty: Feminine Images of God from the Bible to the Early Kabbalah* (Princeton: Princeton University Press, 2002), 119, 232–234, 239–240.

89. Arthur Green, "Shekhinah, the Virgin Mary, and the Song of Songs: Reflections on a Kabbalistic Symbol in Its Historical Context," *AJS Review* 26:1 (2002): 1–52.

90. Pope Benedict XVI, *Jesus of Nazareth: From the Baptism in the Jordan to the Transfiguration* (New York: Doubleday, 2007); idem, *Jesus of Nazareth. Part Two, Holy Week: From the Entrance into Jerusalem to the Resurrection* (San Francisco: Ignatius Press, 2011).

91. S. J. Carlo Maria Martini, "Christianity and Judaism: A Historical And Theological Overview," in *Jews and Christians: Exploring the Past, Present, and Future,* ed. James Charlesworth (New York: Crossroad, 1990), 19.

Chapter 6

1. Aharon Oppenheimer, "The Attitude of the Sages towards the Arabs," *Jewish Studies in a New Europe*, Sixth EAJS Congress, Toledo (July 19–23, 1998): 572–579.

2. Carol Bakhos, *Ishmael on the Border: Rabbinic Portrayals of the First Arab* (Albany: State University of New York Press, 2006), 207; *Reuven Firestone, Journeys in Holy Lands: The Evolution of the Abraham-Ishmael Legends in Islamic Exegesis* (Albany: State University of New York Press, 1990).

3. Flavius Josephus, "Antiquities of the Jews," *Josephus: The Complete Works* (Nashville: Thomas Nelson, 1998), 1:214.

4. Robert G. Hoyland, *Seeing Islam as Others Saw It: a Survey and Evaluation of Christian, Jewish, and Zoroastrian Writings on Early Islam* (Princeton: Darwin Press, 1997).

5. James Kugel, *Potiphar's House: the Interpretive Life of Biblical Texts* (San Francisco: HarperSanFrancisco, 1990).

6. William Brinner, *Prophets & Patriarchs* (Albany: State University of New York Press, 1986), 207.

7. Carol Bakhos, "Abraham Visits Ishmael: A Revisit," *Journal for the Study of Judaism* 38: 4–5 (2007): 553–580.

8. A Synoptic Version of *Pirqe De-Rabbi Eliezer* §30, University of North Carolina Charlotte, http://religiousstudies.uncc.edu/people/jcreeves/pre30text.html.

9. Yehudah Even-Shmuel, *Midreshey Ge'ullah*, 2nd ed. (Jerusalem: Mosad Bialik, 1954), 268–86. For discussion of this work, see Moses Buttenwieser, *Outline of the Neo-Hebraic Apocalyptic Literature* (Cincinnati: Jennings & Pye, 1901), 41. An important translation and study was prepared by Bernard Lewis, "An Apocalyptic Vision of Islamic History," *BSOAS* 13 (1949–51): 308–38; its main arguments are accepted by Salo M. Baron, *A Social and Religious History of the Jews*, 2nd ed. (New York and Philadelphia: Columbia University Press and the Jewish Publication Society, 1952–83), 3:93, 274n27.

10. Tudor Parfitt, ed., *Israel and Ishmael: Studies in Muslim-Jewish Relations* (New York: St. Martin's Press).

11. Yohanan Friedmann, *Tolerance and Coercion in Islam: Interfaith Relations in the Muslim Tradition* (New York: Cambridge University Press, 2003).

12. David Nirenberg, "What Can Medieval Spain Teach Us about Muslim-Jewish Relations?" *CCJR Journal: a Reform Jewish Quarterly* 49 (Spring/Summer 2002): 17–36, http://data.ccarnet.org/journal/702dn.pdf.

13. William M. Brinner, Benjamin H. Hary, John L. Hayes, and Fred Astern, *Judaism and Islam: Boundaries, Communications, and Interaction: Essays in Honor of William M. Brinner* (Brill Academic Publishers, 2000); David M. Freidenreich, "Comparisons Compared: A Methodological Survey of Comparisons of Religion from 'A Magic Dwells' to *A Magic Still Dwells*," *Method and Theory in the Study of Religion* 16 (2004): 80–101.

14. Mark R. Cohen, *Under Crescent and Cross: The Jews in the Middle Ages* (Princeton: Princeton University Press, 1994); Bernard Lewis, *The Jews of Islam* (Princeton: Princeton University Press, 1984); Bernard *Septimus*, "*Better under Edom than under* Ishmael: The History of a Saying" [Hebrew], *Zion* 47 (1982): 103–111; idem, "Hispano-Jewish Views of Christendom and Islam," in *In Iberia And Beyond: Hispanic Jews Between Cultures: Proceedings of a Symposium To Mark The 500th Anniversary Of The Expulsion Of Spanish Jewry*, ed. Bernard Dov Cooperman (Newark: University of Delaware Press, 1998), 43–65; Norman Stillman, "Myth, Countermyth, and Distortion," *Tikkun* 6: 3 (May–June 1991): 60–64.

15. J. Blau, *Scripta Judaica: The Emergence and Linguistic Background of Judaeo-Arabic; A Study of the Origins of Middle Arabic* (London: Oxford University Press, 1965), 159–160.

16. Jonathan P. Decter, "Rendering Qur'anic Quotations in Hebrew Translations of Islamic Texts," *Jewish Quarterly Review* 96: 3 (2006): 336–358.

17. Yair Schiffman, "The Differences Between the Translations of Maimonides' Guide of the Perplexed by Falaquera, Ibn Tibbon and al-Harizi, and their Textual and Philosophical Implications," *Journal of Semitic Studies* 44 (1999): 47–61.

18. Al-Ghazzali, *Balance of Human Action (Mizan al-amal),* trans. Abraham ibn Hasdai (1839, reprinted 1975): 222.

19. Ibid., 343–344.

20. Judah al-Harizi, *The Book of Tahkemoni: Jewish Tales from Medieval Spain,* trans, David Simha Segal (London: Littman Library of Jewish Civilization, 2001), 107:7.

21. Ibid., 348.

22. Marc B. Shapiro, "Islam and the Halakhah," *Judaism* (Summer, 1993): 332–343.

23. Heribert Busse, *Islam, Judaism and Christianity: The Theological and Historical Affiliations* (Princeton: Marcus Weiner, 1998); Quran 49/46–61/58 also 4:153–162/160. S 6:155, 7:101–133

24. Ignác Goldziher and Bernard Lewis, *Introduction to Islamic Theology and Law* (Princeton: Princeton University Press, 1981); Ignaìc Goldziher and S. M. Stern, *Muslim Studies* (Chicago: Aldine, 1973).

25. Camilla Adang, *Muslim Writers on Judaism & the Hebrew Bible from Ibn Rabban to Ibn Hazm* (Leiden: Brill, 1996).

26. For the current state of the relationship of the Bible and Koran studies, see John C. Reeves, *Bible and Quran: Essays in Scriptural Intertextuality* (Atlanta: Society of Biblical Literature, 2003); Idem, "Israel and the Torah of Muhammad," in *Quran and Bible: Essays in Scriptural Intertextuality,* ed. John Reeves (Atlanta: Society of Biblical Literature, 2003); Uri Rubin, *Between Bible and Quran: The Children of Israel and the Islamic Self-Image* (Princeton: Darwin Press, 1999); Sidney H. *Griffith,* "The Gospel in Arabic: An Inquiry into Its Appearance in the First Abbasid Century," in *Quran and Bible: Essays in Scriptural Intertextuality,* ed. John Reeves (Atlanta: Society of Biblical Literature, 2003); M. Mir, "The Qur'anic Story Of Joseph: Plot, Themes And Characters," *The Muslim World* LXXVI (1986): 1–15; Marilyn Robinson Waldman, "New Approaches To 'Biblical' Materials In The Qur'an," *The Muslim World* LXXV (1985); Roberto Tottoli, "Origin and Use of the Term Israiiyyat in Muslim Literature," *Arabica.* 46.2 (1999): 193–210; Uri Rubin, *Between Bible and Qur'ān: The Children of Israel and the Islamic Self-Image* (Princeton, NJ: Darwin Press, 1999); Jane Dammen McAuliffe, *Story-telling in the Framework of Nonfictional Arabic Literature,* ed. S. Leder (Wiesbaden: Harrassowitz Verlag, 1999); Tabarī and Franz Rosenthal, *General Introduction, And, from the Creation to the Flood* (Albany: State University of New York Press, 1988).

27. Camilla Adang, *Muslim Writers on Judaism & the Hebrew Bible from Ibn Rabban to Ibn Hazm* (E. J. Brill, 1996), 194–5.

28. Camilla Adang, *Muslim Writers on Judaism & the Hebrew Bible;* Theodore Pulcini, *Exegesis of Polemical Discourse Ibn Hazm on Jewish and Christian Scriptures* (Oxford University Press, 2000).

29. Saadyah ben Joseph, *Book of Beliefs and Opinions* (New Haven: Yale University Press, 1984), 152, 147, 163.

30. Haggai, Ben-Shammai, "The Attitude of Some Early Karaites towards Islam," *Studies in Medieval Jewish History and Literature Pt. 2* (Cambridge: Harvard University Press, 1984), 3–40.

31. Judah Halevi, *The Kuzari,* trans. H. Hirschfield (New York: Shocken, 1964), I 6–9.

32. Ibid., 11, 83.

33. David *Hartman* and Abraham Halkin, *Crisis and Leadership: Epistle to the Jews of Yemen* (Philadelphia: Jewish Publication Society of America, 1993); Moshe Perlmann, "The Medieval Polemics Between Islam and Judaism," in *Religion in a Religious Age*, ed., S. D. Goitein (Cambridge, MA, 1974); Ronald Kiener, "The Image of Islam in the Zohar," *Mehkerei Yerushalayim be-MahshevetYisrael* 9 (1989): 43–65; See Bernard Septimus, "Petrus Alfonsi on the Cult of Mecca," *Speculum* 56 (1981): 530–531; see also the comprehensive discussion by Sarah Lazarus-Yafeh, "Ha-Problematikah ha-Datitshel ha-Aliyah la-Regel ba-islam," *Divre ha-Akedemyah ha-Leumit ha-Yisraelit le-Mada'im* 5, no. 11 (1976): 222–243;Yehuda Shamir, "Allusions to Muhammed in Maimonides' Theory of Prophecy in his Guide," *Jewish Quarterly Review* 54 (1974): 212–224.

34. Moses *Narboni*, "Commentary on *Guide*," in *Sheloshah Kadmonei Mefarshei Hamoreh*, ed. J. Goldenthal (Vienna, 1852).

35. Gitit Holtzman, "Truth, Tradition and Religion. The Association between Judaism and Islam and the Relation between Religion and Philosophy in Medieval Jewish Thought," *Al-Masaq: Islam and the Medieval Mediterranean* 18:2 (2006): 191–200.

36. Zekhariyah al-Dahiri, *Sefer ha-Musar*, ed. Y. Ratzhaby (Jerusalem: Ben Zvi, 1965), 126–7.

37. Hava Lazarus-Yafeh, *Intertwined Worlds Medieval Islam and Bible Criticism* (Jerusalem: Bialik Institute, 1998).

38. Solomon Aderet, *Shut ha-Rashba* (Jeruslem: Mekhon Or ha-Mizrahò, MekhonYerushalayim, 1996), 75–77; Solomon Ibn Aderet, *Ma'amar al Yishma'el*, ed., Bezalel Naor (Spring Valley: Orot, 2008); Camilla *Adang*, "A Jewish Reply to Ibn Hazm: Solomon b. *Adret's* Polemic Against *Islam*," in *Judíos y musulmanes en al-Andalus y el Magreb: Contactos Intelectuales*, ed. María Isabel Fierro (Madrid: Casa de Velázquez, 2002).

39. Solomon Ibn Aderet, *Ma'amar al Yishma'el*, ed. Bezal el Naor (Spring Valley: Orot, 2008), 79–81, 79–81.

40. Ibid., 101.

41. Ibid., 99, 116.

42. R. Pourjavady and S. Schmidtke, *A Jewish Philosopher of Baghdad. 'Izz al-Dawla Ibn Kammuna (d. 683/1284) and His Writings* (Leiden and Boston: E. J. Brill, 2006); Moshe Perlman, *Sa'd B. Mansur ibn Kammuna's Examination of the Inquiries into the Three Faiths: A 13th Century Essay in the Comparative Religion* (Berkeley, CA: University of California, 1967).

43. Ibid., 76–77, 105.

44. Ibid., 143, 106–7, 122.

45. Ibid., 148–9.

46. Samau'al al-Maghribi, *Ifham Al-Yahud: Silencing the Jews*, trans., Moshe Perlmann (New York: American Academy for Jewish Research, 1964).

47. See Bernard Septimus, "Petrus Alfonsi on the Cult of Mecca," *Speculum* 56 (1981): 530–531. Hiddushei ha-Ran (Jerusalem, 1958), Sanhedrin 61b; Compare R. Nissim, She'elot u-Teshuvot R. Nissim ben Gerondi, 45. R. Nissim on Alfasi, Avodah Zarah, 26b.

48. Maimonides, *Teshuvot ha-Rambam*, no. 448; Septimus, "Petrus Alfonsi," pp. 522–23.

49. David Ibn Abi Zimra, *Responsa*, (Leghorn, 1652), fols. 30–31, no. 92; Isaac Elhanan Spektor, *Eyn Yitzhaq, orah hayyim*, (Jerusalem: Machon Yerushalayem, 2004), 45 §, 11; Abraham Isaac Kook, *Mishpat Kohen* (Jerusalem: Mossad ha-Rav Kuk, 1966), 167–70 § 89; Obadyah Yosef, *Yabah Omer*, pt. 4, *yoreh deah* (Jerusalem, 1993), p. 226–8 § 12; Yekutiel Y. Halberstamm, *Divrey Yeziv, orah hayyim*, I, 1, (Jerusalem, 1996), p. 171–5 §90.

50. Yosef Karo, *Avkat Rokhel* 68, declares that Muslims never used images. See also Mahari ben lev 1:118 Ovadiah Yosef, *Yabiah Omer* 7 yoreh deah 12, is one to allow mosques— also 5 yoreh deah 10 and *Yehaveh Daat* 5, 54.

51. David Zvei Hoffman, *Melamed Lehoil* 2:55.

52. Tzitz Eliezer–yoreh deah 18:47–14:91—bans going to mosques; See also Ateret Paz 1:2 yoreh deah 7.

53. Gideon Libson, *Jewish and Islamic Law: A Comparative Study of Custom during the Geonic Period* (Cambridge, MA: Islamic Legal Studies Program, Harvard Law School, 2003).

54. Zeev Meghen, *After Hardship Cometh Ease: The Jews as Backdrop for Muslim Moderation* (New York: W. de Gruyter, 2005), 3, 203.

55. Ibid., 9–15.

56. Ibid., 70–73, 85; Brannon Wheeler, "The New Torah," *Graeco-Arabica* 7–8 (1999–2000), 571–605.

57. Teshuvot Ha-Geonim (*Harkavi* edition), siman 278; B. M. Levin, *Otzar Hageonim* (Jerusalem: Hotsaat H. Vagshal, 2001).

58. B. M. Levin *Otzar Hageonim* (Jerusalem: Hotsaat H. Vagshal, 2001).

59. Marc B. Shapiro, "Islam and the Halakhah," *Judaism* (Summer 1993): 332–343.

60. Ibid.

61. Paul Fenton, "Jewish Attitudes to Islam: Israel Heeds Ishmael," *Jerusalem Quarterly* 29 (Fall 1983): 98; Moses de León, *Sefersheqel ha-kodesh*, ed. Charles Mopsik (London, 1911), 65.

62. Paul Fenton, "Jewish Attitudes to Islam: Israel Heeds Ishmael," *Jerusalem Quarterly* 29 (Fall 1983): 98.

63. Jacob Mann, "A Polemical Work against Karaites," *Jewish Quarterly Review* 12 (1922): 146–147.

64. "Etz Hadaat Tov" section Tehilim 124.

65. *Zohar*, III, 16b.

66. Hayyim Ibn 'Attâr, *'Ôr ha-Hayyim*, on Lev. 6: 3.

67. R. Joseph Hayyim, *Da'at u-Tevunah* (Jerusalem: Mekor Hayim, 1964), 25b–26a.

68. Vincent Cournell, "Theologies of Difference and Ideologies of Intolerance," in *Religious Tolerance in World Religions*, ed. Jacob Neusner and Bruce Chilton (West Conshohocken, Templeton Foundation Press, 2008), 274–296.

69. Obadyah Maimonides, *Treatise of the Pool*, trans. Paul Fenton (London: Octagon Press, 1981).

70. Khaled El-Rouayheb, "Heresy and Sufism in the Arabic-Islamic World, 1550–1750: Some Preliminary Observations," *Bulletin of the School of Oriental and African Studies* 73 (2010): 357–380.

71. See the introduction to Obadyah Maimonides, *Treatise of the Pool*, trans. Paul Fenton (London: Octagon Press, 1981), especially pp. 8–10.

72. Abraham Maimonides, *The High Ways to Perfection Vol. II*, ed., S. Rosenblatt (Baltimore: The Johns Hopkins Press, 1938), 266, 320.

73. Menahem di Lonzano, *Shetey Yadôt*, Venice 1618, fol. 65d and 141b.

74. Ibid., fol. 9ʙ.

75. Ariel Bension, *The Zohar in Moslem and Christian Spain* (London: G. Routledge, 1932), 34, 40–47.

76. Issachar Ben-Ami, *Folk Veneration of Saints Among the Jews of Morocco* (Jerusalem: Magnes Pr., Hebrew University, 1984); Alex Weingrod, *The Saint of Beersheba* (Albany: State University of New York Press, 1990); Yoram Bilu, *Without Bounds: The Life and Death of Rabbi Ya'aqov Wazana* (Detroit: Wayne State University Press, 2000).

77. Translated selections in Vera Moreen, ed., *Queen Esther's Garden: An Anthology of Judeo-Persion Literature* (New Haven: Yale University Press, 2000), 262–264. Above are six stanzas out of thirty.
78. Ibid., 272–273.

Chapter 7

1. Ignaz Goldziher and Raphael Patai, *Ignaz Goldziher and His Oriental Diary* (Detroit: Wayne State University Press, 1987), 20.
2. Martin Kramer, "Introduction," in *The Jewish Discovery of Islam: Studies in Honor of Bernard Lewis*, ed. Martin Kramer (Tel Aviv: The Moshe Dayan Center for Middle Eastern and African Studies, 1999), 1–48.
3. Abraham Geiger, *Judaism and Islam*, ed. M. Pearlman (New York: Ktav, 1970).
4. Jacob Lassner, "Abraham Geiger: A Nineteenth Century Jewish Reformer on the Origins of Islam," in *The Jewish Discovery of Islam: Studies in Honor of Bernard Lewis*, ed. Bernard Lewis and Martin Kramer, 103–136 (Tel Aviv: The Moshe Dayan Center for Middle Eastern and African Studies Tel Aviv University, 1999); Susannah Heschel, *Abraham Geiger on the Origins of Christianity*, 1990.
5. Abraham Geiger, Judaism and Islam, Prolegomenon by Moshe *Pearlman* (Hoboken: Ktav, [1898] 1970), xvi.
6. Ibid., xviii.
7. Ibid., xvii, xx, xxi.
8. Charles Torrey, *The Jewish Foundation of Islam: Introd. by Franz Rosenthal* (New York: Ktav, 1967).
9. Abraham I. Katsh, *Judaism in Islam*, 1.
10. Abraham I. Katsh, *Judaism in Islam: Biblical and Talmudic Backgrounds of the Koran and Its Commentaries* (New York: Sepher-Hermon Press, 1980); Hartwig Hirschfeld, *Judische Elementeim Koran (Leipzig: Verlag von S. Hirzel, 1865).*
11. Katsh, *Judaism in Islam*, 5–6.
12. Katsh, *Judaism in Islam*, 67.
13. Brannon M. Wheeler, *Moses in the Quran and Islamic Exegesis* (London: Routledge-Curzon, 2002); idem, "Israel and the Torah of Muhammad," in *Bible and Quran: Essays in Scriptural Intertextuality*, ed. John Reeves (Atlanta: Society of Biblical Literature: Scholars Press, 2003).
14. James Kugel, in *Potipher's House: the interpretive life of biblical texts* (Cambridge, MA: Harvard University Press, 1994), 28–65.
15. See endnote 26 in Chapter 6 above.
16. Drory Rina, "Literary Contacts and Where to Find Them: On Arabic Literary Models in Medieval Jewish Literature," *Poetics Today* 14.2 (1993): 277–302, esp. 277–279.
17. Reuven Firestone, *Children of Abraham: An Introduction to Judaism for Muslims* (Hoboken, NJ: Ktav, 2001), 4–8, 157.
18. Bradford E Hinze and Irfan A. Omar, *Heirs of Abraham: The Future of Muslim, Jewish, and Christians Relations* (Maryknoll, NY: Orbis Books, 2005).
19. Jonathan Ray, "Beyond Tolerance and Persecution: Reassessing Our Approach to Medieval 'convivencia'." *Jewish Social Studies* 11.2 (2005): 1–18.
20. Steven M. Wasserstrom, *Between Muslim and Jew: The Problem of Symbiosis under Early Islam* (Princeton: Princeton University Press, 1995), 203, 28–33.
21. Joel L. Kremer, *Humanism in the Renaissance of Islam: the Cultural Revival During the Buyid Age: Second Revised Edition* (Brill: Leiden, 1992), 93, 123, 128.

22. David Nierenberg, "What Can Medieval Spain Teach Us about Muslim-Jewish Relations?" *CCJR Journal* (Spring/Summer 2002), 17–36.

23. Ibid., 7, 21.

24. Ibid., 23–24.

25. Ibid., 24–28, 30, 32.

26. Raphael Patai, *Jadid al-Islam: The Jewish "New Muslims" of Meshhed* (Detroit: Wayne State University Press, 1994); Daniel Tsadik, "Religious Disputations of Imāmī Shī'īs against Judaism in the late Eighteenth and Nineteenth Centuries," *Studia Iranica*. 24.1 (2005): 95–134.

27. Ian Almond, *History of Islam in German Thought from Leibniz to Nietzsche* (New York: Routledge, 2010).

28. W. A. Cristaudo, "Rosenzweig's Stance toward Islam: the Troubling Matter of Theo-Politics in the Star of Redemption," *Rosenzweig Jahrbuch (Rosenzweig yearbook)* (Munich, Karl Alber, 2007), 2: 43–86; Franz Rosenzweig, Gesine Palmer, and Yossef Schwartz, *Innerlich Bleibt Die Welt Eine: Ausgawählte Texte Zum Islam* (Berlin: Philo, 2003); Paul R. Mendes-Flohr, *Divided Passions: Jewish Intellectuals and the Experience of Modernity* (Detroit: Wayne State University Press, 1991), 295–6.

29. Franz Rosenzweig, *The Star of Redemption* (Notre Dame, IN: University of Notre Dame Press, 1985), 116–118.

30. H. E. Ambassador Dr. Akbar Ahmed et al. (2006), "Open Letter to his Holiness Pope Benedict XVI" (PDF). *Egypt State Information Service*, Center for Inter-Civilizational Dialogue, http://www.sis.gov.eg/PDF/En/Arts&Culture/072607000000000010001.pdf. (Retrieved July 23, 2009); Ralph M. Coury, "A Syllabus Of Errors: Pope Benedict XVI on Islam at Regensburg," *Race & Class* Institute of Race Relations 50.3 (2008): 30–61; Spengler [pseud. David P. Goldman] "Christian, Muslim, Jew: Franz Rosenzweig and the Abrahamic Religions," *First Things: A Monthly Journal of Religion and Public Life* (October 2007).

31. Trude Weiss-Rosmarin, "Towards Jewish-Muslim Dialogue" *Jewish Spectator* (1967).

32. Ibid., 6–7.

33. Ibid., 9.

34. Ibid., 44.

35. Ibid., 40–41.

36. Ibid., 10.

37. Ibid., 11.

38. Ibid., 30–31.

39. Ibid., [42–43].

40. Dr. Avraham Elqayam, "The Religion of Mercy: Encounters with Islam," *Deot* 19, (2004): 6–8.

41. Interreligious Dialogue: The Website of the Journal of Inter-Religious Dialogue, "Embracing the Challenge: Reuven Firestone on Jewish-Muslim Dialogue, An Interview by Joshua Stanton," http://irdialogue.org/articles/on-campus-articles/embracing-the-challenge-reuven-firestone-on-jewish-muslim-dialogue-an-interview-by-joshua-stanton/.

42. Reuven Firestone, *Journeys in Holy Lands: The Evolution of the Abraham- Ishmael Legends in Islamic Exegesis* (Albany: State University of New York Press, 1990), 135.

43. Reuven Firestone, "The Qur'an and the Bible: Some Modern Studies of Their Relationship," *Bible and Qur'an: Essays in Scriptural Intertextuality*, ed. John C. Reeves (Atlanta: Society of Biblical Literature, 2003), 1–22; Brie Loskota, "Challenges in Jewish-Muslim Dialogue: The American Context," *Muslim-Jewish dialogue in a 21st Century world*, ed. Humayun Ansari and David Cesarani (Egham, Royal Holloway,

University of London, 2007), 135–158; Greenberg, Brad A. "An Appreciation of Islam: Q&A with Rabbi Reuven Firestone," *JewishJournal.com*, March 11, 2009, http://www.jewishjournal.com/community/article/an_appreciation_of_islam_qa_with_rabbi_reuven_firestone_20090311/ (accessed July 10, 2011).

44. Reuven Firestone, *Children of Abraham: An Introduction to Judaism for Muslims* (Hoboken, NJ: KTAV, 2001), 3.

45. Ibid., 42–3, 237.

46. Jacob Neusner and Tamara Sonn, *Judaism and Islam: Comparing Religions through Law* (London & NY: Routledge, 1999), 234; Jacob Neusner, Tamara Sonn, and Jonathan Brockopp, *Judaism and Islam in Practice. A Sourcebook for the Classical Age* (London: Routledge, 2000).

47. John Calvert, *Sayyid Qutb and the Origins of Radical Islamism* (New York: Columbia University Press, 2010); Benny Morris, "Qutb and the Jews: As the Progenitor of Modern-Day Islamic Fundamentalism, Sayyid Qutb's Advocacy for Jihad against the Hedonistic West Laid the Groundwork for 9/11," *National Interest* (2010): 64–69. Compare Yusuf al-Qaradawi, *The Lawful and Prohibited in Islam* available online http://www.witness-pioneer.org/vil/Books/Q_LP/ (accessed July 10, 2011).

48. Rabbi Eliezer Melamed, "Islam Lives by the Sword," July 15, 2009, *Arutz Sheva IsraelNationalNews.com*, http://www.israelnationalnews.com/Articles/Article.aspx/8917.

49. "Rabbi calls for annihilation of Arabs," BBC News, Tuesday, April 10, 2001, http://news.bbc.co.uk/2/hi/middle_east/1270038.stm.

50. Yair Ettinger and Yoav Stern, *Haaretz* correspondents, *Haaretz* Service and Agencies, "Sephardic Chief Rabbi Shlomo Amar Criticizes Pope's Remarks," September 17, 2006, *Haaretz.com*, http://www.haaretz.com/hasen/spages/763593.html.

51. Ibid.

52. Rabbi Menachem Froman, "Judaism as the West-Judaism as Unique and Universal" *Haaretz* [no longer available online]; idem, "Maybe, We Do Have Someone to Talk To," *Common Ground News Service*, Common Ground News Service, February 16, 2006, http://www.commongroundnews.org/article.php?id=1443&lan=en&sid=0&sp=0 (accessed July 10, 2011).

53. Rabbi Haim Ovadia, "It's time to (re)open dialogue with Islam," *JewishJournal*.com, January 10, 2008, http://www.jewishjournal.com/opinion/article/its_time_to_reopen_dialogue_with_islam_20080111/ (accessed July 11, 2011); For others who proclaim that we should return to the concept of Arabic Jews, see David Shasha, "Sephardim and Israel Today: The 'Levantine Option' on Shaky Ground," *Tikkun* 23.3 (2008): 74–75; Anouar Majid, *We Are All Moors: Ending Centuries of Crusades against Muslims and Other Minorities* (Minneapolis: University of Minnesota Press, 2009).

54. Eric H. Yoffie, "Remarks to the ISNA: Remarks as prepared to the Islamic Society of North America 44th Annual Convention, Chicago, Illinois," *Union for Reform Judaism*, August 31, 2007, http://urj.org/about/union/leadership/yoffie/isna/.

55. Alon Goshen-Gottstein, "Abraham and 'Abrahamic Religions' in the Contemporary Interreligious Discourse: Reflections of an Implicated Jewish Bystander," *Studies in Interreligious Dialogue* 12.2 (2002): 163–183; Jon D, Levenson, "The Idea of Abrahamic Religions: A Qualified Dissent," *Jewish Review of Books*, 2010, http://www.jewishreviewofbooks.com/publications/detail/the-idea-of-abrahamic-religions-a-qualified-dissent.

56. Mark R. Cohen, "Islam and the Jews: Myth, Counter-Myth, History," *The Jerusalem Quarterly*, no. 38 (Spring 1986): 125–137; idem., "The Meaning of 'Cordoba': Can It Really Symbolize Religious Tolerance?" *The Huffington Post*, September 9, 2010, http://www.huffingtonpost.com/mark-r-cohen/the-meaning-of-cordoba_b_707973.html.

57. David Rabeeya, *A Guide to Understanding Judaism and Islam: More Similarities than Differences* (Philadelphia: Maimuna Press, 1992).

Chapter 8

1. Carl W. Ernst, "Situating Sufism and Yoga," *Journal of the Royal Asiatic Society*, Series 3, 15:1 (2005): 15–43, quote on page 15.

2. For the larger context of this translation movement, see Carl W. Ernst, "Muslim Studies of Hinduism? A Reconsideration of Persian and Arabic Translations from Sanskrit," *Iranian Studies* 36 (2003): 173–95.

3. Bruce B. Lawrence, "The Use of Hindu Religious Texts in al-Birūni's India with Special Reference to Patanjali's Yoga-Sutras," in *The Scholar and the Saint: Studies in Commemoration of Abu 'l Rayhan al-Bīrūnī and Jalal al-Din al-Rūmī*, ed. Peter J. Chelkowski (New York: New York University Press, 1975), 29–48; Shlomo Pines and Tuvia Gelblum, "Al-Birūni's Arabic Version of Patañjali's Yogasūtra: A Translation of his First Chapter and a Comparison with Related Sanskrit Texts," *Bulletin of the School of Oriental and African Studies* 29 (1966): 302–325; Shlomo Pines and Tuvia Gelblum, "Al-Birūni's Arabic Version of Patañjali's Yogasūtra: A Translation of the Second Chapter and a Comparison with Related Texts," *Bulletin of the School of Oriental and African Studies* 40 (1977): 522–549; Shlomo Pines and Tuvia Gelblum, "Al-Birūni's Arabic Version of Patañjali's Yogasūtra: A Translation of the Third Chapter and a Comparison with Related Texts," *Bulletin of the School of Oriental and African Studies* 46 (1983): 258–304; Carl W. Ernst, "The Islamization of Yoga in the Amrtakunda Translations," *Journal of the Royal Asiatic Society*, Series 3, 13:2 (2003): 199–226.

4. Yohanan Friedmann, "Medieval Muslim View of Indian Religions," *Journal of the American Oriental Society* 95, no. 2 (Apr.–Jun., 1975): 214–221; *Yohanan Friedmann, Tolerance and Coercion in Islam: Interfaith Relations in the Muslim Tradition (Cambridge University Press, 2003);* Yohanan Friedmann, "Classification of Unbelievers in Sunnī Muslim Law and Tradition," *Jerusalem Studies in Arabic and Islam* 22 (1998): 163–195; *Jamsheed Choksy, Conflict And Cooperation: Zoroastrian Subalterns And Muslim Elites in Medieval Iranian Society (*New York: Columbia University Press, 1997).

5. Julius Guttmann, *Philosophies of Judaism: The History of Jewish Philosophy From Biblical Times to Franz Rosenzweig* (New York: Holt, Rinehart and Winston, 1964), 59.

6. Julius Guttmann, *Philosophies of Judaism*: 58–59; *Joel L. Kramer, Humanism in the Renaissance of Islam*, 2nd rev. ed. (Leiden: E. J. Brill, 1993); David Sklare, "Responses to Islamic Polemics by Jewish Mutakallimun in the Tenth Century," in *The Majlis Interreligious Encounters in Medieval Islam*, ed. Hava Lazarus-Yafeh et al. (Wiesbaden: Harrassowitz, 1999), 137–161.

7. Samuel Rosenblatt, Saadia *Gaon: The Book of Beliefs and Opinions* (New Haven: Yale University Press, 1989), 16.

8. Ibid., 172.

9. Yehudah Halevi, *Kuzari* I:19; I:60–61.

10. Shem Tov ibn Falaquera, *Ethical Epistle (Iggeret ha-Musar)*, ed. A. M. Habermann, *Kovetz Al Yad* 1 (n.s.) (Jerusalem, 1936): 76–78, cited in Abraham Melamed, "The Image of India in Medieval Jewish Culture," *Jewish History* 20:3–4 (December 2006): 299–314.

11. Moritz Steinschneider, *ZDMG*. xxiv. 327.

12. Menachem Meiri, *Mishlei* (Jerusalem: 1974): 34; *Composition on Repentance.* (Jerusalem: 1974): 232.

13. Y. Tzvi Langermann, *Yemenite Midrash: Philosophical Commentaries on the Torah,* Sacred Literature Series (San Francisco: Harper San Francisco, 1996), 276–77.

14. Dov Schwartz, *Aṣtrologyah u-magyahba-hagut ha-Yehudit bi-Yeme ha-Benayim.* (Ramat-Gan: Universitat Bar-Ilan, 1999), 170.

15. Ibid., 214.

16. Menasseh ben Israel, *The Conciliator,* ed. E. H. Lindo (London, 1842 reprinted New York: Hermon Press, 1972) citing *Source and Relaciones de Pedro Teixeira* (1610).

17. Menashe ben Israel, *Nishmat Haayim* 4:21.

18. *Zohar* I:99b–100a; Aryeh Kaplan, *Sefer Yetzirah* (York Beach: Weiser, 1990), xiii–xiv.

19. Benjamin of Tudela, *The Itinerary of Benjamin of Tudela,* trans. Marcus Nathan Adler (London: Oxford University Press, 1907), 138–143.

20. David D'Beth Hillel, *Unknown Jews in Unknown Lands: The Travels of Rabbi,* ed. Walter J. Fischel (New York, NY: *Ktav,* 1973), 116–117.

21. Jacob Saphir, *Even Saphir: masotav ha-muflaimshelYaaḳov Saphir ha-Leyi be-Teman* (Jerusalem: Yehoshua Kohen, 1989), 51.

22. Idem., 116.

23. Idem., 54.

24. Maurice Fluegel, *Philosophy, Qabbala and Vedanta. comparative Metaphysics and Ethics, Rationalism and Mysticism, of the Jews, the Hindus and Most of the Historic Nations, as Links and Developments of One Chain of Universal Philosophy* (Baltimore: H. Fluegel, 1902).

25. Doctrines, God, Ain-Soph.

26. Fleugel, *Philosophy, Qabbala, and Vedanta,* 195.

27. Ibid., 225.

28. Ezriel Gruenzig, "Hindu Philosophy and Kabbalah," *Ha-Eshkol* 3 (Cracow: 1900): 40–48.

29. The first Prime Minister of India, Pandit Jawaharlal Nehru had his autobiography written in 1936, which was then translated into Hebrew soon after its publication. To many, there seemed an affinity of both national movements seeking self-determination against the British empire; H. E. Arun K. Singh, "Israel and India in the Era of Globalization" (Seminar, Tel Aviv University, March 8, 2006).

30. Irving M. Bunim, *Ethics from Sinai; An Eclectic, Wide-ranging Commentary on Pirke Avoth* (New York: P. Feldheim, 1966), Chapter 6.

31. Azriel Carelbach, *India: Account of a Voyage* [Hebrew] (Tel Aviv: 1956); Shalom Goldman and Laurie Patton, "From All Their Habitations—Indian Love Call: Israelis, Orthodoxy, and Indian Culture," *Judaism* 50 (2001): 351.

32. Ḥayim Shpilberg, *Hodu: Emunotye-Deot* (Tel Aviv: Hadar, 1985). Cf. Peretz Hirschbein, Indye: fun maynrayze in Indye (Vilna: 1929 reprinted Amherst MA, 2000).

33. Darya Maoz, "When Images Become 'True', The Israeli Backpacking Experience in India," *Karmic Passages, Israeli Scholarship on India,* ed. David Shulman and Shalva Weil (Oxford University Press: New Delhi, 2008), 214–231.

34. Elḥanan Nir, *Me-Hoduye-adkan: hogimYiśreelimkotvim al Hoduyeha-Yahadutshelahem* (Jerusalem: Reuven Mass, 2006).

35. Rivka Miriam, "On Two Conflicting Visits to India," *From India Till Here,* 41–2, 45. On finding God in all things, *Tikunei Zohar,* Tikun 57 (91b) and Tikun 70 (122b).

36. David Zeller, *The Soul of the Story: Meetings With Remarkable People* (Woodstock: Jewish Lights, 2005).

37. Ibid., 142–3, 193.

38. Miriam Bokser Caravella, *The Holy Name: Mysticism in Judaism* (Punjab, India: Radha Soami Satsand Beas, 1989), xvi.

39. Ibid., 4.
40. Ibid., 49.
41. Ibid., 73, 90–1, 94.
42. Ibid., 107.
43. Ibid., 164–5.
44. Ibid., 215.
45. Alon Goshen-Gottstein, "The Jewish Encounter with Hinduism Personal and Theological Reflections" (Unpublished manuscript).
46. Yechezkel *Landau, Nodeh Beyehudah* (New York, 1960), 10.
47. Zvei Pesah Frank, Yoreh Deah 41:4.
48. Hayyim David Halevi, *Mekor Hayim: piske halakhotha-nehutsot be-yoter* (Tel Aviv: 1983), 179.
49. Ibid., 180.
50. Matityahu Glazerson, *From Hinduism to Judaism* (Jerusalem: Himelsein, Glazerson, 1984), 1–3, 16–17, 74.
51. Full collection of rabbinical sources is available at: http://www1.cs.columbia.edu/~spotter/sheitel/.
52. Benjamin Fleming and Annette Yoshiko Reed "From Tirupati to Brooklyn: interpreting Hindu Votive Hair Offerings," "Interpreting Tonsured Hair as 'Offering'" *Studies in Religion* (2011): 1–36.
53. Daniel Sperber, "The Halachic Status of Hinduism" (Unpublished Manuscript).
54. Nathan Katz, "Jerusalem in Benares" *Tikkun* 22:3 (May–June 2007): 23–25, 68–70.
55. Ellen S. Goldberg and Nathan Katz, *The Last Jews of Cochin: Jewish Identity in Hindu India* (Columbia, S.C.: University of South Carolina Press, 1993), 54.
56. Efrayim En Es, *Sraddhalu* (Articles of Faith), Hitahadutyotse Hodube-Yiśrael, 7 (1989).
57. Cochin Synagogue, *Commemoration Volume; Cochin Synagogue Quartercentenary Celebrations,* December 15, 16, 17, 18, & 19, 1968, ed. P. S. Velayudhan, et al. (Cochin Kerala History Association and the Cochin Synagogue Quatercentenary Celebration Committee, 1971).
58. Barbara A. Holdrege, *Veda and Torah: Transcending the Textuality of Scripture* (Albany: State University of New York Press, 1996).
59. Hananya Goodman, "Judaism and Hinduism: Cultural Resonances," *Between Jerusalem and Benares: Comparative Studies in Judaism and Hinduism,* ed. Hananya Goodman (Albany: SUNY Press, 1994); Gershom Scholem, *On the Mystical Shape of the Godhead* (New York: Schocken Books, 1991), 174, 194.
60. The documents are available at many websites including: http://www.yoga-in-daily-life.org/articles/show.asp?id=20070211001; http://equalitybasedonthesoul.com/jewhinsign.aspx.
61. Ibid.
62. Hindu-Jewish Leadership Summit in Jerusalem, February 17–20, 2008.
63. Ibid.
64. Nathan Katz, "Jewish-Hindu Dialogue: Learning from Each Other-Hindus and Jews," *Hinduism Today* 16, 7 (July 1994).
65. Adin Steinsaltz, "Peace without Conciliation: The Irrelevance of 'Toleration' in Judaism," *Common Knowledge* 11:1 (2005): 41–47.
66. Eliezer Berkovits, *God, Man, and History* (New York: Jonathan David, 1959), 33.
67. Alon Goshen-Gottstein, "Encountering Hinduism: Thinking through Avodah Zarah," in Alon Goshen-Gottstein and Eugene Korn, *Jewish Theology and World Religions* (Portland, OR: Littman Library 2012). Alon Goshen-Gottstein is working on a long book tentatively

entitled *Identity and Idolatry: The Jewish Encounter with Hinduism*. This chapter is based on an earlier draft of that book; Alon Goshen-Gottstein, "The Jewish Encounter with Hinduism Personal and Theological Reflections" (Unpublished manuscript).

68. See Vasudha Narayanan, "Diglossic Hinduism: Liberation and Lentils," *JAAR* 68: 4, (2000), 767.

69. Alon Goshen-Gottstein, "The Jewish Encounter with Hinduism Personal and Theological Reflections" (Unpublished manuscript).

70. David Shulman, preface to *Between Jerusalem and Benares*, ed. Hananya Goodman (Albany: SUNY Press, 1994).

71. Maimonides, *Laws of the Foundation of the Torah*, Chapter 1, 1–6.

72. Alon Goshen-Gottstein, "The Jewish Encounter with Hinduism Personal and Theological Reflections" (Unpublished manuscript).

73. Ibid.

Chapter 9

1. Abraham Isaac Kook, *Shemonah Kevetzim* 5: 47–8; This approach to Theravada Buddhism was still presented as recently as the late 1970s in Ninian Smart, *The Long Search* (Boston: Little, Brown, 1977).

2. Thomas A. Tweed, *The American Encounter with Buddhism, 1844–1912 Victorian Culture and the Limits of Dissent* (Bloomington: Indiana University Press, 1992).

3. Johan Elverskog, *Buddhism and Islam on the Silk Road* (Philadelphia: University of Pennsylvania, 2010).

4. *Islam and Tibet Interactions along the Musk Routes*, ed. Anna Akasoy, Charles Burnett (London: Ashgate, 2010); Anna Akasoy "The Buddha and the Straight Path: Islamic Concepts and Terminology in Rashīd al-Dīn's Life of the Buddha," in *Rashid al-Din as an Agent and Mediator of Cultural Exchanges in Ilkhanid Iran*, ed. Anna Akasoy, Charles Burnett and Ronit Yoeli-Tlalim (London: Warburg Institute Press, forthcoming 2012); Ronit Yoeli-Tlalim, "Rashid al-Din's Life of the Buddha—Some Buddhist Perspectives," in *Rashid al-Din as an Agent and Mediator of Cultural Exchanges in Ilkhanid Iran*, ed. Anna Akasoy, Charles Burnett, and Ronit Yoeli-Tlalim (London: Warburg Institute Press, 2012).

5. Meoreot Zvi (Lvov 1804), usually listed as Yaakov Sassporti, *Sipur Ḥalomot Kez Ha-Pelaot: aser Nilqaṭ Min Sifre Ḥakme Dorot Ha-Rishonim* (Lemberg, 1804). I thank Prof. Zvi Mark for the reference, who also identified the correct author as Rabbi Israel Yafee (or Yafah). I thank Profs. Isrun Engelhardt of Munich and Donald Lopez of the University of Virginia for identifying the corrupted words and places. In their generosity, I was also informed that these passages can only be a rather distorted version of Johannes Grueber's report of his visit to Lhasa in 1661. These reports were compiled by Athanasius Kircher and found in Chapter 4 of Athanasius Kircher, *China Illustrata* (Amstelodami: oannem Janssonium à Waesberge & Elizeum Weyerstraet, 1667). The first paragraph is from Orazio della Penna, *Breve Notizia del regno del Thibet*, 1730, in the translation from Latin or French in Thevenot by Thomas Astley, *A New General Collection of Voyages and Travels*, vol. IV (London, 1747); Donald S. Lopez, *Prisoners of Shangri-La: Tibetan Buddhism and the West* (University of Chicago: Chicago, 1998).

6. Alexandra David-Neel, *Magic and Mystery in Tibet* (Paris: Plon, 1929).

7. Samson HaLevi Bloch, *Shevilei Olam* (Zolkiew, 1822), 119, 135, 72–74.

8. Samuel Alexandrov, *Mikhteve meḥkar u-viḳoret: al devar ha-Yahadut yeha-rabanut ba-zeman ha-aḥaron* (Jerusalem: 1931): 33–34.

9. Abraham Isaac Kook and Tzvi Feldman, *Rav A. Y. Kook: Selected Letters* (Ma'aleh Adumim, Israel: Ma'aliot Publications of Yeshivat Birkat Moshe, 1986).

10. Samuel Alexandrov, *Mikhteve meḥḳar u-viḳoret*, 48, 28.

11. Sandra Lubarsky, *Tolerance and Transformation: Jewish Approaches to Religious Pluralism* (Cincinnati: Hebrew Union College Press, 1990), 39.

12. Ibid., 120.

13. Kaufman Kohler, *Jewish Theology, Systematically and Historically Considered* (New York: Macmillan, 1918).

14. Martin Buber, *Chinese Tales: Zhuangzi: Sayings and Parables and Chinese Ghost and Love Stories* (Atlantic Highlands: Humanities Press, 1991).

15. Martin Buber, *The Origin and Meaning of Hasidism* (New York: Horizon Press, 1960), 228.

16. Idem., 231.

17. Martin Buber, *The Origin and Meaning of Hasidism*, 239.

18. Idem., 236.

19. Jonathan Herman, *I and Tao: Martin Buber's Encounter with Chuand Tzu* (Albany: State University of New York Press, 1996), 76.

20. Idem., 76–77.

21. Jacob Yuroh Teshima, *Zen Buddhism And Hasidism: A Comparative Study* (Lanham: University Press of America, 1995).

22. Daniel Matt, *God and the Big Bang: Discovering Harmony Between Science and Spirituality* (Woodstock: Jewish Lights, 1996), 47–58.

23. Thray Sithu U Ba Khin, *The Real Values of True Buddhist Meditation* (Yegu, Rangoon: Buddha Sasana Council Press, 1962) written on the occasion of the visit of their Prime Minister Mr. Ben Gurion to Rangoon Burma, available as e-book: http://onlinebooks. library.upenn.edu/webbin/book/lookupid?key=olbp11101.

24. Ben-Gurion "Race and Rights," *New York Times*, April 29, 1962.

25. Rami Shapiro, *Open Secrets: The Letters of Reb Yerachmiel ben Yisrael* (Monkfish, 2004).

26. Alan Lew, *This Real and You Are Completely Unprepared* (Boston: Little, Brown, 2003), 16.

27. Idem., 190.

28. Ibid, *One God Clapping: The Spiritual Path of a Zen Rabbi* (New York: Kodansha International, 1999), 154.

29. Idem., 287.

30. Idem., 296, 297. The discussion of Ju-Bu and especially the defense of Lew's combination of meditation practice and Judaism was formulated in extensive emails and blog comments from Len Moskowitz, an Orthodox rabbi with extensive zazen training and personal friend of Alan Lew and Norman Fischer.

31. Paul Williams, *The Unexpected Way* (Edinburgh: T &T Clark, 2002).

32. Paul Knitter, *Without Buddha I Could Not Be A Christian* (Oxford: Oneworld, 2009).

33. Jerome Gellman, "Judaism and Buddhism: A Jewish Approach to a Godless Religion," in *Jewish Theology and World Religions*, ed. Alon Goshen Gottstein and E. Korn (Portland: Littman Library, 2012). For his knowledge of Buddhism, Gellman relies on the modern interpreter Thich Nhat Hanh, in his *Thundering Silence: Sutra on the Better Way to Catch a Snake* (Berkeley, CA, 1993) and *The Heart of Understanding: Commentaries on the Prajnaparamita Heart Sutra*, trans. Thich Nhat Hanh (Berkeley, Calif., 1998).

34. Stephen Batchelor, *Buddhism Without Beliefs* (New York, 1997); For an overview of Nagarjuna on God, see Hsueh-Li Cheng, "N{a-}g{a-}rjuna's Approach to the

Problem of the Existence of God," *Religious Studies*, 12 (1976), 207–16; Richard P. Hayes, "Principled Atheism in the Buddhist Scholastic Tradition," *Journal of Indian Philosophy*, 16 (1988), 5–28.

35. Chaim Brovender, "Ask the Rabbi: Can Jews Eat in 'Idolatrous' Restaurants?" *Jerusalem Post Online Edition*, August 21, 2007.

36. E-mail communication August 30, 2011 also see http://asimplejew.blogspot.com/2007/12/guest-posting-by-rabbi-dovid-sears-part_13.html.

37. Michael Pollak, *The Jews of Kaifeng: Chinese Jews on the banks of the Yellow River* (Tel Aviv: Bet Hatefutsoth The Nahum Goldman Museum of the Jewish Diaspora, 1984), 138.

38. Idem., 137.

39. Michael Pollak, *Mandarins, Jews, and missionaries: the Jewish experience in the Chinese Empire* (Philadelphia: Jewish Publication Society of America, 1980), 289.

40. One prominent contemporary Rosh Yeshiva stated that Judaism is closest to Confucianism in its pattern of accepting tradition, respect for the wise, and emphasizing correct action. On this approach, see Herbert Fingarette, *Confucius: The Secular as Sacred* (New York: Harper & Row, 1972).

41. *Chinese Gleams of Sufi Light: Wang Tai-yü's Great Learning of the Pure and Real and Liu Chih's Displaying the Concealment of the Real Realm* (SUNY Press, 2000); and with the collaboration of William C. Chittick and Tu Weiming, *The Sage Learning of Liu Zhi: Islamic Thought in Confucian Terms* (Harvard University Press, 2009).

Selected Bibliography

Abu-Nimer, Mohammed. *Dialogue, Conflict Resolution, and Change: Arab-Jewish Encounters in Israel*. Albany: Albany State University of New York Press, 1999.

———. *Reconciliation, Coexistence, and Justice: Theory and Practice*. New York: Rowman & Little Field, 2001.

Abu-Nimer, Mohammed, and Muhammad Shafiq. *Interfaith Dialogue: A Guide for Muslims*. Herendon: International Institute for Islamic Thought, 2007.

Adang, Camilla. "A Jewish Reply to Ibn H azm: Solomon b. Adret's Polemic against Islam." In *Judíos y musulmanes en al-Andalus y el Magreb: Contactos Intelectuales*. Ed., María Isabel Fierro. Madrid: Casa de Velázquez, 2002.

———. *Muslim Writers on Judaism & the Hebrew Bible from Ibn Rabban to Ibn Hazm*. Leiden: Brill, 1996.

Aderet, Solomon Ibn. *Ma'amar al Yishma'el*. Ed., Bezalel Naor. Spring Valley: Orot, 2008.

———. *Shut ha-Rashba*. Ed. H. Dimotrvsky Jerusalem: Mekhon Or ha-Mizrahò, Mekhon Yerushalayim, 1996.

Al-Ghazzali, Abu Hamid. *Balance of Human Action (Mizan al-amal)*. 1839. Trans., Abraham ibn Hasdai. Jerusalem: Rare Judaica Pub. House, 1975.

Al-Harizi, Judah. *The Book of Tahkemoni: Jewish Tales from Medieval Spain*. Trans., David Simha Segal. London: Littman Library of Jewish Civilization, 2001.

Almond, Ian. *History of Islam in German Thought from Leibniz to Nietzsche*. New York: Routledge, 2010.

Agus, Jacob. *Modern Philosophies of Judaism: a Study of Recent Jewish Philosophies of Religion*. New York: Behrman's Jewish Book House, 1941.

———. *Dialogue and Tradition: The Challenges of Contemporary Judeo-Christian Thought*. London: Abelard-Schuman, 1971.

Baeck, Leo. *Judaism and Christianity*. Philadelphia: Jewish Publication Society of America, 1948.

———. *Essence of Judaism*. New York: Schocken Books, 1961.

Bakhos, Carol. "Abraham Visits Ishmael: A Revisit." *Journal for the Study of Judaism* 38, 4–5 (2007): 553–580.

———. *Ishmael on the Border: Rabbinic Portrayals of the First Arab*. Albany: State University of New York Press, 2006.

Banki, Judith H., and Eugene J. Fisher. *A Prophet for Our Times*. New York: Fordham University Press, 2002.

Barth, Karl, Geoffrey William Bromiley, and Thomas F. Torrance. *Church Dogmatics, Vol. 2: The Doctrine of God Part 2*. Edinburgh: Clark, 1957.

Batnitzky, Leora. "Dialogue as a Judgment, Not Mutual Affirmation: A New Look at Franz Rosenzweig's Dialogical Philosophy." *The Journal of Religion* 79, 4 (1999): 523–544.

Bellah, Robert N. *The Broken Covenant: American Civil Religion in a Time of Trial*. New York: Seabury Press, 1975.

Ben Israel, Menasseh. *The Conciliator*. Ed., E. H. Lindo. London, 1842. Reprinted. New York: Hermon Press, 1972.

———. *Sefer Nishmat Hayim*. Leipzig: Shemuel Zakhaim, 1861.

Ben-Shammai, Haggai, "The Attitude of Some Early Karaites towards Islam." In *Studies in Medieval Jewish History and Literature Pt. 2*. Cambridge: Harvard University Press, 1984.

Berger, Marshall. "Rabbi Joseph Soloveitchik's 'Confrontation': A Reassessment." *CCJR Journal* 1 (2005–6): 151–169.

Berkovits, Eliezer. *Faith after the Holocaust*. New York: KTAV Pub. House, 1973.

———. *God, Man, and History: A Jewish Interpretation*. New York: Jonathan David, 1959.

Besancon, Alain. "What Kind of Religion is Islam?" *Commentary* (May, 2004).

Bilu, Yoram. *Without Bounds: The Life and Death of Rabbi Ya'aqov Wazana*. Detroit: Wayne State University Press, 2000.

Borg, M. J. *Meeting Jesus Again for the First Time*. San Francisco, HarperSanFrancisco, 1994.

Boyarin, Daniel. *A Radical Jew: Paul and the Politics of Identity*. Berkeley: University of California Press, 1997.

———. *Borderlines*. Philadelphia; University of Pennsylvania Press, 2004.

———. "Gospel of the Memra: Jewish Bintarianism and the Prologue of John." *The Harvard Theological Review* 94, 3 (July, 2001): 243–284.

———. *The Jewish Gospels*. New York, The New Press, 2012.

Boys, Mary C. *Has God Only One Blessing? Judaism as a Source of Christian Self-Understanding*. New York: Paulist Press, 2000.

Brill, Alan. "Triumph Without Battle: The Role of Dialectic Theology in Rabbi J.B. Soloveitchik's Theology of the Culture." In *Rabbi in the New World: The Influence of Rabbi J.B. Soloveitchik on Culture, Education, and Jewish Thought*. Eds., Avinoam Rosenak and Naftali Rothenberg. Jerusalem: The Hebrew University Magnes Press Ltd., 2011.

———. *Judaism and Other Religions: Models of Understanding*. New York: Palgrave Macmillan, 2010.

Brinner, William M. *Judaism and Islam: Boundaries, Communications, and Interaction: Essays in Honor of William M. Brinner*. Eds., Benjamin H. Hary, John L. Hayes, and Fred Astern. Leiden: Brill, 2000.

Brumberg-Kraus, Jonathan D. "A Jewish Ideological Perspective on the Study of Christian Scripture." *Jewish Social Studies* 4, 1 (Autumn, 1997).

Bruteau, Beatrice. *Jesus through Jewish Eyes: Rabbis and Scholars Engage an Ancient Brother in A New Conversation*. Maryknoll: Orbis Books, 2001.

Buber, Martin. *Chinese Tales: Zhuangzi: Sayings and Parables and Chinese Ghost and Love Stories*. Atlantic Highlands: Humanities Press, 1991.

———. *The Origin and Meaning of Hasidism*. New York: Horizon Press, 1960.

———. *Two Types of Faith*. New York: Harper, 1961.

———. "The Question to the Single One." In *Between Man and Man*. Boston: Beacon Press, 1955.

Busse, Heribert. *Islam, Judaism and Christianity: the Theological and Historical Affiliations*. Princeton: Marcus Weiner Publishers, 1998.

Campbell, Joseph, with Bill Moyers. *The Power of Myth*. New York: Doubleday, 1988.

Carelbach, Azriel. *India: Account of a Voyage* [Hebrew]. Tel Aviv, 1956.

Charvit, Yossef. "From Monologues to Possible Dialogue: Judaism's Attitude towards Christianity According to the Philosophy of R. Yéhouda Léon Askénazi (Manitou)." In *Interaction Between Judaism and Christianity in History, Religion, Art, and Literature*. Eds., Marcel Poorthuis, Joshua Schwartz, and Joseph Turner. Leiden: Brill, 2009.

Chazen, Robert. *Reassessing Jewish Life in Medieval Europe*. New York: Cambridge University Press, 2010.

———. *Fashioning Jewish Identity in the Medieval Western Christendom.* Cambridge: Cambridge University Press, 2003.

Clark, Victoria. *Allies for Armageddon: The Rise of Christian Zionism.* New Haven: Yale University Press, 2007.

Clarke, James Freeman. *Steps of Belief.* Boston: American Unitarian Association, 1890.

Clooney, Francis X. *Comparative Theology: Deep Learning across Religious Borders* (Hoboken: Wiley-Blackwell, 2010).

———. "The Emerging Field of Comparative Theology: a Bibliographical Review (1989–95)." *Theological Studies* 56, 3 (September, 1995): 521–550.

Cohen, Arthur Allen. *The Myth of the Judeo-Christian Tradition.* New York: Harper & Row, 1969.

Cohen, Jeremy. *Essential Papers on Judaism and Christianity in Conflict: From Late Antiquity to the Reformation.* New York: New York University Press, 1991.

Cohen, Mark R. *Under Crescent and Cross: The Jews in the Middle Ages.* Princeton: Princeton University Press, 1994.

Cournell, Vincent. "Theologies of Difference and Ideologies of Intolerance." In *Religious Tolerance in World Religions.* Eds., Jacob Neusner and Bruce Chilton. West Conshohocken: Templeton Foundation Press, 2008.

Cousins, Ewert. "Judaism-Christianity-Islam: Facing Modernity Together." *Journal of Ecumenical Studies* 30, 3–4 (Summer–Fall, 1993): 417–425.

Crescas, Hasdai. *The Refutation of the Christian Principles.* Trans., David J. Lasker. Albany: State University of New York Press, 1992.

Decter, Jonathan P. "Rendering Qur'anic Quotations in Hebrew Translations of Islamic Texts." *Jewish Quarterly Review* 96, 3 (2006): 336–358.

DiNoia, J. A. "Religion and the Religions." In *The Diversity of Religions: A Christian Perspective.* Washington: Catholic University of America Press, 1992.

Dunn, James D. G. *Jesus, Paul, and The Law: Studies In Mark And Galatians.* Louisville: Westminster/John Knox Press, 1990,

———. *The New Perspective on Paul.* Grand Rapids: W. B. Eerdmans Publishing, 2007.

Dupuis, Jacques. *Toward a Christian Theology of Religious Pluralism.* Maryknoll: Orbis Books, 2001.

Eckardt, A. Roy. "Telling Tales: Making Sense of Christian and Judaic Nonsense: The Urgency and Basis for Judeo-Christian Dialogue." *Theology Today* (October1993): 502–3.

Eckstein, Yechiel. *The Journey Home: An Orthodox Rabbi and a Christian Journalist See Israel Through Each Other's Eyes and Strengthen Their Faith.* Chicago: Shavti House, 2001.

Edelman, Lily. *Face to Face: A Primer in Dialogue.* Washington: B'nai B'rith, Adult Jewish Education, 1967.

Eisenbaum, Pamela. *Paul was Not a Christian: The Original Message of a Misunderstood Paul.* New York: HarperOne, 2009.

Eliade, Mircea. *The Sacred and the Profane.* New York: Columbia University Press, 1992.

Ellenson, David. "A Jewish Legal Authority Addresses Jewish-Christian Dialogue: Two Responsa of Rabbi Moshe Feinstein." *American Jewish Archives Journal* 52 (1999): 112–28.

Elqayam, Avraham. "The Religion of Mercy: Encounters with Islam" *Deot* 19 (2004): 6–8.

Elverskog, Johan. *Buddhism and Islam on the Silk Road.* Philadelphia: University of Pennsylvania Press, 2010.

Ernst, Carl W. "Situating Sufism and Yoga," *Journal of the Royal Asiatic Society*, Series 3, 15,1 (2005): 15–43.

———. "Muslim Studies of Hinduism? A Reconsideration of Persian and Arabic Translations from Sanskrit," *Iranian Studies* 36 (2003): 173–95.

―――. "The Islamization of Yoga in the Amrtakunda Translations." *Journal of the Royal Asiatic Society* 3, 13:2 (2003): 199–226.

Fenton, Paul. "Jewish Attitudes to Islam: Israel Heeds Ishmael." *Jerusalem Quarterly* 29 (Fall 1983): 98.

Firestone, Reuven. *Children of Abraham: an introduction to Judaism for Muslims.* Hoboken: KTAV Pub. House, 2001.

―――. *Journeys in Holy Lands: The Evolution of the Abraham-Ishmael Legends in Islamic Exegesis.* Albany: State University of New York Press, 1990.

―――. "The Qur'an and the Bible: Some Modern Studies of Their Relationship" In *Bible and Qur'an: Essays in Scriptural Intertextuality.* Ed., John C. Reeves. Atlanta: Society of Biblical Literature, 2003.

Fisher, Eugene J. *Twenty Years of Jewish-Catholic Relations.* New York: Paulist Press, 1986.

―――. *Visions of the Other: Jewish and Christian Theologians Assess the Dialogue.* New York: Paulist Press, 1994.

Flannery, Edward. *The Anguish of the Jews.* New York: Paulist Press, 1985.

Flusser, David. *Jesus.* New York: Herder and Herder, 1969.

Fluegel, Maurice. *Philosophy, Qabbala And Vedanta. Comparative Metaphysics And Ethics, Retionalism And Mysticism, Of The Jews, The Hindus And Most Of The Historic Nations, As Links And Developments Of One Chain Of Universal Philosophy.* Baltimore: H. Fluegel & Co, 1902.

Freidenreich, David M. "Comparisons Compared: A Methodological Survey of Comparisons of Religion from 'A Magic Dwells' to 'A Magic Still Dwells.'" *Method and Theory in the Study of Religion* 16 (2004): 80–101.

Friedheim, Emmanuel. "Sol Invictus In The Severus Synagogue At Hammath Tiberias, The Rabbis, and Jewish Society: A Different Approach" *Review of Rabbinic Judaism* 12, 1 (2009): 89–121

Friedmann, Yohanan. "Classification of Unbelievers in Sunnī Muslim Law and Tradition." *Jerusalem Studies in Arabic and Islam* 22 (1998): 163–195.

―――. "Medieval Muslim View of Indian Religions." *Journal of the American Oriental Society* 95, 2 (April–June, 1975): 214–221.

―――. *Tolerance and Coercion in Islam: Interfaith Relations in the Muslim Tradition.* New York: Cambridge University Press, 2003.

Friedlander, Michael. *The Jewish Religion.* New York: Pardes Pub. House, 1946.

Fredriksen, Paula. *Augustine and the Jews: A Christian Defense of Jews and Judaism.* New Haven: Yale University Press, 2010.

―――. *Jesus of Nazareth, King of the Jews: A Jewish Life and the Emergence of Christianity.* New York: Vintage Books, 2000.

Geiger, Abraham. *Judaism and Islam.* Ed., M. Pearlman (New York: KTAV Publishing House, 1970).

Gellman, Jerome. "Judaism and Buddhism: A Jewish Approach to a Godless Religion." In *Jewish Theology and World Religions.* Eds., Alon Goshen-Gottstein and Eugene Korn. London: Littman Library of Jewish Civilization, 2012.

Glazerson, Matiyahu. *From Hinduism to Judaism.* Jerusalem: Himelsein, Glazerson, 1984.

Goldberg, Ellen S. and Nathan Katz. *The Last Jews of Cochin: Jewish identity in Hindu India.* Columbia: University of South Carolina Press, 1993.

Goldman, Shalom, and Laurie Patton. "From All Their Habitations—Indian Love Call: Israelis, Orthodoxy, and Indian Culture." *Judaism* 50 (2000): 351.

Goldstein, Morris. "Toledoth Yeshu." In *Jesus in the Jewish Tradition.* New York: Macmillan, 1950.

Goldziher, Igác. *Ignaz Goldziher and His Oriental Diary.* Trans., Rapael Patai. Detroit: Wayne State University Press, 1987.

Goldziher, Ignác, and Bernard Lewis. *Introduction to Islamic Theology and Law.* Princeton: Princeton University Press, 1981.

Gordis, Robert. "The Judeo-Christian Tradition-Illusion or Reality." In *Judaism in a Christian World.* New York: McGraw-Hill, 1966.

Goshen-Gottstein, Alon. "Abraham and 'Abrahamic Religions' in the Contemporary Interreligious Discourse: Reflections of an Implicated Jewish Bystander." *Studies in Interreligious Dialogue* 12, 2 (2002): 163–183.

———. "Encountering Hinduism: Thinking Through *Avodah Zarah.*" In *Jewish Theology and World Religions.* Eds., Alon Goshen-Gottstein and Eugene Korn. London: Littman Library of Jewish Civilization, 2012.

———. "God the Father in Rabbinic Judaism and Christianity: Transformed Background or Common Ground?" *Journal of Ecumenical Studies* 38 (2001): 85.

———. "Judaisms and Incarnational Theologies: Mapping Out the Parameters of Dialogue." *Journal of Ecumenical Studies* 39, 3 (2002): 219–247.

———. "The Jewish Encounter with Hinduism Personal and Theological Reflections." In *Identity and Idolatry.* Unpublished manuscript.

———. "Thinking of/With Scripture: Struggling for the Religious Significance of the Song of Songs." *The Journal of Scriptural Reasoning* 3, 2 (August, 2003).

Graf, Fritz. "Roman Festivals in Syria Palestine." In *The Talmud Yerushalmi and Greco-Roman Culture Volume 3* (CITY: J.C.B. Mohr, 2002).

Green, Arthur. 'Shekhinah, the Virgin Mary, and the Song of Songs: Reflections on a Kabbalistic Symbol in Its Historical Context." *AJS Review* 26:1 (2002): 1–52.

Greenberg, Irving. *For the Sake of Heaven and Earth: The New Encounter between Judaism and Christianity.* Philadelphia: Jewish Publication Society, 2004.

Griffith, Sidney H. "The Gospel in Arabic: An Inquiry into Its Appearance in the First Abbasid Century." In *Quran and Bible: Essays in Scriptural Intertextuality.* Ed., John C. Reeves. Atlanta: Society of Biblical Literature, 2003.

Grossman, Louis. *Some Chapters on Judaism and the Science of Religion.* New York: Putnam 1888.

Gruenzig, Ezriel. "Hindu Philosophy and Kabbalah." *Ha Eshkol* 3 (1900): 40–48.

Guttmann, Julius. *Philosophies of Judaism: The History of Jewish Philosophy from Biblical Times to Franz Rosenzweig.* New York: Holt, Rinehart, and Winston, 1964.

Halevi, Ḥayyim David. *Meḳor Ḥayim: Piske Halakhot* Tel Aviv: 1983.

Halevi, Judah. *The Kuzari.* Trans., Hartwig Hirschfield. New York: Schocken, 1964.

Harkins, Franklin T., ed. *Transforming Relations: Essays on Jews and Christians throughout History in Honor of Michael A. Signer.* Notre Dame: University of Notre Dame Press, 2010.

Hartman, David, and Abraham Halkin. *Crisis and Leadership: Epistle to the Jews of Yemen.* Philadelphia: Jewish Publication Society of America, 1993.

Heim, S. Mark. "The Depth of the Riches: Trinity and Religious Ends." In *Christianity and the Religions: A Dialogue.* Ed., Viggo Mortensen. Grand Rapids: Eerdmans, 2003.

———. Salvations: Truth and Difference in Religion Maryknoll NY: Orbis Books, 1995.

Herman, Jonathan. *I and Tao: Martin Buber's Encounter with Chuand Tzu.* Albany: State University of New York Press, 1996.

Hertz, Joseph H. *The Pentateuch and Haftorahs.* London: Soncino Press, 1963.

Heschel, Abraham Joseph. *The Prophets.* New York: Harper & Row, 1962.

———. *Moral Grandeur and Spiritual Audacity: Essays.* New York: Farrar, Straus, & Grioux, 1996.

Heschel, Susannah. *Abraham Geiger on the Origins of Christianity.* Chicago: University of Chicago, 1998.

Hezser, Catherine. "Jews and Gentiles in Yerushalmi Avodah Zarah." In *The Talmud Yerushalmi and Greco-Roman Culture Volume 3* (CITY: J.C.B. Mohr, 2002).

Hick, John. *God Has Many Names.* London: Macmillan, 1980.

Hick, John, and Brian Hebblethwaite. *Christianity and Other Religions: Selected Readings.* Philadelphia: Fortress Press, 1980.

Hinze, Bradford E, and Irfan A. Omar. *Heirs of Abraham: The Future of Muslim, Jewish, and Christians Relations.* Maryknoll, NY: Orbis Books, 2005.

Hirsch, S.R. *Commentary on the Pentateuch with Commentary of Samson Raphael Hirsch.* Trans., Isaac Levy. New York, Judaica Press, 1971.

———. *Horeb: A Philosophy on Jewish Laws and Observances.* London: Soncino Press, 1962.

Holdrege, Barbara A. *Veda and Torah: Transcending the Textuality of Scripture.* Albany: State University of New York Press, 1996.

Holtzman, Gitit. "Truth, Tradition and Religion. The Association between Judaism and Islam and the Relation Between Religion and Philosophy in Medieval Jewish Thought." *Al-Masaq: Islam and the Medieval Mediterranean* 18, 2 (2006): 191–200.

Holwerda, David E. *Jesus & Israel: One Covenant or Two?* Grand Rapids: Eerdmans, 1995.

Hoyland, Robert G. *Seeing Islam as Others Saw It: a Survey and Evaluation of Christian, Jewish, and Zoroastrian Writings on Early Islam.* Princeton: Darwin Press, 1997.

Hutchison, William. *Religious Pluralism in America.* New Haven: Yale University Press, 2003.

Idel, Moshe. *Ben: Sonship and Jewish Mysticism.* New York: Continuum Books, 2007.

Issac, Jules. *The Teaching of Contempt; Christian Roots of Anti-Semitism.* New York: Holt, Rinehart and Winston, 1964.

Jocz, Jakób. *The Jewish People and Jesus Christ: A Study in the Relationship between the Jewish People and Jesus Christ.* London: SPCK, 1954.

Kaplan, Yosef. *From Christianity to Judaism: the Story of Isaac Orobio de Castro* Oxford: Littman Library, 1989.

Kasimow, Harold. *No Religion is an Island: Abraham Joshua Heschel and Interreligious Dialogue.* Maryknoll: Orbis Books, 1991.

Katsh, Abraham I. *Judaism in Islam: Biblical and Talmudic Backgrounds of the Koran and Its Commentaries.* New York: Sepher-Hermon Press, 1980.

Katz, Nathan. "Jewish-Hindu Dialogue: Learning From Each Other—Hindus and Jews." *Hinduism Today* 16, 7 (July 1994).

Kendall, R. T., and David Rosen. *The Christian and the Pharisee: Two Outspoken Religious Leaders Debate the Road to Heaven.* New York: Faith Words, 2007.

Kiener, Ronald. "The Image of Islam in the Zohar," *Mehkerei Yerushalayim be-Mahshevet Yisrael* 9 (1989): 43–65.

Knitter, Paul F. *Introducing Theologies of Religions.* Maryknoll, NY: Orbis Books, 2002.

———. *Without Buddha I Could Not Be A Christian.* Oxford: Oneworld, 2009.

Kohler, Kaufman. *Jewish Theology, Systematically and Historically Considered.* New York: Macmillan, 1918.

Kook, Abraham Isaac. *Igrot ha-Re'iyah.* Jerusalem: Mosad ha-Rav Ḳuḳ, 1062.

———. *Li-Nevokhei ha-Dor.* Unpublished Manuscript, 2010.

———. *Shemonah Kevatsim.* Jerusalem: 2004.

———. *The Lights of Penitence.* New York: Paulist Press, 1978.

Kook, Abraham Issac, and Tzvi Feldman, *Rav A.Y. Kook: Selected Letters.* Israel: Ma'aliot Publications of Yeshivat Birkat Moshe, 1986.

Kraemer, Hendrik. *Religion and the Christian Faith.* Philadelphia: Westminster Press, 1957.

Kraemer, Joel L. *Humanism in the Renaissance of Islam: The Cultural Revival During the Buyid Age.* Leiden: Brill, 1993.

Kramer, Martin. "Introduction." In *The Jewish Discovery of Islam: Studies in Honor of Bernard Lewis.* Eds., Bernard Lewis and Martin Kramer. Tel Aviv: The Moshe Dayan Center for Middle Eastern and African.

Kugel, James. *In Potipher's House: the Interpretive Life of Biblical Texts.* Cambridge: Harvard University Press, 1994. Studies, Tel Aviv University, 1999.

Langermann, Y. Tzvi. *Yemenite Midrash: Philosophical Commentaries on the Torah, Sacred Literature Series.* San Francisco: Harper San Francisco, 1996.

Lasker, David J. *Jewish Philosophical Polemics Against Christianity in the Middle Ages.* New York: KTAV Pub. House, 1977.

Lapide, Pinchas. "Jesus in Israeli Textbooks." *Journal of Ecumenical Studies* 10 (Summer, 1973): 515–531.

———. *Paul, Rabbi, and Apostle.* Minneapolis: Augsburg Pub. House, 1984.

Lapide, Pinchas, and Jurgen Moltmann. *Jewish Monotheism and Christian Trinitarian Doctrine: A Dialogue.* Philadelphia: Fortress Press, 1981.

Lapide, Pinchas, and Karl Rahner. *Encountering Jesus, Encountering Judaism: A Dialogue.* New York: Crossroad, 1987.

Lassner, Jacob. "Abraham Geiger: A Nineteenth Century Jewish Reformer on the Origins of Islam." In *The Jewish Discovery of Islam: studies in honor of Bernard Lewis.* Eds., Bernard Lewis and Martin Kramer. Tel Aviv: The Moshe Dayan Center for Middle Eastern and African Studies Tel Aviv University, 1999.

Lawrence, Bruce B. "The Use of Hindu Religious Texts in al-Birūni's India with Special Reference to Patanjali's Yoga-Sutras." In *The Scholar and the Saint: Studies in Commemoration of Abu'l Rayhan al-Bīrūnī and Jalal al-Din al-Rūmī.* Ed., Peter J. Chelkowski. New York: New York University Press, 1975.

Levenson, Jon D. *The Death and Resurrection of the Beloved Son.* New Haven: Yale University Press, 1993.

———. "The Agenda of *Dabru Emet.*" *Review of Rabbinic Judaism* 7, 1 (2004): 1–26.

———. *The Death and Resurrection of the Beloved Son: The Transformation of Child Sacrifice in Judaism and Christianity.* New haven: Yale University Press, 1993.

———. "The Idea of Abrahamic Religions: A Qualified Dissent." *Jewish Review of Books.* Jewish Review of Books, 2010.

———. "The Same God? Who do Christians and Muslims Worship?" *The Christian Century* 121, 8 (2004):32–33.

———. *Sinai and Zion.* New York: HarperOne, 1987.

Lazarus-Yafeh, Hava. "Ha-Problematikah ha-Datit shel ha-Aliyah la-Regel ba-islam." *Divre ha-Akedemyah ha-Leumit ha-Yisraelit le-Mada'im* 5, 11 (1976): 222–243.

———. *Intertwined Worlds Medieval Islam and Bible Criticism.* Jerusalem: Bialik Institute, 1998.

Lévinas, Emmanuel. "Simone Weil against the Bible." In *Difficult Freedom: Essays on Judaism.* Baltimore: Johns Hopkins University Press, 1990.

———. "Judaism and Kenosis." In *In The Time of Nations.* Ed., Michael B. Smith. Bloomington: Indiana University Press, 1994.

———. *Totality and Infinity: An Essay on Exteriority.* Pittsburgh: Duquesne University Press, 1969.

Levine, Amy-Jill. *The Misunderstood Jew: The Church and Scandal of the Jewish Jesus.* San Francisco, HarperSanFrancisco, 2006.

Lew, Alan. *One God Clapping: The Spiritual Path of a Zen Rabbi*. New York: Kodansha International, 1999.

———. *This Real and You Are Completely Unprepared*. Boston: Little, Brown and Co., 2003.

Lewis, Bernard. "An Apocalyptic Vision of Islamic History." *BSOAS* 13 (1949–51): 308–38.

———. *The Jews of Islam*. Princeton: Princeton University Press, 1984.

Libson, Gideon. *Jewish and Islamic Law: A Comparative Study of Custom During the Geonic Period*. Cambridge, Mass: Islamic Legal Studies Program, Harvard Law School, 2003.

Lubarsky, Sandra. *Tolerance and Transformation: Jewish Approaches to Religious Pluralism*. Cincinnati: Hebrew Union College Press, 1990.

Maimonides, Abraham. *The High Ways to Perfection Vol. II*. Ed., S. Rosenblatt. Baltimore: The Johns Hopkins Press, 1938.

Maimonides, Obadyah. *Treatise of the Pool*. Trans., Paul Fenton. London: Octagon Press, 1981.

Mann, Jacob. "A Polemical Work Against Karaites." *Jewish Quarterly Review* 12 (1922): 146–147.

Maritain, Jacques. *The Mystery of Israel and Other Essays*. Paris: Desclée, De Brouwer, 1965.

Martin, Bernard. "Scriptural Authority, Scriptural Interpretation & Jewish-Christian Relations." In *Evangelicals and Jews in Conversation on Scripture, Theology and History*. Trans., Marc H. Tanenbaum, Marvin R. Wilson, and A. James Rudin. Grand Rapids: Baker Book House, 1978.

Martini, Carlo Maria, "Christianity and Judaism: A Historical and Theological Overview." In *Jews and Christians: Exploring the Past, Present, and Future*. Ed., James Charlesworth. New York: Crossroad, 1990.

Marty, Martin. *Modern American Religion: Under God, Indivisible, 1941–1960*. Chicago: University of Chicago Press, 1986.

Matt, Daniel. *God and the Big Band: Discovering Harmony between Science and Spirituality*. Woodstock: Jewish Lights Pub., 1996.

McAuliffe, Jane Dammen. "Assessing the Isra'iliyyat: An Exegetical Conundrum." In *Story-Telling in the Framework of Nonfictional Arabic Literature*. Ed., S. Leder. Wiesbaden: Harrassowitz Verlag, 1999.

Meghen, Zeev. *After Hardship Cometh Ease: The Jews as Backdrop for Muslim Moderation*. New York: W. de Gruyter, 2005.

Melamed, Abraham. "The Image of India in Medieval Jewish Culture." *Jewish History* 30, 2–4 (December, 2006): 299–314.

Mendelssohn, Moses. *Jerusalem and Other Writings*. Trans., Alfred Jospe. New York: B'nai B'rith, 1969.

Mendes-Flohr, Paul R. *Divided Passions: Jewish Intellectuals and the Experience of Modernity*. Detroit: Wayne State University Press, 1991.

Moreen, Vera, ed. *Queen Esther's Garden: an Anthology of Judeo-Persian Literature*. New Haven: Yale University Press, 2000.

Müller, Max. *Introduction to the Science of Religion*. London: Longmans, Green, 1873.

Murciano, Prosper. *Simon Ben Zemah Duran, Keshet U-Magen: A Critical Edition*. Diss. New York University. Ann Arbor: Xerox University Microfilms, 1975.

Mussner, Franz. *Tractate on the Jews: The Significance of Judaism for Christian Faith*. London: SPCK, 1984.

Narboni, Moses "Commentary on *Guide*." In *Sheloshah Kadmonei Mefarshei Hamoreh*. Ed., J. Goldenthal. Vienna, 1852.

Neusner, Jacob. *Judaism and Christianity in the Age of Constantine: History, Messiah, Israel, and the Initial Confrontation*. Chicago: University of Chicago Press, 1987.

———. *Rabbi Talks with Jesus*. Montreal: McGill-Queen's University Press, 2000.

———. *Telling Tales, Making Sense of Christian and Judaic Nonsense: The Urgency and Basis for Judeo-Christian Dialogue*. Louisville: Westminster/John Knox Press, 1993.

Neusner, Jacob, and Tamara Sonn. *Judaism and Islam: Comparing Religions through Law*. London & NY: Routledge, 1999.

Neusner, Jacob, Tamara Sonn, and Jonathan Brockopp, *Judaism and Islam in Practice: A Sourcebook for the Classical Age*. London: Routledge, 2000.

Niebuhr, Reinhold. *The Nature and Destiny of Man: A Christian Interpretation*. New York: C. Scribner's Sons, 1941.

———. *The Self and the Dramas of History*. New York: Scribner, 1955.

Nir, Elhanan. *Me-Hodu ye-ad kan : hogim Yiśraelim kotvim al Hodu ye-ha-Yahadut shelahem*. Jerusalem: Reuven Mass, 2006.

Nirenberg, David. *Communities of Violence: Persecution of Minorities in the Middle Ages*. Princeton: Princeton University Press, 1996.

———. "What Can Medieval Spain Teach Us About Muslim-Jewish Relations?" *CCAR Journal* (Summer, 2002): 17–36.

———. "The Birth of the Pariah: Jews, Christian, Dualism, and Social Science." *Social Research* 70, 1 (Spring, 2003): 201–236.

———. "Enmity and Assimilation: Jews, Christians, and Converts in Medieval Spain." *Common Knowledge* 9 (2003): 137–155.

Novak, David. *Jewish-Christian Dialogue: A Jewish Justification*. New York: Oxford University Press, 1989.

Ochs, Peter W. "The God of Jews and Christians." In *Christianity in Jewish Terms*. Ed., Tikvah Frymer-Kensky. Boulder: Westview Press, 2000.

Oesterreicher, John M. *Why Judeo-Christian Studies*. Newark: Institute of Judeo-Christian Studies, 1954.

Oppenheimer, Aharon. "The attitude of the Sages towards the Arabs." *Jewish Studies in a New Europe*. 6th EAJS Congress. (July, 1998): 572–579.

Pailin, David. *Attitudes to Other Religions: Comparative Religion in the 17th and 18th Century Britain*. Manchester: Manchester University Press, 1984.

Panikkar, Raimundo. *The Unknown Christ of Hinduism: Towards an Ecumenical Christophany*. Maryknoll: Orbis Books, 1981.

Parfitt, Tudor, ed. *Israel and Ishmael: Studies in Muslim-Jewish Relations*. New York: St. Martin's Press, 2000.

Parkes, James. *Prelude to Dialogue: Jewish-Christian Relationships*. New York: Schocken Books, 1969.

———. *The Conflict of the Church and the Synagogue: A Study in the Origins of Anti-Semitism*. Cleveland: World Pub. Co., 1961.

Patai, Raphael. *Jadid Al-Islam: The Jewish "New Muslims" of Meshhed*. Detroit: Wayne State University Press, 1997.

Pawlikowski, John T. *Christ in the Light of the Christian Jewish Dialogue*. New York: Paulist Press, 1982.

———. *Jesus and the Theology of Israel*. Wilmington: Michael Glazier, 1989.

Pawlikowski, John T., and Judith Banki. *Ethics in the Shadow of the Holocaust: Christian and Jewish Perspectives*. Franklin, WI: Sheed & Ward, 2001.

Perlman, Moshe. "The Medieval Polemics between Islam and Judaism." In *Religion in a Religious Age*. ed., S. D. Goitein. Cambridge: Association for Jewish Studies, 1974.

———. *Sa'd B. Mansur ibn Kammuna's Examination of the Inquiries into the Three Faiths: a 13th Century Essay in the Comparative Religion*. Berkeley, CA: University of California Press, 1967.

Perry, Tom. *Radical Difference: A Defence of Hendrik Kraemer's Theology of Religions.* Waterloo: Canadian Corp. Studies in Religio, 2001.

Pines, Shlomo, and Tuvia Gelblum. "Al-Birūni's Arabic Version of Patañjali's Yogasūtra: A Translation of his First Chapter and a Comparison with Related Sanskrit Texts." *Bulletin of the School of Oriental and African Studies* 29 (1966): 302–325.

———. "Al-Birūni's Arabic Version of Patañjali's Yogasūtra: A Translation of the Second Chapter and a Comparison with Related Texts." *Bulletin of the School of Oriental and African Studies* 40 (1977): 522–549.

———. "Al-Birūni's Arabic Version of Patañjali's Yogasūtra: A Translation of the Third Chapter and a Comparison with Related Texts." *Bulletin of the School of Oriental and African Studies* 46 (1983): 258–304.

Pollak, Michael. *Mandarins, Jews, and Missionaries: the Jewish Experience in the Chinese Empire.* Philadelphia: Jewish Publication Society of America, 1980.

———. *The Jews of Kaifeng: Chinese Jews on the banks of the Yellow River.* Tel Aviv: Bet Hatefutsoth The Nahum Goldman Museum of the Jewish Diaspora, 1984.

Pulcini, Theodore. *Exegesis of Polemical Discourse Ibn Hazm on Jewish and Christian Scriptures.* New York: Oxford University Press, 2000.

Race, Alan. *Christians and Religious Pluralism: Patterns in the Christian Theology of Religions.* Maryknoll, NY: Orbis Books, 1983.

Ratzinger, Joseph. *Jesus of Nazareth: From the Baptism in the Jordan to the Transfiguration.* New York: Doubleday, 2007.

———. *Jesus of Nazareth. Part Two, Holy Week: From the Entrance into Jerusalem to the Resurrection.* San Francisco: Ignatius Press, 2011.

———. *Many Religions, One Covenant: Israel, the Church, and the World.* San Francisco: Ignatius Press, 1999.

Ray, Jonathan. "Beyond Tolerance and Persecution: Reassessing Our Approach to Medieval 'Covivencia.'" *Jewish Social Studies* 11, 2 (2005): 1–18.

Reeves, John C., ed. *Bible and Quran: Essays in Scriptural Intertextuality.* Atlanta: Society of Biblical Literature, 2003.

———. "Israel and the Torah of Muhammad," in *Quran and Bible: Essays in Scriptural Intertextuality.* Ed., John C. Reeves. Atlanta: Society of Biblical Literature, 2003.

Reinhartz, Adele. *Befriending the Beloved Disciple: A Jewish Reading of the Gospel of John.* New York: Continuum, 2001.

Ricoeur, Paul. *The Course of Recognition.* Cambridge: Harvard University Press, 2005.

Rina, Drory. "Literary Contacts and Where to Find Them: On Arabic Literary Models in Medieval Jewish Literature." *Poetics Today* 14, 2 (1993): 277–302.

Riskin, Shlomo. "Shabbat Shalom: Parshat Shemini Leviticus 9:1–11:47." *Ohr Torah Stone.* 29 Mar 2003. http://www.ohrtorahstone.org.il/parsha/5763/shemini63.htm.

———. "Covenant and Conversion: The United Mission to Redeem the World." *Institute for Theological Inquiry.* http://www.yale.edu/ris/theologyconference/documents/ Shlomo_Riskin.pdf.

Rosen, David. "Christians and Jews in a Radically New Relationship." Human Rights Oration given in Sydney, Australia. Sydney, Australia. 13 May 2001. http://www. jcrelations.net/en/displayItem.php?id=956.

———. "Dabru Emet': Its Significance for the Jewish-Christian Dialogue." 20th Anniversary Celebration of the Dutch Council of Christians and Jews (OJEC). Tillburg, Netherlands. 06 Nov 2001. http://www.jcrelations.net/en/displayItem.php?id=1477.

Saadia ben Joseph. *Gaon: the Book of Beliefs and Opinions.* New Haven: Yale University Press, 1989.

Rosenstock-Huessy, Eugen, and Franz Rosenzweig. *Judaism Despite Christianity: The Letters on Christianity and Judaism Between Eugen Rosenstock-Huessy and Franz Rosenzweig*. University of Alabama: University of Alabama Press, 1969.

Rosenzweig, Franz. *The Star of Redemption*. New York: Holt, Rinehart, and Winston, 1971.

Rothschild, Fritz A., ed. *Jewish Perspectives on Christianity: Leo Baeck, Martin Buber, Franz Rosenzweig, Will Herberg, and Abraham J. Heschel*. New York: Crossroad, 1990.

Rubiés Joan Pau. "Theology, Ethnography, and the Historicization of Idolatry." *Journal of the History of Ideas* 67, 4 (2006): 571–596.

Sanders, E. P. *Paul and Palestinian Judaism: A Comparison of Patterns of Religion*. Philadelphia: Fortress Press, 1977.

Schäfer, Peter. *Mirror of His Beauty: Feminine Images Of God From The Bible To The Early Kabbalah*. Princeton: Princeton University Press, 2002.

Schecter, Solomon. *Aspects of Rabbinic Theology*. New York: Schocken Books, 1961.

Schiffman, Yair. "The Differences Between the Translations of Maimonides' Guide of the Perplexed by Falaquera, Ibn Tibbon and al-Harizi, and their Textual and Philosophical Implications." *Journal of Semitic Studies* 44 (1999): 47–61.

Schoeps, Hans Joachim. *The Jewish-Christian Argument: a history of Theologies in Conflict*. New York: Holt, Rinehart, and Winston, 1963.

———. *Jewish Christianity: Factional Disputes in the Early Church*. Philadelphia: Fortress Press, 1969.

Scholem, Gershom. *Major Trends in Jewish Mysticism*. New York: Schoken Book, 1954.

———. *On the Mystical Shape of the Godhead: Basic Concepts in the Kabbalah*. New York: Schoken Books, 1991.

Schwartz, Dov. *Aṣtrologyah u-magyah ba-hagut ha-Yehudit bi-Yeme ha-Benayim*. Ramat-Gan: Univerșitat Bar-Ilan, 1999.

Segal, Alan. *Two Powers in Heaven: Early Rabbinic Reports About Christianity and Gnosticism*. Leiden: E.J. Brill, 1977.

Sendor, Meir. "The Violence of the Neutral in Interfaith Relations." In *Jewish Theology and World Religions*. Ed., Alon Goshen-Gottstein & E. Korn. Portland: Littman Library, 2012.

Septimus, Bernard. "*Better under Edom* than *under Ishmael*: The History of a Saying" [Hebrew] *Zion* 47 (1982): 103–111.

———. "Hispano-Jewish Views of Christendom and Islam." In *In Iberia And Beyond: Hispanic Jews Between Cultures: Proceedings of a Symposium To Mark The 500th Anniversary Of The Expulsion Of Spanish Jewry*. Ed., Bernard Dov Cooperman. Newark: University of Delaware Press, 1998.

———. "Petrus Alfonsi on the Cult of Mecca," *Speculum* 56 (1981): 530–531.

Shamir, Yehuda. "Allusions to Muhammed in Maimonides' Theory of Prophecy in his Guide." *Jewish Quarterly Review* 54 (1974): 212–224.

Shapiro, Marc B. "Islam and the Halakhah." *Judaism* (Summer, 1993): 332–343.

Sharpe, Eric. *Comparative Religion: A History*. New York: Scribner's, 1975.

———. *Nathan Soderblom and the Study of Religion*. Chapel Hill: University of North Carolina Press, 1990.

———. *The Theology of A. G. Hogg*. Madras: Published for the Christian Institute for the Study of Religion and Society, Bangalore by the Christian Literature Society, 1971.

Sherbok, Dan Cohn. *Judaism and Other Faiths*. New York: Palgrave Macmillan, 1994.

Silk, Mark. *Notes on the Judeo-Christian Tradition in America*. Philadelphia: American Studies Association, 1984.

———. "Numa Pompilius and the Idea of Civil Religion in the West." *Journal of the American Academy of Religion* 72, 4 (2004): 86–896.

Sklare, David. "Responses to Islamic polemics by Jewish Mutakallimun in the tenth century." In *The Majlis* Interreligious Encounters in Medieval Islam. Eds., Hava Lazarus-Yafeh et al. Wiesbaden: Harrassowitz, 1999.

Smith, Wilfred Cantwell. *The Faith of Other Men*. New York: Harper, 1972. Reprinted as *Patterns of Faith Around the World*. Oxford: Oneworld, 1998.

———. *Towards a World Theology: Faith and the Comparative History of Religion*. London: Macmillan, 1980.

Smock, David. *Interfaith Dialogue and Peacebuilding*. Washington: United States Institute of Peace Press, 2002.

Soderblom, Nathan. *The Living God: Basal Forms of Personal Religions (Gifford lectures, 1931)*. New York: AMS Press, Inc., 1933.

Soloveitchik, Joseph B. *And From There You Shall Seek*. Trans., Naomi Goldblum. Jersey City: KATV Pub. House, 2008.

———. "Confrontation." & "On Interfaith Relationships." In *A Treasury of Tradition*. Eds., Norman Lamm and Walter S. Wurzburger. New York: Hebrew Publishing Company, 1967.

———. *Halakhic Man*. Philadelphia: J. P. S., 1983.

———. "Sacred and Profane: Kodesh and Chol in World Perspective." Reprinted in *Shiurei HaRav: A Conspectus Of The Public Lectures Of Rabbi Joseph B. Soloveitchik*. Ed., Joseph Epstein. Hoboken: KTAV Pub. House, 1994.

———. *The Lonely Man of Faith*. New York: Doubleday, 1992.

———. *Community, Covenant, and Commitment: Selected Letters and Communications of Rabbi Joseph B. Soloveitchik*. Jersey City: KTAV, 2005.

Steinsaltz, Adin. "Peace Without Conciliation The Irrelevance of 'Toleration' in Judaism." *Common Knowledge* 11, 1 (2005): 41–47.

Stendahl, Krister. *Paul Among Jews and Gentiles and Other Essays*. Philadelphia: Fortress Press, 1977.

Stillman, Norman. "Myth, Countermyth, and Distortion." *Tikkun* 6, 3 (May–June, 1991): 60–64.

Stroumsa, Guy. "John Spencer and the Roots of Idolatry." *History of Religions* 40 (2001): 1–23.

Sweeney, Marvin A. "Why Jews are Interested in Biblical Theology: A Retrospective on the Work of Jon D. Levinson." *Jewish Book Annual* 55–55 (1997–99): 135–68.

Talmage, Frank. *Disputation and Dialogue: Readings in the Jewish-Christian Encounter*. New York: KTAV Pub. House, 1975.

Teshima, Jacob Yuroh. *Zen Buddhism and Hasidism: A Comparative Study*. Lanham: University Press of America, 1995.

Tillich, Paul. *Christianity and the Encounter of the World Religions*. New York: Columbia University Press, 1963.

Todorov, Tzvetan. *Morals of History*. Minneapolis: University of Minnesota Press, 1995.

Torrey, Charles C. *The Jewish Foundation of Islam: Introduction by Franz Rosenthal*. New York: KTAV Pub. House, 1967.

Tottoli, Roberto. "Origin and Use of the Term Israiiyyat in Muslim Literature." *Arabica* 46, 2 (1999): 193–210.

Touati, Charles. "Le Dossier Sur Le Christianisme." *Revue des Etudes Juives* 160, 3–4 (July–December, 2001): 495–497.

Tracy, David. *The Analogical Imagination: Christian Theology and the Culture of Pluralism*. New York: Crossroad, 1981.

Tsadik, D. "Religious disputations of Imāmī Shī'īs against Judaism in the late eighteenth and nineteenth centuries." *Studia Iranica* 24, 1 (2005): 95–134.

Tweed, Thomas A. *The American Encounter with Buddhism, 1844–1912: Victorian Culture and the Limits of Dissent.* Bloomington: Indiana University Press, 1992.

Van Der Leeuw, Gerardus. *Religion in Essence and Manifestation.* New York: Harper & Row, 1963.

Volf, Miroslav. *Allah: A Christian Response.* New York, HarperOne, 2011.

Waldman, Marilyn R. "New Approaches to 'Biblical' Materials in the. Qur'an." *Muslim World* 75 (1985).

Wasserstrom, Steven M. *Between Muslim and Jew: the Problem of Symbiosis under Early Islam.* Princeton: Princeton University Press, 1995.

Weiss-Rosmarin, Trude. "Towards Jewish-Muslim Dialogue." New York: *Jewish Spectator* (1967).

———. *Judaism and Christianity: The Differences.* New York: The Jewish Book Club, 1943.

Werner, Jacob Cahnman. "Schelling and the New Thinking of Judaism." In *German Jewry: Its History and Sociology; Selected Essays.* Brunswick: Transaction Publishers, 1989.

Wheeler, Brannon M. "Israel and the Torah of Muhammad." In *Bible and Quran: Essays in Scriptural Intertextuality.* Ed., John Reeves. Atlanta: Society of Biblical Literature: Scholars Press, 2003.

———. *Moses in the Quran and Islamic Exegesis.* London: Routledge Curzon, 2002.

———. "The New Torah." *Graeco-Arabica* 7–8 (1999–2000): 571–605.

Van Buren, Paul M. *A Theology of the Jewish Christian Reality.* New York: Seabury Press, 1980.

Vermès, Géza. *Jesus and the World of Judaism.* Philadelphia: Fortress, 1983.

———. *Jesus the Jew.* London: S. C. M., 2001.

———. *The Changing Faces of Jesus.* New York: Viking Compass, 2001.

Williams, Paul. *The Unexpected Way.* Edinburgh: T & T Clark, 2002.

Wright, N. T. *Jesus and the Victory of God.* Minneapolis: Fortress, 1996.

———. *Paul: Fresh Perspectives.* London: SPCK, 2005.

Wurzburger, Walter. *Judaism and the Interfaith Movement.* Eds., Walter Wurzburger and Eugene Borowitz. New York: Synagogue Council of America, 1967.

Wyschogrod, Michael. *Abraham's Promise: Judaism and Jewish-Christian Relations.* Grand Rapids: William B. Eerdmans, 2004.

Zeller, David. *The Soul of the Story: Meetings with Remarkable People.* Woodstock: Jewish Lights Pub., 2005.

Index